Brokering Europe

Since the 1960s onwards, the nature and the future of the European Union have been defined in legal terms. Yet, we are still in need of an explanation as to how this entanglement between law and EU polity-building emerged and how it was maintained over time. While most of the literature offers a disembodied account of European legal integration, *Brokering Europe* reveals the multifaceted roles Euro-lawyers have played in EU polity, notably beyond the litigation arena. In particular, the book points at select transnational groups of multipositioned entrepreneurs that have elevated the role of law in all sorts of EU venues. In doing so, it draws from a new set of intellectual resources (field theory) and empirical strategies only very recently mobilized for the study of the EU. Grounded on an extensive historical investigation, *Brokering Europe* provides a revised narrative of the 'constitutionalization of Europe'.

Antoine Vauchez is a research professor at the Centre européen de sociologie et de science politique, Université Paris 1-Sorbonne / CNRS.

Cambridge Studies in European Law and Policy

This series aims to produce original works which contain a critical analysis of the state of the law in particular areas of European law and set out different perspectives and suggestions for its future development. It also aims to encourage a range of work on law, legal institutions and legal phenomena in Europe, including 'law in context' approaches. The titles in the series will be of interest to academics; policy-makers; policy formers who are interested in European legal, commercial and political affairs; practising lawyers, including the judiciary; and advanced law students and researchers.

Books in the series

Brokering Europe: Euro-Lawyers and the Making of a Transnational Polity
Antoine Vauchez

Referendums and the European Union: A Comparative Enquiry
Fernando Mendez, Mario Mendez, Vasiliki Triga

International Trade Disputes and EU Liability
Anne Thies

The Limits of Legal Reasoning and the European Court of Justice
Gerard Conway

New Governance and the Transformation of European Law: Coordinating EU Social Law and Policy
Mark Dawson

The Lisbon Treaty: A Legal and Political Analysis
Jean-Claude Piris

The European Union's Fight Against Corruption: The Evolving Policy Towards Member States and Candidate Countries
Patrycja Szarek-Mason

The Ethos of Europe: Values, Law and Justice in the EU
Andrew Williams

State and Market in European Union Law
Wolf Sauter and Harm Schepel

The European Civil Code: The Way Forward
Hugh Collins

Ethical Dimensions of the Foreign Policy of the European Union: A Legal Appraisal
Urfan Khaliq

The Evolving European Union: Migration Law and Policy
Dora Kostakopoulou

Implementing EU Pollution Control: Law and Integration
Bettina Lange

The Transformation of Citizenship in the European Union: Electoral Rights and the Restructuring of Political Space
Jo Shaw

European Broadcasting Law and Policy
Jackie Harrison and Lorna Woods

The European Convention on Human Rights: Achievements, Problems and Prospects
Steven Greer

The Constitution for Europe: A Legal Analysis
Jean-Claude Piris

Social Rights and Market Freedom in the European Constitution: A Labour Law Perspective
Stefano Giubboni

EU Enlargement and the Constitutions of Central and Eastern Europe
Anneli Albi

Brokering Europe

Euro-Lawyers and the Making of a Transnational Polity

Antoine Vauchez

CAMBRIDGE
UNIVERSITY PRESS

CAMBRIDGE
UNIVERSITY PRESS

University Printing House, Cambridge CB2 8BS, United Kingdom

Cambridge University Press is part of the University of Cambridge.

It furthers the University's mission by disseminating knowledge in the pursuit of education, learning and research at the highest international levels of excellence.

www.cambridge.org
Information on this title: www.cambridge.org/9781107042360

First published 2015

A catalogue record for this publication is available from the British Library

Library of Congress Cataloging in Publication Data
Vauchez, Antoine, author.
Brokering Europe : Euro-lawyers and the making of a transnational polity / Antoine Vauchez.
pages cm. – (Cambridge studies in European law and policy)
ISBN 978-1-107-04236-0 (Hardback)
1. Law–European Union countries. I. Title.
KJE947.V379 2015
341.242′2–dc23
2014026680

ISBN 978-1-107-04236-0 Hardback

Contents

Series Editors' preface

In this groundbreaking addition to the series *Studies in European Law and Policy*, Antoine Vauchez invites the reader to rethink the interconnection of law and the polity of Europe. How exactly, he asks, did Europe come to be defined in legal terms?

Vauchez argues that the shift away from a set of treaties which simply provided technocrats and politicians with the technical expertise in comparative law needed to bring about an alignment of economic interests through common economic laws towards a set of arrangements comprising various sources of law (treaties, legislation, case law, etc.) which can be seen as an overarching constitutional settlement requiring the crucial agency of humans: Euro-lawyers. But this is not a book as such about those personalities and personages, better or worse known, but rather about the power of law itself which displays a brokering capacity helping to hold together Europe's rather disorganized and disjointed polity.

Thus, in contradistinction to political science narratives which have identified various (essentially) external factors, which contribute to law's power, Vauchez's is an internal analysis, underpinned by legal and social theory. Empirically, this is fleshed out by a uniquely wide-ranging set of sources about law, legal activities and lawyers, including biographical details, archival information from the European institutions and legal scholarly outputs. This, therefore, is a theoretically informed book, but not a book about theory. We commend it warmly as an important edition to our series.

Jo Shaw
Laurence Gormley

Acknowledgements

Before turning into its present form, this book has had many lives that span over almost a decade. Its origins can be traced back to many heated discussions over Europe's polity and transnational fields within a small group of friends (Antonin Cohen, Mikael Madsen, Guillaume Sacriste) and, later, within a more formal research network named Polilexes ('Politics of Legal Expertise in European Societies') and financed by the French *Agence nationale de la recherche*. Throughout its development, the critical input that I received from Yves Dezalay and his tireless passion for transnational research have been widely inspirational. All these exchanges grew into an individual project parallel to the collective and collaborative one, on which I started working during my stay at the European University Institute in Florence as a Marie Curie fellow. There, I greatly benefited from the critical mass of EU scholarship and the interdisciplinary atmosphere that is so particular to that place. Many discussions and debates with wonderful scholars such as Bruno de Witte, Yves Mény, Christian Joerges, Karen Alter, Kiran Patel and Heike Schweitzer have helped me a lot. Eventually, the project was turned into an *Habilitation à diriger des recherches* that I presented at the Université Paris 1-Sorbonne in March 2010, with the support of Bastien François. Along the way, some early parts of this overall research were published in a variety of disciplinary fields including law (the *European Law Journal* and *Law and Social Inquiry*), sociology (the *American Journal of Sociology* and *International Political Sociology*) and political science (*European Political Science Research*, *Revue française de science politique*, etc.), and I am therefore indebted to my co-authors and co-editors (Bruno de Witte, Antonin Cohen, Didier Georgakakis, Mikael Madsen, Stephanie Mudge and Cécile Robert) as much as to various referees for pushing me forward. I turned most of the *Habilitation* into a book entitled *L'Union par le droit. L'invention d'un programme institutionnel pour l'Europe* published in 2013 in a series co-directed by Patrick Le Gales at the Presses de Sciences Po. As the present book was progressively taking shape, I had countless opportunities to present sections of the manuscript in many venues. In particular, I benefited from early book talks at Sciences Po-Lille, Lyon, Strasbourg and Paris, the American Bar Foundation in Chicago, the London School of Economics, Siena University, the Central European University, and Berlin's *Wissenschaft Zentrum*. It was, however, during the academic year 2013–14 that I completed the English-language version of this manuscript (Meg Morley was the main translator of the text, and I wish to thank her here), as I benefited from invitations from Columbia University Law School (as an Alliance visiting professor during the Fall semester) and from New York University Law School (as a Senior Emile Noël fellow during the spring semester). That year spent in New York proved instrumental to my completing this project, and again I benefited immensely from feedback after talks given at New York University, Columbia, Cornell, Princeton and the American University in Washington, and discussions with scholars and experts of the EU such as Grainne de Búrca, Daniel Kelemen and Peter Lindseth. Of course, all these years spent in the academic trenches have a special *fil rouge*, Stéphanie Hennette-Vauchez, with whom I have loved to share this intellectual and personal journey.

Introduction

By any standards, Europe is a lawyers' paradise.[1] Many figures illustrate the extent to which 'Europe' is juridified and could well be called upon here: the number of pages of European regulation in any given field, the percentage of national legislation originating in EU norms, the ever-increasing caseload of the European Court of Justice (ECJ, or 'the Court'), etc. Figures, however, fail to grasp the very deep entanglement between Europe and the law that has kept the European integration process rolling over time. In a political context in which the pan-European horizon is fading away, it seems that 'Europe is nowhere so real as in the field of law', to quote a recent 'wise men' report on the reform of the French Constitution.[2] Strikingly, while political scientists, historians and even economists in the field of European studies are still having a hard time agreeing on the 'nature of the beast', EU law appears to be this very unique type of knowledge capable of providing some forms of certainty when it comes to making sense of what the European Union is about and how it ought to function. In fact, 'the law' is so instrumental to Europe's very existence and identity that it has become almost 'natural' to continuously draw on a whole set of legal concepts, categories and theories when thinking about Europe's nature and future. Elevated to the rank of

1 While the book puts a lot of emphasis on the *political* significance of the symbolic unification of European constructions into one consistent and historically constant reality named 'Europe', I use – for the sake of simplicity in writing – the terms 'Europe', 'European Union' and 'European Communities' (and, similarly, the terms 'European law', 'EC law' and 'EU law') as synonymous. Similarly, while I study the transformation of the founding Treaties into a *de facto* Constitution of Europe, I still follow the commonly shared convention of EU official documents that use capital letters in order to distinguish the founding European Treaties from ordinary international agreements.

2 Comité de réflexion sur le préambule de la Constitution – 'Comité Veil', *Rapport au président de la République*, Paris, La documentation française, 2008, p. 47.

founding rock, or even to that of the *raison d'être* of the Union (a 'Union of law'), the law seems so well acclimated in Europe's polity that it has become difficult to see its pervasive presence as anything other than a self-evident fact.

The truth of the matter is that, over the years, EU law, and its underlying constitutional paradigm, has affirmed a strong hold on Europe's political imagination. Strikingly, despite the fact that all constitutional treaties (from the 1954 *Communauté politique européenne* to the 2005 constitutional treaty and the 1984 Spinelli treaty) have failed to be approved in national political fields, Europe still seems to be thinking of itself in constitutional terms. Need it be recalled here that the many reformist ambitions that aimed to address Europe's 'deficits' (lack of: democracy, common values, budgetary and economic coordination, etc.) have developed into a corresponding number of *constitutional* projects, from the Constitutional Treaty to the Charter of Fundamental Rights or the more recent budgetary 'golden rule' of the 2012 Fiscal Compact? How can one then account for this structural preference for law and the related resilience of a constitutional paradigm that seems to maintain itself throughout all the Union's re-foundings and reorientations ever since the 1960s?

For a long time, this symbiotic relationship between Europe and the law did not receive much attention. While lawyers would simply state that the European Union *is* a 'Union of law' (and that the European Treaties *are* a 'constitutional charter', or that the ECJ and the European Commission *are* the institutions that embody the EU's general interest, etc.), historians considered this constitutional path undertaken by Europe as essentially unproblematic and uneventful[3] (after all, no State- or quasi-State-building could be conceived of without the support of legal technologies). Yet, the presence of law's names and symbols (a '*de facto* Constitution', 'a court', 'judges', legal scholars, etc.) at the European level conveys a false sense of resemblance to national polities.[4] In fact, this apparent permanence of law from national to European settings clouds our perception of the *specific*

[3] But for more recent developments of EU historiography on transnational networks, cf. Wolfram Kaiser, Brigitte Leucht and Morten Rasmussen (eds.), *The History of the European Union: Origins of a Trans- and Supranational Polity 1950–72*, London, Routledge, 2008; and on the history of European law, see also the special issue edited by historians Bill Davies and Morten Rasmussen, 'Towards a New History of European Law', in *Journal of Contemporary European History*, 21(3), 2012.

[4] See Pierre Bourdieu, *On the State: Lectures at the Collège de France*, London, Polity, 2014.

political and social arrangement that is 'Europe' where the law has come to play a highly singular function.

Certainly, over the past two decades, a rich strain of interdisciplinary literature, initially inspired by American legal scholars and political scientists, has contributed to dispel the not very discreet charm of this 'Law State'[5] and has provided an overarching paradigm for the wide-ranging legalization of the terms and scope of the European project.[6] This stream of research has pointed in particular at the formation in the mid-1960s of a constitutional doctrine at the ECJ which, by a series of forceful jurisprudential blows, has constructed the conceptual and procedural frameworks of a genuine legal federalism. In turn, then, the ECJ's case law opened up institutional opportunities for multinational enterprises, transnational interest groups and EC institutions to circumvent and undermine national forms of regulation. The progressive, if somewhat chaotic, movement through which national courts eventually rallied the broad principles established by the ECJ consolidated the movement[7] – and this judicial consolidation itself generated new opportunities for the Court to further broaden the scope of its case law to new domains such as anti-discrimination, the environment, fundamental rights, etc. These further moves triggered an implacable iterative mechanism associating interest groups, multinational enterprises, EU institutions, States and the ECJ in a virtuous (or vicious) circle of judicialization with no single author or source, but to which each entity contributed in its own way. Or so have the neo-functionalist account of integration and its later neo-institutionalist variant[8] claimed, thus

[5] Daniel Kelemen, *Eurolegalism: The Transformation of Law and Regulation in Europe*, Cambridge, MA, Harvard University Press, 2011.

[6] The bibliography is immense, but seminal papers or books certainly include: Anne-Marie Burley and Walter Mattli, 'Europe Before the Court: A Political Theory of Legal Integration', *International Organization*, 47(1), 1993, pp. 177–209; Joseph Weiler, 'A Quiet Revolution: The European Court of Justice and Its Interlocutors', *Comparative Political Studies*, 26(4), 1994, pp. 510–34; Alec Stone, *The Judicial Construction of Europe*, Oxford, Oxford University Press, 2004; Karen Alter, *Establishing the Supremacy of European Law: The Making of an International Rule of Law in Europe*, Oxford, Oxford University Press, 2001; Rachel Cichowski, *The European Court and Civil Society*, Cambridge, Cambridge University Press, 2007; for an overview, see Alec Stone, 'The European Court of Justice and the Judicialization of EU Governance', *Living Reviews and European Governance*, http://europeangovernance.livingreviews.org/Articles/lreg-2010-2 (accessed 15 May 2013).

[7] Karen Alter, *Establishing the Supremacy of European Law: The Making of an International Rule of Law in Europe*, Oxford, Oxford University Press, 2001.

[8] Neil Fligstein and Alec Stone, 'Constructing Polities and Markets: An Institutionalist Account of European Integration', *American Journal of Sociology*, 107(5), 2002, pp. 1206–43.

shedding much-needed light on the specific contribution of law to the European integration project and process.

Yet, in its very attempt to break with a legal-centric reading of legal integration by bringing *external* factors back into explanations and theories of its sweeping dynamics, this scholarship has, I argue, missed an important point: in the European Union, even more than anywhere else, there is no possible distinction between the 'law' and the 'society'. There are no areas of Europe's politics, economics, bureaucracy or civil society that have not been produced or co-produced to some extent by lawyers, whatever their guises may be. Legal Europe is *co-extensive* with Europe itself, and it is hardly possible to think about the Union and its 'system', its institutions and their 'logic', its markets and their 'functioning', its civil society and its 'causes', without delving into the impressive corpus of *ad hoc* legal theories and methodologies of Europe.[9] Consequently, the very categories that are considered as *explanatory* factors for the legalization of Europe (institutions' 'rationales', professional groups' 'interests', sector-specific 'frontiers' between the 'national' and the 'European', or between the 'legal' and the 'political', etc.) have actually been produced *alongside* the history that this literature is trying to account for. At the time of the ECJ's first landmark cases (1963–4), Europe's law had no inherent logic of its own, the ECJ itself was hardly perceived as a 'court' worth its name, companies and interest groups had no view of 'Europe' as making up one open land of opportunities, and there was certainly no institutional terrain 'out there' that would have been mechanically derived from the mere signing of the Rome Treaties, or even from a sudden judicial *coup* coming from the judges in Luxembourg.

The fact of the matter is that we are still in need of an explanation as to how the law and the polity of Europe have been interconnected, and how they have been shaping and informing one another. We actually know very little about the manner in which 'Europe' has initially come to be defined in *legal* terms (a *de facto* 'Constitution', an *acquis*, a supranational court, etc.) rather than economic or political ones, and how this particular path was actually chosen (and consolidated) for *the institution of Europe*. As is well known and often recalled, the European Communities had a primarily *economic* (if not merely commercial) scope that did not call for any sort of overarching mission for the law. There were good reasons for

[9] On this, see Antoine Vauchez, 'The Force of a Weak Field: Law and Lawyers in the Government of the European Union (for a Renewed Research Agenda)', *International Political Sociology* 2(2), 2008, pp. 128–44; and Julie Bailleux, *Penser l'Europe par le droit. L'invention du droit communautaire en France*, Paris, Dalloz, 2014.

that: the European Communities were set up in a context of a marked depreciation of the authority of law and of legal professions in national political, bureaucratic and economic spheres.[10] Conversely, other bodies of knowledge (in particular, political economy and sociology of organizations) and techniques of regulation (such as economic planning) were deemed better suited to face the challenge of the 'modernization' of European States and economies. Even though legal experts arguably played an important role in the drafting of the Treaties,[11] they left no trace of a European 'Constitutional Charter', of a 'Supreme Court', nor any mention of a new type of international legal order. The Treaties often and mostly appealed to the *rapprochement*, the *harmonization* or even the *unification* of national legislations in terms that hardly differed from those present in the founding documents of other European organizations such as the Organization for European Economic Co-operation or the Council of Europe. Accordingly, the initial expectation was that law would essentially provide politicians with the technical expertise in *comparative law* they needed to shape the common economic laws of the Common Market.

By what 'miracle', then, have the variegated set of European Treaties, institutions, groups and policies been able to take shape and grow into one unique transnational polity that constitutes a relatively stable order of practice and meaning? Through what processes have they come to coalesce into one unified 'constitutional settlement'? This book does not intend to answer these questions by retrospectively assigning a single intrinsic *economy* or *logic* to the Paris or Rome Treaties. On the contrary, it takes a radically different stance: instead of assuming that an 'institutional terrain' had even existed from the outset of the European Communities, it explores the *institution* of Europe's polity as the contingent and conflictual *historical* process of symbolic, cognitive and practical unification of a variegated set of European constructions (treaties, institutions, policies, etc.) and groups into one single *order* endowed with its own specific rationality.

The book's central claim is that the broad definitional power that law is generally endowed within the context of the European Union actually

[10] This overall decline can be traced in many settings starting with the decline in the share of members of Parliament with a law degree or coming from the legal professions: cf. Maurizio Cotta and Heinrich Best (eds.), *Democratic Representation in Europe: Diversity, Change and Convergence*, Oxford, Oxford University Press, 2007.

[11] Anne Boerger, 'Negotiating the Foundations of European Law: The Legal History of the Treaties of Paris and Rome', *Journal of Contemporary European History*, 21(3), 2012, pp. 339–56.

has to do with (and reveals) EU law's historically acquired 'brokering capacity'. By this expression, I wish here to refer to the ways in which law has come to stand as the major unifying glue and core integrative programme that holds together Europe's complex, disjointed and multilevel polity. For that reason, *Brokering Europe* is not just another narrative of Europe's legal integration. Its ambition is to provide a deeper understanding of Europe's own specific way of polity (its own specific modes of legitimacy, its own specific types of political and professional authority, etc.), a question that the perpetual jousting between intergovernmentalists and neo-functionalists over Europe's major *integrative* force (diplomats or international secretariats? States or international courts? National or transnational civil society?, etc.) has to date essentially left in a dead end.

The formulation of this project has required a number of methodological moves and choices. The first one is a historical *détour* that takes the story this book tentatively retells back to the very early years of the European Communities. The motives for this sociogenetic turn stand distant from any sort of historical *point d'honneur*; nor are they the result of merely erudite interest in the history of European ideas. Rather, they lie in the notion that such a detour is the most efficient denaturalizing device, as it takes us back to a moment in time when there was precisely no common sense about what Europe's polity was about and what its connection with the law ought to be. Yet, I do not engage in historical investigation in the same way a historian would do; in fact, my goal here is not to write a full history of European integration. Some readers may be surprised that canonical episodes of European historiography are mentioned only in passing – if at all. In line with historical institutionalism[12] but with a deeper commitment to the broader tradition of historical sociology,[13] I have chosen to focus on critical junctures and long-term processes that have defined a particular constitutional function for the law in Europe's polity, and the ways in which this progressive imposition has correlatively marginalized other possible futures.

This historical turn called for a second move towards a denser description of the law; one that would allow the tracking of the many political and social connections that have been built *through* the practice of law. In

[12] In a large literature, see Paul Pierson and Theda Skocpol, 'Historical Institutionalism in Contemporary Political Science', in Ira Katznelson and Helen Milner (eds.), *Political Science: The State of the Discipline*, New York, Norton, 2002, pp. 693–721.

[13] For a general theoretical and historical framework, see Pierre Bourdieu, *On the State: Lectures at the Collège de France 1989–92*, London, Polity, 2014.

its attempts to identify the set of *external* factors that keep Europe's *judicial* dynamics moving, political science literature has sacrificed (more often than not) the analysis of the law itself – that is, of the people who set law in motion and the arenas in which law is produced, debated and interpreted. On the mainstream account, lawyers seem to act merely as transmission belts: they are nearly invisible proxies for a variety of contending players who, for their part, are assumed to be very real (States, EU institutions, companies, interest groups, NGOs, etc.).[14] Along-side the Weberian tradition and against this thin description of law,[15] the present book argues that law exists as a specific and relatively autonomous social world – one that is made of specific professional conceptions of worth and wealth, commonsensical ideas about the political and social importance of law and even, under certain historical circumstances, an agenda of its own. *Brokering Europe* therefore inserts living, acting people into what has so far tended to remain a disembodied narrative of reified actors ('the Court', 'the Commission') pursuing abstract goals and *ex ante* defined interests. Rather than contemplating the 'cathedral' of European law from the outside, this book goes inside the edifice and sheds light on the assembly of clerks on which the EU law controversies exercise a calling.[16] Thus shifting the focus on real life and historically situated actors, the book seeks to identify how their legal *and* non-legal undertakings have been shaped and informed by their

[14] See, however, the work of the Polilexes research group (www.polilexes.com) and the recent edited volume, Antoine Vauchez and Bruno de Witte (eds.), *Lawyering Europe: European Law as a Transnational Social Field*, Oxford, Hart Publishing, 2013.

[15] For a similar critique, see Christian Joerges, 'Taking the Law Seriously: On Political Science and the Role of Law in the Process of European Integration', *European Law Journal*, 2(2), 1996, pp. 105–35; Grainne de Búrca, 'Rethinking Law in Neofunctionalist Theory', *Journal of European Public Policy*, 12(2), 2005, pp. 310–36; and Jo Shaw, 'The European Union: Discipline Building Meets Polity Building', in P. Cane and M. Tushnet (eds.), *Oxford Handbook of Legal Studies*, Oxford, Oxford University Press, 2003, pp. 325–52.

[16] On this tradition of political sociology, see Max Weber, *On Law in Economy and Society*, Cambridge, MA, Harvard University Press, 1954; Pierre Bourdieu, 'Genèse et structure du champ religieux', *Revue française de sociologie*, 12(2), 1971, pp. 295–334; 'Une interprétation de la théorie de la religion selon Max Weber', *Archives européennes de sociologie*, 12, 1971, pp. 3–21; and Ernst Kantorowicz, 'Kinship Under the Impact of Scientific Jurisprudence', in M. Clagett, G. Post and R. Reynolds (eds.), *Twelfth-Century Europe and the Foundation of Modern Society*, Madison WI, University of Wisconsin Press, 1961, pp. 89–111; and, for the sake of this book, Antoine Vauchez, 'The Force of a Weak Field: Law and Lawyers in the Government of the European Union (for a Renewed Research Agenda)', *International Political Sociology* 2(2), 2008, pp. 128–44; and Antonin Cohen, 'Legal Professionals or Political Entrepreneurs? Constitution Making as a Process of Social Construction and Political Mobilization', *International Political Sociology*, 4(2), 2010, pp. 107–23.

individual backgrounds, their social and professional socialization and their oft-interlocking networks within and outside the legal field. Euro-implicated lawyers (hereinafter, 'Euro-lawyers') are therefore followed way beyond the litigation arenas, in their manifold capacities as jurisconsults-diplomats, corporate lawyers, EU institutions' legal advisers, 'politicians of the law', institution-builders, academics, etc. In particular, the book envisages lawyers as knowledge-producers: relatedly legal theories and methodologies are not considered as just esoteric forms of knowledge but also as the standard-bearers of specific representations of the Union (its own form of government and principles of legitimacy) in areas as different as antitrust policy, market regulation, supranational administration, human rights control, Euro-parliamentarism, etc.[17]

It is not, however, my intention to substitute a 'grand *legal* narrative' for the similarly grand economic or political master-plans that have dominated most of Europe's historiography, granting the first role to 'great men', audacious master-plans or visionary institutions. There is no hero or 'invisible college' in this tale that does not seek to replace the old heroic figures by new ones – lawyers, judges or law professors in lieu of the former politicians, civils servants and diplomats usually presented as Europe's founding fathers. Hence the third and last move towards the framing of a conceptual toolbox that would be able to account for the social and political conditions for law's authority without locating it in its purportedly eternal capacity to reconcile antagonisms, or in its intrinsic depoliticizing virtues. To this aim, this research draws particularly on Pierre Bourdieu's field-theory, a set of analytical instruments only recently mobilized for the study of the European Union. Here is not the place to discuss its general scope and value.[18] Suffice it to point out that field-theory is particularly well suited for the EU context in which, more than in any other research area, there is a need to consider the power

[17] For a similar view on the political texture of law, see Peter Lindseth, *Power and Legitimacy: Reconciling Europe and the Nation-State*, Oxford, Oxford University Press, 2011.

[18] Recent overviews of this lively stream of research include Adrian Favell and Viriginie Guiraudon, 'The Sociology of the European Union: An Agenda', *European Union Politics*, 10 (4), 2009, pp. 550–76; Michel Mangenot and Jay Rowell (eds.), *A Political Sociology of the European Union: Reassessing Constructivism*, Manchester, Manchester University Press, 2010; Niilo Kauppi and Mikael Madsen (eds.), *Transnational Power Elites: The New Professionals of Governance*, London, Routledge, 2013; Didier Georgakakis (ed.), *The Field of Eurocracy: Mapping EU Actors and Professionals*, Basingstoke, Palgrave, 2013; and Antoine Vauchez and Bruno de Witte (eds.), *European Law as Transnational Social Field*, Oxford, Hart Publishing, 2013.

relations (competing forms of authority and types of social capital) that cut across the political and administrative sites of command. Field-theory enables us to locate law and lawyers in the wider historical competition that took place in the post-Second World War period over the definition of the types of policy instruments, expertise and, ultimately, elites that would be best suited for leading the unification of Europe. As the book traces back the steps and actors in the formation of a specifically European legal field, it is able to unearth the highly singular and enduring form of this transnational field which has remained over time a weakly structured and largely heteronomous social space. Being deeply enmeshed in national fields of power and deprived of strong units of internal governance, it is best described as a 'weak field'[19] located at the very edge of national and European political, administrative, economic and academic fields. The book contends that the 'brokering capacity' of European law to act as the operator of a symbolic and practical unification of 'Europe' originates precisely in this *interstitial* position. The '*weak* field' of European law is analyzed as the privileged *locus* of a transformative process whereby Europe's '*strong* integration programme' – namely, the constitutional paradigm of Europe[20] – progressively crystallized.[21] By these notions of 'strong programme' and 'constitutional paradigm', I do not mean a mere set of abstract ideas: they involve commonsensical assumptions regarding Europe's standard operating modes (institutional roles, policy instruments, groups' identities) that function at a deeper level than any given theory; they allude to taken-for-granted cognitive tools that help decipher and make sense of an otherwise complex and dispersed polity such as the EU (a *de facto*

[19] On the notion of a 'weak field' applied to the study of transnational spaces, see Stephanie Mudge and Antoine Vauchez, 'Building Europe on a Weak Field: Law, Economics, Scholarly Avatars in Transnational Politics', *American Journal of Sociology*, 118(2), 2012, pp. 449–92. On transnational fields as 'crossroads', see also Yves Dezalay and Bryant Garth, *The Internationalization of Palace Wars: Law, Economics and the Transformation of Latin America*, Chicago IL, University of Chicago Press, 2002; and Mikael Madsen, 'Transnational Fields: Elements of a Reflexive Sociology of the Internationalization of Law', *Retfaerd*, 3(114), 2006, pp. 23–41.

[20] By many standards, the notion of 'Constitution' is a slippery one, in the EU context even more than elsewhere (cf. Chapter 6 for more references on these possible confusions). Therefore, I have made no prior assumptions regarding what its 'authentic' meaning ought to be; rather, I have followed the emergence of a constitutional rhetoric and tracked the competing meanings that have been given to it.

[21] This constitutional paradigm can be ideal – typically opposed to what could be labelled a 'weak integration programme' that holds European Treaties to be ones among many inter-State agreements, and sees the law as no more than an instrument serving diplomatic missions and the European Council.

autonomous constitutional order); benchmarks and rationales against which Europe's future is *assessed* (a fully fledged constitutional polity); and a transnational power map locating the ability and responsibility for the 'rational guidance' of European integration in particular institutions (Commission, Court, etc.), blends of professionals (lawyers, economists, diplomats, EU civil servants, etc.) and sets of techniques (legal, political, economic, the *acquis*, Eur-lex, etc.).

In order to seize the coalescence of this constitutional paradigm, *Brokering Europe* suggests new empirical strategies. Over the years, the study of EU legal integration has drawn more and more extensively on large-N quantitative studies, mostly drawn from the ECJ's case law.[22] While these statistical studies have sometimes proved enlightening, I argue they have reached the point of decreasing output, as they fail to grasp the fine-grained processes through which law and Europe have historically built (and rebuilt) each other in a continuous and perpetually reinforcing entwinement. Because much of this history happens through a transnational competition over the interpretation of Europe's nature, the book follows Euro-implicated actors as they build bridges and connexions between Europe and the law. In his search for the formation of a cross-sectoral and cross-institutional common sense about Europe, the researcher is compelled not to choose *one* level of analysis over the others (the legal over the political, or the European over the national, etc.), but rather to pay special attention to what lies precisely *in-between* them. As he casts the connectedness of Europe's legal field with its neighbouring fields, he progressively maps out the overall 'hermeneutic space'[23] in which this interpretative struggle is taking place, reaching out to a variety of social and professional universes and microcosms, apparently a stranger to the field of law, but oft critical to understanding its dynamics. As he traces the arenas in which intellectual and interpersonal connections or oppositions have been produced, the inquiry progressively turns into a transnational *jeu de piste*, from level to level and from empirical *corpus* to empirical *corpus*. Hence, the very diverse set of oft-unexplored empirical resources that this research has dug up over the years – biographical data, in-depth coverage of European law scholarly or professional conferences, ECJ cases' documents and commentaries,

[22] For an overview of the profusion of quantitative inquiries and a discussion of the rather contradictory results, see Lisa Conant, 'The Politics of Legal Integration', *Journal of Common Market Studies*, 46(2), 2008, pp. 293–314.

[23] Nathalie Heinich, *Glory of Van Gogh: An Anthropology of Admiration*, Princeton, NJ, Princeton University Press, 1996.

forgotten doctrinal controversies, interviews with key legal practitioners, archival files from the Commission's Legal Service and secretariat general, commemorative material from the ECJ (eulogies, *Festschriften*, jubilees, etc.), among others.

The book is divided into two parts. The first part explores the genesis of Europe's polity, providing a detailed examination of the historical processes through which Europe's nature and future have been defined on legal grounds. Focusing on specific historical sequences during which the 'strong integration programme' crystallized, it shows how European law acquired its brokering capacity. A significant portion of this first part is thus devoted to investigating the early period of EC institutions when their core principles and *modus operandi* were first defined. It examines how a variety of pan-European actors who were otherwise engaged in political, economic, bureaucratic or academic undertakings seized the opportunity of the early verdicts of the ECJ in order to redirect the course of European integration along a legal/constitutional path. The second part then examines medium- and long-term processes of consolidation of this early constellation. Following the specific trajectories of three legal constructs ('jurisprudence', the '*acquis*' and the 'Constitution' project) as they were formalized as foundational pillars of the European Union, it accounts for the resilience of the constitutional paradigm as the inescapable frame of the EU polity in the face of the diplomatic big bangs and centrifugal forces that have periodically attempted to reopen the space of political possibilities in Europe.

Part I

Unity through law: inventing Europe's 'integration programme'

> In the realm of State structure, jurists are contained and dominated by political authorities, for at the present time there no longer exists any government, in any State, that is in the hands of specialists in law. In all modern countries power belongs to the representatives of public opinion, and it is they who enact laws and dominate jurists. In international organizations, we see jurists occupying a place that they have lost in the internal [national] order. States want to abandon the smallest possible number of sovereign prerogatives when they agree to be bound by the terms of treaties instituting international organizations. They therefore ask jurists to prepare complex magical formulas that will allow the organizations to function while preserving as many privileges as possible for the State structures ... To implement these treaties, courts of justice, judicial committees and legal services are required, and they have characteristically flourished in international organizations ... Their work is not finished, however, for they will subsequently incorporate themselves into the bodies of the monsters they have created. Paul Reuter[1]

The Rome Treaties were signed on 25 March 1957. At the time, nothing would have led one to think that a first transnational polity would grow up between the lines of this international agreement, attracting a multitude of political, administrative, economic, academic and other actors. The three Treaties (ECSC, EEC, Euratom) and the supplementary Convention regarding 'certain institutions common to the European Communities' represented a dense set of texts comprising respectively 100, 248,

[1] 'Techniciens et politiques dans l'organisation internationale', in *Politique et technique*, Paris, PUF, 1958, p. 195. A renowned professor of international public law at the law faculty of the Sorbonne, Paul Reuter had been the legal adviser (*jurisconsulte*) of the French government in the drafting of the European Coal and Steel Community Treaty in 1951. Unless otherwise indicated, all quotations from non-English-language books and journals are translated by the author.

225 and 8 articles. At the outset, this collection did not appear to offer a palette of immediately available opportunities, and even less a unique institutional *system* endowed with a specific rationale. The Treaties were the product of a heterogeneous set of diverse diplomatic forces and ideological influences, and were not immediately intelligible as an 'institutional terrain' creating relationships between and giving meaning to all the groups, institutions and policies that they brought into existence.[2] Likewise, they did not in one fell swoop redraw the lines of the dominant beliefs and representations with regard to the spheres of political mediation, nor did they by themselves upset the organizational practices that determine the national echelon as the natural locus for the aggregation of interests.

There are several explanations for this. After decades of ritual commemoration of this 'founding moment', we have forgotten that the Rome Treaties were greeted with a certain degree of indifference. At the time, few professional groups, companies, labour and employer organizations, political parties or academic disciplines felt that the Treaties' provisions were relevant to them. It must be said that the road to the unification of Europe was already quite congested. The Europe embodied by the European Communities was just one of the forms of transnational political and economic cooperation that were springing up at the time, and that were debated in various forums simultaneously: the Greater Europe forged by the Organization for European Economic Co-operation, the proposed free-trade zones that would give birth to the European Free Trade Association, the Atlantic Europe of NATO and international institutions such as the GATT or the IMF. As noted by Laurent Warlouzet, 'the principal organization of European economic cooperation in which the Six were engaged in 1955 was not the ECSC but the [Organization for European Economic Co-operation], and the latter handled the development of trade for all economic sectors in Western Europe with considerable success'.[3] In other words, the EC institutional framework was just one of several European stages on which politicians and diplomats acted simultaneously. Of course, the importance of the Common Market is not to be under-estimated; but, although the dismantling of customs and tariff barriers was organized in detail by the Rome Treaties, the prospect of 'market merger' leading to harmonization of national economic and

[2] Neil Fligstein and Jason McNichol, 'The Institutional Terrain of the European Union', in Wayne Sandholtz and Alec Stone (eds.), *European Integration and Supranational Governance*, Oxford, Oxford University Press, 1998, pp. 59–91.

[3] Laurent Warlouzet, *Le choix de la CEE par la France. Les débats économiques de Pierre Mendès-France à Charles de Gaulle (1955–1969)*, Paris, CHEFF, 2011.

professional regulations was a distant and frankly improbable outcome. The signatories who gathered at the Capitoline Hill in March 1957 certainly had ambitions for the political unification of Europe. But, as the Rome Treaties were explicitly founded on the renunciation of the constitutional aims linked to the European Defence Community, from the start it was hard to mobilize the nebulous pan-European formation on this basis. Worse still, the adoption of the Treaties opened deep divisions within Europe, with a maximalist faction around the Italian socialist, Altiero Spinelli, who scathingly decried the 'Common Market hoax',[4] and a pragmatic faction around Paul-Henri Spaak, who saw in the Treaties the seeds of a future political unity.[5]

It must be said that nothing in the Treaties hinted at the premises of a new political centre. As the Treaties pursued essentially economic goals, they ultimately left to one side the institutional system intended to organize the Common Market policies. Indeed, commentators pointed out that, in contrast to the Treaty of Paris, the EC institutions were relegated to the fifth and final section of the text. The low level of political content in the new Treaties is reflected in the expression 'Common Market' that was most often used to designate the Communities in ordinary parlance. The 1957 Rome Treaties contain far fewer declarations of values and statements of principles than the 1951 Paris Treaty. After the Coal and Steel Community – which the Paris Treaty pledged would create 'the basis for a broader and deeper European Community among peoples long divided by bloody conflicts' – came a European Economic Community with the 'task' first and foremost of 'establishing a common market ... and to promote throughout the European Community a harmonious development of economic activities' (article 2). In practical terms, the 'basis' of this new European Community was merely a customs union (article 9). But there is something even worse. The singular form (the Rome *Treaty*) which is commonly used today notwithstanding, three international instruments were signed in Rome on 25 March 1957 – the EEC and Euratom Treaties, and a supplementary Convention. These documents mark the existence of three distinct entities on the institutional level, the ECSC, Euratom

4 Altiero Spinelli, 'La beffa del Mercato comune. 24 sett. 1957', in *L'Europa non cade dal cielo*, Bologna, Il Mulino, 1960, pp. 282–7.

5 On the political rifts that divided the European Movement at the time the Rome Treaties were implemented, see Daniela Preda, 'The Movements for European Unity (1958–1972)', in Antonio Varsori (ed.), *Inside the European Community: Actors and Policies in the European Integration 1957–1972*, Baden-Baden, Nomos, 2006, pp. 177–93.

and the EEC. It was clear to all that the institutional characteristics of the two new Communities differed profoundly from those of the ECSC. This ensemble was held together by just one thread, the supplementary Convention to the Treaties, a spare document of eight articles that ensures no more than the *coordination* of the three Communities by setting up a couple of shared institutions, principally the Court of Justice and the Parliamentary Assembly, which as commentators pointed out would nevertheless have different competencies and act according to different procedures under the different Treaties. As it turned out, the absence of a *unified* institutional system in no way impeded the formation of several sector-specific networks that brought together business managers, emerging transnational interest groups, high-level civil servants and other experts representing the Member States.[6] These nascent networks sought to flesh out the skeleton of the various chapters (transport, fisheries, agriculture, social policy, etc.) that made up the new Treaties. It remains, nonetheless, that at the outset no shared and cross-sectoral framework of understanding of 'Europe' was available. The Paris and Rome Treaties had created a set of cursorily defined institutions, an index of (possible) European public policies, and a list of objectives to attain, but hardly any 'political system'.

The first part of this book explores the transformative process through which this rather inchoate set of Treaties, Communities, institutions and policies was turned into one 'constitutional settlement', thereby providing us with a unitary understanding of this emerging transnational polity. It traces the coalescence of a constellation of pan-European actors fostering a constitutional interpretation of the founding Treaties and building the Court's and the Commission's political capacity to defend this settlement, in a context in which the idea that EC law would be granted a constitutional function had little traction. It does so by tracking the conflicts that arose as 'meaning' and 'scope' were given to the Rome and Paris Treaties. The issue of the objective traits of these Treaties did not exist *per se*, but only insofar as it was brandished by a variety of advocates who seek to establish or consolidate a certain vision of Europe, in line with their personal trajectories and their social and professional positions. In other words, defining Europe's institutional platform was at one and the same time a debate over the relative

[6] Neil Fligstein and Jason McNichol, 'The Institutional Terrain of the European Union', in Wayne Sandholtz and Alec Stone (eds.), *European Integration and Supranational Governance*, Oxford, Oxford University Press, 1998, pp. 59–91.

legitimacy of different groups of actors (and their respective credentials, *savoir-faire* and techniques of government) in leading the emerging government of Europe. In this regard the Treaties are first of all a terrain for the confrontation between different definitions of 'Europe', its institutions, its operational dynamics and its modes of legitimization, and, *in fine*, between different types of competencies and credentials expected from the statesman of this emerging polity.[7] On this stage are found, in addition to diplomats and political leaders, various sectoral communities and specialists wielding many sorts of expertise – economic, legal and others – all of whom have an interest in formalizing the 'logic' (intergovernmental or supranational) underlying the Treaties, and the political, economic and legal questions relevant to the functioning of the Treaties.[8] As I track this competitive and collective process of definition of the authentic meaning of the Treaties, I am able to unearth the process whereby 'Europe' has emerged as a tangible political *reality* possessing its own rationale distinct from that of national and international political orders, and as a shared 'institutional terrain' for the variety of Treaties, institutions, and ultimately policies (competition, transport, free movement, the Common Agricultural Policy, etc.) that are implemented in its name. Chapter 1 follows EC institutions and policies as they start up in Luxembourg, Strasbourg and Brussels at the turn of the 1950s, tracing the institutional strategies of various Euro-implicated 'entrepreneurs' as they try to give life and meaning to the Rome Treaties. Chapter 2 analyzes the emergence, at the intersection of these European undertakings, of a transnational legal field whose 'denizens' act as 'brokers' for this transnational institutional sphere as it takes shape. This analysis of legal and judicial spaces as Europe's 'weak field' will enable readers to follow the arguments in Chapter 3 and see how a full-blown political metaphysics of Europe was built up, inscribing in one framework all the heterogeneous and sometimes conflicting groups, institutions and policies that make up the European entity.

[7] See the work of Antonin Cohen for a similar interpretation, in particular 'Constitutionalism without Constitution: Transnational Elites between Political Mobilization and Legal Expertise (1940s–1960s)', *Law and Social Inquiry*, 23(1), 2007, pp. 109–35.

[8] The use of initial capital letters when referring to those treaties which set out EU primary rules (the Treaties of Paris and of Rome, the Single European Act, the Maastricht, Amsterdam and Nice Treaties, the Constitutional Treaty and the Lisbon Treaty) – a convention that we use throughout this text – is in itself indicative of the efforts made to mark the constitutional nature of Europe's fundamental rules.

1 Three Treaties, one Community: institution-building and legal strategies to unify Europe

The four institutions that were officially constituted on 1 January 1958 to carry out the creation of the Common Market – 'an Assembly, a Council, a Commission, a Court of Justice' as succinctly announced in article 4 of the EEC Treaty – were born in a somewhat hazy context. The precedent furnished by the ECSC provided a marker for exploring this *terra incognita*, but this parallel was not always adequate. The 'supranationalism' that was meant to be the specific hallmark of the institutional system created under the Paris Treaty was poorly regarded since the failure of the European Defence Community, so much so that it was close to being 'subject to a ban' at the turn of the 1950s.[1] This notion did not seem readily transposable to the Rome Treaties under which the EEC Commission had no federal vocation, and not even the executive capacity held by the ECSC High Authority. In the absence of trail markers, the most seasoned constitutionalists and political scientists were disturbed by the institutions created under the Rome Treaties. The words used to describe them were certainly familiar, but the objects they referred to were only distantly related to the 'things' habitually designated by this same terminology in national spheres. The Court of Justice of the European Communities, for instance, appeared to be merely an *ersatz* of a supreme jurisdiction, and it was a far stretch from the European Parliamentary Assembly to the genuinely transnational parliamentary representation that some observers hoped to see emerge in Strasbourg. Even the Common Market, which this whole institutional apparatus was developed to serve, looked to be

1 Pierre Pescatore, 'Le traité CECA. Origine et modèle de l'unification européenne', in *CECA (1952–2002)*, Luxembourg, Office des publications officielles des Communautés européennes, 2002, p. 184. For a general perspective, see Julie Bailleux, 'How Europe Came to Law', *Revue française de science politique*, **60**(2), 2010, pp. 295–318.

a figment of the imagination as long as the economies of the six Member States remained almost exclusively under national regulatory frameworks. The labels attributed to the new institutions that were set up in Brussels, Luxembourg and Strasbourg looked more like 'pseudonyms' than titles corresponding to established practice.[2] The awkwardness was palpable: commentators felt obliged to have recourse to multiple rewordings ('quasi-legislative', '*de facto* Constitution', etc.), quotation marks and neologisms in order to qualify the organs whose effective functions 'are not to be found where the analogy with the State model would lead one to expect them'.[3] For those accustomed to the classic architecture of national constitutional edifices, reading the Treaties caused a perpetual 'mental refocusing'.[4] Let us take a look: here the executive has two branches, the legislative function eludes the Parliament, no organ has an exclusive function, no function is exercised by just one organ, etc. The baroque features of these institutional arrangements could make the specialists almost dizzy. Could one really talk of 'political control' in the case of an essentially consultative European Parliamentary Assembly? Could an institution lacking any legislative function be called a parliament? Further still, how could the Commission truly be an 'executive branch' of the Communities when at the same time it shared a 'legislative function' with the Council of Ministers? What sort of court could have the attributions of an administrative court to oversee the legality of the acts of EC institutions, those of a constitutional court to ensure the balance of power between institutions, and those of an arbitral tribunal to resolve conflicts arising from the creation of the Common Market? The most sceptical critics denounced the optical illusion of political institutions that scarcely masked the forceful return of governments in the EC decision-making process; the most indulgent critics saw a confusion of roles characteristic of all international organizations. All, however, pointed out the dearth of traditional landmarks (separation of powers, specialized functions, parliamentarism, etc.) and the absence of criteria shared by the countries for making judgments, thus underscoring the

[2] Fernand Dehousse, *L'avenir institutionnel des Communautés européennes*, Nancy, Conférences européennes, Centre européen universitaire de Nancy, 1967, p. 9.

[3] Fritz Munch, 'Prolégomènes à une théorie constitutionnelle des Communautés européennes', *Rivista di diritto europeo*, **1**(1), 1961, p. 130.

[4] Pierre Pescatore, 'Les objectifs de la Communauté européenne comme principes d'interprétation dans la jurisprudence de la Cour de justice', in *Miscellanea Ganshof van der Meersch*, Brussels, Bruylant, 1979, p. 331.

many uncertainties that weighed on this phase of the implementation of EC institutions.[5]

Our subject here is this newborn Europe emerging from the Rome Treaties, this short historical sequence where these institutions can be seen as they take shape, trying out all sorts of pathways and identities. It is fair to say that at first not many political or social actors took an interest in the Rome Treaties, preferring the national echelon as the most suitable for achieving their objectives. Nonetheless, first microcosms of EC political, administrative, legal and market professionals began to form at the heart of the new institutions, or on their immediate periphery, with the intention of giving *supranational* flesh and bones to the words and fictions of the Treaties. These entrepreneurs of Europe, the first 'tenants' of these EC institutions, sought – for various reasons – to protect the institutions from the pressures of inter-State manoeuvres. Far from representing a single group or project (neo-liberal, federalist or otherwise), these enterprises took on features as varied as the national power structures from which they derived and the transnational networks (political, economic, legal, etc.) to which they were connected. They were members of parliament, businessmen, ambassadors, members of the college of European commissioners, high-level civil servants, often practitioners of legal professions, but also law professors, judges and auditors of the Court, or business lawyers. Their professional and institutional projects were relatively independent of each other, and sometimes even contradictory, reflecting the diversity of the social spaces in which they unfolded. From an administrative point of view, the aim was to cast the foundations of a genuinely supranational bureaucracy that would be a structure embodying Europe's 'general interest', rather than just an international secretariat charged with the technical aspects of setting up common markets. In a more political outlook, the objective was to establish the basis of an authentic European parliamentary system. From a judicial perspective, it was the truly 'jurisdictional' character of the ECJ that was at stake, a court that many saw as no more than an instance for international arbitration. Economically speaking, the issue was to breathe life into the ambitions for a *common* market, with Brussels' institutions as the guarantor and regulator of open trade and free competition.

[5] Piers Ludlow, 'Value, Flexibility and Openness: The Treaty of Rome's Success in Historical Perspective', in Julio Baquero Cruz and Carlos Closa Montera (eds.), *European Integration in Historical Perspective from Rome to Berlin (1957–2007)*, Brussels, Peter Lang, 2009, pp. 17–39.

As I follow the emergence of these institutional strategies as they try to live up to the expectations created by the fictions present in the Treaties, we see a generation of entrepreneurs of Europe; they did not have to imagine, as did the post-Second World War pan-European advocates, the possible outlines or ideals of a European project, embodied in a corresponding number of draft Constitutions, assembly resolutions and other declarations of intent, but henceforth had to bring institutions and policies into concrete existence. In this respect, everything remained to be invented: as set forth in the Rome Treaties, the roles, the scope and the rank of the various institutions were quite vague. Due to this lack of precision regarding the rules of conduct for 'policies' that were essentially stated in terms of objectives, and the relatively indeterminate operational boundaries of each of the 'institutions', the early years of existence of the European Communities had a strong agonistic dimension as each institutional group had to mark its status and define its missions.

In the absence of a unanimously recognized scope of action, and lacking leverage to act within the Member States themselves, the success of these various institution-building strategies would play out to a large extent on the only terrain that gave them legitimacy when confronting diplomats and ministers – the terrain of the Treaties themselves. The Rome Treaties thus became the central object of value for a group of judges, commissioners, members of parliament, entrepreneurs and European business lawyers for whom this shared paper foundation anchored and gave support to their claims of competency. Thus these initial entrepreneurs of Europe were led to produce a set of in-house legal and political doctrines (narratives, rationalizations, theories, etc.) that would interpret the European Treaties as providing them with a degree of autonomy, even if relative. In this context, these first legal and political discourses and theories on the European Treaties were not esoteric discourses produced by actors concerned exclusively with the legal stakes, but constituted a fundamental lever for a highly diverse set of institutional undertakings. This study follows the deployment of lay legal theories of Europe both within and at the margins of the Commission, the Parliamentary Assembly, the ECJ and the Common Market.

Claiming objectivity: the European Commission and the guardianship of the Treaties

If there is one opinion shared by the first commentators on the Rome Treaties, it is the view that these new texts sacrificed to a large extent the driving role of the EC Executives that was so cherished by Jean

Monnet. Citing the failure of the ECSC, the French delegation to the negotiations for the Rome Treaties had been careful to avoid constructing two new Executives – the Commission of the EEC and the Commission of Euratom – according to the supranational model of a High Authority endowed with significant decision-making power. Accordingly, the EEC administrative services that took up their quarters at the intersection of the Avenue de la Joyeuse Entrée and the Rue de la Loi in Brussels on 1 January 1958 had a low profile. An 'Executive' without executive powers, an 'administration' without enforcement powers, the EEC Commission had very little splendour. Its first president, Walter Hallstein, had this laconic comment: '[I]t is not the power of decision that essentially characterizes the role of the Commission in the institutional system of the treaty. . .'.[6] But this was not all. Not only was this emerging European bureaucracy weak, but it was fragmented into three separate entities. In practice, three 'EC Executives' – the High Authority, the EEC Commission and the Euratom Commission – now coexisted. Furthermore, they were geographically dispersed, the High Authority remaining in Luxembourg while the other two set up in Brussels, the provisional capital of the new Communities. Without shared administrative services (with a few exceptions) or a unified status for civil servants (the first dating from 1968), there were very few institutional ties that could ensure coordination across the three Communities in the decade that followed the adoption of the Rome Treaties (up to the merger of the three Executives on 1 July 1967). Adding to the confusion, a muted rivalry smouldered between the ECSC High Authority in Luxembourg and the emerging Brussels pole of the EEC Commission and Euratom, each seat claiming to embody the true EC ambition.[7] While the formation of a transnational bureaucracy thus seemed greatly jeopardized, the political path towards a supranational political Europe did not appear to be any more practicable. Following a diplomatic line already taken during the negotiations for the Rome Treaties, the French government would repeatedly refuse to see these Executives as anything other than 'international secretariats' in charge simply of coordination and technical implementation. This was strikingly confirmed by the French Fouchet projects of 1961–2 that

[6] Walter Hallstein, *Débats de l'Assemblée parlementaire commune du 23 juin 1958*, Luxembourg, Official Journal of the European Communities, 1959, p. 159.

[7] See Daniela Preda, 'Hallstein e l'amministrazione pubblica europea', in *Storia amministrazione costituzione, annale dell'Istituto per la scienza dell'amministrazione pubblica*, 8(1), 2000, pp. 79–104.

envisaged the creation of a fourth EC, which for the government led by Michel Debré would be a fully "inter-governmental" one.[8]

Impossible administration, improbable government, the EEC Commission needed to invent a new role for itself. In the following section, I track how a novel institutional pathway was invented. Instrumental to this invention was the encounter between an EEC Commission president who was an ardent advocate of a constitutional reading of the Rome Treaties, and a Legal Service that tasked itself with the mission of carrying on a 'legal policing' of their rightful implementation. Taking advantage of the then strong osmosis between the 'administration' level (the directors general) and the 'political' level (the commissioners),[9] these European entrepreneurs founded the Commission's institutional identity on a claim of 'supplement of objectivity'[10] *vis-à-vis* Member States enmeshed in the partisan politics and in diplomatic considerations. This mission of objectivity – watching over the European general interest – was rooted in the fictional grounds of a 'Constitution-Treaty', a unified and objective standard, independent of the Member States. Thereby, these first European entrepreneurs devised the equation of a Commission that affirmed its leadership on the playing field of law.

The constitutional doctrine of Professor Hallstein

This propensity to define the Commission's mission in terms of objectivity and law is undoubtedly in part related to the profile of the first commissioners and top civil servants of the three EC Executives (ECSC, Euratom, EEC). In both categories, the appointees were in most cases law graduates, and indeed often directly experienced in legal professions.[11] Their preference for law was emblematically personified by the first president of the EEC Commission, Professor Walter Hallstein, a zealous legal theoretician. Indeed, the former law professor and vice-chancellor

[8] On this topic see Marie-Thérèse Bitsch, 'Les institutions communautaires face au projet d'union politique (1958–62)', in *La construction européenne. Enjeux politiques et choix institutionnels*, Brussels, Peter Lang, 2007, p. 126.

[9] Didier Georgakakis and Marine de Lassale, 'Where have all the lawyers gone? Structure and transformations of the top European Commission officials' legal training', in Antoine Vauchez and Bruno de Witte (eds.), *Lawyering Europe: European Law as a Transnational Social Field*, Oxford, Hart Publishing, 2013, pp. 137–52.

[10] Pierre Pescatore, *Le droit de l'intégration. Emergence d'un phénomène nouveau dans les relations internationales selon l'expérience des Communautés européennes*, Leiden, Sijthof, 1974, p. 80.

[11] During the period 1952–67, 50 per cent of the commissioners held law degrees, and 22.5 per cent were in legal professions. See Andrew MacMullen, 'European Commissioners: National Routes to a European Elite', in Neil Nugent (ed.), *At the Heart of the Union: Studies of the European Commission*, Basingstoke, Palgrave Macmillan, 2000, pp. 28–50.

of the University of Frankfurt, who purportedly made a point of using the title of professor in all circumstances, saw the president's role as an intellectual magisterium, to the point that the German press often reproached him for his 'professorial attitude' and 'juridical turn of mind'.[12] In the course of his mandate, he continued to lecture and to attend conferences at American and European universities: he was present, among others, at the congress of the International Law Association in Hamburg in August 1960, at Harvard University in 1962, at Padua University in March 1962, at the Max-Planck Institute in July 1963, at the *Académie des sciences morales et politiques* in Paris in 1963, at the Royal Institute of International Affairs in London in December 1964, at the British Institute of International and Comparative Law in March 1965, at the *Institut d'études juridiques européennes* at the University of Liège in June 1965, etc. It is true that Walter Hallstein had a number of academic titles to his credit. Before his surprise nomination as head of the German delegation charged with negotiating the Treaty of Paris in 1950, he had followed an exclusively academic career, from the University of Berlin where he studied international private law, to the University of Frankfurt from 1941 onwards, with stints at the University of Rostock where he taught from 1931 to 1941 and at Georgetown University (Washington DC) in 1948–9.[13] Far from severing his ties with German law faculties, Hallstein's entry into politics as the head of the Foreign Affairs Secretariat (the *Auswärtiges Amt*) of the Federal Republic of Germany (1952–7) led him to draw on law, and particularly on German legal doctrine, as the preferred terrain for his political undertakings. Hallstein's commitment to the Law as both an ideal and an instrument was well known: Ernst Steindorff, his former university assistant, would expound this in the following way: '[I]f the jurist Hallstein speaks of the EC as a creation of the law and of legality, it is because he sees the law not only as a means to realize the ideal of the Law, but also as a tool for harmonizing the law for all the people living in the European states'.[14] Even more explicitly, over his years at the *Auswärtiges Amt*, Hallstein helped define the 'legal doctrine' of

[12] Wilhelm Grewe, 'The Lawyer as Diplomat', *Society of International Law Proceedings*, **54**, 1960, pp. 232–6, p. 233.

[13] On Walter Hallstein, see the contributions compiled in Wilfried Loth, William Wallace and Wolfgang Wessels (eds.), *Walter Hallstein: The Forgotten European?*, Basingstoke, Macmillan Press, 1998. See also Corrado Malandrino, *'Tut etwas Tapferes'. Compi un atto di coraggio. L'Europa federale di Walter Hallstein (1948–1982)*, Bologna, Il Mulino, 2005.

[14] Ernst Steindorff, 'Der Beitrag Walter Hallstein zur europäische integration', in Ernst Steindorff (ed.), *Probleme* des *Europäische Recht. Festschrift für Walter Hallstein zu seinem 65 Geburstag*, Frankfurt am Main, Klostermann, 1966, p. 3.

German diplomacy, exalting the constitutionality of the European commitments made by the Federal Republic of Germany that had been born a few months earlier under the sign of a limited sovereignty.

The Auswärtiges Amt and its Jurist-diplomats' constitutional doctrine

When it came to defining European Treaties as constitutional, Hallstein could call upon a handful of jurist-diplomats who were active both in the European talks that marked the 1950s and in the main German academic journals devoted to law. Among these were:

- Carl Friedrich Ophüls, professor of international public law, who had been legal adviser to the German delegation to the ECSC negotiations, then to the European Defence Community, and who headed the 'Europe' department at the Foreign Affairs Secretariat throughout the 1950s before he became the first ambassador of the Federal Republic of Germany to the Communities in 1958, thus accompanying Walter Hallstein to Brussels;
- Karl Carstens, who joined the Foreign Affairs Secretariat in 1954 before becoming a law professor in 1960, then Secretary of State for Foreign Affairs between 1960 and 1964, thereby pursuing a long political and academic career that led him to the presidency of the Federal Republic of Germany (1979–84);
- Wilhelm Grewe, also a professor of international law, legal adviser to Konrad Adenauer, subsequently head of legal affairs, and later political affairs, at the *Auswärtiges Amt* during the 1950s, and finally the German ambassador to Washington in 1962, and then to NATO.

Other members of this group were former colleagues and assistants at the Frankfurt law school, including:

- Ernst Steindorff, who had previously been Hallstein's assistant and his intern in 1950–1 during the Paris Treaty negotiations, and who was at the time a professor and also legal adviser to the European Commission and first president of the German chapter of the International Federation for European Law (*Fédération internationale pour le droit européen*, or FIDE; see below);
- Hermann Mösler, international law professor, Steindorff's colleague at the University of Frankfurt, who headed the Legal Service of the *Auswärtiges Amt* from 1949 to 1954 before being appointed by the German government to the European Court of Human Rights in 1959, and then to the International Court of Justice in 1976.[15]

[15] On this group and its academic activism, see Bill Davies, *Resisting the European Court of Justice: West Germany's Confrontation with European Law (1949–1979)*, Cambridge, Cambridge University Press, 2012, pp. 44–88.

> Collectively, they upheld the 'constitutional' character of the entire set of European commitments contracted during the 1950s by the Federal Republic of Germany, meaning by this that they ranked above federal law and that they were directly applicable. This was already the case at the signing of the European Convention on Human Rights in 1950 when the German delegation, led by Walter Hallstein, invoked the 'constitutional' nature of the Convention.[16] It was again the case in the days following the signature of the ECSC Treaty, when these jurist-diplomats published articles in the German law journals in support of the idea that a 'European structure of a constitutional nature' had been born – running counter to dominant German legal scholarship.[17] While they would disperse after the signing of the Rome Treaties, becoming professors, high-level civil servants, diplomats, judges or politicians, the group of jurist-diplomats formed at the *Auswärtiges Amt* maintained close ties with president Hallstein, as is attested by their contributions to the *Festschrift* that honoured Hallstein in 1966 on the occasion of his sixty-fifth birthday.[18] In the various positions that they occupied at the start of the 1950s, they continued to espouse in chorus the constitutionalist interpretation, extending it to the Rome Treaties.

In his new functions at the head of the EEC Commission, Professor Dr Juri. Walter Hallstein reiterated the constitutional doctrine forged by German diplomats during the 1950s, extolling this time not the imperious nature of the international commitments of the Federal Republic of Germany that aspired to full membership in the 'international community', but rather the figure of a Commission invested with a mission of guardian of a new objective constitutional order created by European Treaties. The intention of Hallstein was certainly not exclusively legal: his speeches show a constant preoccupation with the *political* character of the Rome Treaties: '[T]he existing European Communities are called "economic". But the work of the European Communities is not economic. It does not integrate the decisions of producers, employers and

[16] On this point, see Stéphanie Hennette-Vauchez, 'Divided in Diversity: National Legal Scholarship(s) and the European Convention on Human Rights', in Antoine Vauchez and Bruno de Witte (eds.), *Lawyering Europe: European Law as a Transnational Social Field*, Oxford, Hart Publishing, 2013, pp. 117–36.

[17] Carl Friedrich Ophüls, 'Juristische Grundgedanken des Schumanplans', *Neue Juristische Wochenschrift*, 15 April 1951, pp. 288–92; Hermann Mösler, 'Der Vertrag über die Europäische Gemeinschaft für Kohle und Stahl', *Zeitschrift für Ausländisches Recht und Volkerrecht*, **14**, 1951, pp. 3–22; Ernst Steindorff, 'Schuman-Plan und Europäischer Bundesstaat', *Politisches Archiv*, 20 May 1951, pp. 3955–86.

[18] Ernst Steindorff (ed.), *Probleme des Europäische Recht. Festschrift für Walter Hallstein zu seinem 65 Geburstag*, Frankfurt am Main, Klostermann, 1966.

workers, farmers, bankers and shopkeepers. It is the economic policies, the social policies of the States that are integrated and merged … Our Communities are thus themselves already the beginnings of a real and full "political Union"'.[19] But this 'political union in the area of the economy'[20] is grounded in an objective and incontrovertible source, namely, the *constitutional* character of the Rome Treaties: '[T]he Communities resemble a constitutional construction much more than a classic sort of international organization, because their objectives are to be fulfilled by institutions endowed with sovereign rights'.[21] In that framework, the political authority of the European Commission would derive from its constitutional role as guardian of Europe's general interest. Similarly, the objective mission of the 'German-style' of bureaucracy – permanent, hierarchical and specialized[22] – that Walter Hallstein and his entourage intended to build in Brussels was deeply grounded on the belief that Europe itself was now an objective constitutional order of its own.

A ministry of law

This 'Hallstein doctrine' was strongly relayed in the ambitions displayed by the Legal Service under the aegis of its director, Michel Gaudet, a department that was in a pivotal position in the heart of the newborn EC administration.[23] Nothing predisposed Gaudet, a jurist steeped in State

[19] Walter Hallstein, 'L'unité de l'action européenne (discours du 15 Octobre 1964 aux VIIème états généraux des communes d'Europe)', Lausanne, Centre de recherches européennes, 1965, pp. 10–11.

[20] Walter Hallstein, 'The European Economic Community', *Political Science Quarterly*, **78**(2), 1963, p. 165.

[21] Walter Hallstein, 'Zu den Gründlanden und Verfassungsprinzipien der Europäischen Gemeinschaften', in *Zur Integration Europas, Festschrift für Carl Friedrich Ophüls*, Karlsruhe, CF Müller, 1965, p. 5.

[22] See Daniela Preda, 'Hallstein e l'amministrazione pubblica europea', in *Storia amministrazione costituzione, annale dell'Istituto per la scienza dell'amministrazione pubblica*, 8(1), 2000, pp. 79–104.

[23] In the framework of my *Habilitation à diriger des recherches* defended at the Sorbonne (Political Science Department, March 2010), I started an exploration of the Legal Service of the EC Executive, whose role had until then been neglected in favour of studies on the ECJ. The study of this subject has now gained momentum and important new works have been produced recently that are only partly accounted for in this section: see in particular the recent PhD defended in June 2012 by Julie Bailleux, *Penser l'Europe par le droit. L'invention du droit communautaire en France*, Paris, Dalloz, 2014; for a summary of some of these findings in English, see Julie Bailleux, 'Michel Gaudet as a Law Entrepreneur: The Role of the Legal Service of the European Executives in the Invention of EC Law', *Common Market Law Review*, **50**(2), 2013, pp. 359–67. See also Morten Rasmussen, 'Establishing a Constitutional Practice of European Law: The History of the

law, to embrace the supranational doctrine of the German law professor. Son of a lawyer working before the *Conseil d'État*, a graduate of the Paris Law school and the *École libre des sciences politiques*, appointed to the French *Conseil d'État* in 1942, Gaudet followed in the footsteps of his colleagues at the *Conseil d'État*, alternating positions in the *Conseil* as *auditeur* and the *maître de requêtes*, and positions in government service as legal adviser to the French protectorate in Morocco (1945) and as cabinet secretary to the Secretary of State for the Economy and Finances, Léon Tinguy du Pouët (1946–7). His appointment as head of the Legal Service of the High Authority, upon the recommendation of Maurice Lagrange, his colleague at the *Conseil d'État* and a collaborator of Jean Monnet, are therefore essentially a continuation of a rather classic career of *serviteur d'État*. However, Michel Gaudet progressively made a name for himself in Luxembourg as a guardian and promoter of the 'supranational spirit' of the Communities, in the course of a 'conversion' process that has been efficiently described by Julie Bailleux.[24] As she explains, Michel Gaudet became, immediately upon his arrival in Luxembourg in 1952, part of a small circle of very close collaborators of Jean Monnet, thereby acquiring a role lawyers rarely play in international organizations. Undoubtedly helped by the initial organization of the High Authority as a 'task administration' (*administration de mission*) where the members of the ECSC Executive and high-level civil servants worked closely together in 'working groups',[25] Michel Gaudet was directly and continuously associated with the decisions of the High Authority college.[26] After the departure of Monnet (June 1955) and of many of his closest collaborators (François Duchêne, Max Kohnstamm and Pierre Uri), Michel Gaudet remained one of the last, if not *the* last, representative of Monnet's legacy within the ECSC institutions, all the more so as he had maintained a very strong relationship to Jean Monnet during these years. His designation by the new president of the High Authority, René Mayer, another former colleague of his from the *Conseil d'État*, as

Legal Service of the European Executive (1952–1965)', *Contemporary European History*, **21** (3), 2012, pp. 375–97.

24 Julie Bailleux, 'Michel Gaudet as a Law Entrepreneur: The Role of the Legal Service of the European Executives in the Invention of EC Law', *Common Market Law Review*, **50**(2), 2013, pp. 359–67.

25 On this initial structuring, see Francesco Bonini, 'Studi, materiali e prospettive per una storia delle amministrazioni comunitarie', in *Storia amministrazione costituzione, annale dell'Istituto per la scienza dell'amministrazione pubblica*, **8**, 2000, pp. 57–67, p. 57.

26 Dirk Spierenburg and Raymond Poidevin, *Histoire de la Haute autorité de la CECA. Une expérience supranationale*, Brussels, Bruylant, 1993.

the institution's representative in the group assigned to draft the Rome Treaties, marked another step in his embracing the role of a staunch promoter of pan-European ideals.[27]

There is much evidence, however, that this central position of the High Authority's Legal Service was threatened as two new European Communities were created. At that time still director of that Legal Service, Michel Gaudet immediately saw the dangers inherent in the splitting up of the Communities. In a very enlightening epistolary exchange with a New York lawyer, Michel Gaudet expressed his fears. On 31 December 1957, he wrote:

> I fear that the establishment of the two new Communities will in fact delay, if not stop, that progressive evolution of our Court towards a federal Court . . . Will the judges confirmed the invoked opposition between the Treaties, thus weakening the progress towards United Europe? . . . At present, I can think of only one way for the Court to avoid the danger described above. That is to ensure a coordination between the three Treaties by the three Commissions or Authority themselves before they fix their positions before the Court (and this is also true for their positions before the Assembly or the Council of Ministers). A few divisions, and at any rate, the legal one, must be put in common by the High Authority and the new Communities with a view to ensuring coherence in the interpretation of the three Treaties.[28]

In the weeks following the entry into force of the Rome Treaties on 1 January 1958, as the organizational charts of the new Euratom and EEC Commissions were being drawn up, hastily but sheltered from government influence,[29] Gaudet addressed many notes to the colleges of the three Executives. He directed the colleges' attention to the risks of 'sterile divergence' and 'useless and prejudicial opposition' in the interpretation of the three Treaties as three separate legal units with distinct interests and potentially competing purposes.[30] In his mind, there was no doubt that such a division would only weaken the Legal Service,

[27] Michel Gaudet, interview with Gérard Bossuat, *INT 603 of 14th April 1988, Voices of Europe Collection*, Archives historiques des Communautés européennes (available online).

[28] 'Correspondence between Michel Gaudet and Donald Swatland' published and introduced by Julie Bailleux in 'Michel Gaudet as a Law Entrepreneur: The Role of the Legal Service of the European Executives in the Invention of EC Law', *Common Market Law Review*, **50**(2), 2013, p. 374.

[29] See Katia Seidel, *The Process of Politics in Europe: The Rise of European Elites and Supranational Institutions*, Basingstoke, Palgrave Macmillan, 2010.

[30] Service juridique de la Haute autorité, 'Concours susceptible d'être apporté aux nouvelles Communautés européennes', Texte No. 2, 4 February 1958, p. 3, in CEAB1/956 HAEU.

whose authority 'in-house' rested precisely on their capacity to invoke the unequivocal and objective legal character of the Treaties. Gaudet's *Note sur l'organisation d'un service juridique commun aux trois Communautés*, submitted in late January 1958, constitutes a tightly formulated argument in favour of the creation of a 'single corps of jurists' endowed externally with the exclusive right to represent the three Executives before the ECJ, and internally with complete control over the interpretation of the law when queried by the directorates general.[31] A few months later, in October 1958, in an in-house memo, Gaudet further insisted that 'all documents' submitted to one of the three colleges should first go through the Legal Service, in the name of the necessary consistency in interpreting the Treaties.[32] This project was ambitious in scope, but it had three vital supporters among the EEC commissioners: Walter Hallstein, Hans von der Groeben and Jean Rey, respectively president of the Commission, commissioner in charge of talks with his counterparts at the EEC and at Euratom on the subject of setting up joint services across the three Communities, and commissioner in charge of the 'Legal Group'. All three held PhDs in law and believed the Commission to be 'by its very nature an *état-major* of economists and jurists'.[33] In fact, the idea of a joint Legal Service shared between the three Communities was rapidly accepted by the Communities and the members of the High Authority.[34] In lieu of the three Legal Services initially envisioned (or, worse still, myriad 'mini legal services' under each DG), a single body of jurists was thus constituted as a *counterweight* to the three-headed organization of the Communities. Pleading for the necessary 'independence' required for an objective analysis of the Treaties,[35] the Legal Service was in addition placed in an 'extra hierarchical' position outside the administrative structure, answering directly to the commissioners, and not to the secretariat general, as is usually the case in international organizations. In this way, the Legal Service escaped the

[31] Michel Gaudet, Legal Service of the High Authority, 'Note sur l'organisation d'un service juridique commun aux trois Communautés', 26 January 1958, p. 1 in CEAB1/956 HAEU.

[32] On this document dated October 1958, see Antonio Grilli, *Le origini del diritto dell'Unione europea*, Bologna, Il Mulino, 2010, pp. 215–20.

[33] Jean Rey, 'Les juristes et le Marché commun', *Journal des tribunaux*, 1961, pp. 1–2.

[34] Service juridique, Service juridique commun aux trois Communautés, letter dated 15 February 1958, 4 pages, Archives historiques des Communautés européennes, CEAB 1/956.

[35] Michel Gaudet, Michel Gaudet, Legal Service of the High Authority, 'Note sur l'organisation d'un service juridique commun aux trois Communautés', 26 January 1958, p. 4 in CEAB1/956 HAEU.

particularly rigid hierarchical organization that was coming into existence at the same time. What is more, the Legal Service used this cross-sector and generalist position to legitimize its role in framing and reining in the ambitions of the various directorates general. Thus the requisite 'consistency of interpretation of the Treaties and in the defence of the Executives before the Court' meant that the Legal Service would have to be 'consulted on all issues of interpretation of the Treaties, on all drafts of legal instruments for the Executives, and in particular on proposals to be submitted to the EEC/EAEC'.[36] This ambitious plan was not a dead letter, if we are to judge by the testimonials that describe Michel Gaudet as an '11th commissioner'.[37] Gaudet reports: 'In my experience of the sessions of the High Authority, and later of the EEC Commission in the 1960s, the Legal Service was present at all the meetings of the executive ... We were constantly asked ... "Does the Treaty allow this?", "Can the Treaty be interpreted in this way?"'.[38] The Legal Service was the only joint administrative service from 1958 until the merger of the EC Executives in 1967 (with the exception of the information department and of the statistics office),[39] and established itself as one of the principal sources of research regarding the structure of the European Communities and the nature of the Rome Treaties. This was all the easier as the Service had few or no competitors, as the Council of Ministers and the European Parliamentary Assembly had at best just a handful of legal advisers. Only the secretariat general of the EEC Commission, under the lead of Guy Mollet's former cabinet secretary Émile Noël, appeared to be in a position to counter Michel Gaudet's ambitions. But, in addition to the fact that the two directors 'were emperors who treated each other with circumspection ... and who knew that they had to treat each other with circumspection',[40] up until the merger of the three Executives Émile Noël had only a partial vision of the Communities, that of the EEC Commission.

[36] Michel Gaudet, 'Note relative aux tâches et à l'organisation du Service juridique', 26 November 1958, CEAB1–956 HAEU.

[37] Jean-Marc Sohier, quoted in Michel Dumoulin *et al.* (eds.), *La Commission européenne 1958–1972*, Luxembourg, Office des publications officielles des Communautés européennes, 2007, p. 225.

[38] Michel Gaudet, Interview with Gérard Bossuat, *INT 603 of 14th April 1988, Voices of Europe Collection*, Archives historiques des Communautés européennes (available online).

[39] Treaty instituting a single Council and a single Commission of the European Communities, signed in Brussels on 8 April 1965 with effect on 10 July 1967.

[40] Gérard Olivier (member of the Legal Service during this period), Interview with Gérard Bossuat and Myriam Rancon, *INT 714 of 4 December 2003*, Archives historiques des Communautés européennes, pp. 35–6.

This non-standard and extra-structural department could also count upon a team of 'State jurists' who were well versed in administrative matters. In a context in which the recruiting process in the European Communities was in most cases still exempt from the rules of competitive entry examinations, thus giving the department heads broad freedom to choose their colleagues, in hiring their staff over the years Michel Gaudet and his deputy director Robert Krawielicki tended to prefer State jurists who had served in government administrations and/or international organizations. Both men had spent nearly all their previous careers in public service – the French *Conseil d'État* for Gaudet, and the Federal Republic of Germany's Justice Ministry for Krawielicki – and they left only meagre pickings for legal practitioners, fiscal advisers or business jurists, professions that were directly qualified to help set up the Common Market. Most of the young recruits in the Legal Service were men who had in common their background in public service, either national (academics, magistrates, legal advisers in ministries, etc.) or international (judges at the Saar International Tribunal, auditors at the ECJ, etc.).[41] At the crossroads of the common markets and supported by jurists disposed to think of Europe as a matter of *public* law, from the outset the joint Legal Service built its doctrine on the promotion of the fundamental unity of European law spanning the three EC Treaties. Displaying the legal unity of the Treaties was in fact an obsession at the Legal Service. Indeed, Michel Gaudet had already invoked, as the basis of his call for a single Legal Service, the need for 'a unity of spirit in the interpretation of the Treaties and in the effort to construct the European edifices', a unity that he saw as 'the most appropriate method when the task at hand is to create *one* body of law common to six countries whose traditions are quite different'.[42] Accordingly, Gaudet sought to bridge the gaps between the ECSC and EEC Treaties even though they differed greatly. The 'institutional relationships between the independent Executives on the one hand, and the Councils, the Assembly or the Court on the other hand', 'the determination of the international legal personality of the European Communities and of their rights and obligations on the international scene', and 'the legal

[41] Among the twenty-four members who worked in the Legal Service between 1952 and 1965, the academic profile of 'pure jurist' remained marginal (two out of twenty-four), and only three had worked as lawyers or legal advisers in companies. By contrast, seventeen came directly from State service or international organizations.

[42] Michel Gaudet, Legal Service of the High Authority, 'Note sur l'organisation d'un service juridique commun aux trois Communautés', 26 January 1958, p. 1 in CEAB 1/956 HAEU.

issues related to their employees' status' – all these are 'fundamental legal questions common to the three Executives [which] must be addressed jointly from the outset'.[43] Likewise, the Legal Service took it upon itself to promote ways to achieve the coordination, harmonization and, *in fine*, the unification of statutes, functions and Treaties. For instance, it called for the merger of the Communities in the early 1960s, and pleaded for adoption 'by the three administrations ... of a single corps of civil servants for the Communities'.[44] Thus, even though they grappled with a set of sectoral issues (nuclear power, economics, agriculture, anti-competitive cartels and monopolies, etc.), the members of the Legal Service worked to build 'Europe' as a single institutional entity, whose intrinsic nature was legal even before it was economic. As jurists of the *res publica* faced with the construction of a common market, in the course of internal consultations, briefs to the Court and scholarly articles, they were keen on building a system of 'Institutions' with a capital 'I' that Michel Gaudet never failed to insert. When Gaudet asked the rhetorical question, 'Can't the Communities just "do business" and leave out all institutional stuff? Perhaps a more matter-of-fact approach might spare all the talk – including my own – on organization, transfer of powers and democracy, which after all is not a necessary contribution to the success of the common market!', he quickly added that 'this learned audience [of legal scholars] knows better than that. To you a common market means much more than a mere trade agreement ... This complex job cannot be accomplished without proper Institutions ... indispensable for establishing, ruling and operating a common market'. And, if the institutional logic embraces more than just the day-to-day management of the common markets, it is because it is anchored in 'the more noble and more essential task [of] completing and implementing EC law as it stands in the Treaties'.[45] The mission of 'overseeing the application of the provisions of the present Treaty and the dispositions taken by the institutions on the basis of this Treaty' (EEC Treaty, article 155) became, in the notes compiled by the Legal Service, a veritable 'policing' of the Treaties in the name of Europe's general interest, thereby taking the EC Executives well beyond the task of organizing

[43] Legal Service of the High Authority, 'Concours susceptible d'être apporté aux nouvelles Communautés européennes', Text No. 1, 4 February 1958, p. 2, in CEAB1/956 HAEU.

[44] Michel Gaudet, 'The Challenge of the Changing Institutions', *Common Market Law Review*, 3(1), 1965–6, p. 150.

[45] *Ibid.*, p. 144.

common markets.[46] In this framework, the identification of 'presumed breaches' that the Legal Service could then refer to the ECJ became an essential lever of the Executives' authority, consolidating by law their role as guardians of the Treaties. The implantation of a Legal Service, placed at the intersection of the EC Executives and granting it the role of monitoring through law the implementation of the Treaties was therefore instrumental to affirming their *political* status as an objective spokesmen of Europe's 'general interest' – a notion incidentally mentioned in the European Treaties but one that had remained vague and undefined until then.[47]

Europe's political laboratory: the European Parliament and the building of a collective expertise in institutional reform

There is little outward splendour about the Strasbourg Assembly. It sits in a building borrowed from the Council of Europe; it is served by ushers borrowed from the parliaments of the six Member States still wearing their national uniforms; it even had to christen itself, having been born with the bland name of "Assembly". Its administrative services located in Luxembourg migrate to Strasbourg at session time. Its standing committees are peripatetic – sitting in Strasbourg, Luxembourg or Brussels. Its legal powers are limited.[48]

This is how the European Parliament appeared to a visitor at its sessions in 1959. Endowed with essentially consultative powers, relegated to the margins of the Commission–Council duopoly where the bulk of the Communities' legislative power was concentrated, the European Parliamentary Assembly was a pale copy of national parliaments. It is true that the Parliamentary Assembly differed from other consultative European assemblies (the Council of Europe, the Western European Union, NATO) in that it possessed an embryonic parliamentary control of the Executives, via its power to adopt a vote of no-confidence in the college of commissioners. But, in the framework of the Rome Treaties, it was the Council of Ministers that was the principal seat of the 'legislative power', and the parliamentary censure was largely illusory. This ambiguity was reflected in the qualification of this entity, that the Treaties did not want

46 Legal Service of the European Executives, Note to MM. Sassen and Rey, 19 October 1961, p. 2, BAC 118/1986-932.

47 Both the Paris and the Rome Treaties mentioned only in passing that 'The members of the Commission [or High Authority] shall, in the general interest of the Communities, be completely independent in the performance of their duties'.

48 Eric Stein, 'The European Parliamentary Assembly: Techniques of Emerging "Political Control"', *International Organization*, **13**(2), 1959, pp. 233–54, p. 233.

to name as an authentic 'Parliament'.[49] One of the most attentive American observers at the European Communities saw this assembly as a cross between a national parliament and an international assembly like the General Assembly of the United Nations, adding that 'its powers over the budget are inferior to those of the United Nations Assembly which determines the budget of the organization'.[50] This initial uncertainty was compounded by a 'fundamental difficulty'. In the words of Pierre-Henri Teitgen, one of the figureheads of this early Euro-parliamentarism, how can one 'bring into existence and develop a political control regarding a specialized action such as that of the EC?'[51] This equation was not fundamentally altered by the signing of the Rome Treaties: the new members of parliament were concerned about the impossible political future of an 'Assembly dedicated to such technical, scientific and economic work', and they exhorted each other to escape from this trap of technicity. 'When we study our tables, when we draw up diagrams and pose financial problems, let us be careful not to neglect human feelings', was the plea of an Italian Christian-Democrat member of parliament.[52] How could a *political* institution be created when the subject-matter was technical and economic through and through?

A solution to this problem was proposed by a group of members of the European Parliament already quite seasoned in the workings of trans-national political venues (pan-European congresses, European parliaments, diplomatic delegations, etc.) as well as closely tied to European law schools (Pierre-Henri Teitgen, Fernand Dehousse, Marinus van der Goes van Naters, among others). Although they would often differ in political affiliations, they all converged in turning institutional-legal expertise into one privileged pathway when it came to asserting Parliament's political utility. This subject was of prime importance, judging by the fact that reforming Europe's institutional architecture was a pre-occupation of the chanceries throughout the decade following the

[49] By a resolution dated 30 March 1962, a veritable '*petit coup d'État*' in the words of Fernand Dehousse, the parliamentarians of the 'European Parliamentary Assembly' claimed the appellation of 'European Parliament' that had been denied to them in the French and Italian translations of the Treaties.

[50] Eric Stein, 'The New Institutions', in *American Enterprise in the European Common Market*, Ann Arbor, MI, University of Michigan Law School, 1960, pp. 55–6.

[51] Pierre-Henri Teitgen, *Rapport fait au nom de la Commission des affaires politiques et des relations extérieures de la Communauté sur les pouvoirs de contrôle de l'Assemblée commune et leur exercice*, ECSC Common Assembly Doc. No. 5, November 1954.

[52] Enrico Roselli, *Débats du mardi 24 juin 1958*, Assemblée parlementaire commune, 1958, p. 172.

signing of the Rome Treaties. From the controversies over the 1960 French proposal for a '*Communauté politique*', better known as the 'Fouchet plan', and the negotiations for the merger of the three Communities (that would eventually end up with the 1965 Merger Treaty that essentially merged the three Executives into one European Commission) to the March 1965 Hallstein proposals, revision of the Treaties was a subject of nearly uninterrupted discussion up to the 'empty chair' crisis.[53] Armed with the many recognized legal experts in its ranks, partly law academy and partly an international law commission, the European Parliamentary Assembly came into its own as a laboratory for institutional thinking.

The politicians of the law

The institutional pathway thus taken by the European Parliamentary Assembly leads us to evoke the premises of a first transnational politics, in which the politicians of the law are a key figure. With the creation of the Consultative Assembly of the Council of Europe in August 1949, parliamentary assemblies took their place alongside diplomatic conferences, technical secretariats and courts of justice in the basic institutional toolkit of European organizations: assemblies were created under the ECSC in 1952, the Nordic Council in 1953, the West European Union in 1954, NATO in 1955 and last but not least in the framework of the Benelux countries in 1957. From plenary sessions to the working groups of various commissions and committees, a full palette of transnational parliamentary activity began to take form. A British member of parliament reported that 'a member of a large country will be a member of three committees, possibly chairman of one, and a member of his political group. Between September 1957 and the first three months of 1959, he attended a total of 69 meetings and spent 191 days outside his own country on European work'.[54] The work load grew very quickly at the new European Parliamentary Assembly born of the Rome Treaties, occupying members' schedules to the extent that it became difficult to belong to more than one assembly simultaneously. This was all the more true now that this supranational politics not only took hold in the parliamentary setting, but was paralleled in the nebulous supranational politics of

[53] Jean-Marie Palayret, Helen Wallace and Pascaline Winand (eds.), *Visions, Votes and Vetoes: The Empty Chair Crisis and the Luxembourg Compromise Forty Years On*, Brussels, Peter Lang, 2006.

[54] Kenneth Lindsay (ed.), *European Assemblies: The Experimental Period 1949–1959*, London, Stevens and Sons, 1960, p. 90.

the European Movement. As noted by one observer, 'it is not only the formal attendance at plenary or bureau meetings, or committee sessions which counts, but also the necessary informal meetings, the need to study documents, often acting as rapporteur to a committee and in some cases the wish to keep contacts with the European Movement, in order to prevent the growth of a rift between the "official" and the "non-official" forces working for Western European federation'.[55]

In academic colloquia and in European Conventions, in parliamentary committees and in general meetings, a small group of professionals of this emerging transnational politics came into existence. It is worth noting that the major political figures in Europe, from Winston Churchill to Edouard Herriot, who had initially shown a strong presence at the podium of the Council of Europe Consultative Assembly, gradually deserted these venues, either through absenteeism or by not seeking to renew their mandate. Their place was taken by parliamentarians who had less prominent political profiles, but who often possessed a technical expertise in European matters that came into its own in the sectoral commissions of the European parliamentary assemblies, to the point that Fernand Dehousse worried about 'national representations that are less and less representative'.[56] This disengagement fostered first and foremost the emergence of jurist-politicians of law at the front ranks of Euro-parlimentarism. By their presence in universities where they held chairs, at the numerous conferences in which they participated and by the doctrinal articles that they continued to write,[57] as in the first party-political networks in Europe,[58] they set the initial framework for this new transnational parliamentary activity. As has been noted by Julien Weisbein, the sociability that took root in the pan-European political nebula 'is defined more by status and quality (top civil servant, expert, intellectual, politician, etc.) than by their numbers or by the population they represent', so that 'the action takes place in a discreet fashion similar to that found in the diplomatic paradigm (production of expert knowledge, more or less informal negotiations,

55 Ivo Daalder, 'The Netherlands', in Kenneth Lindsay (ed.), *European Assemblies: The Experimental Period 1949–1959*, London, Stevens and Sons, 1960, p. 125.

56 Fernand Dehousse, *L'avenir institutionnel des Communautés européennes*, Nancy, Conférences européennes, Centre européen universitaire de Nancy, 1967, p. 14.

57 Marinus Van der Goes van Naters, 'Les fondements du droit parlementaire européen', *Nederlands tijdschrift voor international recht*, 1956, pp. 324–41.

58 On the activity of these first transnational partisan networks, see the work of Wolfram Kaiser on the Christian Democrats, *Christian Democracy and the Origins of European Union*, Cambridge, Cambridge University Press, 2007.

etc.)'.[59] Naturally, not all of the 142 parliamentarians who gathered for the inaugural session of the European Parliamentary Assembly on 19 March 1958 were equally capable of excelling in specific types of politics. The politicians of the law were particularly well equipped for this game involving expertise and political representation. A virtuous dynamic of accumulation existed between these two poles, as shown by Antonin Cohen when he indicates that political centrality, as measured by the number of European parliamentary mandates occupied, would increase with the amount of legal capital.[60] This is particularly true for the French professor of public law and co-founder of the *Mouvement républicain populaire*, Pierre-Henri Teitgen, for the Dutch socialist lawyer and Doctor of Law Marinus van der Goes van Naters, and the Belgian professor of international law and senator Fernand Dehousse. These three each held multiple positions in the highest ranks of the European parliamentary assemblies during the 1950s and 1960s. Teitgen was a member of the Council of Europe Assembly (1948–58) and of the ECSC Assembly (1952–8). Van der Goes van Naters was vice-president of the Council of Europe Assembly (1949–59), a member of the ECSC Assembly, then of the Joint Assembly of the European Communities (1952–67), and vice-president of this Assembly's political commission in the mid-1960s. As for Dehousse, he was a member of the Council of Europe Assembly from 1952 to 1961 and served as its president from 1956 to 1959, and was a member of the ECSC Assembly and then of the European Parliament (1952–71). Their central role in the parliamentary assemblies can also be gauged by the fact that they were frequently chosen to be rapporteurs for various committees, 'a position that carries great political importance and considerable prestige, and [for which] elections are hotly disputed'.[61] Spanning these different transnational parliamentary venues in which they often held the post of president or vice-president, they were the actors of an early form of professionalization in the European political sphere.

59 Julien Weisbein, 'Les mouvements fédéralistes ou les entrepreneurs déçus d'une Europe politique (années 1950–1990)', in Olivier Baisnée and Romain Pasquier (eds.), *L'Europe telle qu'elle se fait. Européanisation et sociétés politiques nationales*, Paris, CNRS Editions, 2007, pp. 35–54, p. 40.

60 Antonin Cohen, 'L'autonomisation du "Parlement européen". Interdépendance et différenciation des assemblées parlementaires supranationales (années 1950-années 1970)', *Cultures et conflits*, **85–6**, Spring 2012, pp. 13–33.

61 Ernst Haas, in Institut d'études juridiques européennes, *Le Parlement européen. Pouvoirs, élections, rôle futur*, Liège, colloquium at the University of Liège, p. 221.

Fernand Dehousse: political and legal craftsmanship in Europe's institutional engineering

The links that were formed between institutional expertise and political authority at the heart of Euro-parliamentarism can be seen, in a nutshell, in the activism of Fernand Dehousse (1906–76) in the course of the eighteen months of talks on the draft European Constitution that was to accompany the construction of the European Defence Community. Before engaging in that debate, Dehousse had pursued a multifaceted career, always moving across the political, diplomatic and academic boundaries: a member of the Belgian delegation to four of the first six sessions of the General Assembly of the United Nations, an associate member of the *Institut de droit international* since 1947, and a member of the Permanent Court of Arbitration, Fernand Dehousse had at the same time been an active member of the European Movement, a member of the *Union européenne des fédéralistes* and of the *Mouvement socialiste pour les États-Unis d'Europe*. A professor of international law at the University of Liège, he became the most renowned expert in engineering European institutions: he would be successively called upon to be secretary general to the *Comité d'études pour la Constitution européenne* (also called the 'Jurists' committee') constituted in May 1952 within the European Movement; chairman of the expert group on international law formed in July 1952 to study the different European constitution drafts;[62] rapporteur for Europe's Political Community project to the Constitutional Commission (Co-Co) created within the *ad hoc* assembly (charged with preparing a draft treaty); and special rapporteur on the reform of EC institutions to the second congress of the European Movement in The Hague in October 1953. This broad range of experiences gave him a veritable authority over the reform of European institutions. His contemporaries readily recognized that Dehousse occupied a 'strategic position'[63] acquired in the course of his work crossing back and forth between pan-European movements and European parliamentary institutions. In a portrait of Dehousse that can in many respects also be read as a self-portrait, Pierre-Henri Teitgen extolled the virtues of the Belgian senator, 'the professor rich in practical experience, the politician faithful to his doctrine, the jurist who is concerned for the fate of Justice . . . and the combativeness of the militant', all qualities that mark the facets of this first European political capital.[64]

62 Philippe Carlier, 'Fernand Dehousse et le projet d'Union politique', in *The European Integration from the Schuman Plan to the Treaties of Rome*, Baden Baden, Nomos Verlag, 1993, pp. 365–77.

63 Robert Bowie and Carl Friedrich (eds.), *Studi sul federalismo*, Milan, Comunità, 1959, p. xxxix.

64 Pierre-Henri Teitgen, 'Préface', in Fernand Dehousse, *L'Europe et le monde. Recueil d'études, de rapports et de discours 1945–1960*, Paris, LGDJ, 1960, p. xv.

This small group of parliamentarians helped elevate institutional engineering to the rank of high art serving this emerging transnational politics. Proof to that effect can be seen in the particular importance of 'reports' in the emerging repertoire of pan-European political activism. Whether they be elaborated by committees of specialists, parliamentary commissions or European Movement working groups, they would clearly mark the success of expert knowledge when it came to envisioning the nature and future of Europe. This was not new on the international scene, as the Geneva multilateralism of the 1920s had likewise fostered the deployment of an 'a-political' repertoire.[65] The emerging Euro-parliamentarism provided a particularly propitious environment for this development, however. The absence or weakness of internal opposition at the Assembly was certainly a contributing factor; the communist parties were excluded up until 1969, as was the populist movement of French politician Pierre Poujade, and the Gaullist parties had only a handful of representatives prior to 1962. As a result, both European assemblies (the Consultative Assembly of the Council of Europe and the Parliamentary Assembly of the ECSC) formed a space with few deep divisions that was particularly favourable to the emergence of a depoliticized knowledge-based repertoire. With the development of parliamentary committees, and more particularly the political affairs and institutional committees, reports bloomed and flourished. Fernand Dehousse said as much when he rejoiced that, in a European Parliament that 'has little political activity, certain reports point it in this direction'.[66] Relying on analyses of different possible institutional scenarios for Europe that sought to be methodical, systematic and even scientific, these reports claimed an objectivity that would rise above the narrow viewpoints of States and political groups. The two Teitgen reports, the first on the European Convention on Human Rights presented on 9 September 1949 to the Legal Affairs Commission of the Consultative Assembly of the Council of Europe, and the second on strengthening the functions of the Parliament in the institutional system under the Treaty of Paris presented on 14 November 1954 to the Political Affairs Commission of the joint ECSC Assembly, and the Dehousse report on the project for a European Political Community drawn up in September 1952 for the

[65] On this point, see Guillaume Sacriste and Antoine Vauchez, 'The Force of International Law: Lawyers' Diplomacy on the International Scene in the 1920s', *Law and Social Inquiry*, 32(1), 2007, pp. 83–107.

[66] Fernand Dehousse, *L'avenir institutionnel des Communautés européennes*, Nancy, Conférences européennes, Centre européen universitaire de Nancy, 1967, p. 12.

Constitutional Commission of the 1952 *ad hoc* Assembly, are models of the genre. The Consultative Assembly of the Council of Europe soon gained a reputation for its 'debates of an academic nature', often 'confused, but of a high calibre', as one vice-president of the ECSC Assembly commented, not without irony.[67] Indeed, the rapporteurs were obliged to defend themselves against the charge of 'examining problems on an academic and abstract level' and had to declare that 'politicians [were guided] by a genuine concern for political effectiveness'.[68] It remained nonetheless that their conclusions were based on 'in-depth study' in comparative legal and institutional engineering. By thus displaying their capacity to construct realistic institutional proposals for a future political Europe, the rapporteurs and their reports outlined an art of European politics in which rational knowledge of the Treaties and institutional mechanics played a central role.

Euro-parliamentarism and the institutional unity of Europe

The political and institutional unity of Europe was the first cause they would espouse. It must be said that the European Parliament itself had narrowly escaped the three-way partition that characterized the EC edifice born of the Rome Treaties. The negotiators at the intergovernmental conference held at Val Duchesse in June and July 1956 had initially pushed for the creation of a new parliamentary assembly that would be in charge of the two new common markets and Euratom Communities, in addition to the ECSC Assembly and that of the Council of Europe. Fernand Dehousse, at the time president of the Assembly of the Council of Europe, and the two other presidents, Hans Furler of the ECSC Assembly and René Pleven of the Western European Union, together led the riposte of the European assemblies that avoided such fragmentation of Euro-parliamentarism. Dehousse instigated a joint meeting of the bureaux of the three assemblies in February 1957, and obtained a meeting with the six foreign affairs ministers chaired by Paul-Henri Spaak. In the face of the ministers' opposition, the Assembly presidents had to give up their initial plan to merge the four Assemblies (ECSC, Council of Europe, the Western European Union and the

[67] Cited in Franco Piodi, *Vers un Parlement unique. L'influence de l'Assemblée commune de la CECA sur les Traités de Rome*, Parlement européen, 2007, p. 206.

[68] See Fernand Dehousse, *Rapport établi au nom de la Commission des affaires politiques et des questions institutionnelles sur l'élection de l'Assemblée parlementaire européenne au suffrage universel direct*, European Parliamentary Assembly, session documents, 30 April 1960, doc. No. 22.

Common Assembly of the two new Communities) which was postponed 'until a later time'.[69] The worst was avoided, however, because they obtained *in extremis* a single assembly for the three communities (EEC, ECSC, Euratom). Although functioning under three distinct legal regimes and three different types of powers, depending on which European Community was operating, the European Parliamentary Assembly was, like the ECJ, one of the few links between the three communities.

It comes as no surprise therefore that the European Parliamentary Assembly, arguably the weakest of the institutions that emerged from the Rome Treaties, found its first *raison d'être* in the promotion of the institutional unity of the Communities, deeming that 'it falls within its purview as a parliamentary institution, common to the three Communities, to see that this unity is progressively achieved'.[70] This enterprise was spearheaded by the Committee for Political Affairs and Institutional Issues which saw itself from the outset as 'the prime locus of a discussion on the future of our institutions and on the development of our European politics'.[71] This commission soon emerged as the most 'political' and generalist of the commissions, first in the order of protocol, guided by experienced parliamentarians (over half of the twenty-six members had belonged to the ECSC Common Assembly) and heavily endowed with legal expertise (half of the members had studied law). While the twelve other committees were assigned to the different domains of the Communities' sectoral competence (transport, energy policy, internal market, trade policy, agriculture, institutional rules, etc.), the Committee for Political Affairs and Institutional Issues would take up the challenge of providing Europe with unificatory institutional devices. Leaving aside the thorny issue of the 'single seat' of the Communities, and the touchstone proposal to institute universal direct suffrage (immediately taken up by Fernand Dehousse), the committee's first reports were devoted to the institutional unity of the Communities and the outcomes at stake. Pushed by two members of parliament, Charles Janssens and Marinus van der Goes van Naters, both doctors of law, the question was on the agenda as early as June 1958. The two pointed out the faulty coordination, redundancies and other malfunctions resulting from the

[69] On this point, see the discussion in Franco Piodi, *Vers un Parlement unique. L'influence de l'Assemblée commune de la CECA sur les Traités de Rome*, European Parliament, 2007, pp. 35–8.

[70] 'Résolution sur la coordination des trois Communautés du 27 juin 1958', *Annuaire de l'APE*, 1958–9, pp. 538–9.

[71] Battista, 'Débats parlementaires', 12 October 1960, p. 9.

three-way partition, all of which were unacceptable in light of the statements 'that, I hope, that you all know [that] our Treaty is a "Constitution"; [and] I believe we are all in agreement on this point'.[72] The focus on coordination soon led to work to prepare plans for the 'merger of the Communities', which was the topic of successive parliamentary reports under the impetus of members such as Marinus van der Goes van Naters, Maurice Faure and Fernand Dehousse, paving the way for the Merger Treaty, which would ultimately be signed in April 1965.[73] Alas, the political aspirations of these politicians of the law were largely dashed, as these projects were rapidly quashed by the Member States. The six Member States did reach agreement on the merger of the three European Executives in February 1964, but this was *à institutions constantes*, meaning that the *relance européenne* envisioned by both the Parliament and the Commission, notably in budgetary matters, came to naught.[74] What was worse, the January 1966 'Luxembourg compromise' that put an end to the 1965 'empty chair' crisis even condoned a marginalization of the Parliament–Commission duopoly, compared to the essential role acquired by the Council of Ministers and the Committee of Permanent Representatives (Coreper). Yet, even though this whole body of institutional expertise that had been produced in the framework of the European Parliament had dramatically failed to influence the treaty revision process that remained in the hands of diplomats, it did define the profile of Euro-parliamentarism, the authority of which was now linked to its expert capacity in designing Europe's institutional future.

A supreme court? The European Court and its constitutional doctrine

With the entry into force of the Rome Treaties, a new court, the Court of Justice of the European Communities, began work on 7 October 1958, replacing the ECSC Court of Justice. It was not born under favourable auspices, and the prognosis of observers was not particularly optimistic, judging by the opinion voiced by the American political scientist Stuart

[72] Marinus van der Goes, *Débats du 24 juin 1958*, European Parliamentary Assembly, 24 June 1958, p. 167.

[73] Marinus van der Goes van Naters, *Note sur l'unicité des trois Communautés*, Archives du Groupe socialiste au Parlement européen, Florence, 22 July 1959–16 October 1959.

[74] Piers Ludlow, 'De-Commissioning the Empty Chair Crisis: The EC Institutions and the Crisis of 1965–66', in Jean-Marie Palayret, Helen Wallace and Pascaline Winand (eds.), *Visions, Votes and Vetoes: The Empty Chair Crisis and the Luxembourg Compromise Forty Years On*, Brussels, Peter Lang, 2006.

Scheingold when he visited Luxembourg in the early 1960s. 'There is a great chance', wrote Scheingold, 'that the Court will function more as an arbitration tribunal than as a court'.[75] Just as it was no simple matter to generate political debate out of the technical intricacies related to the implementation of the Common Market, it was likewise not easy to ferret out 'the pure gold of constitutional issues under the heaps of scrap iron and coal'.[76]

The impossible Court of Justice

The preceding ECSC Court of Justice, flatly called the 'coal and steel court',[77] had been for the most part restricted to the role of an economic court specialized in judging highly technical matters, and did not inspire optimism. This Court affirmed 'as early as possible and with a certain ardour' an economic doctrine that was marked by 'enthusiasm for a competitive market' and a belief in the 'general efficacy of the rationalizing pressure of natural market forces'.[78] By contrast, it had a reserved attitude in the repertoire that most suits supreme courts, that of broad legal principles. How could it act otherwise, knowing that it had to rule on the acts of the ECSC High Authority, an institution defined by one of its creators as a 'manager', an 'expert', a 'banker', a 'referee'?[79] All the evidence indicates that, apart from the presiding judge and the two advocates general who were meant to embody the *ratio juris*, the six other members of the Court were appointed – as is usually the case for arbitration courts – on the basis of their technical expertise, in this instance private international law, trade law and economics. As noted by Antonin Cohen, the composition of the ECSC Court of Justice gave pride of place to economists, labour-union representatives and high-level civil servants specialized in economic law. On the bench were Petrus Serrarens, a figurehead of the international Christian labour movement; Louis Delvaux, a lawyer and former member of parliament, who had worked in various positions in banking; Jacques Rueff, professor of economics and former member of the economic and financial secretariat

[75] Stuart Scheingold, *Law and Politics in Western European Integration*, University of California Berkeley, PhD dissertation, 1963, pp. 29–30.

[76] Pierre Pescatore, 'La Cour en tant que juridiction fédérale et constitutionnelle', in *Institut für das Recht der Europäischen Gemeinschaften, Zehn Jahre Rechtsprechung des Gerichtshofs der Europäischen Gemeinschaften*, Cologne, Carl Heymanns Verlag, 1965, pp. 520–58, p. 522.

[77] Henri Rolin, 'La Cour du charbon et de l'acier', *Journal des tribunaux*, June 1951.

[78] Stuart Scheingold, *Law and Politics in Western European Integration*, University of California Berkeley, PhD dissertation, 1963, pp. 362–3.

[79] Paul Reuter, *La Communauté économique du Charbon et de l'Acier*, Paris, LGDJ, 1957, p. 47.

of the League of Nations; and Adrianus van Kleffens, a Dutch jurist who had served before the war as head of the foreign trade department at the Dutch economic affairs ministry.[80] In addition, member governments had agreed with the two major European labour confederations to reserve a seat for a trade unionist on the Court, as they had done in the case of the High Authority.[81] With this roster, the Court rather resembled the High Authority,[82] the EC judges drawing their legitimacy from their proximity to those who were to be judged, as is true for arbitrators, and not from their distance, as is the case for national judges.

Furthermore, the experience of the ECSC Court of Justice apparently did not convince the negotiators of the Rome Treaties that a European *jurisdiction* would be absolutely necessary. Citing the essentially technical and economic nature of the Common Market, the French delegation, in the person of Georges Vedel, the delegation's expert on institutional questions, initially pleaded for the constitution of a simple arbitration panel deemed to be better suited to the economic and technical scope of the Rome Treaties.[83] Although a Court of Justice was, *in fine*, retained in the Treaties, its capacity to produce[84] authentic jurisprudence was far from enacted, not only because the Court ruled on cases of little legal import, but also because it was not evident that the Court would be able to construct a single corpus of jurisprudence, valid for the three Communities, given the major institutional differences between the ECSC and the two other Communities. The risk of a three-way partition in EC jurisprudence was evoked in early commentary. In a letter written to an American lawyer on the eve of the entry into force of the Rome Treaties,

80 Antonin Cohen, 'Ten Majestic Figures in Long Amaranth Robes: The Formation of the Court of Justice of the European Communities', *Revue française de science politique*, **60**(2), 2010, pp. 227–46.

81 Cf. Letter from H. G. Buiter, Secretary General of the Secrétariat syndical européen, and J. Kulakowski, Secretary of the European organization of the Confédération internationale des syndicats chrétiens, to the members of the Council of the European Communities, 1 August 1958, CM2/1958/548.

82 *Ibid.*

83 In a note dated 11 September 1956 to prepare the French communication to the meeting of the delegation heads, Georges Vedel, foreign affairs legal adviser, challenged the very idea of a Court of Justice for a common market whose technicity 'would more appropriately and more efficiently relate to arbitration'. On this point, see the many insights given by Anne Boerger-de Smedt in 'Negotiating the Foundations of European Law (1950–1957): The Legal History of the Treaties of Paris and Rome', *Contemporary European History*, **21**(3), 2012, pp. 339–56.

84 Antonin Cohen, 'Ten Majestic Figures in Long Amaranth Robes: The Formation of the Court of Justice of the European Communities', *Revue française de science politique*, **60**(2), 2010, pp. 227–46.

Michel Gaudet expressed his fear 'that the establishment of two new Communities could be of a nature to delay, if not halt, the progressive transformation of the Court of the Communities into a truly federal court . . . In the face of divergent and even opposing views coming from the two Communities, what will the judges do? Will they attempt to impose a conception for the three Communities, and if so to what extent will federalism prevail?'[85] In a public query regarding the path that would be followed by the Court in this context, ECJ advocate general Maurice Lagrange worried about the possibility of maintaining a consistent jurisprudence across the three Communities: 'Will the Court opt to maintain the interpretation of the Treaties in its original framework (three-way partition) or on the contrary will it seek to establish a *rapprochement* in order to propose identical solutions to similar problems?'[86]

This concern over the capacity to construct a single judicial point of view on the three EC Treaties was undoubtedly justified. The Court was not immune to the various political blockages that hamper the capacity of international courts to embody the judicial ideals of impartiality and independence to the same degree as national jurisdictions. Since the birth of the Permanent Court of International Justice, international jurisdictions have all complied with the same nearly diplomatic imperative that ties their legitimacy to a balance between the powers within the courts' make-up, or – in the euphemistic terms of the 1922 Statute of the Permanent Court of International Justice – 'representation of the main forms of civilization and of the principal legal systems of the world'. The ECJ was no exception to this rule. The savvy 'diplomatic equilibrium' reached following the Treaty of Paris balancing 'the principle of equality between countries (one judge per country) and the unwritten but fundamental principle of parity between France and Germany'[87] was thus renewed, with a few minor adjustments, in the months after the signature of the Rome Treaties. As with other international courts, this geographical weighting was seen as an essential precondition ensuring the viability of the ECJ. Pierre Pescatore, who was then Head of the political affairs' department at Luxembourg's ministry of foreign affairs,

[85] Letter from Michel Gaudet to Donald Swatland, 31 December 1958, cited by Julie Bailleux, *Penser l'Europe par le droit. L'invention du droit communautaire en France*, Paris, Dalloz, 2014.

[86] Maurice Lagrange, 'Le rôle de la Cour de justice des Communautés européennes tel qu'il se dégage de sa jurisprudence', *Revue du Marché commun*, **4**(32), 1961, p. 33.

[87] Maurice Lagrange, 'La CJCE du Plan Schuman à l'Union européenne', in *Mélanges Fernand Dehousse*, Paris, Nathan et Labor, 1979, pp. 127–37, p. 129.

remarked that it would be 'impossible in the long term to maintain the community ties as tightly as stipulated by the Treaties ... if the Member States are unable to have the conviction that the Court of Justice includes for each case, at the very least, one member with direct knowledge of the national law and of the particulars of the national interests involved'.[88] Even more threatening for the judicial legitimacy of the ECJ, this dependence on the dynamics of international politics also manifested itself in an inequality between parties before the court. While the Member States are not required to justify their 'interest in bringing an action' in order to file suit with the Court, individual persons must be 'directly and individually' concerned in order to mount an attack on an EC decision (article 173 of the EEC Treaty), leading the former minister and Belgian lawyer Marcel Grégoire to speak of 'the pathetic protection of individual rights in the Common Market'.[89] Worse still, individual suits are simply ruled out when the contested decisions relate to the 'legislative' activity of the Council of Ministers. Appointed directly by the Member States, and well connected in national and transnational political and diplomatic circles, the ECJ judges showed restraint, securing a political sanctuary to the inter-State decision-making process. Without such a sanctuary, protected from judicial meddling by individuals, the political consensus upholding international treaties would have been jeopardized. Former member of the French *Conseil d'État* and a legal adviser to Jean Monnet during the negotiations of the Paris Treaty, ECJ advocate general Maurice Lagrange said as much when he underscored the 'extremely grave consequences that would follow from even a partial annulment of texts that [have] "quasi-legislative character" and [have] been adopted with considerable difficulty, and sometimes after a compromise reached in the Council'.[90] This eminently *political* prudence was the justification for the Court's self-limitation, as attested by remarks made by Andreas Donner, the president of the Court from 1958 to 1964, in the wake of the 'empty chair' crisis:

> People have regretted that, in recent years differences between France and its partners, the legal implications of the French absence in the Council were never

[88] Pierre Pescatore, in Institut für das Recht der Europäischen Gemeinschaften, *Zehn Jahre Rechtsprechung des Gerichtshofs der Europäischen Gemeinschaften*, Cologne, Carl Heymanns Verlag 1965, p. 614.

[89] *Le Soir* (belgium), 3 October 1957.

[90] Opinion of the Advocate General Maurice Lagrange, 'Confédérations nationales des producteurs contre Conseil des CEE, Affaire 16-62, 14 décembre 1962', in European Court of Justice, *Reports of Cases before the Court*, Luxembourg, Curia, 1962, p. 486.

submitted to the Court. That is much too legal an approach; it would have been the definite end of the Communities as Communities if the opposing parties had gone to law and asked for a ruling of the Court on details that were no more than the juridical top of a political iceberg. Under the existing conditions, the capacity of the legal framework to support the weight of such controversies is yet only a limited one – just as political science teaches us that no constitution has the unlimited ability to withstand any social or political disintegration.[91]

Fully cognizant of the political imperatives that weighed on inter-State relationships, the ECJ judges allowed themselves only a limited scope of intervention in disputes concerning the Communities.

A contested interpreter

Thoroughly enmeshed in the politics of European integration and constrained by the essentially economic mission of the European Communities, the Court initially struggled to affirm a recognized authority for the interpretation of the Rome Treaties. Even without discussing here the disdain of some international jurists who continued to call for the transformation of the Court into a mere chamber of the International Court of Justice,[92] it must nonetheless be observed that the ECJ was kept at a distance regarding the disputes of legal and political interpretation that grew up around the new Treaties. National jurisdictions were reluctant to recognize the Court as a genuine 'interlocutor' in this area.[93] It would be nearly three years after the Rome Treaties took effect before the Court was notified of its first case related to the Treaties, and close to a decade before the national origins of the preliminary rulings began to diversify (until the end of the 1960s, almost all such preliminary rulings came from the Netherlands).[94] Oral accounts report that the judges broke out the champagne each time a new appeal was notified.[95] And, when the 'dialogue' was finally engaged, it was expressed in terms of rejection. National supreme courts, the guardians *par excellence* of the judicial ideal, regarded this new jurisdiction with suspicion. When the

[91] André Donner, *The Role of the Lawyer in the European Communities*, Chicago, IL, Northwestern University Press, 1968, p. 63.

[92] J. P. A. François, 'La juridiction européenne dans la communauté internationale', in *Mélanges offerts à Henri Rolin. Problèmes de droit des gens*, Paris, Pedone, 1964, pp. 95–103.

[93] On this point, see Karen Alter, *Establishing the Supremacy of European Law: The Making of an International Rule of Law in Europe*, Oxford, Oxford University Press, 2001.

[94] The procedure initially foreseen in article 177 allowed a national court to rest its judgment on the interpretation of a point of EC law by the ECJ.

[95] Anecdote reported in Catherine Barnard and Elenor Sharpston, 'The Changing Face of Article 177 References', *Common Market Law Review*, **34**, 1997, p. 1117.

highest-ranking magistrates of the six Member States came to Luxembourg for the first time in June 1965, some did not hide their irritation, as manifested by the president of the French *Cour de cassation* who questioned his ECJ colleagues in highly undiplomatic language: 'How does one explain that everyone – this seems to me to be a principle of democracy, if I may employ the term – is not placed on an equal footing when addressing the EC Court?' This defiance is also found in the first judicial decisions concerning the new Treaties: ranging from the order handed down by the fiscal court of the Palatinate emphasizing that the Treaties did not conform to the Basic Law of Germany (November 1963) and the ruling of the Italian Constitutional Court in *Costa* v. *ENEL* that denied any primacy of EC law (March 1964), to the decision by the French *Conseil d'État* in *Shell-Berre* (June 1964) affirming its own competence to interpret the Rome Treaties when they were 'self-explanatory' (a doctrine known as the *théorie de l'acte clair*), the Member States' jurisdictions were loath to consider the ECJ as a full-fledged member of the 'society of courts'.

Just as the national supreme courts openly displayed their scepticism regarding the ECJ, the political actors in the EC listened only distractedly to the Court and only occasionally deferred to its authority to decide the inter-institutional conflicts that emerged in the interpretation of the Rome Treaties. Indeed, it was not until December 1961, close to three years after the new Treaties took effect, that the Court pronounced its first verdict pertaining to the Rome Treaties.[96] In practice, the inter-institutional conflicts that grew up were settled for the most part outside the Court's jurisdiction. This was the case in 1959 in the dispute that sought to resolve whether it was possible for the Euratom Commission to claim 'implied powers' in addition to those explicitly granted to it under the Treaties. Rather than referring the matter to the Court to resolve this legal dispute, a conciliation panel was ultimately set up between the Euratom Council and the Euratom Commission to find a political compromise between the institutions.[97] And, when there was recourse to the Court, it was, apparently, in the framework of broader political negotiations, with the result that a significant proportion of cases initially submitted to the Court were withdrawn because the conflict had been

[96] 'Commission de la CEE contre gouvernement de la République italienne, Affaire No. 7-61', in *Recueil de la jurisprudence de la Cour*, Luxembourg, Curia, 7, 1961, p. 633.

[97] On this episode, see Eric Stein, 'The New Institutions', in Eric Stein and T. L. Nicolson (eds.), *American Enterprise in the European Common Market*, Ann Arbor, MI, University of Michigan Press, 1960, p. 75.

resolved upstream of the Court (twelve cases out of forty-seven for the period 1952–60).[98]

Judicializing the Court

In this context, the judicialization of the Court, that is, its approximation to national standards of justice, was not a simple matter. Its long-standing advocates were for a long time in the minority in Luxembourg. The advocate general Maurice Lagrange, Jean Monnet's former legal adviser in the drafting of the Paris Treaty, was the main spokesperson for this cause in Luxembourg. Over a period of ten years in Luxembourg, Maurice Lagrange transformed his function of advocate general into a veritable chair of EC law, linking narrowly the debate over the nature of the Court (in part constitutional, he would claim) and that over the nature of the Rome Treaties (quasi-constitutional, he would argue).[99] In one of the very first cases brought before the Court, *Fédéchar* v. *High Authority*, he faced some of the most eminent internationalists of the time, including Professor Henri Rolin, who was defending the Belgian coal federation. Lagrange clearly invoked the *specificity* of the Treaty of Paris to distinguish the ECSC Court of Justice from ordinary international jurisdictions. He regarded the latter to be 'more timid when it came to departing from a literal interpretation [of the Treaties]': '[O]ur Court is not an international jurisdiction, but the jurisdiction of a Community created by six States, along lines that are much closer to those of a federal organization than to those of an international organization'.[100] At the time, however, the Court did not follow his opinion.

The first chair in European law: Maurice Lagrange as ECJ advocate general

Born in 1900, with a father who was a member of the *Conseil d'État*, himself appointed to the French administrative supreme court in 1924, Lagrange spent most of his career there, leaving the *Conseil d'État* only to assist – with a certain bureaucratic zeal – the wartime Vichy government in the

(cont)

[98] Stuart Scheingold, *Law and Politics in Western European Integration*, University of California Berkeley, PhD dissertation, 1963.

[99] On this point, see Lauren Clément-Wilz, *La fonction de l'avocat général prés la Cour de justice des Communautés européennes*, Brussels, Bruylant, 2011.

[100] Conclusions of the Advocate General Maurice Lagrange, 'Fédération charbonnière de Belgique c. Haute autorité de la CECA, Affaire No. 8/55', in *Recueil de la jurisprudence de la Cour*, Luxembourg, Curia, 1, 1955, p. 263.

administrative implementation of the status of Jews in public service.[101] Reaching the rank of full-fledged *conseiller d'État* in 1945 (he had only received a minor administrative sanction – a '*blame*' – the previous year for his role in Vichy), Maurice Lagrange was chosen to assist Jean Monnet in the drafting of the Paris Treaty in 1950. The only one of the nine members of the ECSC Court of Justice to have taken part in the Paris Treaty negotiations, Jean Monnet's former legal adviser was from the outset the herald of a 'constitutional' reading of the jurisdiction which was on all points opposed to the status of specialized economic jurisdiction to which many actors in Europe seemed to want to limit the court.[102] As early as November 1953, in a discourse at the *École nationale d'administration* (ENA), he stated in clear terms 'the supranational feature of ECSC powers'.[103] In the course of the sixty Opinions that he delivered as advocate general, from the ruling in *France* v. *High Authority* in 1954 to the ruling in *Costa* v. *ENEL* in July 1964 (he left the Court in October of the same year),[104] Lagrange paved the way for a 'judicialization' of the Court, elevated to the rank of supreme jurisdiction of a new constitutional order. This undertaking was not without its ambiguities. As seen above, the former member of the *Conseil d'État* fully recognized the *political* limits of the court's jurisdiction, maintaining a restrictive stance of individual access to the ECJ. Nor did he accept the constitutionalism of the jurist-diplomats of the *Auswärtiges Amt*, pointing out the many ambiguities of the constitutional rhetoric. In this regard, he warned that 'one must be wary of analogies that go too far', because 'if in some respects our Court does in effect have the role of a constitutional judge in the Communities, the Treaties do not attribute to the Court the full attributes of such a judge'.[105] But, embodying, by his function as advocate general and his experience in French administrative jurisprudence, the '*general* principles of law' in a court long dominated by the preoccupations of *sectoral* law, Lagrange worked, in his Opinions and doctrinal articles, to prise the Court free of the constraining internationalist and economic framework in which it seemed condemned to remain. His strategy rested on an interpretation of the EC Treaties as a

[101] On Maurice Lagrange in Vichy, see Marc-Olivier Baruch, *Servir l'État français. L'administration en France de 1940 à 1944*, Paris, Fayard, 1997, pp. 325–6; and Laurent Joly, *Vichy dans la 'Solution finale'. Histoire du commissariat général aux questions juives (1941–1944)*, Paris, Grasset, 2006, pp. 89–92.

[102] On this point, see Antonin Cohen, 'Ten Majestic Figures in Long Amaranth Robes: The Formation of the Court of Justice of the European Communities', *Revue française de science politique*, **60**(2), 2010, pp. 227–46, who characterizes him as 'the architect of a silent revolution'.

[103] Cf. Julie Bailleux, *Penser l'Europe par le droit. L'invention du droit communautaire en France*, Paris, Dalloz, 2014.

[104] Rosa Greaves, 'The First Advocate General: Maurice Lagrange', in Noreen Burrows and Rosa Greaves (eds.), *The Advocate General and EC Law*, Oxford, Oxford University Press, 2007, pp. 59–88.

[105] Conclusions of the Advocate General Maurice Lagrange, 'NV Algemeine Transport Van Gend en Loos contre Administration fiscale néerlandaise, Affaire No. 26-62', in *Recueil de la jurisprudence de la Cour*, Luxembourg, Curia, 9, 1963, pp. 85–6.

unique and specific 'constitutional order'. He had already laid down markers with respect to the Paris Treaty. As early as his first findings delivered in the first *France* v. *ECSC High Authority* case in 1954, he promoted a teleological interpretation 'in relation to the Treaty as a whole' and in particular to its 'philosophy'.[106] He was not followed by the Court, which preferred a more textual method of interpretation. With this extensive reading of the Paris Treaty as a Treaty-Constitution, Lagrange was one of the spokespersons for the 'dissidents' of international law who were proponents of a supranational reading of the European Community in the 1950s and into the 1960s.

His position, long in the minority, would however find a new echo within the Court in the years following the adoption of the Rome Treaties. At this time, there was a notable change in the Court's membership with new recruits that were more concerned with ensuring a full-fledged judicial legitimacy for the institution. It must be said that the lawyers of the '*groupe juridique*' tasked with drafting the Rome Treaties in the spring of 1957 had managed to obtain a higher standard of juridical requisites for the judges, they would henceforth be aligned with those of the judges of the International Court of Justice for which 'a recognized juridical or judicial competence' is required.[107] The choice of candidates was still left, *in fine*, to the sovereign appreciation of each of the Member States, but there seemed to be an increasing sensitivity among Member States towards the legal credentials of the future judges. Just a few months after the entry into force of the Rome Treaties, Louis Joxe, secretary general to the French foreign ministry, wrote in a telegram to his *chargé d'affaires* in Bonn or the need to require 'an improvement in the composition of the Court':

I would be obliged if you could indicate to the federal government that we are highly preoccupied by the insufficient quality of the Court in its current composition ... [T]here is no reason for a trade unionist to sit on a Court of

106 Conclusions of the Advocate General Maurice Lagrange, 'Gouvernement de la République française contre Haute autorité de la CECA, Affaire No. 1-54', in *Recueil de la jurisprudence de la Cour*, Luxembourg, Curia, 1, 1955, pp. 53–5. On these first ten decisions and the role played by Maurice Lagrange, see the discussion by Antonin Cohen, 'Ten Majestic Figures in Long Amaranth Robes: The Formation of the Court of Justice of the European Communities', *Revue française de science politique*, **60**(2), 2010, pp. 227–46.

107 This was not the case for the ECSC Treaty that required only that judges be recruited 'among persons of recognized independence and competence' (article 32). On this episode, see Pierre Pescatore, 'Les travaux du "groupe juridique" dans la négociation des Traités de Rome', *Studia diplomatica*, **24**(1–4) 1981, pp. 159–78, p. 167.

Justice charged with interpreting the Treaties; training as a trade unionist gives no qualification to be a good judge of European Treaties. This principle must therefore be rejected and a seventh judge's seat attributed to someone who is truly competent, in replacement of the present trade unionist ... It will be advisable to have the Italian government understand that it should designate only candidates of great personal value; for your information I point out that this is not the case at present.[108]

The practice of including a trade unionist among the judges came to an end in 1958 with the departure of the Dutch judge Petrus Serrarens, former secretary general to the International Confederation of Christian Trade Unions. This departure, and the progressive withdrawal of the economist judge Jacques Rueff who was retained for other functions in Paris, reflect this perspective that considerably reinforced the legal capital of the ECJ. With one exception, the five new judges appointed between 1958 and 1962 had pursued almost exclusively careers in law. In 1958, Andreas Donner, a young professor of administrative law and son of a very high-ranking Dutch magistrate, and Nicola Catalano, legal adviser to the Italian State and former member of the ECSC Legal Service, joined the Luxembourg court. In 1962, Riccardo Monaco, principal legal adviser to the Italian foreign affairs ministry and eminent professor of international law at *La Sapienza* in Rome, and Alberto Trabucchi, an undisputed authority on Italian civil-law scholarship, were appointed to the Court. Robert Lecourt, also appointed in 1962, stands out in this group. He came to the Court after a top-level political career in the *Mouvement républicain populaire* party throughout the Fourth Republic in France (he served notably as justice minister), but he held a doctoral degree in law and had practised as a lawyer for nearly fifteen years in Paris and Rouen before the war. All the appointees were confirmed jurists, and were also deeply attached to the EC project. Steeped in a *jus naturalis* juridical culture, judge Alberto Trabucchi, brother of a Christian-Democrat minister, extolled the European *jus commune* of which the EC Treaties would be an expression. Robert Lecourt, who today is sometimes elevated to the rank of a 'second Robert Schuman' for his role at the head of the Court (1967–76),[109] was a former member of the

108 French Ministry of Foreign Affairs to Mr Leduc, French chargé d'affaires in Bonn, 20 June 1958, in Commission de publications des documents diplomatiques, *Documents diplomatiques français: 1958*, vol. 1, Paris, Imprimerie nationale, p. 810. I would like to thank Kiran Patel for indicating this document to me.

109 Pierre Pescatore, 'Robert Lecourt (1908–2004)', *Revue trimestrielle de droit européen*, 3, July–September 2005, p. 990.

Nouvelles equipes internationales network, the transnational network of Christian Democrats. Coming to the Court in the very same year in which the *Mouvement républicain populaire* ministers left the Gaullist government due to a profound disagreement over the government's orientation towards European integration, Lecourt put a missionary spirit into his new function. Nicola Catalano, formerly at the Legal Service of the High Authority, soon revealed himself to his colleagues at the Court as 'possessed by the European idea and an idea that has shone like a flame through all his activity'.[110]

The ideas of a Maurice Lagrange, extolling the authentically judicial, and even constitutional, character of the ECJ, found new support in Luxembourg in the years following the implementation of the Rome Treaties. The new judges were equally attached to the causes of law and the European Community, and, in their turn, concerned themselves with the construction of an in-house doctrine. Indeed, in a setting in which litigation remained limited, the doctrinal path was seen as an additional component needed to affirm the Court's institutional identity. Exciting little interest in national legal and judicial circles, and therefore acting in a semi-public sphere, the Court's own staff (clerks and judges) were among the few who took the trouble to chronicle the Court's jurisprudence in law journals. Via the twin pathways of rulings and commentaries on those rulings, the judges and their clerks tended to monopolize discussion of the Court. They did not all necessarily follow Maurice Lagrange on the constitutional path, when he wrote, for instance, that 'the Court appears as clearly invested with a mission of a constitutional nature, and, insofar as the Treaty system is likened to a federal system, it is permissible to state that the role of the Court is likewise assimilated to that of a federal judge'.[111] But they joined with him in exalting a Court whose mission was henceforth to emphasize the legal and political unity of the three Communities. While he would concede prudently that even the more reluctant judges, such as advocate general Roemer, who indicated in a May 1960 Opinion that 'it is not possible to speak of a legal unity of the three Communities', would, however, concede that 'their spiritual unity constitutes a reality that calls for a greater juridical unification'.[112] And the Court would actually follow him wholeheartedly, affirming in its subsequent ruling the

[110] Andreas Donner, *Audience solennelle du 8 mars 1962 à l'occasion du départ de M. le juge Nicola Catalano et de la prise de fonctions de M. le juge Alberto Trabucchi*, Luxembourg, Curia, 1962, p. 18.

[111] *Ibid.*, p. 36. [112] Aff. 27-59, 10 May 1960, Rec. 1960, vol. VI, p. 847.

principle of 'the operational unity of the [three] European Communities', justified by the great common vision of European unification for which the Luxembourg Court wished to be the interpreter. The ECJ was no longer the arbitration court to which EC actors only occasionally had recourse. Instead, it was emerging as a supreme court willing to take charge of the variegated set of economic, administrative *and* constitutional conflicts inherent to the functioning of a quasi-federal regime.

A supranational market? Euro-lawyers and Europe's economic constitution

What exactly was this 'Common Market' in the name of which so many institutions were set into motion? Did the normative ideal inscribed in the Treaties suffice to give birth to an 'institution' within the meaning given to the term in economic sociology ever since Karl Polanyi, that is, a relatively unified set of rules and social conventions pertaining to the forms, goods and actors of economic exchange? There is room for reasonable doubt. Like any other social institution, the 'market' cannot be created by decree, no more than it emerges spontaneously from the development of economic exchanges.[113] While the Rome Treaties are particularly precise about the 'dismantling of customs and tariffs' and the constitution of a free-trade zone for the circulation of people, capital, goods and services, for which the Treaties provide a detailed roadmap, they are by contrast singularly vague about the development of a form of EC economic regulation in Brussels. To use the terms consecrated in European studies, while 'negative integration' is well orchestrated in the texts, the concrete mechanisms of 'positive integration' (harmonization of legislation, competition policy rules, etc.) that would imply a full merger of market legislations and regulations remain a distant prospect. The 'institutional market', this new type of law-based market diametrically opposed to the Manchesterian *laissez faire* market, that Jacques Rueff had enthusiastically detected as incipient in the Rome Treaties, had only a sketchy existence.[114] Very few economic and political actors of the six Member States seemed to pay attention at first to the provisions of the EEC Treaty regarding the regulation of cartels and monopolies (articles

[113] Cf. Neil Fligstein and Iona Mara-Drita, 'How to Make a Market: Reflections on the Attempt to Create a Single Market in the European Union', *American Journal of Sociology*, 102(1), 1996, pp. 1–33.

[114] Jacques Rueff, 'Une mutation dans les structures politiques. Le marché institutionnel des Communautés européennes', *Le Monde*, 9–10 February 1958, p. 5.

85–86). Either they preferred, like French employers' federations, to see nothing more than a loose coordination of national policies in this area, or they sought to minimize as much as possible this aspect of the Treaties, in the manner of the French government which at the time was hostile to any reinforcement of the competencies held by the European executives.[115] All in all, the legal instruments for the organization of economic markets (patents, property rights, taxation, State subsidies, etc.) remained in the hands of the States whose sovereignty in matters of economic regulation was intact.

Far from creating a *single* market, the Common Market left the legal, professional and institutional structures of the national economies almost untouched. For proof, we have the example of the professions of business consultancy (legal, fiscal, patrimonial, etc.); these firms continued to be structured around national professional orders and deontological rules that differ greatly from one country to the next. To be sure, there were 'modernizers' in each of these national professions who saw early on the business opportunities that the Common Market was opening. This first impetus spurred various interest groups, employers in particular, to open offices in Brussels.[116] But the hopes placed in the Common Market were soon dampened. The reform-minded members of the legal professions rapidly had to rein in their ambitions. Hopes for a speedy modernization of the legal structures in the economy via the EC were dashed by two failures. First, the plan to create the status of a 'European commercial company' initially backed by the Commission became quickly mired in disagreements between various Member States. Second, under the auspices of the Consultative Commission of European Bar Associations set up in Brussels in 1961, the members of the bar in the different countries exerted coordinated pressure to postpone *sine die* the adoption of a directive concerning the rights of lawyers to establish offices within the territories of the Member States. Thus it seemed that neither the regulation of the economy nor the market for business consultancy would be able to take on a European dimension.

In this context, it was only in Brussels that an embryonic and truly supranational market seemed to be emerging following the lead of two groups of actors equally inclined to take the Rome Treaties as the basis of

115 Laurent Warlouzet, *Le choix de la CEE par la France. Les débats économiques de Pierre Mendès-France à Charles de Gaulle (1955–1969)*, Paris, CHEFF, 2011, p. 563.

116 Guillaume Courty and Hélène Michel, 'Interest Groups and Lobbyists in the European Political Space: The Permanent Eurocrats', in Didier Georgakakis (ed.), *The Field of Eurocracy: Mapping EU Actors and Professionals*, Basingstoke, Palgrave, 2013, pp. 166–87.

a supranational regulation of the European economies. There were multinational corporations, in particular those based in the United States, who were ready to bet on the emergence of a new regulatory echelon in Brussels and who flocked to the Belgian capital. And there were the high-level civil servants of the competition DG who were laying the groundwork of an antitrust policy that was centralized in the hands of the Commission. Between these two poles, there emerged a generation of young lawyers who were American or who had trained in the United States, who had close ties to the new European administration, and who became the first practitioners and the zealous theoreticians of this embryonic market-based Europe. Thereby, they contributed to defining a boundary of action for the Euro-lawyer far wider than those of most of its national counterparts.

Brussels as a new marketplace

The first signs of a European economic regulation began to appear. In the temporary quarters of the new EEC Commission, a small group of high-level civil servants in the competition DG, most of whom shared an ordoliberal faith, devised a European regulatory system to oversee cartels and monopolies. The profile of the first commissioner in charge of competition policy had something to do with this orientation. Hans von der Groeben was a jurist of long-standing ordoliberal conviction, a former 'Schuman Plan' bureau chief in a German economic ministry dominated at the time by ordoliberal notions,[117] a member of the pan-European Europa Union movement and deputy head of the German delegation charged with negotiating the Common Market (1956–7) to which he contributed to help give it a markedly liberal stamp.[118] In Brussels, he formed a small team of civil servants and advisers, all of whom came from this movement which was then in its golden age in Germany. Hermann Schumacher, director of the cartels and monopolies office, Ernst Albrecht, his cabinet secretary, and Ernst-Joachim Mestmäcker, his special adviser, all had close ties to this milieu: the first was the son of an important ordoliberal economist, and the third had

[117] On the importance of ordoliberalism to the West German Economy Ministry under the direction of Ludwig Erhard (1949–1963), see B. Löffler, *Soziale Marktwirtschaft und administrative praxis. Das Bundeswirtschaftsministerium unter Ludwig Erhard*, Stuttgart, Steiner, 2002.

[118] On his contribution to the neo-liberal orientation of the Treaties, see François Denord and Antoine Schwartz, 'L'économie (très) politique des Traités de Rome', *Politix*, **23**(89), 2010, pp. 35–56.

obtained his doctorate with one of the figureheads of German ordoliberalism, Franz Böhm, a former colleague of Ludwig Erhard when the latter worked for the Anglo-American occupation authority after the war.[119] They had in common lengthy legal studies (in some cases including a doctorate), publishing in 1958 a joint commentary on the European Treaties, *Kommentar zum EWG-Vertrag* that was destined to become a reference work in German. They were also undoubtedly marked by the decade of debate over the German antitrust law that led to the creation of the *Bundeskartellamt* (BKA), an independent administrative authority with considerable power, and they shared a 'constitutional' view of competition policy.[120] The 'free-market interventionism' that they advocated depended on a fully independent authority entrusted with the power to ensure, in law and under a quasi-jurisdictional procedure, the liberal economic order, by attacking practices that restricted competition. This was exactly the mission of the German BKA, a quasi-tribunal protected from political pressure that from 1958 undertook very close oversight of industrial cartels in Germany.

One essential way to promote this mandatory reading of EC competition policy actually consisted in interpreting the Treaty as containing an economic constitution. It seems that the German ambassador to the EC, the renowned international law professor Carl Friedrich Ophüls, whom we saw earlier promoting the constitutional nature of the Paris Treaty in the early 1950s, was the first to promote this constitutional reading in the domain of European economic integration, mentioning as early as 1962 the existence of a 'European Economic Constitution'.[121] He was followed in this particular way by Ernst-Joachim Mestmäcker, the legal adviser to the commissioner Hans von der Groeben, who would become

119 On this group, see Katia Seidel, 'DG IV and the Origins of a Supranational Competition Policy: Establishing an Economic Constitution for Europe', in Wolfram Kaiser, Brigitte Leucht and Morten Rasmussen (eds.), *The History of the European Union: Origins of a Trans- and Supranational Polity 1950–72*, London, Routledge, 2008.

120 Readers are referred to the important work done by David Gerber, 'Constitutionalizing the Economy: German Neo-liberalism, Competition Law and the "New" Europe', *American Journal of Comparative Law*, **42**(1), 1994, pp. 25–84; and by Christian Joerges, 'The Market without the State? The "Economic Constitution" of the European Community and the Rebirth of Regulatory Politics', *European Integration Online Papers (EIoP)*, Vol. **1**, 1997; and, more recently, the important edited volume at the crossing between law and history by Kiran Patel and Heike Schweitzer (eds.), *Historical Foundations of EU Competition Law*, Oxford, Oxford University Press, 2013.

121 Carl Friedrich Ophüls, 'Grundzlige Europäischer Wirtschaftsverfassung', *Zeitschrift für das gesamte Handelsrecht und Wirtschaftsrecht*, **124**, 1962, pp. 136–66.

one of the most active *doctrinaires* of this view.[122] Thus, contrary to the dominant interpretation among top civil servants, law professors and employers in France who saw articles 85–86 of the Rome Treaties as no more than a simple roadmap that would have to bend to political winds and to particular national circumstances, the ordoliberals of the competition DG held these same articles to be truly constitutional, thereby laying the groundwork for a supranational regulation fully independent of the Member States. As Hans von der Groeben himself said in a speech before the European Parliament, in their eyes 'the economic order is not established by itself, but only through an adjustment of the economic order of competition'.[123] Therefore, only a constitutional predicament – whose respect would be monitored by a court, the ECJ – could free this essential policy from the tutelage of States viewed as excessively sensitive to their social and political clienteles. With the benefit of divisions among European employers' federations and the Member States, and singularly of the isolation of the French government in its refusal to endow the Commission with new powers,[124] von der Groeben managed to impose his views in the course of 1961, by way of Regulation 17/62 that conferred upon the Commission quasi-jurisdictional powers to oversee cartels. This regulatory text, which remained in essence in effect until it was superseded by Regulation 1/2003, erected a centralized oversight system that left little room to national authorities when confronting cartels 'affecting free circulation' (article 85).[125] An ambitious notification system obliged enterprises to directly inform the Commission of their cartels, in effect bypassing national authorities. The Commission alone had the authority to grant exemptions to the principle

[122] See in particular his contribution to the *Festschriften* on honour of the most prominent ordoliberal legal scholar, Franz Böhm: Ernst-Joachim Mestmacker, 'Offene Märkte im System Unverfälschten Wettbewerbs in der Europäischen Gemeinschaft', in Heinrich Kronstein and Joachim Mestmächer (eds.), *Wirtschaftsordnung und Rechtsordnung. Festschrift zum 70 Geburstag von Franz Böhm*, Karlsruhe, Verlag C. F. Müller, 1965, pp. 345–91.

[123] Hans von der Groeben, 'La politique de la concurrence, partie intégrante de la politique économique dans le Marché commun', Speech delivered before the European Parliament, 16 June 1965, quoted in François Denord and Antoine Schwartz, *L'Europe sociale n'aura pas lieu*, Paris, Raisons d'agir, 2009, p. 72.

[124] See Laurent Warlouzet, *Le choix de la CEE par la France. Les débats économiques de Pierre Mendès-France à Charles de Gaulle (1955–1969)*, Paris, CHEFF, 2011, pp. 507–644.

[125] Hubert Buch-Hansen and Angela Wigger, 'Revisiting 50 Years of Market-Making: The Neoliberal Transformation of EC Competition Policy', *Review of International Political Economy*, **16**(4), 2009, pp. 20–44.

that banned cartels, as the French government had been able to obtain only a purely consultative committee of representatives of the Member States. Regulation 17/62 consecrated a major success for the 'constitutional' reading of the Treaties, conferring an effective juridical scope to articles 85 and 86, under the authority of an institution that was largely independent from the Member States. The specific identity of the competition DG was built on this paradigm to a point that it became for three decades the province of jurists who had worked with Hans von der Groeben. Personalities such as Ernst Albrecht, Manfred Caspari and Claus-Dieter Ehlermann, who succeeded each other at the head of this directorate almost without interruption from 1967 to 1995, had respectively been cabinet secretary, cabinet member and a colleague who incidentally took over the editorship of *Kommentar zum EWG-Vertrag* when von der Groeben retired.

During these same years, a multitude of multinational corporations took offices not far from the Commission's premises. The months following the enactment of the Rome Treaties saw a veritable rush to the Belgian capital by investors, in particular by American investors. Already enhanced by the success of the World's Fair in 1958, now the 'provisional capital' of the institutions of the Common Market, Brussels emerged as an essential pole for the internationalization strategies of major corporations. Driven by the spectacular economic growth of the United States during this period, a wave of investment swept across all of Europe in the 1950s and 1960s. This American foreign investment flowed primarily to the six Member States, rising from US$970 million in 1958 to US$2,063 million in 1962.[126] Just as in Europe economic modernization meant tackling the 'American challenge', in the United States business internationalization meant engaging with the economies of the six: 'going international' entailed coming to grips with the many problems of doing business both with and within the Common Market.[127] We may recall the best-selling book written by Jean-Jacques Servan-Schreiber, who warned of a 'Common Market Europe that has become a new Far West for American business'.[128] Indeed, American corporations concluded no fewer than 530 acquisitions and 582 joint

126 Mira Wilkins, *The Maturing of Multinational Enterprise: American Business Abroad from 1914 to 1970*, Cambridge, MA, Harvard University Press, 1974, p. 331.

127 Arthur Selwyn Miller, 'Foreword', in *Doing Business in the Common Market*, co-sponsored by George Washington University and Commerce Clearing House Inc., 1963, p. iii.

128 Jean-Jacques Servan-Schreiber, *Le défi américain*, Paris, Denoël, 1967, p. 23.

ventures in the six Member States between 1958 and 1965.[129] Responding to the extremely advantageous fiscal measures set up by the Belgian government, American investors were particularly drawn to Brussels.[130]

Brussels, a new capital for business law?

The most internationalist segments of the American legal and business elite – members of the international chapter of the American Bar Association, members of the International Law Association and members of the economic networks of the American Chamber of Commerce in Brussels[131] – all were drawn to Brussels at the urging of the US State Department, which championed the EC cause[132] and highlighted the considerable opportunities of the Common Market to both businessmen and lawyers. In the early 1960s, major business law congresses were held in Brussels, consecrating this city as a new international venue. The International Law Association held its bi-annual convention in Brussels in 1962, attended by many high-ranking EC civil servants and commissioners. Financed in part by the large multinational corporations that were then emerging (Shell, British Petroleum, Iran Petroleum, the US Steel Foundation, and Lever), the members of this association represented the segment of the Western legal professions most closely tied to international trade (Walter Hallstein was a member). In 1963, the Antitrust Law section of the American Bar Association also held a very large conference over four days, straddling Luxembourg and Brussels and attended by the full array of top EC personalities who came together to promote the potential of competition policy in the Common Market. Alongside the vice-presidents of the Commission (Robert Marjolin) and the High Authority (Albert Coppé) and the president of the ECJ (Andreas Donner) were the competition commissioner and his director general (Hans von der Groeben and Peter Verloren van Themaat), the directors of the European Commission's Legal Service, and numerous EC civil servants.[133]

129 Sigmung Timberg, 'Antitrust in the Common Market: Innovation and Surprise', *Law and Contemporary Problems*, **37**(2), 1972, pp. 329–40.

130 American investment in Belgium represents 1.9 per cent of GDP, compared to 1.1 per cent in France and in Germany; cf. Eric Stein, *American Enterprise in the European Common Market*, Ann Arbor, MI, University of Michigan Press, 1960, p. 29.

131 See Maria Green Cowles, 'The EU Committee of AmCham: The Powerful Voice of American Firms in Brussels', *Journal of European Public Policy*, **3**(3), 1996, pp. 339–58.

132 On the State Department networks and their diplomatic action regarding the construction of Europe, see the recent work by Kenneth Weisbrode, *The Atlantic Century: Four Generations of Extraordinary Diplomats Who Forged America's Vital Alliance with Europe*, Cambridge, Da Capo Press, 2009.

133 Section on antitrust law, American Bar Association, 'Conference on Antitrust and the European Communities. Brussels September 23–25, Luxembourg, September 25–26. Program', CEAB 1, No. 24, 1963.

Euro-lawyers as corporate brokers

Between these two microcosms, the competition DG on the one hand, and the multinational corporations established in Brussels on the other, burgeoned an entire generation of American and Belgian lawyers. They were all educated in East Coast law schools and were at the same time closely linked to the EC institutions, thus setting themselves up as natural intermediaries of the emerging EC market that was thus dominated by the 'American way of law'.[134] Indeed, American lawyers arrived in Brussels close on the heels of American corporations at the end of the 1950s. Between 1958 and 1965, all the major Wall Street firms opened offices in the Belgian capital: Baker & McKenzie (1958), Cleary Gottlieb (1960), Simons and Simons (1962), Archibald (1963), Couderts Brothers (1965), Dewey Ballantine, Dilley and Custer (1967), White and Case (1967), Clifford Chance (1968), etc. Until then, for the most part concentrated in Paris that in the interwar period had served as the European headquarters for many New York law firms (in part due to the presence of the International Chamber of Commerce in the French capital), these firms now saw the 'new Eldorado'[135] in Brussels and redeployed an internationalization strategy that was still in its infancy. 'They saw the notification procedures (rule 17/62) before the Commission', recalls a Belgian lawyer, 'and they said to themselves that there would be an American-style market there'.[136] They encountered many obstacles in their Brussels adventures, however. Fearing unfair competition from these American lawyers, the Council of the Brussels Bar Association considerably restricted their professional freedom of action in the European capital: they were not allowed to put up a professional nameplate, were banned from pleading before a Belgian court, and were required to apply for a professional activity card that was granted sparingly. This protectionist regime was coupled with a *de facto* ban on pleading before the ECJ, as only members of the bar of one of the six Member States were accepted in Luxembourg. In this context, the development strategy of the American law firms also involved co-opting local lawyers who could act as permanent representatives of American branches in Brussels. Many Belgians therefore tried their luck in these American law firms that set up in the European capital after 1958 and sought to bring in European recruits who, as indicated by the founder of

[134] Yves Dezalay and Bryant Garth, 'Re-structuring States by Exporting Law: American Law Firms and the Genesis of a European Legal Market', in Hanne Petersen *et al.* (eds.), *Paradoxes of European Legal Integration*, Aldershot, Ashgate, 2008, pp. 76–88.

[135] Interview No. 3, Brussels, October 2008. [136] *Ibid.*

Cleary Gottlieb himself, 'had, without exception, the most distinguished record in the European law schools where they had earned their diplomas, and most of whom had also attended an American law school, and English university or the Inns of Court, where they excelled'.[137] The future 'great men' of EU competition law, Jean Blondeel, Walter van Gerven, Jean-Pierre de Bandt, Ivo van Bael and Michel Waelbroeck trained in the Cleary Gottlieb firm for the first two, at Frank Boas for the third, and at Dewey Ballantine for the last. Their recruitment was not by chance: they had graduated from one or another of the five law faculties that existed in Belgium, and they also had finished their training in the crucible of American legal excellence, that is, at Harvard (Jacques Blondeel, Jean-Pierre de Bandt, Jean-Pierre Lagae, Luc Hinnekens, Pierre Osterweil), New York University (Michel Waelbroeck), the University of Chicago (Walter van Gerven) and the University of Michigan (Ivo van Bael). Belgium thus had a pool of lawyers trained on the other side of the Atlantic thanks to a major university exchange system set up by the Belgian–American Educational Foundation immediately after the First World War.

This Belgian–American microcosm could not have numbered more than a few dozen people, in a Brussels bar that registered more than 1,000 lawyers. But it appeared very much as a threat to the hierarchs of the Brussels Bar who were little inclined to accept this 'extra-territorial enclave' in the very heart of the Belgian capital. In taking up quarters in the Belgian capital, these lawyers – with their multiple facets and professional roles – transgressed 'the extreme punctiliousness manifested by the national legislator in the organization of the legal professions (lawyers, barristers, solicitors, bailiffs, notaries, etc.)'.[138]

Cleary Gottlieb, the first Euro-law firm

Let us consider the American firm Cleary Gottlieb, one of the first firms to set up in Brussels and in which several generations of Belgian business lawyers would be trained. The example is undoubtedly a singular one due to the close relationship between Jean Monnet, the first president of the High Authority, and one of the partners in the firm, George Ball, an eminent member of the

[137] Leo Gottlieb, *Cleary, Gottlieb, Steen & Hamilton: The First Thirty Years*, New York, Cleary Gottlieb, 1993, p. 243.

[138] Conseil de l'ordre, 'Installation des juristes étrangers à Bruxelles', *Ordre des avocats. Barreau de Bruxelles*, March 1968, p. 47.

foreign policy establishment.[139] Ball was a former general counsel to the post-war French Supply Agency when Jean Monnet was the director of this public entity tasked with negotiating the buying of war furniture in the name of the French government in Washington (1945–6). Subsequently, he took an active part in the launching of a new Wall Street law firm, Cleary Gottlieb Friendly & Cox. Through his close ties with Jean Monnet (who had returned to France as the head of the *Commissariat général au Plan*), this new firm became the representative of the French government's economic and financial interests in the United States in the framework of the Marshall Plan. Retained in 1953 by Jean Monnet (now head of the ECSC High Authority) to take charge of the interests of the High Authority, the American firm did not limit itself to giving legal advice, but had a much broader role as a broker between the European Communities and the American elite, one that was more akin to the role lawyers played at the time in the United States well beyond a strictly legal scope (legal advice, public relations, lobbying, etc.). The firm negotiated the loans that the EC contracted with American banks, founded and directly managed the EEC information office in Washington, drew up briefs for 'key members of Congress and of the Executive Department', ensured that 'the itineraries of qualified representatives of the EC who visit the United States include meetings with small groups of key members of American financial institutions',[140] 'organized the visits of American personalities to Luxembourg', etc. It was 'most ardently' wished, within the Luxembourg institutions, that, 'given the distance from Washington', 'Mr Ball, in whom we have the utmost confidence, should have there the global responsibility of our representation to the United States'.[141] Trusted by Jean Monnet and his successors, to the point that he would take part directly in High Authority meetings when he visited Luxembourg,[142] George Ball and his law firm were in the position of the 'High Authority's authorized agent',[143] assigned 'tasks of a political nature',[144] and acted throughout the 1950s as a veritable platform for EEC interests in the United States.[145]

139 On the connections between Jean Monnet and George Ball, see Jean Monnet's *Memoirs*, London, Collins, 1978, pp. 227–8, and a recent publication by Hannah Gurman, *The Dissent Papers: The Voices of Diplomats in Cold War and Beyond*, New York, Columbia University Press, 2012, pp. 119–27.

140 Law Firm Cleary, Gottlieb, Friendly and Ball, *Report to the President of the High Authority on the European Coal and Steel EC in American Opinion*, 10 February 1955, p. 6. CEAB 05-316 HAEU.

141 Legal Service, Note to MM. Balladore Pallieri *et al.*, 11 December 1957, in CEAB 05-316 HAEU.

142 Procès-verbal de la 282ème réunion de la Haute autorité, Luxembourg, 28 September 1955, CEAB 05-316.

143 Piero Malvestiti, Letter to George Ball, 27 October 1960, in CEAB5–922, HAEU.

144 Division des relations extérieures, Note pour Messieurs les membres de la Haute autorité, 3 November 1958, p. 1, in CEAB5-316, HAEU.

145 The appointment of George Ball in 1961 as Deputy Cabinet Secretary for economic affairs under President Kennedy marked the end of this special relationship between

This particularly broad spectrum of tasks taken on by the American-style lawyer in Brussels questioned the traditional and rather limited roles that the *avocat, avvocato* or *rechtanwalt* would be able to play. What probably made the emergence of this *Euro*-lawyer possible in the Brussels' enclave was that these young Belgian lawyers had all the characteristics of 'young Turks': if they could without too much risk disregard the structures of the Brussels bar, that saw in the law firms an unfair competition, and could do so without causing controversy, it was because they remained, through their families and/or university mentors, the 'heirs' of various Belgian political and/or legal dynasties. They were relatives and/or protégés of the Belgian 'grand masters' of European and international law at the time (Henri Rolin, de Visscher father and son, Walter Ganshof van der Meersch and George van Hecke), and they benefited from the indulgence often granted to unruly heirs, to the extent that, in the words of one of them, 'one didn't dare consider me to be a traitor [to the Brussels Bar]'.[146] This group included: Walter van Gerven at Cleary Gottlieb, son of a senator and former president of the bar in Dendermonde, who had studied under Jossé Mertens de Wilmars (himself a lawyer, senator, president of the European Movement in Belgium, and future judge and president of the ECJ of the European Community); Michel Waelbroeck at Dewey Ballantine, son of a high-level civil servant at the International Labour Board, first cousin once removed and protégé of the Socialist senator and top international law professor Henri Rolin, and also one of the students closest to Walter Ganshof van der Meersch, professor and attorney general at the Court of Cassation, who would join the European Court of Human rights in 1973; John Kirkpatrick, great-grandson of Gustave Rolin-Jaequemyns, minister of the interior and founder of the *Institut de droit international*, as well as cousin to Michel Waelbroeck; and, finally, Bavo Cool, also at Cleary Gottlieb in the 1960s, son of August Cool, a central figure in Belgian Christian trade unionism and at the time president of the European organization of Christian trade unions.

These first Euro-lawyers quickly imposed themselves as mandatory intermediaries between the multinational corporations and the competition DG. They were in fact the permanent staff of these first Brussels offices, if only because the 'European tour of duty of the

the EC and the law firm. After resigning from this position, George Ball became chairman of the board at Lehman Brothers International.

146 Interview No. 1, Florence, October 2008.

American lawyer'[147] was a stint of only a few years (about three years) that was not long enough to build up real expertise in EC law, and even less so in the Belgian law that was nonetheless often required in the first cases that related to the establishment of distribution and export networks. At the end of the 1960s, with the ebb of American firms disappointed by the development of the Commission's economic powers that they found too modest, these Euro-lawyers became the true bridgeheads of multinational corporations in Brussels. Pooling both their expertise in European business law and their address books of American contacts and clients, these Belgian lawyers soon founded the first two law firms specializing in EC law. A first group of former students from the Catholic University of Louvain joined the firm of seasoned international lawyer George Van Hecke who had been their teacher, forming the firm Bandt-Van Hecke-Lagae & Van Bael, in 1969; some former students at the Free University of Brussels came together in 1965 to create the firm Liederkerke Waelbroeck & Kirkpatrick. Partly structured along the lines of American law firms, they became indispensable relays for clients outside the EC. As one of these lawyers recalls, 'those who came to us were non-Europeans . . . [T]hey were in need of new lawyers for their business in Europe, and they tended to seek them in Brussels. French companies called exclusively upon French lawyers'.[148] In addition, English firms 'were slow to get involved in European law, and therefore they sent me their cases. They liked having someone in Brussels, we had a geographic advantage'.[149] Henceforth, they appeared as the natural legal correspondents for multinational enterprises from outside the EC. 'We had splendid cases', recalls one lawyer, 'lots of people went to see Waelbroeck, he was very well-known in the United States and in England'.[150]

Inevitable relays for multinational corporations in Brussels, they also had close relationships within the political and government spheres of the EC. Members of a prestigious lineage, an inseparable mesh of family and professional ties that linked them to the major internationalist figures in post-war Belgium, they were very early on familiar with the forums, actors and debates of European law matters, as they had been successively the students, university assistants and interns of these internationalist jurists. Even before coming to Dewey Ballantine, both Michel Waelbroeck and his cousin John Kirkpatrick had done

[147] Leo Gottlieb, *Cleary, Gottlieb, Steen & Hamilton: The First Thirty Years*, New York, Cleary Gottlieb, 1993, p. 200.

[148] Interview No. 3, Brussels, October 2008.

[149] Interview No. 2, Brussels, October 2008.

[150] Interview No. 4, Brussels, October 2008.

internships at the firm of their former professor and 'cousin' Henri Rolin, while the latter was in charge of the defence of the influential Belgian steel mills federation, Fédéchar, before the ECJ, or the Belgian State before the International Court of Justice in the important *Barcelona Traction* case (1969). The young Michel Waelbroeck also assisted another former professor and mentor at the Free University of Brussels, Walter Ganshof van der Meersch, when as prosecutor general at the Court of Cassation he prepared his Opinion in the *Fromageries Franco-Suisses Le Ski* case (27 May 1971) that marked the beginnings of the shift of the Belgian Court of Cassation towards the doctrine of the supremacy of EC law. The young lawyer and professor, Walter van Gerven, for his part, clerked with George van Hecke, the highly reputed dean of the law faculty or the Catholic University of Louvain under whom he had studied, and then worked for as an assistant. Van Hecke had himself studied at Harvard in the 1920s, and was at the time one of the most renowned international antitrust lawyers, notably at the ECJ before which the Commission and corporations often made use of his services.

These Euro-lawyers provided this supranational milieu with an initial meeting place for developing a structure around the Common Market – the university. Often pursuing careers both in law schools and at the bar, they had solid connections in the academic world. 'There were close contacts between the *Université libre de Bruxelles* and the Commission', recalls one of the actors. 'People were invited to give courses in the Evening Conferences and continuing education programmes. There were civil servants from the Commission there'.[151] Placed between the multinational corporations and the Commission, the American and Belgian lawyers were in a position to jointly lay the groundwork for a market of European business law that was just in its beginnings.

It was no easy task, however; although Regulation 17/62 (and its supplement, Regulation 17/65), supported by Hans von der Groeben, had indeed laid down the basis of an EC regulatory system, very few decisions had been handed down, by either the Commission or the Court. To make matters worse, the notification system advocated by the competition DG very quickly revealed the limitations of the directorate, incapable of handling the flow of notifications, that numbered

[151] Interview No. 2, Brussels, October 2008.

over 36,000 in less than one year.[152] Against this backdrop, the *Grundig–Consten* case took on great importance for that little microcosm, and the various stages of this litigation constituted a full-blown judicial saga, from the ruling by the Commercial Court of the Seine in 1962 and the European Commission decision in 1964, up to the judgment pronounced by the ECJ in July 1966. This case, pertaining to the legality of an exclusive contract for the French market between the manufacturer, Grundig, and a distributor, Consten, was the vertical inauguration of articles 85 and 86 of the Rome Treaties.[153] It was the occasion for the first sanctions handed down by the competition DG, more than two years after approval of Regulation 17/62. It was also the occasion for a first decision from the ECJ on the fundamental substance of the rules of EC competition policies; previously, the Court had only incidentally considered this part of the Rome Treaties. In this way, the *Grundig–Consten* case put to the test the ambitions of those – multinational corporations, law firms and the competition DG foremost among them – who had since 1958 bet on the emergence of regulatory authority in Brussels. In November 1966, just a few months after the Court's ruling, a colloquium organized by Michel Waelbroeck with an American business lawyer, Homer Angelo, gave an idea of the expectations placed in the Court. The 164 participants in the audience who were invited to discuss 'Patents and brands under competition law in Europe and the United States' included twenty-three professors and seventy-one multinational corporations (secretaries general, heads of patent departments, etc.). For the most part, these enterprises were American (Coca-Cola, Shell, General Motors, Phenix Works, Procter and Gamble, Pfizer Europe, ITT Europe and Philips) and large European companies (Pechiney, Unilever, Pétroles d'Aquitaine, Petrochim and Nestlé). Also in attendance were nineteen civil servants from the Commission, mostly from the competition DG (and, to a lesser extent, from the Legal Service), twelve American lawyers

152 Laurent Warlouzet, *The Rise of European Competition Policy, 1950–1991: A Cross-Disciplinary Survey of a Contested Policy Sphere*, Florence, European University Institute/RSCAS, 2010.

153 Recently, historians have dug into the dynamics of the *Grundig–Consten* case, bringing detailed accounts of its underlying legal and political dynamics: see Sigfrido Ramirez and Sebastian van de Scheur, 'The Evolution of the Law on Articles 85–86 EEC: Ordoliberalism and Its Keynesian Challenge', in Kiran Patel and Heike Schweitzer (eds.), *Historical Foundations of EU Competition Law*, Oxford, Oxford University Press, 2013, pp. 19–54; and Brigitte Leucht and Mel Marquis, 'American Influences on EEC Competition Law: A Belated Europeanization through Convergence?', in Kiran Patel and Heike Schweitzer (eds.), *Historical Foundations of EU Competition Law*, Oxford, Oxford University Press, 2013, pp. 54–88.

with offices in Brussels, seventeen lawyers at the Brussels Appellate Court and twelve lawyers from other European countries.[154] All were there to discuss the outlook for the Commission and the Court. With its declaration that 'the EC competition regime does not tolerate abusive use of rights proceeding from national rights for brands that would counter the EC law on cartels', the Court did not disappoint this audience. The Court thus confirmed the full sovereignty and supremacy of the Commission to oversee 'agreements likely to affect trade between Member States', and attested its capacity to call into question national economic regulations (in this case, national patent laws) when these regulations impeded the proper functioning of free competition. The condemnation of the exclusive contract, in the name of its incompatibility with free circulation, had the quality of a first victory,[155] and soon became the keystone of a legal and economic doctrine that made free competition a core definition of the Common Market.[156] Immediately raised to the rank of a 'landmark in the law of the European Communities',[157] this decision at the same time bolstered the competition DG that found a way to handle its work overload,[158] and confirmed the Brussels Euro-lawyers who had anticipated the formation of a supranational regulatory system at the intersection of the Court and the Commission.

Conclusion

The Commission, the Parliament, the Court and the Common Market thus found in the construction of in-house legal doctrines an essential

154 Homer Angelo and Michel Waelbroeck (eds.), *Brevets et marques au regard du droit de la concurrence en Europe et aux États-Unis. Colloque organisé les 15 et 16 novembre 1966*, Brussels, Presses universitaires de Bruxelles, 1968.

155 Competition litigation was very rare: only four decisions were handed down by the Commission between 1964 (the date of the *Grundig–Consten* ruling) and the end of the transition period for the industrial common market, in July 1968; cf. Laurent Warlouzet, *The Rise of European Competition Policy, 1950–1991: A Cross-Disciplinary Survey of a Contested Policy Sphere*, Florence, European University Institute/RSCAS, 2010.

156 Philippe Maddalon, *La notion de marché dans la jurisprudence de la Cour de justice des Communautés européennes*, Paris, LGDJ, 2007.

157 Ernst Steindorff, 'The Grundig–Consten Case, a Landmark Decision of the European Court of Justice on Common Market Antitrust Law', *American Journal of Comparative Law*, 15(4), 1966, pp. 811–22.

158 The principles established by the ECJ were explicitly used as the basis for a rule proposed by the competition DG a month later (26 August 1966) that enabled the DG to set aside a significant proportion of the 32,000 authorization applications it had received.

lever for their institutionalization strategies. These strategies comprised in particular the invention of a series of transcendancies – 'Europe's Community of law', 'Europe's economic Constitution', 'general interest' – and teleologies – 'the economic union', 'integration', 'the ever-closer union of peoples', etc. – concepts that helped found the various components of Europe's emerging polity. Pointing at the 'general economy', the 'philosophy' of the European Treaties, they outlined the existence of a single European *reality* that integrated the three Communities, the various treaties and the multiple policies that were enacted in its name. While this exemplifies the emerging entanglement between European law and Europe's polity-building, this is still not enough to account for the legal identity of the nascent EC polity. There was still far to go, from these multiple uses of the law to the genesis of a genuine 'institutional programme' under the Treaties. This study must therefore delve deeper to understand the social and political dynamics that turn the constitutional paradigm into Europe's core unificatory paradigm. This will be the subject of the next two chapters. Chapter 2 is devoted to the formation of a field of European law which we see functioning as a crossroads for a variegated set of EC-related political, economic, administrative and academic undertakings.

2 The force of a weak field: the transnational field of European law and the formation of Europe's polity

In the previous chapter, we saw that Brussels at the beginning of the 1960s was an impressive melting-pot of institutional experiments and legal constructs, political strategies and academic theories, and it is not always possible to discern which of these preceded the others. The capital of Europe was the locus of convergence for highly varied endeavours that granted equally a logic or a nature to the Rome Treaties in the service of, respectively, the judicialization of the Court, the parliamentarization of the Parliament, the authority of the Commission, or the formation of a supranational market. Observers were not indifferent to this teeming activity that bubbled through the EC enclave, as shown in this account by an American law professor and early promoter of EC law among American lawyers after one of his frequent stays in the EC capital:

> [O]f all the cities hosting international organizations, Brussels is unique in having developed an explosively productive "critical mass" of legal talent. Neither New York, nor Geneva, the principal seats of UN administration, has managed to provide an atmosphere of sustained and organized interaction among the legal staff of the UN bodies, the local bar and law faculties. But in Brussels, the early leading figures of the European Communities – Hallstein, Rey, Von der Groeben, Gaudet, Verloren van Themaat – personally set a pattern of extensive scholarly writing, lecturing and teaching, and they frequently sought outside advice from legal scholars and practitioners'.[1]

In other words, in the crucible of the emerging EC institutions, a subfield of debate and conflict over the legal interpretation of the Rome Treaties was progressively emerging. Born in the continuity of the

[1] Eric Stein, 'European Communities', *American Journal of Comparative Law*, 22(3), 1974, p. 573.

undertakings to institutionalize Europe, this transnational legal field appeared as an interstitial space of the EC polity where, under the aegis of law, all sorts of agents coexisted, jurists by profession or training but nonetheless direct participants in one or another of the sectoral-specific policies that emerged from European Treaties. Thus, far from being exterior to the many struggles that made up European integration at the time, the field of European law was actually their prolongation; as such, it constituted a space for exchange and mobilization where many sorts of specific sectoral legitimacies and competencies were built up and nurtured. By virtue of this unique position at the crossroads of Europe, it is possible to look at this field not only for the law it produced but also for the work of brokering that it enabled which turned Euro-lawyers into authentic professionals of European interdependence.

The genesis of a transnational legal field

State knowledge and European heresies

What should be clear from the previous chapter is that an essential part of the institutional strategies of Europe's (political, administrative, economic) entrepreneurs relied on their capacity to convincingly provide new theories of the Paris and Rome Treaties. The stakes were high, considering that the in-house doctrines that they produced did not take effect in a theoretical vacuum, and that they constituted authentic heresies when compared to the more established definitions of what 'judicial power', 'Constitution', 'separation of powers' or 'sovereignty' traditionally meant in the various Member States. It is easy to see that things could hardly have been otherwise. Indeed, how could one justify the term 'Parliament' for an assembly that had no legislative capacity without subverting the very concept of parliamentarism? How could a 'constitutional function' be granted to an international court without at the same time undermining the very notion of State sovereignty? How could one call an international treaty a 'Treaty-Constitution' without having an effect on the idea of constitutionalism?

The making of the EC *sui generis*

The construction of Europe therefore required a veritable decoupling of concepts to allow a court, a bureaucracy, a political sphere and a market to exist at the European level without necessarily referring to the meanings that the national corpus of State knowledge attributes to these canonical terms of modern polities. Many lawyers had actually initiated such a decoupling with the Paris Treaty, promoting the intrinsically unique nature of this treaty. The report delivered on 8 December 1952 by the jurisconsults of the German, French and Italian ministries of foreign affairs (respectively, Carl Friedrich Ophüls, Paul Reuter and de Rossi) to the joint secretariat of the ECSC and Council of Europe parliamentary assemblies, argued that the specificity of the Paris Treaty lay in the transfer of sovereignty that had been accepted by the Member States. Similarly, the collaborative work undertaken by the *Institut des relations internationales de l'Université de Bruxelles* with leading international law scholars such as Fernand Dehousse, Heinrich von Bretano and Riccardo Monaco indicated that 'the EC, while presenting some features of a federal State, can not be assimilated to any pre-existing legal category and therefore forms a *sui generis* Union of States'.[2]

However, these initial efforts to set the Paris Treaty apart from 'ordinary' international treaties would be somewhat suspended after the political rejection of this 'supranational' reading of the ECSC institutional system with the rejection by the French Assembly of the European Defence Community in 1953. In a context, that of the entry into force of the Rome Treaties, where the 'supranational' lexicon turned into a taboo, the scholarly debate over the nature of the European Treaties started all over again. It is therefore not surprising to see the president of the Court, constitutional law professor Andreas Donner, exhort the judges and the professors 'to leave behind the too-narrow framework of the sacrosanct notions of traditional constitutional law'.[3] Likewise, advocate general Maurice Lagrange addressed internationalist jurists just a few weeks after the Rome Treaties came into effect, asking that 'they not hesitate, as the case may be, to revise [their doctrinal positions]' because 'the dynamic force of the treaty requires equally dynamic legal thinking'.[4] The president of the Commission, Walter Hallstein, was no less of a proponent of this view, recalling that 'legal concepts must keep pace with reality'.[5] The constitutional traditions of the different Member

2 On these two reports, see the developments by Antonio Grilli, *Le origini del diritto dell'Unione europea*, Bologna, Il Mulino, 2010, p. 83.

3 Andreas Donner, 'La Cour de justice des Communautés européennes', *Recueil des cours de l'Académie de droit international de La Haye*, 118(2), 1965, p. 7.

4 Maurice Lagrange, 'L'ordre juridique de la CECA vu à travers la jurisprudence de sa Cour de justice', *Revue de droit public*, 84, 1958, pp. 841–65, p. 865, quoted in Julie Bailleux, 'How Europe Came to Law', *Revue française de science politique*, 60(2), 2010, pp. 295–318.

5 Walter Hallstein, 'Economic Integration: An Example of the Association of States', *International Law Association Conference Report. August 1960*, 1960, pp. 13–32, p. 19.

States (parliamentarism, legislative power, political accountability, 'separation of powers', etc.) thus looked to be outdated doctrines, incapable of reflecting the new forms of regional integration for which the different functions – legislative, judicial and executive – were jointly exercised under a system of permanently interdependent organs. The Court, supported in this by a legal doctrine that was seeking to bring meaning to the *terra incognita* of the Treaties, was not long in coining a new notion, that of 'institutional balance', which was not written into the Treaties but would be steadily developed by the Court as a European substitute for the 'separation of powers', starting with the *Meroni* ruling of 13 June 1958. This manoeuvre to avoid the most classic constitutional categories went hand in hand with a process of voiding the very essence of these principles, a veritable effort of sabotage of nationally entrenched notions of public law. The continuous recourse to 'quasi' or *de facto* – 'quasi-State', 'quasi-federation', '*de facto* Constitution', 'quasi-legislative' – exemplifies such a strategy, as it helped maintain an apparent continuity with State knowledge and national political lexicons, while in fact subverting the meaning of these terms by placing very different meanings behind the same words.

From this point of view, the many efforts to qualify the European Communities as an institutional system *sui generis* and thereby not subject to State knowledge, can be seen as a symbolic *coup de force*. Far from mirroring a sort of pre-existing nature inherent to the European Communities, the *sui generis* is actually first and foremost the historical product of strategies designed to break with the traditional categories of understanding of State-building processes. By organizing a conceptual void around EC institutions, it became imperative to erect a whole new set of intellectual constructs. French diplomacy's jurisconsult, Paul Reuter, had sensed this necessity to emancipate Europe from national traditions of political thought when he suggested to Jean Monnet and Robert Schuman to use the term 'Community' to label the future ECSC institutional system which, as he said at the time, 'did not mean anything legally, except for wedding and churches',[6] and would therefore allow a concrete advancement along the path of integration without the tutelage of historically established notions of international public law. Walter Hallstein himself felt this necessity very vividly, positing in 1962 that

[6] Quoted in Antonin Cohen, *Histoire d'un groupe dans l'institution d'une 'communauté' européenne (1940–1950)*, PhD in political science, Université Paris 1-Sorbonne, September 1999.

'the European Community is *sui generis*, a new kind of political animal ... Just as language precedes grammar, so politics precedes political theory'.[7] This constitutional *tabula rasa* opened up all sorts of institutional possibilities. In effect, it authorized a decoupling of European polity-building from national constitutional traditions, and thereby opened up considerable room for manoeuvring for the different entrepreneurs working to build EC institutions. As early as July 1960, the judges of the ECJ added their stone to this edifice, by refusing to accord any legal value to national Constitutions or to the jurisprudence of supreme courts. 'It is not the Court's responsibility to enforce the rules of internal law, even constitutional, in effect in one or another of the Member States', stated the *Nold* ruling, and this was supported ten years later in 1970 in *Internationale Handelsgesellschaft*, in which the Court refused to consider itself bound 'by the fundamental rights as they are formulated by the Constitution of a Member State (or by the) principles of a national constitutional structure'. By these efforts to set aside national constitutional constraints, by exhorting politicians 'to recognize, purely and simply, that the traditional separation of powers is not capable of properly explaining the EC ensemble',[8] Euro-lawyers helped confound the historically stabilized definitions and roles of the relationship between law and politics.

As erudite and sophisticated as they may appear, however, the bold positions taken by Waelbroeck, von der Groeben, Lagrange, Dehousse, Gaudet and Hallstein could not initially rely upon an academic discipline or even a supreme court ready to fully embrace their representations of the emerging European polity. Constructed in the course of action, their doctrines were at first more avatars of science and jurisprudence, as understood by the American sociologist Andrew Abbott, i.e. scholarly formalizations constructed by and for practice itself.[9] Above all, they existed as juridical or judicial 'theories' able to found 'Europe' on a firm ground only on the condition that they met with the two-fold approval, on the one hand, of the academics who alone could grant (or refuse) the label of scientific validity, and, on the other hand, of the judges who alone could give them substance in law. Yet, this academic and judicial

[7] Walter Hallstein, *United Europe: Challenge and Opportunity*, Cambridge MA, Harvard University Press, 1962, p. 29.

[8] Pierre Pescatore, 'L'Exécutif communautaire. Justification du quadripartisme institué par les traités de Paris et de Rome', *Cahiers du droit européen*, 1978, p. 393.

[9] Andrew Abbott, 'Linked Ecologies: States and Universities as Environments for Professions', *Sociological Theory*, 23(3), 2005, p. 266.

homologation was far from assured. As they reinvented the legal categories that traditionally organized 'political power' at the national level, these in-house doctrines called into question much more than just 'principles' or 'ideas'; they touched more broadly upon the vast array of isomorphic policy instruments, professional identities and the institutional functions that had grown out of State-building processes.

The academic and judicial guardians of the States

It is no surprise then that the high courts and law faculties, organized into professional disciplines and bodies, often zealous guardians of national and international State sovereignty, erected a solid social and intellectual barrier to the various in-house doctrines that were being constructed in Luxembourg, Strasbourg and Brussels.

The discipline of international law that had been primarily institutionalized around a Westphalian reading of international affairs was particularly reluctant to accept the European set of doctrinal innovations.[10] It is true that the post-Second World War period was marked by much activity in the field of international protection of human rights, involving the notions of *jus cogens* and access by individual plaintiffs to international courts.[11] But the so-called 'contractualist' approach – that recognizes only States as the subjects of international law and thus preserves their entire and exclusive sovereignty in the international sphere – continued very largely to predominate outside the small circle of the first practitioners of the European Court of Human Rights. Europe's high-level civil servants and members of the High Authority had the bitter experience of being confronted with this attitude. Julie Bailleux has clearly demonstrated this: as they were trying to ground 'in legal rationality' a notion, that of supranationality, that had been made politically fragile by the failure of the European Defence Community, it was quite natural that they (civil servants and members of the High Authority) turned to the most authoritative scholars of international affairs at the time, namely, the international law community.[12] The impressive international congress devoted to the study of the ECSC

[10] Generally, on the history of internationa law's paradigms, see Marti Koskenniemi, *The Gentle Civilizer of Nations: The Rise and Fall of International Law*, Cambridge, Cambridge University Press, 2001.

[11] On this point, see Stéphanie-Hennette Vauchez, 'L'Europe au service (du droit) des droits de l'homme', *Politix*, 1, 2010, pp. 57–78.

[12] On the Stresa congress, see Julie Bailleux, 'How Europe Came to Law', *Revue française de science politique*, 60(2), 2010, pp. 295–318.

held in Stresa from 31 May to 9 June 1957 was conceived by the High Authority as a scholarly high mass intended to anoint the High Authority with the academic unction of international law, in the presence of the different stakeholders of the ECSC (major steel industry companies, Member States' representatives, etc.). However, the organizers of the conference (the High Authority) were obliged to give top billing to the international law scholars in the scientific discussion, and thus they concretely felt their isolation: the supranationality that they claimed as the foundation of a new international law and of a new type of European integration was essentially defended by the EC institutions' lawyers themselves (the advocate general Maurice Lagrange, ECJ judge Louis Delvaux, and constitutional law professor and member of the European Parliament, Pierre Wigny, etc.) but was relegated to the status of a *political* option based on shaky academic reasoning by the most established international law scholars of the time. The observations of one of these proponents during the conference says it well: '[T]he old conceptions of the State and its absolute sovereignty' erected 'a theoretical barrier'.[13] The congress exemplified that the scholarly field of international law was not propitious to the consecration of the new principles purported to found 'Europe'.

National supreme courts and law faculties also firmly opposed the in-house doctrines that were being constructed in Brussels and Luxembourg. No doubt, the first promoters of a constitutional Europe were fully aware of how controversial their theories were at the national level. They compared the differences in the level of the 'opening' of national legal elites to their constructions: while former ECJ judge Nicola Catalano viewed the Netherlands as best, 'where the difficulties seem to be solved', France would come in second place;[14] Italy was considered by advocate general Maurice Lagrange to be 'a victim of its professors';[15] and the German scholarship and jurisprudence was viewed by international law professor and German ambassador to the EC, Carl Friedrich Ophüls, 'as influenced by the ruins of the mythology of sovereignty'.[16]

[13] Giorgio Balladore Pallieri, 'Problèmes juridiques de la CECA', in Centre italiano di studi giuridici, *Actes officiels du congrès international sur la CECA, Milan-Stresa, 31 mai–9 juin 1957*, 7 vols., vol. 1, Milan, Giuffrè, 1959, p. 95.

[14] Nicola Catalano, in *Droit communautaire et droit national. Semaine de Bruges 1965*, 1965, Bruges, De Tempel, p. 89.

[15] Maurice Lagrange, 'Les obstacles constitutionnels à l'intégration européenne', *Revue trimestrielle de droit européen*, 5(2), 1969, p. 242.

[16] Carl Friedrich Ophüls, in *Droit communautaire et droit national. Semaine de Bruges 1965*, Bruges, De Tempel, 1965, p. 89.

As a matter of fact, the constitutional reading of the European Treaties espoused in the 1950s by the German *Auswärtiges Amt* jurist-diplomats – around Walter Hallstein – was very clearly in the minority at the annual colloquium of the *Vereinigung der Deutschen Staatsrechtslehrer*, the influential association of public law professors whose members saw in this reading a threat to parliamentary sovereignty.[17] In 1953, and then repeatedly up to the middle of the 1960s, the leading names in German public law would underscore that the transfer of sovereignty enacted under the Paris and Rome Treaties, to the benefit of a system without guarantees of fundamental rights without securing the oversight function of the *Bundestag*, was not in compliance with the German Basic Law. From the beginning of the 1960s, the German courts kept up a sceptical posture *vis-à-vis* the institutional system born of the Rome Treaties. Two decisions of a German tax court, dated 14 November 1963 and 25 March 1965, kicked off the debate in a spectacular fashion, listing the defects of constitutional form in the EC political system, starting with the dispossession of the German Parliament in favour of a regime, the European Communities, that had no separation of powers. The 1974 ruling of the German Constitutional Court, better known as the *Solange I* ruling, would follow the same line, declaring that, *as long as* the Communities had no democratically elected parliament and no protection of fundamental rights, the German Constitutional Court would claim the right to verify the constitutionality of EC rules.[18] Acting as guardians of State's sovereignty, many high magistrates and professors of law were opposed to the new set of concepts on which the institutionalization of the Rome Treaties had been grounded.

If we cast off the intellectualist vision of science as simply sets of theories and ideas, we are obliged to see that this conceptual barricade was not just theoretical, but effectively worked as 'a brake'.[19] When academics contested the scientific or judicial reality of the in-house doctrines conceived by the entrepreneurs of a supranational Europe, the entire institutional edifice was menaced by this resistance. For, above and beyond their differences, the common feature of the EC enterprises

[17] On this episode, see Bill Davies, *Resisting the European Court of Justice: West Germany's Confrontation with European Law (1949–1979)*, Cambridge, Cambridge University Press, 2012, pp. 44–88, pp. 46–88.

[18] See, in the vast literature, Peter Lindseth, 'The Law–Regulation Distinction and European Integration. Reflections on the German Jurisprudence from the 1960s to the Present', *Jus Politicum*, 2(4), 2009, www.juspoliticum.com/The-Law-Regulation-Distinction-and.html.

[19] Maurice Lagrange, 'L'ordre juridique de la CECA vu à travers la jurisprudence de sa Cour de justice', *Revue de droit public*, 84, 1958, pp. 841–65, p. 865.

was that they all rested upon a constitutional reading of the Rome Treaties. The exaltation of the ECJ as the 'Supreme Court of the Communities', the consecration of the Commission as 'guardian of the general EC interest', the elevation of the competition DG to the rank of chief regulator of the new Common Market, or the accession of the European Parliament Assembly to the family of Parliaments, are all inseparably linked to the reading of the Rome Treaties as Treaty-Constitutions. Without a formal endorsement of these theories by academic and jurisdictional authorities, these institutions were at risk, in the words of the president of the ECJ himself, of being no more than 'a variation on the old story of Baron Münchhausen who dragged himself out of the mud by pulling on his own hair'.[20]

Academic and judicial endorsement

In this light, the development of an EC judicial scene and the flourishing of transnational academic arenas relatively sheltered from the scepticism of national legal elites were means of getting around this 'theoretical barrier'. Born as a by-product of the strategies for the institutionalization of the Rome Treaties, and financially supported by the Communities, these venues opened up a durable space for scientific discussion and judicial debate that was relatively independent of the States and of national legal traditions, and thereby more favourable to the development of a genuinely European vision of law. These transnational academic and judicial spheres constituted 'neutral places' where different avatars could be discussed, revised and ultimately validated.

A courtroom for Europe

The formation of these transnational arenas was not an effortless process. As we saw above, the ECJ long turned a deaf ear to the pleas of its advocate general Maurice Lagrange, who urged the Court to mark its difference with classical international jurisdictions. In fact, the Court was initially the receptacle of an 'internationalist' judicial style, by which is meant types of actors, standard operating models, and methods of interpretation that distinctively characterized international courts. Proof of this is the fact that, in the same way as their counterparts at

[20] Andreas Donner, 'Les rapports entre la compétence de la Cour de justice des Communautés européennes et les tribunaux internes', *Recueil des cours de l'Académie de droit international de La Haye*, 115(2), 1965, pp. 1–61, p. 57.

Table 1 *The ten most frequent plaintiffs before the Court, 1954–1978 (by number of interventions commissioned over this period)*

Plaintiff	Number of interventions
EC Executives	1,082
Council of Ministers	113
Italy	56
Parliament	40
The Netherlands	19
France	18
Germany	18
Meroni & Co.	17
United Kingdom	16
Lemmerz-Werke GmbH	10

the International Court of Justice or the European Court of Human Rights, professors, and particularly professors of international law, initially played an important role at the ECJ: there were no fewer than nine professors among the fourteen lawyers who were the most active practitioners before the Coal and Steel Court (1954–8).[21]

Nonetheless, a process of autonomization of this EC judicial space got underway. Starting in 1958, the proportion of professors to lawyers began to shift in favour of the latter: by 1972, there were only three professors for twenty-one lawyers among ECJ most active 'players'. This acquisition of autonomy was bolstered by the EC Executives, who played an essential part at the Luxembourg Court. The Executives were the only repeat players in this emerging judicial arena: alone, they commissioned 40 per cent of the 2,710 'interventions' by jurists (legal advisers in the institutions or outside consultants) before the Court between 1952 and 1978. This predominance had no equivalent, as the 1,216 other interventions were instigated by close to 700 different clients (individuals, companies and Member States). With the rare exception of a few States and companies (Meroni & Co., Lemmerz-Werke, among others), no other actor was a recurring litigator before the Court. Table 1 lists the ten most frequent plaintiffs before the Court in the period 1954–78.

This is a significant fact. First and foremost, it signifies that the Legal Service alone was in a position to pursue a truly jurisprudential policy,

[21] The following quantitative data are published in Christèle Marchand and Antoine Vauchez, 'Lawyers as Europe's Middlemen? A Sociology of Litigants Pleading to the European Court of Justice (1954–1978)84', in Michel Mangenot and Jay Rowell (eds.), *What Europe Constructs?*, Manchester, Manchester University Press, 2010, pp. 68–87.

concretely fulfilling the definition that Mark Galanter gives of the 'repeat player' in a celebrated article: 'a unit which has had and anticipates repeated litigation, which has low stakes in the outcome of any one case, and which has resources to pursue its long-run interests'.[22] To be sure, the pool of members of the Legal Service were experienced practitioners of the European Treaties, while the litigation departments of national ministries and major companies accorded it only sporadic attention. Having poached four out of nine legal clerks (*référendaires*) from the ECSC Court of Justice in 1958, Michel Gaudet and his team of legal advisers were the only ones with the capacity to develop judicial strategies that matched the specific opportunities and constraints of the jurisprudence developed by the Court since 1952. This state of play did not go unnoticed by the practitioners at the Court, who observed that 'the plaintiffs only rarely obtained confirmation of their arguments ... because the Court took care, and rightly so, to avoid unnecessarily attacking the brand-new institutions, on the contrary seeking to reinforce as much as possible their credibility'.[23] Addressing the trade federations of the steel industry, another seasoned observer gave them warning in these terms: 'Going to the Court of Justice is like going to Waterloo'.[24]

But this was not all. Not only was the European Commission in the best position when it came to shaping a body of jurisprudence tailored to its desires, it also contributed to the structuring of the corps of ECJ specialists by its frequent recourse to outside legal consultants called in to support the Commission in its litigation strategies. Here it must be remarked that, initially, the members of the Legal Service of the Executives, often surprisingly young and with little experience, could hardly hold their own against seasoned practitioners of international courtrooms such as the professors and legal advisers, Henri Rolin (Case No. 1-54), Riccardo Monaco (Case No. 2-54) and Wilhem Riphagen and J. H. M. Verzilj (Case No. 6-54) who came to Luxembourg to defend variously the coal federations, the Netherlands, Italy, etc. Consequently, the Commission sought from the start to reinforce its position at the Court by frequently calling upon external legal consultants chosen from the rosters of national faculties and bars. Nearly one-third of the 1,082

[22] Mark Galanter, 'Why the Have's Come Out Ahead: Speculations on the Limits of Legal Change', *Law and Society Review*, 9(1), 1974, p. 102.

[23] Jossé Mertens de Wilmar, 'Souvenirs externes sur les débuts de la Cour', *XXXV anni (1952–1987)*, Luxembourg, Curia, 1987, p. 49.

[24] Paul Reuter, quoted in *ibid.*

interventions by jurists before the Court commissioned by the Commission between 1952 and 1978 were made by outside lawyers. In this way, the EC Executives imposed themselves as the main suppliers of cases in an EC litigation market that was still small and did not allow for a high degree of specialization in law firms. Fewer than one-quarter of the 460 lawyers who pleaded before the Court between 1952 and 1978 appeared three times or more; for the most part, they were 'one-shotters', to use the expression coined by Mark Galanter. In these conditions the fact that the Commission employed many outside consultants can be seen as a co-optation. Statistical data show the same. Those who had worked at one time or another for the Commission were also those whose activities before the Court were most significant between 1952 and 1978: more than one-quarter of these seventy-five lawyers, twenty-one in all, who were most active in Luxembourg had the Commission as their main client. Even more significantly, those who pleaded for the Commission were also those whose clientele was the most diverse (States, companies, interest groups, individuals, etc.) and who had the most long-standing practice before the Court. Regularly consulted by the Commission, which had often given them a leg up by 'offering' them their first case in Luxembourg, lawyers including Jean Coutard (France), Wijckerheld Bisdom (Netherlands), Alex Bonn (Germany) and George van Hecke (Belgium) were rapidly ensconced as the uncontested masters of the European courtroom. The imprimatur of the Commission thus consecrated a reputation and expertise to which companies, interest groups and to a lesser extent States had recourse when they went to defend their causes in Luxembourg. In designating its 'defenders' throughout the 1950s and 1960s, the Commission therefore indirectly chose its future 'opponents'.

This was not without consequences, considering that these lawyers, frequently co-opted on the basis of personal ties to members of the Legal Service, and acclimated to the legal reasoning of the 'EC Institutions', were inclined to inscribe their pleas within the space that the Court and the Commission had together delineated. In this way, they helped consolidate the foundations of a European courtroom that was in part protected from the scepticism of professors of international law and of high court judges. This is undoubtedly one of the most tangible effects of the institutionalization of the Court as a specific judicial arena, i.e. organized around its own distinctive rules and operational logic: it imposed upon those who sought to plead successfully a shared set of arguments, the terms of and alternatives to which were necessarily adopted by the State jurists, companies, individuals and Communities who appeared before the Court. As noted today by Loïc Azoulai, 'the closer the plea or observation submitted to the Court was to the language and constraints adopted by the Court itself, the better its chances of being properly received and treated'.[25]

Co-opted academia?

European academia, taken to be the transnational academic space devoted to the study of Europe and the Communities, already existed in an embryonic form when the Rome Treaties were signed. In the wake of the mobilization for the Hague congress (May 1948) and singularly by the impetus of the cultural commission of the European Movement, myriad of local and transnational academic initiatives came to the fore. Spurred by figures in the federalist nebula such as Denis de Rougement and Alexandre Marc, these movements aimed to acculturate national elites to the 'European spirit'.[26] The creation of College of Bruges and the first generation of Institutes of European Studies in Nancy, Nice, Saarbrucken, Strasbourg, Tours and Turin that grew up in its wake (all of them were created between 1950 and 1954) were inscribed in the same perspective of a Europeanization 'from below' aiming at forging a new form of European patriotism via access to a 'European culture' freed from its nationalist roots. In most cases confined to the periphery of universities, populated by educators who owed their presence first to their pan-European commitment, and with an uncertain academic legitimacy, these multidisciplinary teachings were essentially focused on providing a 'civilizational' approach to Europe, thereby granting law as well as economics a secondary position in the required coursework. Moreover, this training was based on a broad understanding of 'Europe', thereby refusing to grant a specific status to the European Communities *vis-à-vis* other European integrations (the Western European Union, NATO or the Council of Europe). Most often dependent on local support from pan-European political leaders, mixing practitioners (politicians, journalists, writers, public intellectuals, etc.) and scholars in highly eclectic curricula, these institutes all claimed a commitment to the

[25] Loïc Azoulai, 'La fabrication de la jurisprudence communautaire', in Pascal Mbongo and Antoine Vauchez (eds.), *Dans la fabrique du droit européen*, Brussels, Bruylant, 2009, pp. 178–97.

[26] On this point, and regarding this paragraph in general, we refer to the first chapter of the doctoral dissertation by Julie Bailleux, *Penser l'Europe par le droit. L'invention du droit communautaire en France*, Paris, Dalloz, 2014.

political unification of Europe. Thereby, their existence was continuously subjected to controversy from both Euro-sceptical national political parties as much as from established academic communities that hardly recognized their scientific legitimacy.

However, the period following the adoption of the Rome Treaties offered a new opportunity for 'European studies' to emerge from the limbo in which they had been since the European Movement had opted for universities as the prime vectors for the rise of a 'European consciousness'. The interest taken by American foundations as well as the emergence of a sustained interest for academic research at the Commission, offered new sources of funding that allowed a transnational academic debate to exist, if not full-fledged core academic disciplines recognized in national curricula. By virtue of the close ties that Jean Monnet had with the Ford Foundation through the former Marshall Plan commissioner John McCloy, the foundation funded the creation of an *Institut de la Communauté européenne pour les etudes universitaires* (with Walter Hallstein as a member), and the creation of a first chair in European integration, in Lausanne in 1957.[27] Above all, those who took an interest in the Communities could henceforth count on the support of the European Communities press and information DG headed by another figure close to Jean Monnet, Jacques-René Rabier, who had been the head of Monnet's cabinet at the French *Commissariat général au Plan* (Planning Commission) and then later at the High Authority. During his nearly eighteen years at the press and information DG (1955–73), Rabier put numerous measures into motion: the creation of European Documentation Centres in universities that would receive free of charge all EC publications and documents; research grants and awards; logistic and financial assistance in setting up national academic associations, etc.[28] The press and information DG directly financed the emergence of university research centres that promoted education on European issues (European Studies Institutes) and national scholarly societies for the study of the European Communities, such as the *Commission pour l'étude*

[27] Giuliana Gemelli, 'American Foundations and European Scientific Integration: Actors and Networks (1920s–1970s)', in Michel Dumoulin (ed.), *Réseaux économiques et construction européenne*, Brussels, Peter Lang, 2004, pp. 55–72.

[28] Recent work by various authors has underscored the multifarious academic forms invested by the Information and Communication Department of the Commission: see in particular the articles by Morgane Le Boulay and Philippe Aldrin in the Symposium entitled 'L'Académie européenne', 89, Politix, 2010; and a recent book by Oriane Caligaro, *Negotiating Europe: EU Promotion of Europeanness since the 1950s*, Basingstoke, Macmillan, 2013.

des Communautés européennes (Cedece, 1965) and the *Arbeitskreise für Europäische Integration* (1969).[29] This continuous support was instrumental in the emergence of transnational spaces that were partly independent of the dynamics of national academic fields.

But let there be no mistake: the formation of an embryo of European academia could in no way be detached from the mobilization of the first political entrepreneurs of supranational Europe, more often than not themselves academics. By their presence within both EC institutions and European studies research centres, they were at once the initiators and the first beneficiaries of the various institutional resources distributed by the Communities (subsidies, internships and awards for their students, but also privileged access to information, etc.). Let us take a closer look. The Cedece was founded in 1965 by the former vice-president of the Assembly of the Council of Europe, Pierre-Henri Teitgen, who was also a professor at the University of Paris and a principal proponent of the institutionalization of EC law in French law schools. The *Arbeitskreise für Europäische Integration* came into being under Professor Walter Hallstein, president of the European Commission. Most European studies research centres were born in similar circumstances. The Europa-Instituut was founded in 1962 at the University of Leiden under the aegis of Ivo Samkalden, then the (socialist) minister of justice of the Netherlands, professor of international law and president of the Dutch chapter of the association of European jurists, the *Fédération internationale pour le droit européen* (FIDE). The *Institut d'études juridiques européennes* (IEJE) was launched in 1964 by the European member of parliament Fernand Dehousse, professor at the University of Liège, who did himself proud for having a few years earlier created the first Licence diploma in European law (1957). And there are other examples.

Likewise, a large part of the doctrinal production was actually a co-production bringing together scholars from within and without the EC institutions. The commentaries on the Rome Treaties that were published in the different Member States were a form of co-production between the EC institutions' lawyers (from the Court, the Council and the Commission) and legal scholars. Examples include the two legal commentaries that were then, and for a long time afterwards,

[29] On this point, see an account by one of the main protagonists involved in the Commission's policies to support European studies: Jacqueline Lastenouse, 'La Commission européenne et les études universitaires', *Temas de Integracao*, 15–16, 2003, pp. 13–36.

authoritative in Germany. The first associated the names of the director of the Council of Ministers' Legal Service, Ernst Wohlfart, and law professor, Ulrich Everling, who was soon to be appointed judge at the ECJ.[30] The second was the work of the European commissioner for competition, Hans von der Groeben, and his colleague with whom he shared responsibility for the ECSC Treaty at the economic ministry, Hans van Boeckh.[31] Likewise, the sole Italian commentary on the Treaties associated (in 1965 and 1970) two judges of the ECJ, Alberto Trabucchi and Riccardo Monaco, with an international law professor, Rolando Quadri. But the most striking example is certainly the Mégret *Commentary*, the fruit of the cooperative efforts undertaken (from 1970 to the present) by professors at the *Institut d'études européennes* at the *Université libre de Bruxelles* and members of the Council's Legal Service under its then director Jacques Mégret. This commentary is known as the French-language 'bible' on the Rome Treaties.[32]

The first academic spaces were thus formed not at a distance, but in direct and continuous contact with political and administrative audiences.[33] The first 'theories' of Europe were born 'in a context of application' and in a close relationship with their end users with whom these academic constructs were discussed, abandoned or reworked. They were conceived first and foremost as contributions destined to equip the emerging figures of the European governing personnel – judges, top civil servants, commissioners, members of Parliament, diplomats, corporate executives – with rationales for their own roles and techniques for the unification of Europe. More broadly, these first transnational academic venues were 'kitchen cabinets'[34] where European decision-makers could test out all sorts of trial balloons and garner all sorts of doctrinal suggestions. They also constituted a pool for the recruitment of 'seconds' who

30 Ulrich Everling and Ernst Wohlfart, *Die Europäische-Wirschaftsgemeinschaft: Kommentar zum Vertrag*, Berlin, Vahlen, 1960.

31 Hans von der Groeben and Hans von Boeckh (eds.), *Kommentar zum EWG-Vertrag*, Baden-Baden, Nomos, 1958.

32 Jacques Mégret, Jean-Victor Louis, Daniel Vignes and Michel Waelbroeck, *Le droit de la Communauté économique européenne. Commentaire du traité et des textes pris pour son application*, vol. 1, Brussels, Presses universitaires de Bruxelles, 1970. The *Mégret Commentary* consists of fifteen volumes and has been reprinted several times.

33 Cécile Robert and Antoine Vauchez, 'L'Académie européenne. Savoirs, experts et savants dans le gouvernement de l'Europe', *Politix*, 89, 2010, pp. 9–34.

34 Karen Alter, 'Jurist Advocacy Movements in Europe: The Role of Euro-Law Associations in European Integration (1953–1975)', in Karen Alter, *The European Court's Political Power: Essays on the Influence of the European Court of Justice on European Politics*, Oxford, Oxford University Press, 2009, pp. 63–91.

were already fervent proponents of the European project and who could be immediately mobilized to positions in the initial European teams – administrative, judicial, economic and political. Last but not least, there is no neglecting the fact that decision-makers and academics gave each other mutual support in maintaining an image that flattered their own role and importance. The academics profited from the presence at their side of European leaders who were very often invited to introduce, preside over, preface or conclude academic debates, and thereby confirmed the utility and credibility of their scholarly work in the historic process of the construction of Europe. The European decision-makers, for their part, found in these transnational venues their first 'captive' audiences that reassured them as to the pertinence of their pan-European strategies.

The Fédération internationale pour le droit européen: the 'private army of the Communities'

The creation of the *Fédération internationale pour le droit européen* (International Federation for European Law, FIDE) in 1961, the main scholarly association in the domain of EC law, is wholly emblematic of the conditions subsisting in the emergence of this European academe. Doubtless scathed by its failures to enlist the big names of international law in support of its cause, the Legal Service of the Commission pushed for the creation of an association with unquestioned pan-European loyalties.[35] FIDE inherited in part the pan-European legal networks of the Association of European Jurists created in 1952 merging them with the group of lawyers who were working for EC institutions (judges, auditors, legal advisers to the Commission), thereby creating an institution that, from its outset, was protected from the criticism of international law professors who were carefully kept out of range. As a result, FIDE could rely on the broad range of jurists that the European integration spawned, who were much more diverse than the traditional specialists of international legal affairs. These included jurists in multinational corporations with business in the Common Market, law professors in the various Institutes for European Studies, jurists in ministries, auditors and judges of the ECJ, as well as pan-European advocates, politicians, etc. A veritable consortium from all quarters of European integration, FIDE did not have the authority of a scholarly society like the *Institut de droit international* (indeed, academics were a minority in FIDE) but its loyalty to the twin causes of law and the political advancement of Europe

[35] On the creation of the FIDE and the role of Michel Gaudet, see Julie Bailleux, *Penser l'Europe par le droit. L'invention du droit communautaire en France*, Paris, Dalloz, 2014.

> was unshakeable. Prevailing for at least two decades as the true 'Mecca of EC jurists'[36] and bringing every two years around 200 practitioners and theoreticians of EC law together for its congresses, FIDE aimed to be 'the private army of the European Communities' in the words of its first president the Belgian high magistrate, Léon Hendrickx,[37] furnishing, in colloquia and journals, the legal arsenal that would ensure the firepower needed for pan-European combat.

Thus, the field of EC law – and in particular here its judicial venues and academic arenas – was born in the continuity of a number of lay endeavours (political, administrative, economic, judicial, etc.) that supported and promoted an extensive and unified reading of the European Treaties. Consequently, these spaces were never beyond the pale of the '*irréductible diplomatique*'[38] that ran through and through the functioning of the EC political and administrative spaces.

The 'irréductible diplomatique'

Nothing could have been more foreign to this emerging 'Europe of law' than an a-national cosmopolitanism. Although not a hard and fast rule, the appointment of members to the High Authority and of commissioners respected a balance between the 'large' countries (France, Germany, Italy) who were entitled to two positions and the 'small' countries (Belgium, Luxembourg, the Netherlands) who had to settle for a single representative; this quasi-diplomatic logic had a tendency to cascade down through all the EC institutions (general secretariat, directorates general, etc.). This was the case in the joint Legal Service of the Executives, where the directors carefully tracked the national distribution of legal adviser positions. This notion of geographic weighting spread well beyond the political and administrative spheres. In a framework where the principles of transnational legitimacy, such as that of specialized expertise, were not sufficiently ensconced to override diplomatic considerations, the prime condition ensuring legitimacy to these first European arenas lay in a geopolitical equilibrium that secured national representativeness. The

36 Hjalte Rasmussen, *On Law and Policy in the European Court of Justice*, Dordrecht, Nijhoff, 1987, p. 266.

37 Léon Hendrickx, quoted in 'Le colloque international de droit européen de Bruxelles', *Journal des tribunaux*, 1962, p. 614.

38 Claude-Albert Colliard, 'L'irréductible diplomatique', *Études de droits des Communautés européennes. Mélanges offerts à Pierre-Henri Teitgen*, Paris, Pedone, 1984.

organizers of scientific meetings and the leaders of FIDE alike took care to ensure, if not equality, at least a form of balance between nationals of the different countries. FIDE organized the discussions at its congresses (Brussels 1960, The Hague 1963, Paris 1965, etc.) on the basis of six national reports drawn up by its six national sections.[39]

There can be no better sign of this quasi-diplomatic sensitivity among Euro-lawyers than the fact that the forms of discrepancies and inequalities never went unnoticed. At a law conference held at the College of Bruges in 1965, some participants voiced regret over 'the henceforth traditional absence of qualified representatives of the French University at these colloquia'.[40] On another occasion, in Lyon in May 1962, some participants would worry that it was important 'not to give the impression that these international meetings are necessarily and exclusively dominated by Franco-Belgian and German law'.[41] Only the pooling of the different national legal traditions of which each national citizen is an expression, willingly or not, could secure the Europeanness of these venues. In other terms, if the FIDE meetings or hearings before the ECJ could claim to constitute a *European* view of law, beyond national allegiances and dependencies, it was on the condition that these forums be composed in equal parts of representatives of different legal traditions.

Legal Europeanness was defined not as a space beyond nations, but through the glorification of the different legal cultures found in the Europe of the Six. This national representativeness condition was also reflected in the working methods and argumentational strategies used by EC lawyers. As one Luxembourg jurist-diplomat remarked, in the days following the signing of the Rome Treaties, interpreting the Treaties would mean 'calling upon underlying notions that can be revealed by comparison of national bodies of legislation and the deepest legal convictions', emphasizing that 'the task of discovering – or rediscovering – this legal commonality is a role that falls to comparative law scholars, an avant-garde role that could usefully be performed by academia'.[42] The

[39] On the role of 'national traditions' in the formation of transnational academic spaces, see also Johan Heilbron, 'Qu'est-ce qu'une "tradition nationale" en sciences sociales?', *Revue d'histoire des sciences humaines*, 18, 2008, pp. 3–13.

[40] Jean-Louis Victor, 'Compte-rendu', *Cahiers du droit européen*, 1, 1965, p. 80.

[41] Pierre Padis, 'Introduction à un colloque de juristes européens', *Problèmes juridiques et pratiques du Marché commun*, Lyon, Imprimerie des petites affiches lyonnaises, 1962.

[42] Pierre Pescatore, 'Les aspects fonctionnels de la Communauté économique européenne, notamment les sources du droit', in Commission Vie et Droit des Affaires, *Les aspects juridiques du Marché commun*, Collection scientifique de la Faculté de Droit de Liège, 1958, p. 74.

Court did precisely this when it chose to interpret the Treaties, not so much on the basis of international doctrine, as by seeking the elements 'brought forth by a comparative study of the law in all the Member States', and notably the set of principles commonly shared across these bodies of national law. This was noted by advocate general Maurice Lagrange, when he underscored that, as from the very first litigation before the Court in 1954, 'the Court adopts ... a method of textual interpretation that is not literal, not based on exegesis of texts, but a global approach directly inspired by the rules in effect in the national jurisdictions for the application of domestic law and that is opposed to the misguided directions habitually followed by international jurisdictions'.[43] Even though expressed euphemistically as the fair representation of different national legal traditions, it was indeed a quasi-diplomatic rationale that impregnated the European legal field, in its very ways of functioning (working methods, forms of reasoning, etc.).

A field at the crossroads of Europe

At first sight, this emerging field of EC law looks like any other national legal field. Functionally speaking, one can find a 'court', 'legal professionals', 'scholarship', 'academic congresses' and 'learned societies', etc. However, taking homonyms for synonyms would be seriously wrong and would cloud our understanding of what constitutes this field's specificity, namely, its particular degree of instability and heteronomy. Born of the endeavours of lawyers engaged in very different political, bureaucratic, economic or judicial sites, the field of EC law blurred the multiple professional boundaries that ordinarily give a 'national' structure to legal and judicial activity at the national level. The numerous caesurae and censorings that traditionally organize the space of possibilities of legal professionals lose some of their social effectiveness at this transnational level. It is as if there were a sort of 'functional decoupling' of jurists, bound by many customs and rules linked to their social and professional role in their national activity, but benefiting from an unaccustomed degree of liberty on the European stage. This emerging transnational field allowed for a set of proximities, circulations and exchanges that would otherwise have been unthinkable. This in turn positioned the field of EC law as the crossroads of European undertakings.

[43] Maurice Lagrange, 'La CJCE du Plan Schuman à l'Union européenne', in *Mélanges Fernand Dehousse*, Paris, Nathan et Labor, 1979, p. 131 (emphasis added).

A functional decoupling

There is one founding paradox of the European Communities that is worth reflecting upon: while the Treaties and subsequent EC rules did set up a series of European legal institutions, they actually never managed to define the legal professionals that were supposed to populate and give life to these institutions. The treaty drafters managed to agree on the creation of a *permanent* jurisdictional institution, but they simultaneously renounced the tackling of the much more sensitive question of defining who the *permanent* members of this permanent court (judges, litigants) had to be and what sort of credentials they should be required to have. This was not the first such occasion: the advisory committee of jurists solicited in 1920 by the League of Nations to draft the statutes of the first international jurisdiction, the Permanent Court of International Justice, had also failed to codify the qualities and characteristics that were expected of these first professionals of international law.[44] From the outset, deeply divergent definitions of what an 'international judge' had to be were in opposition, at the very least between the 'international magistrate judge' drawn from the bar or the courts, a notion defended by the common law countries, and the 'international professor judge' or 'jurisconsult' familiar to civil law countries. The stakes were not just symbolic. This conflict touched upon the different historically rooted systems of professions, potentially putting in question the respective scope of action and domains reserved to legal professions. The solution adopted by the European Treaties and the internal rules of the Court are strikingly similar to that found in 1920: absent an agreement on a single professional canon for the European 'judge' and 'lawyer', all definitions would be accepted, enabling any jurist, whether professor, magistrate, politician of the law or jurist-diplomat, to be appointed as a judge at the Luxembourg Court. It is as if the price to be paid for the creation of a European court was to forego the definition of the European judge and lawyer, and so it fell to each of the national governments to choose the profile – politician, civil servant, magistrate or professor – best suited to fulfilling the EC judicial functions. The result was a wide variety of recruitment pathways that, *in fine*, were a function of national administrative and political arrangements.[45]

[44] Antoine Vauchez, *Transnational Expert Fields as Weak Fields: The Drafting of the First World Court and the Genesis of the International Way of Expertise*, Working Paper EUI, RSCAS, 2014, forthcoming.

[45] On the diversity of recruitment pathways, see Antonin Cohen, 'Ten Majestic Figures in Long Amaranth Robes: The Formation of the Court of Justice of the European Communities', *Revue française de science politique*, 60(2), 2010, pp. 227–46.

This initial lack of definition of professional standards for Euro-lawyering can also be found in the relative imprecision that prevailed as to rules of incompatibility that are such sensitive issues at the national level when it comes to judges. The 'Rueff case' that marked the first months of operation of the new Court in 1958 is particularly emblematic in this regard.[46]

A European judge in Luxembourg, a government expert in Paris: the 'Rueff case' (1959–61)

Jacques Rueff, a top civil servant and renowned free-market economist, had initially been appointed to the ECJ in 1952. When Charles de Gaulle returned to power in 1957, Rueff was called on to take a prominent role in the creation and work of the committee of experts designated in late 1958 to draw up a financial and monetary stabilization plan for France (later adopted under the name of the 'Rueff plan'), and then in the 'Armand–Rueff' committee tasked with analyzing 'obstacles to economic expansion'.[47] Jacques Rueff was therefore at the same time a European judge and a highly important government expert in Paris. While this double appointment triggered embarrassment at the Court, MEPs of strict pan-European obedience were quick to denounce this as a conflict of interest: politician of the law and MEP, Marinus Van der Goes van Naters, decided to draw the attention of public opinion in a written question submitted on 23 June 1959 to the EEC Council, in which he evoked the incompatibility between the functions of a judge at the ECJ and 'the very active role as chairman of a commission of experts mandated to make proposals to the government of a Member State as to measures to be taken by said State in economic and financial matters'.[48] Revising its first draft response which underscored the 'purely occasional and therefore [*sic*] extra-professional character', the Council ultimately gave a laconic response that recognized *de facto* the possibility of multiple mandates, as 'the nature of Mr Rueff's activities does not fall under any of the bans or incompatibilities stipulated' in the statutes of the Court.[49] 'The higher interest of the Communities' – and, in this case, of its Member States – would appear to be sufficient to justify this departure from the rules of judicial deontology; a few years later, Andreas Donner who had been the ECJ president during the 'Rueff case', would endorse this view, stating that, in

(cont)

[46] The 'Rueff case' has been recently explored in more detail by Antonin Cohen, 'Juge et expert. L'Affaire Rueff ou la production des frontières institutionnelles', *Critique internationale*, No. 59, 2013, pp. 69–88.

[47] Cf. Michel-Pierre Chélini, 'Le plan de stabilisation Pinay–Rueff 1958', *Revue d'histoire moderne et contemporaine*, 48(4), 2001, pp. 102–23.

[48] Written Question No. 27 submitted to the Council by Marinus Van der Goes van Naters of the European Parliamentary Assembly, in AHCE, CM2/1959/442.

[49] Reply of 25 July 1959 to Question No. 27 submitted to the Council by Marinus Van der Goes van Naters of the European Parliamentary Assembly, in AHCE, CM2/1959/442.

exercising his governmental functions in Paris, Mr Rueff 'was realizing to Europe the greatest service he could, that of helping the heart of Europe [for which, read "the French economy"] to sustain the effort demanded of it by a new era. He was continuously recalled to Paris to undertake duties as honourable as they were difficult'.[50]

In a context in which many candidates who were approached declined appointments to Luxembourg (starting with Pierre-Henri Teitgen and Paul Reuter),[51] this initial refusal to set strict rules was undoubtedly the price to pay to make the EC judicial function attractive. It allowed ECJ judges to 'never lose sight of the public affairs of their country'.[52]

The same ambiguities prevailed for the European bar. The authors of the Court's internal rules adopted the same prudent attitude and did not risk a foray onto the terrain of a European-wide definition of the profession of lawyer, an attempt that would inevitably have appeared as a form of meddling in the delicate interplay and balances of national systems of professions (*avoués/avocats/notaires* in France, *avvocato/procuratore legale* in Italy, etc.). Declining to set supranational standards for the profession of lawyer, the ECJ's internal rules granted the right to plead before the Court to any person qualified to do so in one of the six Member States, thus remitting the control of access to the EC bar, as well as the deontological oversight of practices, to the national professional bodies, and to them alone. As early as 1960, the most internationalized segments of the European legal professions supported various projects to establish 'a European bar distinct from national bar associations … grouping in a single order lawyers who plead before European jurisdictions … establishing between members of the bars a supranational confraternity where the conceptions of law and the defence of legal rights would be unified in the words of the former president of the Paris Bar'.[53] But these

[50] 'Funeral Oration in Honour of Mr Jacques Rueff Given by Judge A. M. Donner on 11 May 1978', in *Formal Sittings of the Court of Justice. 1978 and 1979*, Luxembourg, Curia, 1979.

[51] See Nicole Condorelli-Braun, *Commissaires et juges dans les Communautés européennes*, Paris, LGDJ, 1972.

[52] 'Address Delivered by the President of the Court of Justice, H. Kutscher, at the Formal Sitting of the Court on 29 March 1979 on the Occasion of the Retirement of Judge Andreas M. Donner', *Formal Sittings of the Court of Justice. 1978 and 1979*, Luxembourg, Curia, 19791979, p. 18. In 1971, Andreas Donner presided over the consultative committee tasked with reforming the constitution of the Netherlands.

[53] René-William Thorp (former head of Paris Bar), *Vues sur la justice*, Paris, René Julliard, 1962, p. 257.

ambitions were quickly stifled within the *Conseil consultatif des barreaux européens* which remained a mere confederative institution with no direct regulation over European lawyers. Similarly, the ambitious projects promoted by the EEC Commission as early as 1961 of a directive that would secure a freedom of establishment for lawyers throughout the Member States would soon be blocked by the impossibility of national bars' representatives to agree on a common definition of what being a 'lawyer' in Europe meant.

Without professional standards applicable throughout the European Community, or at the very least a European system of equivalencies between the different national titles, diplomas and professions, a certain degree of ambiguity reigned as to the meaning and value of these titles (*chargé de cours, bâtonnier, docteur, avocat-notaire*, etc.), diplomas and professions (*notaire, avocat, jurisconsulte*, professor, etc.). The methods of classification differing from one country to another, no one system could prevail without jeopardizing the equal dignity of the jurists of the six Member States that was a core element in the legitimacy of these transnational legal and judicial spaces. This confusion showed up in the rulings of the Court as they were transcribed by the Registrar, in which one may spot ambiguous wording, inconsistencies and errors in the titles and qualifications of lawyers (identified sometimes by their own name, sometimes with that of their partner(s), or even by the name of their firm). This reflects the early beginnings of a formalization of a European legal practice. More broadly, the faltering language also reflects the fact that, in the emerging field of EC law, there coexisted profoundly different definitions of legal professions, their scopes of action, and their roles and positions in political, economic and administrative spaces. All sorts of jurists were gathering under the common banner of European law. These first circles were a colourful array in which the German *Rechtsanwalt* crossed paths with the Italian *Avvocato dello stato*, the French *conseiller d'État* met with the Belgian lawyer-professor, the German law-professor diplomat encountered the American business lawyer, etc.

Caesurae and censorings at the national level

This was not a trivial circumstance, considering that the national legal fields offered little possibility for these types of encounters, and were, on the contrary, highly compartmentalized. National systems of legal professions (how legal work is divided up, professional pathways between occupations, the possibility of multiple mandates, incompatibilities, etc.)

are the outcome of long series of fratricidal battles. As emphasized by Yves Dezalay, 'the division of the world of clerks into rigorously defined subcategories that are for all intents and purposes impermeably sealed off from each other, as it has existed up until now in Europe, hardly facilitates circulation between the different professional positions'.[54] This subdivision of legal and judicial tasks into an infinite number of orders and professional bodies is particularly acute in France and in Italy where legal advisers, solicitors (*avoués*), lawyers at the Court of Cassation, lawyers at commercial courts, notaries and other *commercialisti* constitute so many professions anxious to protect their domain of jurisdiction from the incursions of neighbouring professions.[55] While in Germany the unity of the quasi-bureaucracy of *Juristen* had prevailed since the time of Prussia, a particularly strict geographical compartmentalization had taken hold, and lawyers could not plead outside of the judicial district in which they are registered.[56] In addition to this occupational compartmentalization, the legal fields in the six Member States are traditionally organized along a caesura between public law and private law that is not a purely academic separation, but entails different legal regimes, specific judicial proceedings and distinct professional roles.[57] Placed under tight surveillance, the relations (passages, points of contact, multiple positioning, etc.) between the different legal segments are highly codified in European countries (incompatibilities, bans on multiple occupations, etc.). This is all the more true in view of the fact that the professional boundaries are in most instances protected by the States themselves, which throughout the nineteenth century relayed the construction of national legal professions, granting *numerus clausus*, licences, authorizations and monopolies in exchange for the loyalty of the professional bodies thus created to the regime in place.[58]

[54] Yves Dezalay, *Marchands de droit. La restructuration de l'ordre juridique international par les multinationales du droit*, Paris, Fayard, 1992, p. 259.

[55] On this point, see Yves Dezalay, 'Vendre du droit en (ré)inventant de l'État. Stratégies constitutionnelles et promotion de l'expertise juridique dans le champ du pouvoir d'État', in Antonin Cohen and Antoine Vauchez (eds.), *La Constitution européenne. Élites, mobilisations, votes*, Brussels, Presses de l'Université libre de Bruxelles, 2007.

[56] For a comparative study of legal professions in Europe, see Jean-Louis Halpérin, *Avocats et notaires en Europe. Les professions judiciaires et juridiques dans l'histoire contemporaine*, Paris, LGDJ, 1996.

[57] Ségolène Barbou Desplaces, 'La summa divisio en droit communautaire', in Xavier Bioy (ed.), *L'identité en droit public*, Paris, LGDJ, 2010.

[58] On this point, see the comparative approach proposed by Maria Malatesta, *Professionisti e gentiluomini. Storia delle professioni nell'Europa contemporana*, Turin, Einaudi, 2006.

To this must be added the fact that the multiple separations in the national legal fields of the six Member States are structured around a 'double distancing' from both the world of business and the political sphere. Many writers, from Mark Osiel and Lucien Karpik to Yves Dezalay, have shown in their work how the distance maintained from market actors and dynamics constituted a structural feature of the identity of European legal professions, that are quite different from their American counterparts in this respect.[59] Heirs to an aristocratic conception of their role, informed by a vision of detachment and vocation, the high magistrates of the Court of Cassation, law professors and the elites of European bars thus kept at bay those most directly in contact with business matters (business lawyers, *commercialisti*, commercial agents and notaries) whom they relegated to the margins of the legal field. By glorifying a 'pure' law exempt from the scars and blemishes of practice, an 'ethic of distanciation' and an 'ideology of detachment', these notables of national legal fields preserved a strict hierarchical order.[60] In addition to this separation came that between the political sphere and the world of law. The genesis of the parliamentary State, in which law professionals had directly participated, nonetheless contributed to the structural subordination of these professions to the Parliament – the expression of national sovereignty – that had the monopoly on making laws that magistrates, professors and lawyers were to comment upon or apply.[61] This break between 'law' and 'politics', between practitioners of law and producers of law, is one of the least noticed effects of the affirmation in Europe of parliamentarism. Of course, this boundary did not rule out movement and contact of all sorts. The new political profession that emerged from that parliamentary age of the late nineteenth century drew massively from the ranks of the legal elite, starting with the bar, to the point that one Italian political scientist referred to the legal profession as a 'pre-profession for politics'.[62] But the separation of the legal and the political repertoires remained strong: while the intervention of 'jurists' in public debate was of course still possible, it had to remain within the realm of expertise and pay, at least formally, due

[59] Mark Osiel, 'Lawyers as Monopolists, Aristocrats, and Entrepreneurs', *Harvard Law Review*, 103(8), 1990, pp. 2009–66.

[60] Cf. Alain Bancaud, *La haute magistrature judiciaire entre politique et sacerdoce*, Paris, LGDJ, 1993; Lucien Karpik, *Les avocats entre l'État, le public et le marché: XIIIe-XXe siècle*, Paris, Gallimard, 1995.

[61] See Guillaume Sacriste, *La république des constitutionnalistes (1870–1914)*, Paris, Presses de Sciences Po, 2011.

[62] Paolo Farneti, *Politica e società*, Florence, La nuova Italia, 1979, p. 242.

respect for the popular will as embodied by elected officials, that was meant to found and organize the political regime as a whole. This political censure, inscribed in the models of professional excellence, was manifested quite clearly in the multiple examples of resistance by high magistracies and legal academia of the six Member States to the development of a jurisdictional oversight of the constitutionality of laws. Alain Bancaud has shown how deeply entrenched in the *habitus* of French magistrates was their loyalty to the State and its legitimate government, not to mention of course the members of the *Conseil d'État* which would repeatedly state their *légicentrisme*: '[W]hat remains banned for courts of all sorts, is, in any circumstance whatsoever, a critical appreciation of the law'.[63] Suffice it to mention here the resistance that the development of constitutional courts aroused in European countries, particularly within the legal and judicial professions themselves. The vicissitudes of the late French conversion to constitutional justice in the 1970s are well known today,[64] but this is less the case for Germany and Italy, where the legal and judicial elites – mostly trained during the years of totalitarian regimes that glorified the unity and higher interest of the State – still had a hard time imagining a form of subordination of the politician to the judge – even a constitutional judge – and they initially worked to reduce the scope of these post-Second World War innovations.[65] This was the case for the Italian Constitutional Court that was set up with great difficulty in 1956, nearly ten years after the Constitution took effect in 1948. The Court was long contested by the Court of Cassation, and was itself very prudent in affirming its own role, preferring to see itself, in the words of its first president, 'not so much as an instrument of sanction, as one might think, but of collaboration with all the powers of the State'.[66]

This was one of the collateral effects of the formation of a relatively autonomous transnational field of EC law: to loosen in part the hold of these compartmentalizations between 'law' and 'politics', and between 'the world of law' and 'the world of business', or between that of 'public' and 'private' law. Under the aegis of promoting a European rule of law,

63 'Comments by Achille Mestre under Arrighi, *Conseil d'État*, 3 November 1936', *Recueil Sirey*, 1937, p. 3.

64 Bastien François, 'Le Conseil constitutionnel et la Ve République. Réflexions sur l'émergence et les effets du contrôle de constitutionnalité en France', *Revue française de science politique*, 47(3–4), 1997, pp. 377–404.

65 See Frieder Günther, *Denken vom Staat her. Die bundesdeutsche Staatsrechtslehre zwischen dezision und integration (1949–1970)*, Munich, Oldenbourg2004.

66 Cf. Antoine Vauchez, *L'institution judiciaire remotivée. Le processus d'institutionnalisation d'une 'nouvelle justice' en Italie (1960–2000)*, Paris, LGDJ, coll. Droit et société, 2004.

figures and sectors whose relationships were frequently highly codified at the national level (State jurists, high magistrates, law professors, cause lawyers, business jurists, politicians of the law, jurist-diplomats, commissioners, etc.) were set side by side and would mingle in the name of law.

Proximities and exchanges under the aegis of European law

Absent a supranational definition of European legal professions, the field of EC law – the courtroom of the ECJ, scholarly societies and academic journals, the Legal Committee of the European Parliament, etc. – were home to the relatively undifferentiated figure of the jurist, that of the 'Euro-lawyer', available to take on all sorts of roles – scholarly, expert, political, judicial, business-related or non-profit, etc. – in the name of building Europe and its rule of law. This novelty did not escape the notice of the French members of FIDE, who were pleased to see 'for once, all legal professions working together: jurists in public and private law, magistrates, lawyers, certified ministerial officers, experts recognized by the courts', etc.[67] In a country where the legal field was highly segmented, the French chapter of FIDE brought together ECJ advocate general Maurice Lagrange, the secretary of the European Commission for Human Rights at the Council of Europe, thirty-four lawyers, eleven magistrates in national courts, five members of the French *Conseil d'État*, eight law professors, the presiding judge of the Paris commercial court, two experts, one *notaire*, the president of the *Compagnie des experts judiciaires*, the president of the *Conseil des fédérations commerciales d'Europe* (trade federations), a director from the administration of the Ministry for Public infrastructure, the former minister and negotiator of the Rome Treaties Maurice Faure, and René Mayer, the second president of the ECSC High Authority.

The congresses of FIDE were particularly emblematic of this non-differentiation; in the name of a unified support for European integration and the rule of law, the proceedings ranged from debates over the constitutional nature of the Rome Treaties, to discussions about the economic organization of the Common Market. In the course of the same congress, members might discuss both 'the problem of directly applicable provisions of the Treaties instituting the Communities' (i.e. the direct effect) and 'the statutes of the European commercial company', or 'the guarantees required of companies in the Member States

[67] Adolphe Touffait, 'Maurice Rolland, européen', *Bulletin de l'Association des juristes européens*, 38, 1978, p. 16.

to protect the interests of associated partners and third parties', to mention just some of the topics addressed. Michel Waelbroeck, whom we left organizing, under the auspices of the *Institut d'études européennes* at the *Université libre de Bruxelles*, a conference on 'Patents and *marques* in competition law' with an American lawyer, could just as well be active in the birth of EC antitrust law, and participate fully in the ontological questions surrounding the constitutional (or otherwise) nature of the Rome Treaties.[68] The committee on legal affairs of the European Parliament was another space that facilitated exchange and circulation across professional and sector-specific boundaries. Let us take as an example Arved Deringer, at once a CDU member of Parliament, president of the Parliament's Legal Committee, founder in Cologne in 1962 of a law firm, Deringer-Tessin, which would later become one of the first global law firms, and legal counsel to major American and German corporations. In the European Parliament, he could successively promote the 'harmonization of the legislation of Member States regarding taxes on business income' in a 1963 parliamentary report, and call for setting up full protection of individual rights at the EC level in another parliamentary report in 1968.[69] A Treaty-Constitution as much as a trade treaty, the Rome Treaties allowed the proponents of the cause of EC law to cast off the historically consolidated separation of public law and private law.[70]

The separation between legal professions (judges, lawyers, law professors) and the careers to which law gave access (politics, government service, business responsibilities, etc.) seemed to have been considerably blurred. The profile of the most prominent figures of EC law congresses, such as Walter Hallstein, Fernand Dehousse, Hans von der Groeben and Michel Gaudet, provided concrete examples of such mingling. As a result, the scholarship produced between 1962 and 1995 was the work of practitioners, in non-negligible proportions (and much higher than in national spaces), whether civil servants at the Commission (17 per cent), judges (11 per cent) or lawyers (8 per cent);[71] similarly, only eight of the thirty-two most prolific authors of doctrinal work during this period had

[68] Michel Waelbroeck, *Peut-on parler d'un droit constitutionnel européen?*, Travaux et conférences de l'Université de Bruxelles, 1964.

[69] Guillaume Sacriste, 'L'Europe est-elle un État comme les autres? Retour sur la distinction public/privé au sein de la commission juridique du Parlement européen des années 1960', *Cultures et conflits*, 85–6, 2012, pp. 33–60.

[70] On this point, see Ségolène Barbou Desplaces, 'La summa divisio en droit communautaire', in Xavier Bioy (ed.), *L'identité en droit public*, Paris, LGDJ, 2010.

[71] Harm Schepel and Rein Wesseling, 'The Legal Community: Judges, Lawyers, Officials and Clerks in the Writing of Europe', *European Law Journal*, 3(2), 1997, p. 174.

never worked for EC institutions during their careers. Another indicator is the fact that FIDE meetings were always held when the ECJ was out of session, a way of reserving a special place for the Court in the production of the academic doctrine of EC law. A curious medley of genres thus took hold in the ranks of FIDE and in the columns of European law journals, in congresses and hearings before the European Parliament: a mixture of law practice and academic work, private and public law, and of legal professions from a wide variety of occupations (politics, diplomacy, corporate boards, etc.) As ambassadors met judges, politicians spoke with scholars, business lawyers encountered EC institutions' legal advisers, a 'zone of non-distinction between usually distinct orders of practice' was created, as discussed by Christian Topalov in relation to reform-minded elite circles in late-nineteenth-century France. Without supranational professional regulation, EC law gave its practitioners a chance to partially escape from the rather limited sets of activities lawyers could hope for at the national level.

The degrees of liberty acquired at the European level with respect to national professional orders allowed for career moves and multiple positioning that were improbable, and sometimes unthinkable, at the national level. Under the umbrella of this academic discussion on various aspects (institutional, economic, etc.) of treaty law, the distance between actors coming from different spaces (political, administrative, economic, judicial) of European integration was reduced, and sometimes abolished. The result was a partial non-differentiation of the repertoires of intervention. The boundaries between science and reform, between law and politics, became less distinct. The Euro-lawyer could be both the scholar constructing the rationale behind the emerging EC power and the practitioner testing it in different policy domains, both the politician envisioning new steps for the political unification of Europe and the lawyer providing theories and arguments for the constitutional nature of the Treaties, and so on. In this respect, FIDE resembled less today's national scholarly societies than the sort of broad coalitions that made up learned society in the second half of the nineteenth century, such as the National Association for the Promotion of Social Science in Britain (1857) and the American Social Science Association (1867) whose academic aims were equalled only by their ambition for reform.[72]

[72] Johan Heilbron, Nicolas Guilhot and Laurent Jeanpierre, 'Towards a Transnational History of the Social Sciences', *Journal of the History of Behavioral Sciences*, 44(2), 2008, pp. 146–60.

It comes as no surprise therefore that this intense exchange of ideas and projects fostered an intense exchange of opportunities and resources. The field of EC law acted *de facto* as a facilitator, encouraging forms of exchange and circulation that would otherwise have been unlikely or unthinkable. Colloquia and conferences became the occasion to establish bridgeheads between sectors that were habitually distinct, or, to use the terms of the sociology of networks employed by Ronald Burt, to fill the 'structural hole'[73] between different poles of European integration. As one professor-lawyer has pointed out, 'the relationships with the Commission were made through the FIDE. We maintained friendships in this way'.[74] Another lawyer-professor recounts how he found his way into the world of multinational corporate clients at a colloquium on ... human rights! 'One day', as he tells it, 'I gave a talk in Leiden at a conference on the European Court of Human Rights, there was someone from the legal department at Gulf Oil in the audience, and that's how I started working for them. Then later for other big corporations in the sector: Esso, Mobil, BP'.[75] The itinerary of someone like Michel Gaudet, whom we previously encountered as he presided over the destiny of the Legal Service at the Commission (1952–69), is equally exemplary. After a whole career as a State lawyer (successively serving with equal zeal the French State and the European Commission), he left Brussels through the 'revolving door' for a job in the private sector where he joined the *Fédération française des assurances* (1970–81) before presiding over the arbitration court at the French Chamber of Commerce (1977–88) where he succeeded the former president of the Commission and lawyer from Liège, Jean Rey. In other words, practising in the field of EC law had a "booster" effect: it ensured a high convertibility of resources across social spaces that would often remain segmented at the national level, and allowed for a striking accumulation of concurrent activities and positions (editorial, administrative, academic, economic, judicial, as court expert, etc.).[76] Legal professions thus resumed, at the European scale, the role of crossroads professions that they had long

[73] Ronald Burt, *Structural Holes: The Social Structure of Competition*, Cambridge, MA, Harvard University Press, 1992.

[74] Interview No. 1, October 2008.

[75] Interview No. 2, October 2008.

[76] This highly 'fungible' nature of international capital has already been pointed out by Yves Dezalay, 'Les courtiers de l'international. Héritiers cosmopolites, mercenaires de l'impérialisme et missionnaires de l'universel', *Actes de la recherche en sciences sociales*, 151–2, 2004, pp. 5–35; see also Anne-Catherine Wagner, *Les classes sociales dans la mondialisation*, coll. Repères, Paris, La découverte, 2008.

played in national arenas, offering those who followed them a vast palette of careers and possible conversions, in domains as varied as economics, politics, government service and academia.[77] In the 1960s, a professional passage through these European legal positions was thus a powerful vector enabling those who took this path to flourish outside their original occupational universe and venture into other sectors (administrative, economic, judicial, academic, etc.) of the construction of Europe. Just as, in France, 'State service' at the highest level opens the door to all sorts of careers in politics, economics, courts, etc., in the European Union, it all occurred as if it was 'service in the European law' that would play that role.

Professionals of European interdependence

The resulting paradox is that, while jurists actively contributed to strengthen the autonomy of the EC polity, carving out the theories and categories that would found 'Europe' as a self-standing entity, the field of European law practice itself continued to have little autonomy. As it was indeed 'submerged on all sides by more solidly constituted and marked out fields'[78] such as the administrative, economic, political and judicial fields, national or European. the field of EC law constituted a 'weak field', as defined by Christian Topalov in his analysis of fields of social reformers in late-nineteenth-century France. The weak autonomy and internal differentiation of this transnational field meant, however, that it was at a crossroads in the overall emerging European field of European power.

To fully grasp this interstitial crossroads, it is necessary to consider in more detail the social profiles and professional trajectories of the first generation of lawyers who populated the field of EC law. If one considers how they have progressively accumulated a first European legal capital – hereinafter defined as the authority to speak in the name of the law of the European Treaties – one can identify two patterns. The first pathway, that of 'legal cosmopolitanism', accompanied the development of transnational venues, while the second pathway, that of 'national brokers', followed an intersectoral path within the 'national communities of

[77] On this point, see Christophe Charle, 'Pour une histoire sociale des professions juridiques à l'époque contemporaine. Note pour une recherche', *Actes de la recherche en sciences sociales*, 76–7, pp. 117–19; and Ralf Darendorf, 'The Education of an Elite: Law Faculties and the German Upper Class', *Transactions of the Fifth World Congress of Sociology*, Vol. 3, Louvain, 1964, pp. 259–74.

[78] *Ibid.*, p. 464.

European law'. Beyond their differences in forms of capitalization, it is clear, however, that both types of Euro-lawyers accrued – and certainly did not undermine – their authority as they moved across the communities, institutions, policies and actors that made up 'Europe'. In other words, the European legal capital was first an *intersectoral* capital acquired and amassed for the most part at the intersection of the different levels (national, transnational) and sectors (administrative, political, judicial, economic, academic) with a stake in the law of the Treaties. By contrast with their national counterparts, Euro-lawyers owed their success less to their independence and accumulation of the trophies in a single branch (judiciary, university, bar) than to their capacity to be *professionals of interdependence*, positioning themselves in and between each of the constitutive poles of the emerging European polity.

Legal cosmopolitans

'The army of European jurists, the vanguard whose loyal feats of arms we follow with pleasure',[79] formed not only a new transnational arena in which the urgent concerns and stakes of EC law could be discussed and defined. It also contributed to portray a number of resources that were useful for navigating and for being noticed. Specific traits of excellence and virtuosity came to the fore, outlining the contour of a 'European sensibility that breaks down borders ... and escapes the bonds of narrowly national imperatives'.[80] To put it another way, the pages of EC law journals, the aisles of the convention halls of FIDE, and the ECJ courtrooms were also the locus where a European (legal) civility was shaped, to shed all nationalist reflexes and all *a priori* political assumptions. A first type of distinction emerged at FIDE meetings between 'national' and even nationalist jurists who were shunted back to their unmovable and narrow legal particularisms, and Euro-lawyers who moved between national legal cultures and, thereby, were the only ones capable of rising above these cultures to judge their respective merits objectively and dispassionately. The display of a certain distance regarding one's own country, the capacity to smooth over differences between national legal categories and suggest possible compromises, were qualities that were expected and remarked. Conversely, a lack of familiarity with these usages and customs which proved a form of 'methodological (legal)

[79] Alphonse de Vreese, in Symposium 'Droit communautaire et droit national', *Cahiers de Bruges*, 14, 1965, pp. 399–400.

[80] Arithmos, 'Propos européens', *Cahiers du droit européen*, 1(1), 1965, p. 95.

nationalism' did not go unnoticed and was indeed seen as a handicap. The president of a chamber at the Court of Cassation, André Pépy, was obliged to confess the difficulties of a French jurist in general (who 'does not have a federal mind') and of a French magistrate in particular (who does not possess 'the EC psychology') in apprehending Europe and its law. For this, he attracted the ironic comments of his fellow countryman Michel Gaudet, the director of the Commission's Legal Service, who saluted the 'memorable encounter of M. Pépy with the EC atmosphere'.[81]

The capacity to fully participate in the 'EC atmosphere' and to excel in this setting was most certainly tied to the possession of key resources that not only enabled one to understand the language of the law of other member countries, but also gave them the capacity to speak all these languages with equal fluency. Basic linguistic skills were a key element from this point of view, particularly for those who spoke more marginal languages (Flemish/Dutch, even Italian) and therefore could not easily act in these arenas without mastering one of the two dominant languages, German and (to an even greater extent) French. Cosmopolitans as much as legal practitioners from bilingual or multilingual countries (Belgium, Luxembourg) had an advantage as they could plead, argue and debate in several languages, and thus had access to several national arenas (and clienteles) in which EC law was produced, interpreted and discussed. Jossé Mertens de Wilmars (1912–2002) who, as a lawyer, would defend Belgian, French and Dutch companies before the ECJ, thus gained a reputation as a specialist in EC law (a reputation certainly reinforced by his being president of the Belgian council of the European Movement and former Christian-Social member of Parliament from 1951 to 1961), leading to his appointment a few years later as judge on the ECJ (1967), a jurisdiction that he eventually presided over (1980–4).

Being multilingual was not enough in itself, however, if it did not come with a mastery of the different legal cultures of the six Member States. Anyone who wanted to take part in the construction of a common law of Europe had to be able to debate with nearly equal facility on the major subjects of international law (self-execution, *jus cogens*, direct invocability of international treaties, etc.), on the appropriateness of adopting in EC law the '*théorie de l'acte clair*' from the French *Conseil d'État*, and on the merits of the classical German constitutional debates over the *Transformationslehre*, thereby engaging in a comparative analysis

[81] Michel Gaudet, in College of Bruges, *Droit communautaire et droit national. Semaine de Bruges 1965*, Bruges, De Tempel, 1965, p. 291.

of national legal bodies. In this respect, all ongoing contacts with the foreign legal cultures of the six Member States (academic training, previous working experience, etc.) were the trump cards.

Pierre Pescatore, the cosmopolitan Euro-lawyer par excellence

Pierre Pescatore (1919–2010) whom we saw earlier heading Luxembourg's diplomatic mission and participating in the writing of the Rome Treaties, embodies cosmopolitan legal excellence. Descended from an old and rich Luxembourg family of industrialists, he trained in the different European legal traditions at the universities of Tübingen and Louvain, and obtained his doctorate in international law in 1946. A polyglot (it is said that he spoke French, English, German and Spanish as well as Dutch), in 1946 he entered the diplomatic service as a legal adviser, and in this capacity he participated in negotiations of the charter to establish the OECD (1948), of the Rome Treaties (1956–7), the Benelux treaty (1958) and the Fouchet plan (1963). Head of the 'Political affairs' department at the Luxembourg ministry of foreign affairs at the age of 39 (1958), and then secretary general to that ministry at the age of 45 (1964), he became one of the principal voices of Luxembourg diplomacy, all the while undertaking very active transnational academic activities. Adjunct professor at the University of Liège in the years after the war, he became full professor of law at this same university in 1963, and at the same time teaching various courses in international law all across the six Member States at the *Centre d'études européennes* of Nancy, the Saar University, the Academy of International Law at The Hague and the International Institute of Comparative Law in Luxembourg, among others. His nomination to the ECJ in 1967 – a position he held until 1984, durably influencing EC jurisprudence – did not interrupt his multifarious activism – far from it. *Doctor honoris causa* of the universities of Nancy, Geneva, Tübingen and Leiden, member of the principal scholarly societies of international law (*Institut de droit international*, International Law Association), he elaborated an ample body of doctrine in service of a constitutional vision of the legal order born of the Rome Treaties.[82] Continually crossing the national borders and linguistic boundaries, discussing with ease the respective merits of the different national legal categories and theories in existence, Pierre Pescatore incarnates better than anyone else the cosmopolitan figure of the Euro-lawyer.

It remains, however, that proximity with this ideal type of the 'legal cosmopolitan' was not equally necessary, in part depending on the country or institution of origin. Because, as shown by Anne-Catherine

[82] A selection of his doctrinal work has recently been published: Pierre Pescatore, *Études du droit communautaires (1962–2007)*, Brussels, Bruylant, 2008.

Wagner, 'the balances of power between nations are not abstractions [but] produce concrete effects on the positions of agents, on trajectories and social relationships',[83] the exchange value of languages, diplomas and national professional experience is very unequal. In other words, jurists were not all required to be legal comparativists in the way of a Pierre Pescatore. The considerable weight of the French *conseillers d'État* (Maurice Lagrange, Michel Gaudet, Jacques Mégret, etc.), often considered as the 'founding fathers' of EC law, was only marginally the product of their 'Europeanness'. Other important factors mattered: the central position occupied by France in EC institutions that gave these *conseillers d'État* a direct access to leading roles in European law (advocate general of the ECJ, director of one of the Legal Services at the Commission or at the Council); the preponderance of the French language that vaulted them from the start and almost effortlessly to the heart of the European legal debate that took place mostly in this language; and their membership in an institution, the *Conseil d'État*, which was prestigious well beyond its national borders (four of the five other Member States actually had themselves a *Conseil d'État* and an administrative law built – at least initially – on the 'Napoleonic model'). This meant they did not need to engage in international strategies as much as say a Belgium law professor would need to. In addition to the fact that often they were endowed with fewer international resources, they rarely shaped their strategy in this direction, much less often in any event than their Belgian, Italian, Dutch and even more their Luxembourg counterparts, who on the contrary manifested a much more highly developed spirit of European goodwill (multilingualism, publications in foreign languages, participation in conferences abroad, etc.). This is particularly the case for Maurice Lagrange, who had no previous international or European experience before being asked to draft the Paris Treaty and who would later join the ECJ: this would not stop him from becoming (as we have seen) a figurehead of this first European legal milieu, a veritable 'spiritual father of the function of advocate general' that over 12 years he transformed into 'one of the most eminent chairs of EC law'.[84] This means that, ultimately, legal cosmopolitanism was just one of the

[83] Anne-Catherine Wagner, 'Les stratégies transnationales en France', Skeptronhäften Working Papers, No. 13, 1997, p. 6.

[84] 'Éloge funèbre de Maurice Lagrange prononcé par le président Lord Mackenzie Stuart', in European Court of Justice, *Aperçu des travaux de la Cour en 1986 et 1987 et audiences solennelles*, Luxembourg, Curia, 1988, p. 206.

ways – and still an infrequent one – to constitute one's authority to interpret European law.

National brokers of Europe

While transnational ties were indeed becoming more frequent, the field of EC law remained profoundly embedded in national fields of power. There were at least two reasons for this. The first reason is that access to positions in European law (as *expert national détaché*, member of the Legal Services, judge or clerks at the ECJ, etc.) was subject to various forms of national co-optation, notably affiliation to relatively stable and narrow professional and institutional orders. In other words, lawyers were not randomly 'thrown' into the European legal sites merely by virtue of their competence or pan-European motivation, but rather refracted the idiosyncracies and particular balance of professional powers in national legal fields. Most often, the proximity with the pole of State jurists, whether it be the *Conseil d'État* in France, the *Avvocatura della Stato* in Italy, or the ministries of justice and the economy in Germany proved to be particular critical for accessing positions in the Legal Service or at the ECJ.[85] The second reason was the common situation that objectively linked the jurists of the same country when they were engaged in the same undertaking to enhance the value of their professional experience as a 'Euro-lawyer' at the national level, and when they had to highlight the value of their own 'legal culture' in debates over the definition of European legal categories. In practice, congresses and conferences help draw the symbolic outlines of national groups of EC law experts. The first Italian commentary on the Treaties, the *Trattato istitutivo della CEE. Commentario* published in 1962, was the work of forty-four contributors, all Italian, who in their diversity represented the different spaces in which EC law was produced (law professors, civil servants at the Commission, diplomats, legal experts in various ministries, business lawyers, etc.). The same was true for the different national chapters of FIDE and for the journals of EC law that sprang up in each of the Member States.[86] Certainly, these national communities of jurists were not constituted

[85] On French administrative pathways acceding to EC institutions see Michel Mangenot, *Une Europe improbable. Les hauts fonctionnaires français dans la construction européenne 1948–1992*, PhD in political science, IEP Strasbourg, December 2000.

[86] In Italy, the *Rivista di diritto europeo* (starting in 1961); in the United Kingdom and the Netherlands, the *Common Market Law Review* (1963); in Belgium, *Les cahiers du droit européen* (1965); in France, the *Revue trimestrielle de droit européen* (1965); and, in Germany, *Europarecht* (1966).

in the same way from one country to the next, depending on the architecture of national legal fields. For instance, French law professors who had been progressively sidelined by the members of the *Conseil d'État* when it came to accessing international legal functions (in international organizations and courts) had certainly fewer professional opportunities than had their Italian, Belgian or German counterparts who could be found under many different guises. Although structured differently, the ties established through a variety of national venues (conferences sponsored by the government or the pan-European movement promoting European integration, editorial committees of EC-related book series or journals, FIDE national chapters, etc.) still turned these national communities of Euro-lawyers into a common breeding ground from which to recruit the many legal experts, clerks, legal advisers, lawyers and judges that the construction of Europe required.

National musical chairs in legal Europe: the first generation of Italian Euro-lawyers

These national legal communities enabled a circulation across institutions. Let us look at the astonishing game of musical chairs that occupied for nearly two decades the three Italian judges who served on the ECJ between 1958 and 1976. They took turns in each domain of European integration, handling diplomatic, economic, administrative and political matters, and successively filled all the available roles for Euro-lawyering.

Nicola Catalano (1910–84), doctor of law, joined the *Avvocatura dello Stato* in 1939, a body specialized in the legal defence of the State where he was in charge of international legal affairs serving as Legal agent of his government in the Conciliation Commissions established by the peace treaties (1948–50) and then as legal adviser in the Tangiers international zone (1951–3). He then entered service in the EC institutions as legal adviser at the High Authority of the ECSC in Luxembourg, a position he held from 1953 to 1956 and which led him to defend the interests of the Communities before the ECJ, on several occasions against his own national government. In 1956, the Italian government called him back to participate in the negotiation of the Rome Treaties as jurisconsult in the Italian delegation. Chosen by his government to become a judge at the ECJ in 1958, he became one of the most prolific and well-known advocate publicists of EC law, publishing one of very first manuals of EC law (in both French and Italian, the *Manuel de droit des Communautés européennes*, Dalloz-Sirey, 1962) and chairing the Italian chapter of FIDE. Upon reluctantly leaving the Court in 1962, he pursued an intense doctrinal activity, and at the same time created his own law firm specializing in EC law at the Rome bar, defending companies and EC civil servants before the ECJ and against EC institutions. Unfailing in his 'missionary zeal', he

(cont)

brought his legal expertise to the conception of the Spinelli draft treaty for the 'European Constitution' just a few months before his death in 1984.[87]

Riccardo Monaco (1909–2000), doctor of law at the University of Turin, magistrate from 1931 to 1939, occupied the position of professor of international law in various Italian universities from 1939 to 1948. Returning to Rome after his appointment at the *Consiglio di Stato* in 1948, he was named principal jurisconsult of the Italian foreign affairs ministry. In this capacity, he was a member of many Italian delegations to international conferences, starting with those that preceded the Rome Treaties. He also represented the Italian State in a number of cases before the ECJ between 1954 and 1964. Appointed professor at the *La Sapienza* university in Rome in 1956, he was also one of the most prolific authors on doctrinal questions, publishing a manual (*Primi lineamenti du diritto pubblico europeo*, Milan, 1962), two commentaries on the Treaties (*Trattato istitutivo della Comunità economica europea*, 1965 and *Trattato CECA. Commentario*, 1970) co-edited with Alberto Trabucchi, and various articles written with Nicola Catalano. In 1962, he founded the Italian journal of EC law, *Rivista di diritto europeo*, with the support of a Christian Democrat member of parliament. Already considered for the job in 1958, he was finally appointed judge at the ECJ in 1964, a position he held until 1976. The function of ECJ judge did not prevent him from continuing to 'represent' the Italian State from time to time, as in the arbitration proceedings of *Italy* v. *United States Air Transport Cargo Services* in which he participated in July 1965. As he himself has written, referring to his first years at the Court, 'as the workload at the Court was light and alternated with weeks off, I was able to return to the ministry with some frequency'.[88]

Alberto Trabucchi (1907–98), lecturer (1929), associate professor (1935) and then full professor (1941) at the universities of Padua, Ferrara and Venice, Trabucchi was at the time of the Rome Treaties one of the foremost authorities on Italian civil law scholarship: the publication of his *Manuale du diritto civile* (now in its forty-second edition), the direction of the Institute of Private Law at the University of Padua from 1945, and the founding of the *Rivista di diritto civile* in 1955, all confirm his stature. Regularly called upon by his former colleague for the University of Padua, Giulio Pasetti, who had moved to the ECSC Legal Service, Trabucchi had brought his legal expertise to defend the EC Executives in various cases between 1952 and 1962, including some against the Italian State. In parallel, he also pleaded before the Constitutional Court, where he defended, for instance, the district of Bolzano against the Italian State. Linked to the political field by virtue of his brother, also a Christian Democrat politician and minister of finance between 1960 and 1963, Trabucchi was chosen by the Italian government to be judge at the Court in 1962, a post he would retain until 1976. He is the author of a

[87] Nicola Catalano, 'Le Traité d'Union européenne. Légitimité juridique et institutionnelle', in *Crocodile. Lettre aux membres du Parlement européen*, 11, June 1983.

[88] Riccardo Monaco, *Memorie di una vita, memorie per l'Europa*, Rome, Ledip, 1996, p. 161.

Codice delle comunità europee and of two commentaries on the Treaties with Riccardo Monaco.

Mandated to defend causes as diverse as the definition of the interests and objectives of national diplomacy, the construction of the scholarly premises of EC law, the competencies of the Commission, the protection of business interests, the promotion of Court jurisprudence and the federal projects of pan-European groups, these three Italian Euro-lawyers would successively oppose and unite with each other, depending on the position they occupied at the time. Riccardo Monaco recalls with emotion 'the friendly legal jousting before the Court of Justice' with Nicola Catalano, with whom he wrote an important report on the 'direct effect of EC law' for the Italian chapter of FIDE in 1963,[89] 'me as jurisconsult for the Italian government and he as the counsel of the European Communities'.[90] The situation was reversed a few years later when Nicola Catalano, now a practising lawyer, pleaded before the ECJ on which his friend Riccardo Monaco now held a seat – a network of close ties (scholarly collaborations, joint participation in FIDE, stints in the same institutions, etc.) linked these three jurists whose careers had led them to engage in the legal representation of nearly all the interests involved in the construction of Europe.

While the Italian example may seem to be an extreme case, it reveals a pattern that is less so: this continual circulation between the different poles of the European polity is an essential mechanism in the formation of European legal capital. A form of 'cartelization' of the emerging European legal market around a limited number of actors was at work in the accumulation of resources and titles resulting from this to-and-fro movement. This process was never clearer than in the case of those who, having participated in the negotiation and drafting of the Paris and Rome Treaties, felt 'a bit responsible for the institutional system of the Rome Treaty'.[91] They could legitimately claim to know the spirit and the philosophy of the founding Treaties, and this advantage made them the natural recipients of the first European legal appointments. This type of

[89] The two jurists co-authored the Italian report to the second FIDE congress held in October 1963 on the direct effect of the Rome Treaties: Nicola Catalano and Riccardo Monaco, 'Rapport italien', in FIDE, *Deuxième colloque international de droit européen. La Haye, 1963*, The Hague, W. E. J. Tjeenk Willink, 1966, pp. 115–35.

[90] Riccardo Monaco, 'Nicola Catalano (1910–1984)', *Rivista di diritto europeo*, 23(1), 1984, pp. 104–5.

[91] Nicola Catalano, in Institut für das Recht der europäischen Gemeinschaften, *Zehn Jahre Rechtsprechung des Gerichtshofs der Europäischen Gemeinschaften*, Cologne, Carl Heymanns Verlag, 1965, p. 42.

pathway is no doubt not limited to jurists,[92] but it has particular importance in the field of law, in which it was connected to the essential issue of treaty interpretation. The role of the treaty drafters was all the more central because, as the ECJ did not recognize for legal purposes the 'preparatory work' (declaration of government intentions, records of working group discussions, etc.), the texts of the Treaties were open to exegesis. And six of the sixteen judges who sat on the ECJ between 1951 and 1969, and three of four directors of the Legal Services at the Council (Ernst Wohlfahrt) and the Executives (Michel Gaudet and Robert Krawielicki) had directly participated in the negotiations preceding either the Paris or Rome Treaties. Invested with the authority of their direct experience in the negotiations and by their practical experience of EC institutions, these 'founding fathers' *in pectore* had more than one title to act as interpreters *par excellence* of the meaning of the Treaties.

By highlighting these movements between jobs, I do not mean to denounce any presumed duplicity of these Euro-lawyers, or even to suggest that there is one set of interests (economic, political, bureaucratic or others) supposed to be more real or determinant. The aim is rather to emphasize that the first Euro-lawyers, contrary to a retrospective vision of the 'founding fathers', did not form an epistemic community of denationalized experts united in fervent pan-judicial and pan-European communion. Many of those who figure today in the pantheon of the precursors to Europe's 'Union of law' (Vedel, Monaco, etc.) were frequently also meticulous defenders of the interests of their diplomatic service in their role as jurisconsults, of the Commission as legal advisers, of companies as business lawyers, etc. Putting it another way, the idealism of the academic and the cynicism of the lawyer, the pan-Europeanism of the Commission's counsellor and the legal nationalism of the jurisconsult, the activism of the defender of human rights and the realism of the jurist-expert do not necessarily determine opposing figures, but rather constitute the different repertoires through which the Euro-lawyer would fulfil his or her public office.[93] These movements back and forth across the boundaries between law and politics, between the national and the EC, or between the public and the private sectors are naturally also possible for other actors in Europe – starting with diplomats and high-level civil servants whose

[92] See Katia Seidel, *The Process of Politics in Europe: The Rise of European Elites and Supranational Institutions*, Basingstoke, Macmillan, 2010.

[93] See also Martti Koskenniemi, 'Entre engagement et cynisme. Aperçu d'une théorie du droit international en tant que pratique', in *La politique du droit international*, Paris, Pedone, 2007, pp. 359–90.

careers are often made of a circulation between national and European administrative positions. But, in the case of law, these movements have the traits of professional duty, if not honour, situating legal excellence precisely in this capacity to defend 'in the name of the law' all causes and all interests. This circulation was not without problems however. Take the embarrassing position of Riccardo Monaco in one of the most controversial cases heard by the ECJ, *Costa* v. *ENEL* in July 1964. Jurisconsult to a government (Italy) that refused to recognize the jurisprudence of the ECJ regarding the direct effect of EC law, and at the same time future judge on this same Court (his appointment was at the time already settled), Monaco had no choice but to leave the case so as not to compromise his ties with one and the other:

> By reasons of my functions, it was my job to be the agent of the Italian government; but I did not at all want to assume this responsibility. I had the *Avvocato generale* [Italian government] designate one of my best colleagues; in addition, I also managed to have my illustrious colleague and friend Massimo Severo Gannini placed in the ranks of the Italian defence ... To the surprise of the audience [at the hearing before the ECJ] I refused to take the floor. I had a good reason: it was already rumoured that I would be appointed judge at the Court of Justice in early October.[94]

It is clear, however, that, in managing these multiple or successive social and political loyalties that this circulation implied, Euro-lawyers were in a privileged position. This had previously been underscored by the American sociologist Wright Mills who saw lawyers as 'professional go-betweens of economic, political and military affairs, and who thus act to unify the power elite'.[95] By focusing narrowly on legal know-how exclusively in terms of strictly technical competence, the fact that this competence also and inseparably constituted a social skill is too often neglected. When Luc Boltanski observes that modern legal vocabulary has developed a particularly sophisticated casuistry for thinking, organizing and facilitating relationships between individual persons and the multiple social positions that they occupy (persons/institutions, physical persons/moral persons, boss/company, etc.), he omits to mention that the mastery of this difficult social art is possessed first of all by lawyers themselves.[96] As professionals of these forms, their work is to constantly

[94] Riccardo Monaco, *Memorie di una vita, memorie per l'Europa*, Rome, Ledip, 1996, p. 158.

[95] C. Wright Mills, *The Power Elite*, Oxford, Oxford University Press, 2000 (first edition printed in 1956), pp. 288–9.

[96] Luc Boltanski, 'L'espace multipositionnel. Multiplicité des positions institutionnelles et *habitus* de classe', *Revue française de sociologie*, 1, 1973, pp. 3–26.

break down the subjects they treated into points of fact and points of law, social causes and legal causes, physical persons and moral persons, etc. This turns them into experts who were particularly well armed to play a multipositional game: they manage the positions of their clienteles certainly, to whom they gave a sort of omnipresence by ensuring their representation in various loci of the social space; but they manage also, and perhaps primarily, their own positions, i.e. their capacity to accumulate clients/mandates/employers with interests and objects both diverse and varied, without this accumulation ever appearing to be incongruous or contradictory. This is one of the specific characteristics of 'legal representation', as codified by the jurists over time in the framework of the trial process (judicial representation by lawyers) as well as in the broader set of legal relationships (notions of mandate, representation, delegation, etc.): it enables both the defence of the specific interests and causes of the groups who employ the jurists' services, *and* a distance from these groups operated by the work of re-presentation or re-translation in the terms of the law.

In sum, if there is indeed a 'European legal identity', it lies not only in a heritage of common principles but also in a form of *legal habitus* that leads these law professionals to practice a balance between proximity to the numerous lay interests in their charge, and distance (unequally maintained depending on the case) from these interests, in the name of the Law of which authority they are collectively the guardians. This hypothesis – the existence of a European legal *habitus* – is based on their common acculturation to the exigencies of a legal rationality espoused by all European law faculties from the time they adopted, at the turn of the nineteenth century, juridical models grounded in the increasingly formal science of legal exegesis.[97] Constructed along a model that favours formal systematization (objective, and thereby calculable, legal order) and that in part sweeps aside the substantial issues of ends, values and other meta-justifications, modern legal rationality is naturally 'welcoming'.[98] Under its aegis and in its name, one can regulate and deregulate, politicize and depoliticize, Europeanize or nationalize, shift to the left or anchor on the right, build up an administration or take it to court.

It must be recognized that this specific *habitus*, rooted in European law faculties, was particularly at ease in the emerging EC polity. Unburdened (at least in part) of the numerous caesurae and censorings that

[97] Olivier Beaud and Patrick Wachsmann (eds.), *La science juridique française et la science juridique allemande de 1870 à 1918*, Strasbourg, Presses universitaires de Strasbourg, 1997.

[98] V. Jean-Philippe Heurtin and Nicolas Molfessis (eds.), *Sociologie du droit de Max Weber*, Economica, 2006.

circumscribe their professional practices at the national level, Euro-lawyers in serving law in Europe had an opportunity to serve a broad range of social and professional interests. Armed with technologies and social skills particularly well suited to a multilevel transnational ensemble, they have become the professionals of European independence. This position at the crossroads of European integrations is not only propitious to the accumulation of resources; it also reinforces the legitimacy of Euro-lawyers and, ultimately, that of the ECJ as arbitrator of all EC-related disputes. Henceforth, the 'honest courtier' of Europe is less – as Walter Hallstein had wished – the European Commission itself, than the corps of jurists, as mediators and unavoidable points of passage in this Europe in the making.[99]

'Weak field' of Europe's polity, the transnational field of European law cuts across all EC-implicated sectors, while being simultaneously bound to each one of them by a set of 'weak links'. It is precisely this limited autonomy that makes this transnational legal field a terrain for political mediation that can reintegrate the diversity of private and public, national and European, economic and political interests, that take part in the construction of Europe. Henceforth, it is much more than law that is forged in the halls of law in Europe. Distanced from the diverse professional and social interests present in Europe, and at the same time closely tied to each of these interests, the European legal field forms an intermediate space where are brought together – under the auspices of a disinterested exchange in the service of the law of Europe – a set of sectoral and/or national arenas that are only loosely connected and largely exclusive of each other. In this sense, this field is a critical terrain for discussion of Europe, its nature and reform, among individuals drawn from a diverse range of professional backgrounds and institutions, but who are able to recognize each other, and agree, if not on reform measures, at least on the diagnosis and assessment of possible futures for Europe's polity. Thereby, the 'field effect' is not to be found in the judicial coup of an 'invisible college' of Euro-lawyers taking over power and designing this or that public policy, than in the field's specific contribution in the shaping of cross-sectoral and inter-institutional frames of understanding Europe's fragmented polity, thereby providing a privileged *locus* for the metamorphosis of the inchoate set of treaties, institutions, and groups into one new polity.

[99] Walter Hallstein, *United Europe: Challenge and Opportunity*, Cambridge, MA, Harvard University Press, 1962, p. 21.

3 The 'Van Gend en Loos moment'

The transformation of Europe has its particular 'moment', one in which a constitutional integration programme coalesced and brought into a coherent whole the so far dispersed constitutional doctrines of Europe's nature and future. This foundational moment is quite easy to identify. Suffice it to read the established narrative of European law that dates its creation back to one particular case, *Van Gend en Loos* (6 February 1963) whose fiftieth anniversary was celebrated in 2013.[1] However, just like the *Marbury* v. *Madison* case in the United States, Europe's foundational case is primarily remembered for what it is purported to have inaugurated, rather than for what it actually was.[2] It stands as a unique moment of revelation of Europe's nature (a unified legal order where EC norms have direct effect and prevail over national norms) and future (an incremental process of Europeanization through case law). As with any foundational myth, the principles 'uncovered' in 1963–4 have been 'vindicated and validated again and again'[3] at each of the critical steps of the story of Europe, from the 1973 enlargement to the various projects of a Constitution for Europe from 1984 onwards, and from the Maastricht Treaty to the Lisbon Reform Treaty. The decision appears as the constitutional platform of Europe encapsulating all the successive developments of the EU polity to which they are purported to have paved the way, if not directly to have called for. The consequences of this judicial

[1] Court of Justice of the European Union, *50th Anniversary of the Judgment in Van Gend en Loos (1963–2013). Conference Proceedings*, Luxembourg, Office des publications officielles de l'Union européenne, 2013.

[2] On this, see also a stimulating paper by Damian Chalmers and Luis Barroso, *What Van Gend en Loos Stands For*, Jean Monnet Working Paper 03/14.

[3] Joseph Weiler, 'Rewriting Van Gend en Loos: Towards a Normative Theory of ECJ Hermeneutics', in O. Wiklund (ed.), *Judicial Discretion in European Perspective*, Kluwer Law International, 2003, p. 151.

'discovery' seem so far-reaching that it has become almost impossible to imagine 'what EU law would have been without the decisions of 1963 and 1964'[4] and, consequently, 'what Europe would be without the European Court of Justice'.[5] As a consequence of this dense set of interrelated narratives where *Van Gend en Loos* stands as the cornerstones, it is virtually impossible to reflect upon it without referring to its 'logical' outcomes, be they legal (the formation of a highly integrated legal order), economic (the intense development of intra-EC exchanges) or political (the succession of Treaties reinforcing European integration).[6] Until very recently, this teleological reading has impeded one from engaging in a fine-grained historical analysis of its genesis. Contrary to the *ex post* vision of the Court's decision as a judicial *fiat*, it is not just a thunderstorm in a quiet sky but rather takes place in a very specific *moment* of European integration, that between 1962 and 1966, during which the legal interpretation of the Rome Treaties became a focal point for a variety of academic, political, economic and bureaucratic controversies. While it was becoming clearer and clearer that the prospects for further political integration were less and less plausible, the fate of EC institutions became even more dependent upon the recognition of a constitutional status to the EC Treaties as a whole. While they were not aiming directly at creating a new body of law, the institutional strategies of the European Commission, the European Parliament and the main proponents of the Common Market had a direct stake in securing that an extensive interpretation of the legal reach and scope of the Rome Treaties prevailed as it directly impinged upon their own competences and powers. In other words, the '*Van Gend en Loos* moment', is not just important for the legal principles it contributed to establish:

4 Robert Lecourt, 'Qu'eut été le droit des Communautés sans les arrêts de 1963 et 1964?', in *L'Europe et le droit, Mélanges Boulouis*, Paris, Dalloz, 1991, p. 350.

5 Denys Simon, 'Retour du mythe du gouvernement des juges?', *JurisClasseur-Europe*, February 2006, p. 1. Quotes from this article have been translated by the present author.

6 As with any foundational myth, the *ex post* exegesis of *Van Gend en Loos* and *Costa* offers a selective reading of history. Quite emblematically, the ECJ's selection of its most important decisions presented in the languages of the new Member States that joined the EU in 2004 starts with *Van Gend en Loos*. See http://curia.europa.eu/cs/content/juris/data57/liste.htm (accessed 4 April 2014). Highlighting those decisions that establish the purported emancipation of the ECJ from classic intergovernmental politics, it neglects other ECJ decisions that could well be considered as equally important in defining the Court's jurisprudence. For example, *Confédération nationale des producteurs de fruits et légumes* v. *Council of the EEC*, 14 December 1962 could also qualify as a 'landmark decision', as it gave a very restrictive reading of individual standing, therefore granting Member States with specific privileges and rights within this new legal order.

it relates more broadly to the various controversies around the parliamentarization of the European Parliament, the judicialization of the European Court of Justice, the 'governmentalization' of the European Commission and, last but not least, the emergence of the Common Market as a credible level of governance for national and international economic actors. This chapter shows how the '*Van Gend en Loos* moment' has been the temporal *locus* for the transformation of the EC Treaties from a diverse and heterogeneous set of communities, institutions and policies into one common institutional *terrain* endowed with specific properties and qualities. In other words, it is through the law and, more specifically, through the shaping of a constitutional reading of European Treaties that Europe has built its relative autonomy and its political capacity.

Between predictions and hindsight: the making of a landmark decision

If one wishes to study this moment *for what it is*, and not for what it is supposed to have produced, there is no other way than suspending temporarily taken-for-granted exegesis of *Van Gend en Loos*. More often than not, the decision is indeed considered as a self-explanatory and self-evident decision taken by a compact and solitary Court bringing a full-fledged theory to the external world. Yet, just like any other legal text, *Van Gend en Loos* does not *mean* anything in itself, unless we consider the lengthy, continuous and multilayered process of interpretation that takes place on both sides of the 'event'. In other words, jurisprudence is not just a natural and ahistorical outcome: it is rather the product of collective and concurrent attempts to define their true meaning and extent.[7] This chapter therefore charts the whole 'hermeneutic

[7] In this, I disagree with Alec Stone's reading of *Van Gend en Loos* as a juridical *coup* not so much for the objective he is aiming at – questioning transformations of law's legitimacy of a given political system (my general goal too) – but rather for the conception of social change the idea of '*coup*' conveys. It is hardly possible to conceive of Courts – and of international Courts in particular – as unified and rational actors endowed with one clear and common idea of their objectives. A product of heterogeneous if not opposed conceptions of Law and particularly of EC law, *Van Gend en Loos* is less the sort of inaugural and far-reaching judgment than a still ambiguous text which leaves open a variety of possible interpretations and futures (particularly as far as supremacy is concerned). We argue here that the decision's far-reaching 'content' has been produced throughout the history of the European integration. See Alec Stone, 'The Juridical Coup d'État and the Problem of Authority', *German Law Review*, 8, 2007, pp. 935–40.

space'[8] of this decision, that is, the various social arenas – national as well as European, legal but also bureaucratic, economic and political, etc. – in which its meaning, scope and implications have been commented before, during and after its occurrence. In particular, it shows how the decision has been inserted into a dense web of pre-dictions (structuring the expectations and strategies of the actors *vis-à-vis* the ECJ) and of retro-dictions (granting it with specific meaning and implications). Through this complex interpretative process, *Van Gend en Loos* has been prophesied, associated, contested, stylized and eventually polished and codified into one judicial theory of Europe, solidly grounded on a group of stable legal and political principles – the 'Van Gend en Loos–Costa theory of EC law'.[9]

Mobilizing for judicial fiat

Far from being a thunderbolt in a calm judicial sky, *Van Gend en Loos* had been awaited for a couple of years within the then still-restricted circles of Euro-lawyers. As a matter of fact, the Court's interpretation of the juridical value and effect of the new European Treaties remained uncertain. As early as 1961, the Rome Treaties had started being implemented in national – including judicial – settings. This opened the way for a flow of judicial decisions dealing with the interpretation of the new Treaties.[10] While evidence shows that the issue raised little interest within the national bureaucracies,[11] two groups of actors felt particularly concerned: the Legal Service of the three Executives of the European Communities (hereinafter the 'Legal Service') and the pan-European association of lawyers' association, the *Fédération internationale pour le droit européen* (FIDE). Both groups were closely intertwined: the Legal Service had actually called for, subsidized and co-defined the agenda of FIDE's foundational congress of 1961. On that occasion, 300 legal professionals of all kinds (ECJ and national judges, clerks, professors, jurisconsults, corporate lawyers, etc.) coming from different political,

[8] Nathalie Heinich, *Glory of Van Gogh: An Anthropology of Admiration*, Princeton, NJ, Princeton University Press, 1996.

[9] Eric Stein, 'The Making of a Transnational Constitution', *American Journal of International Law*, 75(1), 1981, p. 12.

[10] See Karen Alter, *Establishing the Supremacy of European Law: The Making of an International Rule of Law in Europe*, Oxford, Oxford University Press, 2001.

[11] Bill Davies, 'Meek Acceptance? The West German Ministries' Reaction to the Van Gend en Loos and Costa Decisions', *Journal of European Integration History*, 2, 2008, pp. 57–76.

administrative, academic, judicial and – to a lesser extent – economic segments of the EC polity had gathered in Brussels. After carefully scrutinizing the first decisions of national courts on the legal effects of EC Treaties,[12] the Legal Service asked the FIDE Board to devote part of its next congress (October 1963) to that specific issue. One of its roundtables accordingly was devoted to 'Le problème des provisions directement applicables (self-executing) des traités internationaux, et son application aux traités instituant les Communautés'.[13]

The initiative concurred with that of the Dutch section of FIDE. Possibly because there was already a tradition of international lawyering in the Dutch bar, possibly because the 1956 constitutional reform had rendered its legal system compatible with the direct effect of international treaties, the Dutch section of FIDE launched a working group tasked with identifying 'which provisions of the Treaty establishing the EC are self-executing' as early as November 1961. While other national sections of FIDE were more keen on drafting proposals for a European statute for companies, the Dutch section of FIDE was putting together legal practitioners from various backgrounds (legal advisers of public and private bodies, lawyers and law professors) to consider the juridical potentialities of the EEC Treaty article by article in terms of litigation.

These multifaceted doctrinal efforts were soon offered a chance to get tested in real judicial life. It must be said that the Rome Treaties famously provide a new 'judicial gadget',[14] that of the preliminary ruling, which allowed for national courts, and in particular lower courts, to solicit directly the ECJ's opinion on matters of treaty interpretation thereby circumventing the traditional diplomatic channels. As a matter of fact, the Dutch FIDE's working group had barely started when the ECJ received its first preliminary ruling and gave a wide interpretation to the range of national jurisdictions allowed to refer cases to it under this procedure (*Bosch*, 6 April 1962). This new legal venue did not go unnoticed by the members of the working group; in fact, the recourse to this new procedure soon became a distinctively Dutch phenomenon,

[12] As of 1961, the Legal Service had a Centre de Documentation scrutinizing the evolution of national jurisprudence on EC law: 'Document de travail interne. Analyse des décisions nationales rendues par les juridictions et les autorités administratives sur le droit des Communautés européennes', 1962, HAEU/COM/BAC.

[13] Louis-Edmond Pettiti, 'Nouvelles diverses sur les travaux de l'Association', *Bulletin de l'Association des juristes européens*, 10, 1962, p. 29.

[14] Pierre Pescatore, 'Les travaux du groupe juridique dans la négociation du Traité de Rome', *Studia diplomatica*, 34(1–4), 1981, pp. 159–78.

spearheaded by FIDE members.[15] Amongst them was L. F. D. Ter Kuile, an international lawyer of the Rotterdam bar since 1955 and legal adviser to an important international bank (the *Bank voor Handel en Scheepvaart*, the Bank of Commerce and Navigation). Ter Kuile managed to engage in two test-cases on the legal effect (direct or indirect) of article 12 of the EEC Treaty. On 21 May 1962, together with another well-established international lawyer and former head of Amsterdam's bar, Hans Stibbe,[16] he defended two firms before the Dutch tax court (*Tariefcommissie*) – the transport company *Algemenende Van Gend en Loos* and the electro-technical equipment company *Da Costa en Schaake NV*. He obtained a preliminary ruling before the ECJ in August 1962.

Michel Gaudet, the head of the Legal Service of the Commission, immediately seized the opportunity opened by his fellow members of FIDE. The brief he submitted in the case was arguably the most far-reaching and ambitious account of the relationship between Law and Europe at the time. A very influential figure in the early years of the EEC, as we saw in Chapter 1, Michel Gaudet was able to have the *Collège des commissaires* fully endorse his daring legal theory of European integration in its 204th meeting on 31 October 1962 on the matter.[17] Described as a 'vast' and 'very impressive analysis of the structure of the EC' by ECJ advocate general in the case, Karl Roemer, the twenty-one-page memo presented by Michel Gaudet before the Court on 29 November 1962 proposed in fact a unique legal doctrine for the three European Treaties, only mentioning the specific facts of the *Van Gend en Loos* case at the very end. Trying to make the case for the irreducible specificity of the 'legal structures established by these Treaties' with regard to international law, he indicated very explicitly that EC law 'ha[d] to be' of direct effect and 'ha[d] to prevail over contrary national law, and even over subsequent rules'.[18]

[15] Out of the first eighteen preliminary rulings notified to the Court during the first six years of the Rome Treaties, fifteen came from Dutch tribunals, one from Luxembourg, one from Germany and one from Italy.

[16] Hans Stibbe's Amsterdam law firm, which he inherited from his father, would become, after several mergers, one of Europe's largest law firms in the field.

[17] On this, see Morten Rasmussen, 'The Origins of a Legal Revolution: The Early History of the European Court of Justice', *Journal of European Integration History*, 4, 2008, pp. 77–99.

[18] Michel Gaudet, 'Note à MM. les membres de la Commission. Objets. Observations de la Commission devant la Cour de justice au sujet des demandes préjudicielles de la "Tariefcommissie" néerlandaise', ronéo, 1963, 21p. I would like to thank Bruno de Witte who was so kind as to lend me his own copy of this precious albeit still unpublished document.

The fact that many actors of the Court itself caught this multifaceted call for a 'judicial *fiat*' coming from both the FIDE lawyers and the Commission's Legal Service is confirmed by the comment of Roger-Michel Chevallier, Robert Lecourt's young *référendaire* and active FIDE member, made a few days before the actual decision: 'When you know that a preliminary reference has recently been made to the Court (the case is under deliberation) concerning a possible direct "applicability" of article 12 ... you understand the huge interest ... not only for the Member States but for any individual if the Court is to give a positive answer to this question'.[19] A landmark judgment was predicted; and expectations were great.

A polysemous decision

However, when the *Van Gend en Loos* decision was eventually delivered, it disappointed many of these expectations of a legal clarification of the EC Treaties' scope. Evidence now shows that the case actually gave way to an open conflict of interpretation within the Court itself between the more classical thesis heralded by the advocate general Otto Riese and the *juge-rapporteur* Charles-Léon Hammes on the one hand and the more ambitious position of Alberto Trabucchi on the other.[20] Testimonies indicate that the majority that eventually ruled on direct effect was very narrow (four to three).[21] As a result, the final decision lay somewhere between Gaudet's grand design and the more circumspect analysis of the German advocate general Karl Roemer. Of course, the Court clearly rejected the allegations of the three Member States (Belgium, the Netherlands and Germany) who had presented memos rejecting on principle any direct applicability of the Treaties.[22] Nonetheless, the judgment only recognized direct effect on the restrictive ground that article 12 entailed a

19 Roger-Michel Chevallier, 'Commentaire d'arrêt 2 et 3/62 de la CJCE', *Gazette du palais*, 19–22 January 1963, p. 1.

20 The position of Alberto Trabucchi is known thanks to the recent publication of the internal memo he circulated among the judges which went against the position taken by the *juge-rapporteur* in the case: G. Perini, 'Note à MM. les juges. Affaire 26/62 Tariefcommissie', in Giuseppe Perini, 'Alberto Trabucchi, giurista europeo. Alle radici del diritto in Europa: una testimonianza inedita', *Quaderni della rivista di diritto civile*, 2008, pp. 174–6.

21 Interview (conducted together with Morten Rasmussen) with Paolo Gori, former *référendaire* of Alberto Trabucchi, Prato, Italy, 20 March 2008. See also Morten Rasmussen, 'The Origins of a Legal Revolution: The Early History of the European Court of Justice', *Journal of European Integration History*, 4, 2008, pp. 77–99.

22 See Eric Stein, 'The Making of a Transnational Constitution', *American Journal of International Law*, 75(1), 1981, p. 12.

'negative' obligation for Member States (namely, an obligation not to act). In other words, large parts of the Treaties according to which States had 'positive' obligations were potentially excluded from the scope of 'direct application' as defined in *Van Gend en Loos*. Furthermore, the decision did not consecrate the intrinsic specificity of the European legal order, merely described as a 'new legal order in international law'.[23] If read together with the former *Confédération nationale des producteurs de fruits et légumes* v. *Council of the EEC*, the decision that had just restricted individual legal standing before the ECJ (December 1962), the judgment could well have been taken to be yet another version of the well-established rules laid out in 1928 by the Permanent Court of International Justice in its Opinion on the access of [certain] individuals to the Danzig courts.[24] Last and not least, *Van Gend en Loos* did not express any opinion on the question of the supremacy of EC law over national laws – contrary to what the Legal Service of the Commission had hoped for.

Thereby, in itself, *Van Gend en Loos* cannot be said to have called for what nowadays is said to be its 'logical' consequence: the affirmation of the principle of supremacy of European law as a whole. Quite to the contrary, and because of its thorough nature and its argumentative richness that have been pointed out by many authors, the judgment actually left open a wide margin of interpretation. The very wavering of the decision's terminology is quite telling in this regard: while the English-language version referred to the 'direct effects', the French version used the words '*effets immédiats*',[25] while the unofficial translation made by the *Common Market Law Reports* mentioned the 'direct effect' (with no plural).[26] To these not irrelevant variations, one may add the wide range of expressions that legal scholars used in their commentaries ('self-executing articles', 'direct applicability', 'direct insertion', etc.). This ambiguity of the decision as well as the fluidity in the lexicon not only indicate that no legal commonsense had yet imposed itself *erga omnes*, it also confirms that a range of possible legal futures were still open for Europe. Only this sense of uncertainty that prevailed among Euro-lawyers can actually explain how an acute and alert lawyer such as

23 The citations herein all come from the judgment as published in *Common Market Law Reports*, 1963, pp. 127–32.

24 See Joseph Weiler, 'Rewriting Van Gend en Loos: Towards a Normative Theory of ECJ Hermeneutics', in Ola Wiklund (ed.), *Judicial Discretion in European Perspective*, The Hague, Kluwer Law International, 2003, pp. 151–63.

25 Cour de justice des Communautés européennes, *Recueil de la jurisprudence de la Cour*, Luxembourg, Publications officielles des CE, 1963, p. 21.

26 *Common Market Law Reports*, 1963, p. 13.

Pierre Pescatore could neglect to even quote the case in a long paper on ECJ case law presented at a conference held in April 1963. Commenting on his text forty-five years after, he acknowledged that 'it is quite obvious that I had not at the time grasped the fundamental importance of this decision'.[27]

Judicial ventriloquism: Van Gend en Loos and its legal entrepreneurs

These uncertainties may actually be the reason why *Van Gend en Loos* was immediately taken up in an interpretative tide sparked by some of those who had been directly implicated in the case: within two months, a number of members or former members of the Court, joined by their *référendaires*, the Commission's Legal Service as well as the lawyer in the case, Ter Kuile. Their activism profoundly transformed the case. Their efforts converged in drawing the attention of a variety of audiences and publics (lawyers, academics, public opinion, etc.) on the historical importance of the decision for European integration, a matter of weeks after the judgment was delivered.

The transnational fabric of a landmark case

The interpretative tide started the very day after the decision had been delivered. On 6 February 1963, at a ceremony held at the Court for his departure, Otto Riese (ECJ judge) indicated that, 'in these days, the Court has delivered an important decision'.[28] On 21 February 1963, Michel Gaudet, head of the Commission's Legal Service, notified the *Conférence du libre barreau de Liège* that 'a decision of the Court of the highest interest' had just been taken.[29] Two days later, Maurice Lagrange, ECJ advocate general, speaking before the French section of FIDE, 'called immediately [their] attention to a recent Court decision, 26/62 of 5 February 1963 ... of the highest importance'.[30] The very same day, in a column in the most authoritative French newspaper, *Le Monde*, Robert Lecourt stressed that, 'in the core of the Brussels crisis, the judicial world has just brought an important stone to the building of the European entity'.[31] A month later, on 6 April 1963, ECJ judge

[27] Pierre Pescatore, 'Note', in *Études de droit communautaire européen (1962–2007)*, Brussels, Bruylant, 2008, p. 61.

[28] Otto Riese, 'Ansprache von Herrn Professor O. Riese anlasslich seiner Verabschiedung am 6 February 1963' in /CEAB 2/1137 HAEU.

[29] Michel Gaudet, 'Incidences des Communautés européennes sur le droit interne des États membres', *Annales de la Faculté de droit de Liège*, 1963, p. 24.

[30] Maurice Lagrange, 'L'organisation, le fonctionnement et le rôle de la Cour de justice des Communautés européennes', *Bulletin de l'Association des juristes européens*, 1963, p. 13.

[31] Robert Lecourt, 'L'Europe dans le prétoire', *Le Monde*, 23 February 1963, p. 1.

Alberto Trabucchi, in a lecture at the University of Ferrara, evoked a 'decision [that] will have a great echo'.[32] In issues published just after *Van Gend en Loos*, various legal journals included comments on the case. Nicola Catalano, a former ECJ judge, referred to 'a rightful, well-founded and cautious decision' in one of the major Italian legal journals, *Foro padano*.[33] He was followed by judge Trabucchi's *référendaire*, Paolo Gori, who considered the decision as 'one of the most important contributions [which] will be remembered as a landmark in the affirmation of EC law'.[34] In the first issue of the Dutch–British EC law journal, the *Common Market Law Review*, the president of the Court, Andreas Donner, referred to the decision as one of 'cardinal importance for the entire operation of the EEC Treaty'.[35] Two months later, in October 1963, the lawyer who had brought the *Van Gend en Loos* case before the Court, L. F. D. Ter Kuile, commented on the decision's extreme relevance in a report to the 1963 FIDE congress on direct effect.[36]

Even though there are no signs of a premeditated collective strategy, four judges and one advocate general, together with their *référendaires*, former judge Nicola Catalano, as well as the director of the Commission's Legal Service Michel Gaudet and the lawyer in the case L. F. D. Ter Kuile swiftly converged in giving *Van Gend en Loos* legal and political salience. Through this process of drawing the attention of various audiences to the case, there came into being a sort of *judicial ventriloquism* ('the Court said that . . .') through which the judgment was put into common parlance in legal circles, by which the actors in the case managed to turn the ambiguous *Van Gend en Loos* judgment into a clear-cut and far-reaching judicial *fiat*. On the whole, it all occurred as if a kind of second judicial deliberation had been initiated – one that would fabricate the overall reach of *Van Gend en Loos* by extending in manifold ways the sense and the validity of its message well above and beyond the relatively prudent and balanced considerations of the decision itself.

32 Alberto Trabucchi, 'Un nuovo diritto', *Rivista di diritto civile*, 9, 1963, p. 259.

33 Nicola Catalano, 'L'inserimento diretto delle disposizioni contenute nel Trattato istitutivo della Comunità economica europea negli ordinamenti giuridici degli Stati membri', *Foro padano*, 1963, p. 32.

34 Paolo Gori, 'Una pietra miliare nell'affermazione del diritto europeo', *Foro italiano*, 1963, p. 10.

35 Andreas Donner, 'National Law and the Case-Law of the Court of Justice of the European Community', *Common Market Law Review*, 1(1), 1963, p. 13.

36 L. F. D. Ter Kuile, 'Le problème des dispositions directement applicables des traités internationaux et son application aux traités instituant les communautés', in *Deuxième colloque international de droit européen: La Haye 1963*, The Hague, NV Uitgeversmij, 1966.

Various elements were crucial in such a pre-empting of the *Van Gend en Loos* hermeneutic space. The first relates to the very position of these Euro-lawyers. As each of them had taken part in the case (as judge, law clerk or litigant in the case of Michel Gaudet and Ter Kuile), they could claim direct access to the 'authentic' sense of the decision. As (almost[37]) no dissenting opinion was expressed publicly in the following weeks,[38] their authority with regard to asserting what *Van Gend en Loos* 'really' meant remained virtually unchallenged. Protected by the secrecy of the judicial deliberations, they were in a privileged position when it came to persuasively stating what 'the decision recognized implicitly'.[39] A second element is the sort of *activism by proxy*, in which judges could engage with the help and participation of their *référendaires*. The latter were indeed in a very favourable position since not only had they been associated (albeit indirectly) with the judicial deliberations, but they had also more statutory freedom to openly speak about the case. This is particularly important as they played a crucial role at the time in the legal commentary of ECJ case law,[40] thereby assuming a position both in the drafting and in the commenting of the Court's decisions. The third element of explanation lies in the position these Euro-lawyers had in the nascent transnational academic circles of EC law. Most of them were key members of that emerging community of scholars, if only because of the critical role

[37] I have identified only one differing opinion to this interpretative activism, namely, that of ECJ *référendaire* Sergio Neri, presumably echoing the viewpoint of his judge, Rino Rossi, who denied the view, held by many Euro-lawyers, that there is any element in the decision enabling to see supremacy of EC law as a logical consequence of *Van Gend en Loos*: 'While the Court has endorsed the Dutch theory of self-executing of *specific* international norms, it is not possible to affirm that it has accepted supremacy': see Sergio Neri, 'Sulla natura giuridica delle Comunità europee', *Rivista di diritto internazionale*, 1964, p. 235.

[38] To our knowledge, three out of the seven ECJ judges (Louis Delvaux, Rino Rossi and Charles Léon Hammes) and one of the two Advocates General (Karl Roemer) did not take part in this *ex post* interpretative activism and remained silent.

[39] Alberto Trabucchi, 'Un nuovo diritto', *Rivista di diritto civile*, 9, 1963, p. 259.

[40] While finishing a PhD at the University of Paris, precisely on ECJ preliminary rulings, Roger-Michel Chevallier, Robert Lecourt's *référendaire*, was writing a regular legal commentary on EC law in the French *Gazette du palais*, and, together with the Belgian Gérard Rasquin (Hammes's *référendaire*), they wrote numerous doctrinal articles on the Court's procedures and case law. Paolo Gori, Alberto Trabucchi's *référendaire*, a PhD in international law from the University of Florence and Harvard Law School, and Sergio Neri, another Italian *référendaire* who also held a PhD in international law, were respectively commenting ECJ decisions for the *Foro italiano* and the *Foro padano*. One could add former ECJ judge Nicola Catalano to this group, for he had just left the Court and had become one of the most active commentators of the Court's decisions in major Italian, French and Belgium law journals.

both the Court and the Legal Service had played in framing (and subsidizing) the nascent milieu through FIDE. It is quite natural then that *référendaires* and judges engaged in a sort of academic tour, spreading the *Van Gend en Loos* word. Two months after the decision, in late April 1963, no fewer than thirteen members of the Court (five judges out of nine, and eight *référendaires* out of nine) took part in the important conference held at the *Institut fur das Recht der Europäische Gemeinschaften* in Cologne on 'Ten Years of ECJ Jurisprudence'. And, at the second FIDE congress in October 1963, three judges and five *référendaires* participated, together with Michel Gaudet and L. F. D. Ter Kuile,[41] all of them actively promoting the relevance of the *Van Gend en Loos* case for interpreting the whole architecture of the Treaties. Last but not least, judges could rely on the variegated sets of national social networks in which they participated. Quite characteristically, these activists of the pan-European legal cause primarily took action in their own national political, legal and academic circles. It comes as no surprise that former minister and member of parliament Robert Lecourt published an enthusiastic Op-Ed in *Le Monde*, and did the same several times during his years in Luxembourg. Similarly, judges Antonio Trabucchi and Andreas Donner, who were both academics, commented the *Van Gend en Loos* judgment in various law journals and conferences in their respective countries. The diversity in the channels of mobilization mirrors the various sorts of social capital that the first ECJ judges could rely on.[42] The range of national but also transnational resources they could collectively count on allowed for a quick enlargement of the social fora implicated in the debate over the relationship between Europe and law.

Manufacturing content: Van Gend en Loos and its 'implications'

Through this interpretative activism, *Van Gend en Loos* was soon divested of its litigation identity and turned into a constitutive principle of an overall doctrine. It ceased to be the mere resolution of a dispute between the transport company NV Algemene-Van Gend en Loos and the Dutch tax authorities, or just an interpretation of article 12 of the EEC Treaty on customs duties. Rather, it came to represent a trail-blazing judgment founding EC law's social and political functions with European

[41] Presumably as a tribute to his achievement in his *Van Gend en Loos* test-case, L. F. D. Ter Kuile was representing the Dutch section of FIDE in that debate.

[42] Antonin Cohen, *Scarlet Robes, Dark Suits: The Social Recruitment of the European Court of Justice*, European University Institute, Working Paper RSCAS 2008/35.

integration. Two elements were particularly crucial in such a multi-faceted exegesis.

First of all, *Van Gend en Loos* became considered as the cornerstone of an altogether new body of law. Because it related to the judicial capacity for 'individuals', Euro-lawyers viewed the decision as paving the way for '*un nuovo diritto*' (in the words of judge Trabucchi). The decision was read as 'the first arch of a bridge meant to entirely overcome the barrier between the sovereignties of the different Member States'.[43] For this transnational group of exegetes, this was just the first step. As they commented on the ground-breaking importance of the decision, they simultaneously set the Court's future challenges, namely, the 'supremacy of EC law'. As indicated by former judge Catalano, 'a decision of the ECJ [in this matter] could well be necessary'[44] to solve the next obstacle – 'the serious problem concerning the coexistence of national and EC law'.[45] Their analysis was at one and the same time descriptive (what *Van Gend en Loos* was or said), prescriptive (what European case law should be now) and performative (making *Costa* happen before it actually did). While Trabucchi's *référendaire* stated that 'the rule *will be* that of general prevalence of EC law and jurisdiction over the law and jurisdiction' of the Member States,[46] the president of the Court himself boldly explained that the issue was almost solved already since the Court 'would presumably have ruled that the EEC Treaty has precedence [supremacy] over national law'[47] in *Van Gend en Loos* had it been questioned on the matter. Caught up in this net of descriptions, predictions, and anticipations, *Van Gend en Loos* thus became not only a foretaste of EC law's future but also a far-reaching manifesto calling for a number of further steps.

A second cognitive salience made its way through this thick pile of interpretative strata: the *political* relevance of the decision in the context of the crisis in the EC institutions. While there is no direct evidence that this heated political context – the French government had adjourned the

[43] Paolo Gori, 'Una pietra miliare nell'affermazione del diritto europeo', *Foro italiano*, 1963, p. 10, p. 17.

[44] Nicola Catalano, 'L'inserimento diretto delle disposizioni contenute nel Trattato istitutivo della Comunità economica europea negli ordinamenti giuridici degli Stati membri', *Foro padano*, 1963, p. 32, p. 36.

[45] Alberto Trabucchi, 'Un nuovo diritto', *Rivista di diritto civile*, 9, 1963, p. 259.

[46] Paolo Gori, 'Una pietra miliare nell'affermazione del diritto europeo', *Foro italiano*, 1963, p. 10, p. 18 (emphasis added).

[47] Andreas Donner, 'National Law and the Case-Law of the Court of Justice of the European Community', *Common Market Law Review*, 1(1), 1963, p. 13.

British membership negotiations only a couple of days earlier on 28 January 1963 – had influenced the Court in its decision, it clearly weighed on its interpretation. Actually, the day immediately after the *Van Gend en Loos* decision was delivered, first references were made to the intergovernmental crisis in the presidential address welcoming a newly elected ECJ judge: '[S]ince the political impetus [for European integration] will possibly slacken for some time to come, it is incumbent upon the organs [of the Communities] to be all the more conscious of their role as the institutionalized carriers of the European idea'.[48] Such transgressions of the separation of political and judicial branches would then repeatedly occur, to the obvious advantage of the judicial realm: '[W]hile the statesmen discuss the political future of Europe, without sparing the weight of their authority and the passion of their convictions, the lawyers of our six countries dedicate themselves to the birth of a European law which is discreet, yet full of promises'[49] – said Michel Gaudet, the director of the Commission's Legal Service, a couple of weeks after *Van Gend en Loos*. ECJ judge and former political leader Robert Lecourt went even further when indicating that the ECJ's case law was one of the possible fuels for a lasting European integration: '[I]n times where the establishment of a political construction is at a standstill, the field is clear to accomplish other, certainly more modest, progresses but ... which might be determinant ... The practical Europe, which evolves under the influence of mere facts, could soon make political Europe inevitable'.[50] On the whole, therefore, *Van Gend en Loos* was given very extensive legal and political potentialities that made it a salient point in the nascent EC polity.

Debating the 'logic' of the European Treaties

Had it not been heralded within the various social fields that made up the European Communities at the time, the emerging legal doctrine of Europe drawn from *Van Gend en Loos* exegeses would have stayed in the realm of abstraction. In a context where the perspectives for political integration appeared less and less plausible, the salience of this emerging

[48] Speech by Andreas Donner on 6 February 1963, quoted in W. Feld, *The Court of the European Communities: New Dimensions in International Adjudication*, Dordrecht, Martinus Nijhoff, 1964, p. 116.

[49] Michel Gaudet, 'Incidences des Communautés européennes sur le droit interne des États membres', *Annales de la Faculté de droit de Liège*, 1963, p. 24 (emphasis in the original).

[50] Robert Lecourt, 'L'unification du droit européen est aussi un moyen de construire l'Europe', *France-Forum*, 1963, p. 31.

doctrine of *Van Gend en Loos* gave a variety of (political, bureaucratic, corporate, etc.) entrepreneurs of Europe an opportunity to ground their pan-European ambitions in new *legal* terms. In this progressive rallying of differently situated actors, a new common sense of the European Communities was consolidated as each of these mobilizations enriched this nascent paradigm with new dimensions and scopes at the core of the EC polity.

Dramatizing the stakes

While extensive interpretations of the *Van Gend en Loos* scope and consequences were emerging and consolidating, a dramatic turn of events suddenly put in question the very possibility of such daring pan-European jurisprudence. In a decision of 7 March 1964, the Italian Constitutional Court explicitly denied the supremacy of EC law over posterior national legislation, thereby putting in doubt the then emerging *Van Gend en Loos* doctrine. Interestingly, the case had emerged from the very hopes and expectations that *Van Gend en Loos* had triggered within specific Euro-lawyers. The very vagueness of the decision left open a variety of possible future paths. Brussels' first business lawyers saw *Van Gend en Loos* as a form of *ex post* confirmation of their correctness in choosing the EC institutions as a new centre for economic regulation; as early as May 1963, a former chairman of the international section of the American Bar Association who had set up his legal office in Brussels two years earlier, Homer Angelo, welcomed *Van Gend en Loos*: 'on February 5, 1963, the Court of Justice handed down an interlocutory ruling which may prove for the European communities to be a landmark equivalent to *Marbury* v. *Madison* or *McCulloch* v. *Maryland* in American constitutional history'.[51] The paragraph in *Van Gend en Loos* on the contribution of 'individuals' to the implementation of the Treaties[52] had been read by others as setting the stage for legal actions against all sorts of violations of the spirit or letter of the Treaties by the Member States or the Commission (including the more political aspects concerning the functioning of the EC institutions and their internal politics). Both lawyers who had initiated the *Costa* v. *ENEL* case that led to the

[51] Homer Angelo, 'Developments in the European Common Market', *International and Comparative Law Bulletin*, 7(2), 1963, p. 12.

[52] As stated in the *Van Gend en Loos* decision: 'The vigilance of individuals concerned to protect their rights amounts to an effective supervision in addition to the supervision entrusted by articles 169 and 170 to the diligence of the Commission and Member States'.

decision of the Constitutional Court were part of the first rank of national lawyers who read *Van Gend en Loos* as a new starting point.

European cause-lawyers and the Costa v. ENEL case

Far from being a rather irrational dispute over a contested 1,925 Italian lire bill issued by the Italian electricity company, ENEL, led by a litigious, if not foolish, individual, Flaminio Costa (as many of the accounts seem to indicate nowadays), the *Costa* v. *ENEL* case originated in a consistently activist conception of a European rule of law. Giangaleazzo Stendardi, a forty-three-year-old constitutional law professor, and Flaminio Costa, a sixty-two-year-old criminal lawyer[53] were both committed liberals (in the European sense of criticism of State intrusion in the area of both individual freedoms and economic markets). On previous occasions, they had argued that individual standing before the two European courts was a critical element for bringing about a *Stato di diritto* in Italy. Costa was among those calling for his government to accept 'with no more delays the individual petition right before the European Court of Human Rights'.[54] Stendardi had theorized the role of individual legal activism before courts as a quasi-substitute for political accountability, particularly at the European level. In various writings before and after the *Costa* case, he indicated that 'it is not necessary to have a Parliament directly elected by the people for the citizen to be protected; it only requires the existence of a procedure capable of protecting the individual *vis-à-vis* the [European] organization'.[55] The test-case was a familiar strategy to him. An early analyst of the Italian Constitutional Court (he published one of the very first books on the newly founded Court), he had immediately seized (however unsuccessfully) the opportunity opened by its creation in 1956 to defend freedom of speech through a preliminary ruling, thus resulting in the court's third decision (23 June 1956). Similarly, when claiming as early as 1958 that ignorance of EC law supremacy was 'a substantial violation of the Treaties', he prophetically stated that 'it will be necessary to plead judicially such an issue, in order to provoke a decision, for example of the European Court of Justice'.[56]

(cont)

53 Giangaleazzo Stendardi took part in the case only when it was before the Italian Constitutional Court, but suggested the recourse to the ECJ. See Giangaleazzo Stendardi, 'Problemi in materia di legittimità di espropriazione d'impresa', *Foro padano*, 5, 1962, pp. 52–60.

54 Flaminio Costa, 'Riforme legislative urgenti per una più efficace tutela giurisdizionale del cittadino nella procedura penale' in *Congresso nazionale giuridico forense: Milan 13–18 settembre 1965*, Milan, Giuffrè, 1966, p. 735.

55 Gian Galeazzo Stendardi, *I rapporti tra gli ordinamenti giuridici italiani e le Comunità europee*, Milan, Giuffrè, 1958, p. 18.

56 *Ibid.*

This strong belief in Law as the paramount tool for citizens (more important even than the vote)[57] was then naturally mobilized in this context against the December 1962 Italian nationalization law. As a matter of fact, Stendardi, who had been adjunct professor at the private Milanese business school, La Bocconi, in the 1950s and was at the time an active member of the Italian liberal party in Milan,[58] was highly critical of the ongoing process of nationalization of a number of private companies in Italy. In an article published in late 1962, Stendardi argued that nationalization was both unconstitutional and contrary to the EC Treaties and that the most likely 'legal consequences of these violations [would be] a preliminary ruling before the European Court of Justice'.[59] It was therefore as a natural continuation of both their professional litigation know-how and their political commitments that the two of them tried a test case (Costa was both the plaintiff and his own lawyer in this case) asking a Milanese lower court for a preliminary ruling before the ECJ (and the Constitutional Court) on the legality of ENEL's nationalization. In a nutshell, the two cause lawyers argued two issues: first, the prevalence of EC law over the posterior Italian nationalization bill; second, the fact that individuals could solicit the Court on the grounds that the obligation of consulting the European Commission before engaging in the nationalization process (articles 93 and 102 of the EEC Treaty), an obligation breached by the Italian government, was not just 'politically' but also 'legally' binding and justiciable. Hence, they tested an extensive interpretation of the scope of direct effect that would have enabled individuals to ask for the legal implementation of the most 'political' part of the Treaties (the inter-institutional dynamics).

In this context, where *Van Gend en Loos* had given rise to high expectations and many prophecies regarding the future of EC law, the decision of the Italian Constitutional Court in *Costa* v. *ENEL* came as a blow. All the more so as other supreme courts had at the same time delivered judgments which refused to acknowledge the specific nature of the Rome Treaties *vis-à-vis* other international treaties. In France, three judicial decisions from the *Cour de cassation* (19 February and 22 October 1964)

[57] He urged each European citizen to 'ask himself: what have I done, what am I doing for the European norms to be implemented?' *Ibid.*, p. 17.

[58] The Partito liberale italiano, a small right-wing party closed to corporate interests, had gained an unprecedented momentum at the time in Milan (around 20 per cent in 1963–4 elections), actively campaigning against the politics of the centre-left government and, particularly, its nationalization policies. Giangaleazzo Stendardi was on the party's list at the municipal elections in Milan in 1963 and eventually entered the municipal council in 1969. See M. Emanuelli, *Accade a Milano 1945–2002*, Milan, Greco e Greco, 2002.

[59] Gian Galeazzo Stendardi, 'Problemi in materia di legittimità di espropriazione d'impresa', *Foro padano*, 5, 1962, p. 60.

and the *Conseil d'État* (19 June 1964) defined the EC Treaties as ordinary international public law instruments. The annual meeting of the German law professors' association, where the proponents of a 'constitutional reading' of European Treaties turned out to be a minority,[60] confirmed that the emerging legal doctrine was hardly capable of convincing national judicial and academic elites. The case had not come to a close, however. Both Milanese lawyers had lodged simultaneously a preliminary ruling before the ECJ and therefore the perspective of a new decision of the same case before the summer triggered an unprecedented transnational legal mobilization. A memo presented by the Legal Service of the Commission in the *Costa* v. *ENEL* case indicated its 'vivid apprehensions' after the Italian and German adverse judicial decisions.[61] The Opinion presented a couple of days later, on 24 June 1964, by ECJ advocate general Maurice Lagrange – the very last Opinion of his more than twelve years at the Court – pointed at the 'disastrous – the word is not too strong – consequences of such a jurisprudence [would have] on the functioning of the institutional system established by the treaty and therefore, on the very future of the Common Market'.[62] Last but not least, only three days before the decision of the Court, the German section of FIDE met in Bensheim for a small seminar with ECJ judges and *référendaires* to talk about the options open to the Court in matters of supremacy of EC law, Hans-Peter Ipsen, at the time one of the leading German academic authorities in the field, presented possible pathways for the relationship between EC law and domestic laws.[63]

Politicizing the issue of the legal logic of the European Treaties

This dramatization of the stakes of ECJ decision could not leave the many EC law-implicated political and bureaucratic entrepreneurs unconcerned, all the more so that pan-European leaders were simultaneously

60 Bill Davies, *Resisting the European Court of Justice: West Germany's Confrontation with European Law (1949–1979)*, Cambridge, Cambridge University Press, 2012, pp. 44–88.

61 Opinion of the Advocate General Maurice Lagrange on *Costa* v. *ENEL*, 25 June 1964, in *Recueil de la jurisprudence de la Cour*, Luxembourg, Curia, 1964, p. 1179.

62 *Ibid.*

63 Wissenschaftliche Gesellschaft für Europarecht, *Aktuelle fragen des europäische gemeinschaftsrechts, Bensheim, 10–14 Juli 1964*, Stuttgart, Enke Verlag, 1965. On the importance of this meeting and the influential role of German law professor Hans Peter Ipsen in shaping the set of possible alternatives for the ECJ judges, see Christian Joerges, 'Europe a Großraum? Shifting Legal Conceptualisations of the Integration Project', in Christian Joerges and Navraj Ghaleigh (eds.), *Darker Legacies of Law in Europe: The Shadow of National Socialism and Fascism over Europe and Its Legal Traditions*, Oxford, Hart Publishing, 2003, pp. 167–91, p. 183, n. 92.

facing a closing down of the perspectives of European *political* integration. The many disagreements and crises that developed between Member States ever since 1962 prevented the rapid development of EC supranational institutions in which federalist political entrepreneurs had put many of their hopes. The failure of the various initiatives to revive European integration (for example, the Fouchet plan of 1961–2 and, most of all, the Hallstein proposals of March 1965), as well as the rejection of the British application for membership (January 1963) illustrated the hardening of the Member States' diplomatic positions and marked a sudden inflexion in the rise of the Commission within the EC institutional system.[64] Similarly, the central cause of the European Parliament, namely, the institution of direct election, was quickly put aside. The Parliamentary Assembly criticized such evolution in a resolution to the Council on 27 June 1963, without, however, any effect. In the meantime, the agreement on the merging of the European Communities (February 1964) was carried out *à institutions constantes*.[65] This progressive closure of the political horizon of European integration, which would progressively become more and more clear, came over the months leading up to the 1965 'empty chair' crisis, and came along with a serious crisis of the pan-European movement itself. While, in the immediate aftermath of the Second World War, the European Movement had been *the* crossroads for all European (political, economic and academic) undertakings, it was now weakened by a series of internal conflicts regarding the best ways to achieve unity of the polity. Ever since the failure of the European Defence Community in August 1954, at least two different streams emerged, one led by Altiero Spinelli which heavily criticized the Rome Treaties and pushed for the establishment of a Constituant Assembly of the European people, and the other promoted by leaders such as Paul-Henri Spaak who defended a more pragmatic point of view on the political potential of the Common Market.[66] As a consequence of these divisions, the pan-European nebula lost much of

[64] Cf. Jean-Marie Palayret *et al.* (eds.), *Visions, Votes and Vetoes: The Empty Chair Crisis and the Luxembourg Compromise Forty Years On*, Brussels, Peter Lang, 2006.

[65] See Piers Ludlow, 'A Supranational Icarus: The Early Commission and the Search for an Independent Role', in Antonio Varsori (ed.), *Inside the European Community: Actors and Policies in the European Integration 1957–1972*, Baden-Baden, Nomos, 2006.

[66] On these divisions, see Daniela Preda, 'The Movements for European Unity (1958–1972)', in Antonio Varsori (ed.), *Inside the European Community: Actors and Policies in the European Integration 1957–1972*, Baden-Baden, Nomos, 2006, pp. 177–93; and Wilfried Loth (ed.), *Crises and Compromises: The European Project 1963–1969*, Baden-Baden, Nomos, 2001.

the political momentum that had marked its early congresses in the immediate post-Second World War period.

This progressive dismantling of both the transnational pan-European milieu and the concrete institutional opportunities for further political integration would not be of direct interest for our present research if many of the pan-European political leaders had not also been jurists often maintaining close relationships with legal academia. Fernand Dehousse, Arved Deringer, Walter Hallstein, Carl Friedrich Ophüls, Jean Rey, Marinus van der Goes van Naters, Ivo Samkalden, Paul-Henri Spaak and Pierre-Henri Teitgen whom we have met earlier in this book as they were engaged in institution-building at the Council, the Commission, the Court or the European Parliament, were at the same time law professors, judges or corporate lawyers related to the legal realm through a number of professional associations, teaching positions, learned societies and law journals. This blurriness of the borders between law and politics in early EC settings is essential to understand how these 'politicians of the law' were able to redirect their own pan-European investments towards the promotion of a new project of Europeanization where the ECJ would play a central political role. In a context where the blockage of the political pathway was becoming more and more flagrant, the judicial terrain appeared like a new land of opportunities.

Thus, the signal coming from Italy in February and the perspective of a decision by the ECJ in July did not remain unnoticed. Walter Hallstein was first among our lawyers to engage publicly with the debate in a speech before the European Parliament in June 1964. That he was critical in converting the judicial issue of supremacy of EC law into a political stake of European integration as a whole is probably not surprising. As indicated in Chapter 1, Hallstein had retained strong links with German legal academia. Evidence shows that he was closely following the ongoing heated debates over EC law principles.[67] In a context where the political development of EC institutions was experiencing its first blockages, the decision of the Italian Constitutional Court indicated that the fate of European integration was also at stake on the judicial scene. Taking advantage of the debate before the European Parliament over the EEC Commission's annual report on 18 June 1964 (that is to say one month before the *Costa* decision by the ECJ), Walter Hallstein presented no less than his own legal doctrine of Europe. His 'theses' were all

[67] See Bill Davies, *Resisting the European Court of Justice: West Germany's Confrontation with European Law (1949–1979)*, Cambridge, Cambridge University Press, 2012, pp. 44–88.

grounded on the fact that 'the regulation of EC law prevails, regardless of the level of the two orders where the conflict appears', thus including prevalence of all EC regulation over national constitutions.[68]

In this context, it comes as no surprise that the *Costa* v. *ENEL* decision delivered by the ECJ was immediately seen as a landmark raising interest and concern beyond the restricted circles of EC law specialists. Even if it is still impossible to speculate on the internal balance within the Court itself,[69] its decision taken on 15 July 1964 resolutely sided with pan-European advocates. Admittedly, *Costa* was assertive and defended most of the arguments that had been expressed by the Commission in its *Van Gend en Loos* brief. Not only did it set out the prevalence of EC law, but this time it did so in a particularly clear, almost provocative manner, with EC law being defined as an 'integral part of the legal systems of the Member States' enshrining a 'permanent limitation [by the latter] of their sovereign rights'.[70] Since the post-*Van Gend en Loos* prophecies had determined anticipations and strategies *vis-à-vis* the Court, the recognition of the principle of supremacy confirmed that *Costa* was read as 'undoubtedly a continuation and development of the [*Van Gend en Loos* dccision]'.[71] One decision being seen as the mere endorsement of the other's 'logical consequences', the commentators of the *Costa* case, fulfilling the predictions they themselves had made in the wake of *Van Gend en Loos*, the two cases became firmly linked together into one unique and coherent doctrine.

However, given the still fragile authority of the ECJ, it is not surprising that its decision in *Costa* was far from being the last word on the now widely debated issue of the legal nature of the Rome Treaties. At the European Parliament, a number of politicians of the law started drawing attention to the political relevance of the subject-matter. The first of them was Marinus van der Goes van Naters, a Belgian Socialist member of parliament, lawyer and former vice-president of the Consultative

68 Walter Hallstein, 'La Communauté européenne, nouvel ordre juridique', in *Les documents de la Communauté européenne*, 27, 1964, p. 5.

69 In between the two decisions, the composition of the Court had undergone only one change with the – to our knowledge, still unexplained – resignation of the German judge Otto Riese, Adenauer's nephew, only one day after the publication of the decision in *Van Gend en Loos* (but after he had taken part in the judicial deliberations). He was replaced by Walter Strauss, former minister of Justice in Adenauer's government.

70 Decision *Costa* v. *ENEL*, *Recueil de la Cour de justice des Communautés européennes*, Luxembourg, Curia, 1964, p. 1141.

71 Paolo Gori, 'La preminenza del diritto delle Comunità europee sul diritto interno degli Stati membri', *Giurisprudenza italiana*, 1964, pp. 1071–86.

Assembly of the Council of Europe between 1949 and 1959. On 11 August 1964, he expressed his deep concerns about the Italian Constitutional Court's *Costa* decision in a question addressed to the Commission. The question initiated an exchange between the Parliament and the Commission that ended with Fernand Dehousse writing a report on the matter in the name of the Legal Committee of the Parliament he was presiding over at the time. Dehousse's report on the 'supremacy of EC law' (15 March 1965) was largely based on *Van Gend en Loos* and *Costa* v. *ENEL* of which he quoted and paraphrased many extracts. Prepared in close collaboration with the Legal Service of the Commission,[72] the report was meant to be 'a cry of alarm'. Forging close links between the highly doctrinal questions (for example, dualist v. monist reading of the relationship between national and international law) and the very survival of European integration, it foresaw that 'legal chaos'[73] would ensue if the dualist perspective heralded by the Italian Constitutional Court prevailed.

A couple of weeks later, on 8–10 April 1965, the locus of mobilization moved to an academic setting. The conference on the relationship between EC law and national law organized by the College of Europe in Bruges in April 1965 brought together a very diverse set of people. Among the two hundred participants, one can find a member of the European Commission (Jean Rey), two directors of the Legal Service (Michel Gaudet and Theodor Vogelaar), four members or former members of the ECJ (Nicola Catalano, Maurice Lagrange, Riccardo Monaco and Joseph Gand), a number of jurisconsults of national diplomacies (Ulrich Everling and Pierre Pescatore), young professor-lawyers (Walter van Gerven and Michel Waelbroeck), etc. To put it in the terms of a participant, there was a diverse 'group of EC law specialists, some being actual "Founding fathers" of the EC, others being former or current members of the Court of Justice, high civil servants of the EC or university professors ... [embodying] the wheeling flank of the army of European jurists'.[74] However, beyond the diversity of the professional positions of the participants, one could see a striking convergence that another observer, the young Jean-Victor Louis, described in the following

[72] Its director Michel Gaudet was heard on 18 February 1965 by the Legal Committee, and a member of its staff was 'lent' for the purpose of the report to the European Parliament.

[73] Fernand Dehousse, *Rapport fait au nom de la commission juridique sur la primauté du droit communautaire*, Parlement européen, documents de séances, 1965, p. 14.

[74] Alphone de Vreese, in Symposium 'Droit communautaire et droit national', *Cahiers de Bruges*, 14, 1965, pp. 399–400.

terms: '[W]hereas the Court of Justice's decision of 5 February 1963 in the case *Van Gend & Loos* has been at the heart of the debates in The Hague in October 1963, this time the decision of 15 July 1964 in the case *Costa* v. *ENEL*, where the Court clearly affirmed the primacy of EC law in a well-founded manner, served as a background to the debates [in Bruges]. Nobody in The Hague challenged the liberal orientation of the decision *Van Gend & Loos*, everybody in Bruges recognized the necessary primacy of EC law'.[75]

Two months later, the debate was brought to the European Parliament through the discussion over the Dehousse report. In the meantime, however, the political context had changed dramatically. The disagreements over the reform of EC institutions had now turned into an overt intergovernmental crisis that would lead to the begining of the 'empty chair' period starting with the 28–30 June 1965 Council of Ministers. In this context, the fact that the parliamentary discussion displayed a large consensus between MEPs and the presidents of the three Executives, all of them 'fully agreeing with the 15 July 1964 ECJ decision'[76] and stressing the importance of *judicial* integration, is of importance. Walter Hallstein had made things even clearer in a booklet published in 1964 by the Office for Official Publications of the European Communities as a follow-up to his June speech to the European Parliament on this subject. The president of the EEC Commission defined Europe as a 'European Community of law'[77] – an expression he had already used in 1962 but in rather vague terms.[78] By that, he meant to describe (on the basis of the two judicial decisions) the quasi-constitutional structure of the European Communities in which individuals and EC institutions have a direct relationship through law and beyond State control. Quite strikingly, in packaging altogether the direct effect ('the individual is a legal subject . . . [who] as a citizen and a subject of the EC is subjected to legal orders in the same way as in the constitutional system of states of federal nature') and the supremacy (if there were no supremacy, the very 'functioning of the EC would be put into question'), he connected them to article 177 as 'the preliminary rulings of the Court of Justice

[75] Jean-Victor Louis, 'Compte-rendu', *Cahiers du droit européen*, 1, 1965, pp. 74–5.

[76] Débats du Parlement européen, Séance des 16–17 juin 1965, 1965, pp. 221–3. See also the resolution: 'Résolution du 22 octobre 1965', Assemblée parlementaire commune, 1966.

[77] Walter Hallstein, 'La Communauté européenne, nouvel ordre juridique', in *Les documents de la Communauté européenne*, 27, 1964, p. 5.

[78] Matthias Schonwald, 'Walter Hallstein et les institutions des Communautés européennes', in Marie-Thérèse Bitsch (ed.), *Le couple franco-allemand et les institutions européennes*, Brussels, Bruylant, 2001, pp. 151–68.

guarantees a uniform interpretation of EC law which is faithful to the finality of the Treaty'.[79] Quoting *Van Gend en Loos* and *Costa* v. *ENEL* no less than six times (he actually only referred to these two decisions), literally paraphrasing some of their formulae in several occasions,[80] he turned this 'direct effect/supremacy' into the very bedrock of the European Communities. What emerges here is a sort of 'magic triangle' connecting direct effect, supremacy and preliminary ruling: taken individually, any of these notions is merely a legal principle or procedure utterly incapable of founding a political order on its own. Taken together, their effects now appear to bring into being a dynamic of circular reinforcement: no effective European Treaties without the supremacy of EC law over the law of Member States; no direct effect without preliminary ruling ensuring the uniform implementation of EC law throughout the Community; and, to the loop, no preliminary references to the ECJ without the recognition of the possibility for individuals to claim justiciability in EC law through the direct effect/supremacy doctrine. It seems now that the whole Community would fall apart, were one of these pillars to be compromised or put in question. Structured as a unique legal matrix, this 'magic triangle' provides a unique cognitive framework for all European Treaties regardless of their different institutional and political setups, elevating law as the unifying glue of Europe.

In turn, probably comforted by the strong endorsement it had received on a variety of academic and political fronts, the ECJ itself became more and more assertive in promoting and diffusing the emerging '*Van Gend en Loos* doctrine'. Among these far-reaching and bold affirmations of the former is the report of ECJ president Andreas Donner in the *Poudres de lait* decision on 13 November 1964 that Pierre Pescatore considers to have 'sealed the finally established unanimity'[81] among ECJ judges, less than three years after the Court had split four against three on *Van Gend en Loos*.[82] The accession of Robert Lecourt, one of the strongest advocates of an extensive reading of *Van Gend en Loos*, appointed to the Court's presidency in 1967 further consolidated the 'holistic' reading of the European

79 Walter Hallstein, 'La Communauté européenne, nouvel ordre juridique', in *Les documents de la Communauté européenne*, 27, 1964, pp. 8–10.

80 *Ibid.*, pp. 10–11.

81 Pierre Pescatore, 'Robert Lecourt (1908–2004)', *Revue trimestrielle de droit européen*, 3, July September 2005, p. 990, p. 995.

82 William Phelan, 'Supremacy, Direct Effect and Dairy Products in the Early History of European Law', EUI Working Paper, 2014/11.

Treaties, Communities, institutions and policies as constitutive of one coherent, unified, and hierarchized legal order.

Europe's integration programme

It is probably not necessary to push further this fine-grained analysis of the debates over the legal interpretation of the EC Treaties. Within three years, and in a context of great political turmoil in Brussels, a genuine corpus of legal–political doctrine had emerged and become consolidated that was now considered as the very foundation of the European Communities themselves. As the Brussels' crisis affected many of the initial political hopes that had been put in the EC, this doctrine offered an opportunity for jurists of various sorts (politicians of the law, legal advisers to EC institutions, business lawyers, ECJ judges, law professors, etc.) to reformulate their variegated pan-European ambitions into one *integration programme*, thereby defining a common institutional terrain for EC institutions.

A new common sense

What is most striking in this progressive coalescence of Europe's integration programme is indeed how convergent it has been across fields and institutions. This is not to say there were no dissenting opinions in Europe. It is well known that, at the national level, many Courts, academics, politicians and other groups did not support a '*Van Gend en Loos* doctrine'.[83] However, at the EC level, a consensus quickly emerged. From Lecourt to Hallstein and Gaudet to Dehousse, from legal academia to political institutions, from the Court to the Commission or the Parliament, the frames of understanding EC Treaties aligned swiftly. Such a redefinition of Europe as a 'Community of law' was so consensual that there was confusion as to which institution was to be recognized as the actual 'author' of such a doctrine. Those who had a more predominantly political role, such as the European commissioner Emmanuel Sassen, started referring to 'the Court's support [in the Costa decision of July 1964] to the Commission's position [expressed in June 1964 by Hallstein before the European Parliament]'. Others, mostly legal academics, would rather draw attention to the creative role of the Court's jurisprudence

[83] Some cases are thoroughly documented in Karen Alter, *Establishing the Supremacy of European Law: The Making of an International Rule of Law in Europe*, Oxford, Oxford University Press, 2001.

and the successive rallying of political institutions to it. The similarity of the arguments of the three European institutions was actually striking enough for the president of the EEC Commission to feel the need to underline that 'there is no conspiracy, but common agreement of freely convinced institutions which are conscious of their responsibility in European affairs'.[84] Equally, commissioner Sassen had to emphasize that 'this concordance is absolutely no conspiracy whatever'.[85]

The synchronization of timelines around the judicial saga of *Costa* and the alignment of the EC institutions' agenda hints again at the position of the transnational field of European law as an interstitial field standing at the crossroads of Europe's many integration paths. Key figures of the EC polity such as Fernand Dehousse (head of the Parliament's Legal Committee and EC law professor), Robert Lecourt (president of the ECJ and a member of the *Nouvelles equipes internationales*, the Christian-democrats' European association), Walter Hallstein (head of the Commission and former international law professor) or Michel Gaudet (*conseiller d'État* and director of the Commission's legal service) were all multi-positioned actors moving across the various social universes that made up Europe at the time. Their multifaceted activities in the various legal, academic, political or administrative sites of the EC polity were integral in producing common cognitive and normative frameworks of European legal integration. As a matter of fact, in managing their personal 'holdings' of memberships and networks, they generated diffuse and almost unnoticed forms of coordination of their various points of view. While one would call for academics to take political imperatives into account, another would simultaneously call for political leaders to draw on the lessons of academic work. As they moved from one position to another, they acted as the 'special functionaries coordinating the game'[86] Norbert Elias referred to in his sociology of complex social settings. Progressively, this convergence of the timing and agendas of EC-implicated actors was authenticated and codified under various forms, such as the jurisprudence of the Court, FIDE proceedings, the Commission's policies or the Parliament's resolutions, etc. On the whole then, this doctrine had no specific author but can be said to have been designed concurrently and collectively through the interplay of reciprocal references and quotations in judicial decisions, hearings and memos

[84] Walter Hallstein, in 'Débats. Compte rendu in extenso des séances', Session 1964–5, 17 June 1965, European Parliament, 1965, p. 218.

[85] Walter Sassen, in *ibid.*, p. 223.

[86] Norbert Elias, *What Is Sociology?*, London, Hutchinson, 1978, p. 86.

as well as in academic conferences and parliamentary debates. Although there was no particular conductor, each of these actors contributed in its own way to further this new definition of Europe and the law.

The emerging theory of Europe took account of the fact that, in the context of intergovernmental rivalries in Brussels, ECJ case law was the most tangible and lasting form of European integration, for it departed from the shaky foundations provided by inter-State agreements. Notably, because it relied on a legal procedure (preliminary rulings) that depended neither on the goodwill of the Member States, nor on that of the Commission, the ECJ appeared to be available to all Euro-concerned interests (be they expressed by individuals, interest groups, companies, etc.). Everyone could take part in the construction of European law through recourse to the ECJ. The fact that the 'empty chair' crisis had not altered the dynamics of intra-European exchanges, which continued to expand swiftly, was considered as a confirmation that the really relevant avenue for integration needed to be a-political.[87] Rapporteur of the *Costa* case within the ECJ, the judge and former prominent French political leader Robert Lecourt, who would be president of the Court from 1967 to 1976, was one of the most committed choirmasters of this renewed understanding of the Court's social and political functions in the integration process. Although there are no accounts of his encounters with the functionalist literature,[88] his 1964 conference before the French section of FIDE, entitled 'The Role of Law in Unifying Europe', is arguably the first systematic conceptualization of the Court's contribution to the dynamics of what would today be referred to as 'integration-through-law'. In this sense, the '*Van Gend en Loos* doctrine' is not just a legal doctrine of Europe. More widely, it is the key to the process of social and economic integration between six countries – a process that, eventually, political leaders will have to endorse:

> The legal method to unify Europe lies in the fact that EC law has the effect of multiplying relations, associations, transactions beyond borders, as well as of triggering narrow interrelations of activities, interests, and human relationships. The resulting interpenetration of populations cements *in concreto* a lively Europe thereby irreversible. Thereby, this process will necessarily call for a political coronation required by the very needs of the population ruled by this unique body of law'.[89]

[87] Joseph Kaiser, 'Das Europarecht in der Krise der Gemeinschaften', *Europarecht*, 1, 1966, pp. 4–24.

[88] It must be noted that the first book engaging in a reflection on the role of the European Court in a functionalist perspective came later: S. Scheingold, *The Rule of Law in European Integration*, New Haven, CT, Yale University Press, 1965.

[89] Robert Lecourt, 'Le rôle du droit dans l'unification européenne', *Bulletin de l'Association des juristes européens*, 17–18, 1964, pp. 5–23, p. 22.

Table 2 *Contending doctrines in Europe and law in the early 1960s*

	International harmonization	Judicial functionalism ('*Van Gend en Loos–Costa* doctrine')	European citizenship
Central EC actor	Commission and Council of Ministers	European Court of Justice	Individuals/civil society
Dominant figure of lawyer	Jurisconsulte	Judge	Cause-lawyer
Fuel of integration	Political and administrative initiative	Economic and social groups' interests	Individual rights
Channel	EC policies	Preliminary ruling procedure (article 177)	Direct judicial action
Role of the ECJ	Incidental	Regulatory	Instrumental
Type of legal integration	Europeanization-through-codification	Europeanization-through-case law	Europeanization-through-legal-activism

Note: These models are ideal-types. Thereby, they do not intend to *mirror* reality and they cannot be observed *as such* in social life. Rather, this table aims at providing a stylization of specific cleavages over the possible political functions given to law and lawyers in the integration process in the early years of European integration. The relevance and respective weight of these three models then have to be measured empirically.

Potentially mobilized by Europe's civil society, the ECJ was soon pictured as the new cornerstone of economic, social and eventually political integration. As the natural receptacle of this 'real' Europe, the ECJ therefore appeared to be in a privileged position when it came to engaging in the highly political task of regulating interests and groups. In this vein, functionalism was no longer related to economics but to law – essentially private law that was endowed with a particular ability to build Europe. Judicial functionalism therefore emerged as a new way of conceiving the articulation between Europe and the law,[90] thereby marginalizing two other possible paths for legal integration that would be left off, or at least played down in the course of history: the 'international harmonization' one for which the Member States–Commission

[90] On this, see also the interesting developments by Peter Lindseth, *Power and Legitimacy: Reconciling Europe and the Nation-State*, Oxford, Oxford University Press, 2011.

duet would monitor an overall programme of harmonization of national legislations through political decision-making, and the 'European citizenship', heralded by Stendardi and Costa, which gave individuals (and civil society in general) the lead through extensive *direct* petitioning before the ECJ. Instead, it is the ECJ which is elevated to the role of mediator and moderator between the claims of individuals (considered to be potentially 'excessive' and thereby disruptive of the fragile diplomatic agreement) and inter-States politics (deemed incapable of providing Europe with a lasting integrative momentum). As a result, the ECJ and 'its interlocutors' have the role of a channel, if not the engine, of Europeanization itself. Table 2 sets out these contending doctrines in Europe and law in the early 1960s.

A Community of law

In that it ties together law and politics, the ECJ and European integration, this judicial theory of European integration is more than just an abstract reflection on the future of Europe. The variegated set of its promoters intended it to be performative, thus to effectively redesign the allocation of authority and legitimacy within the EC polity. More particularly, they contributed to elevate legal competence as a necessary precondition for anyone to fully and persuasively participate in EC debates. The fact that Europeanization became seen as a matter of law implied that anyone willing to hold a position of responsibility within the European Communities (be it political, economic, bureaucratic and of course judicial) had to be able to engage in legal discussions. By acknowledging each other as crucial interlocutors beyond the ordinary divisions that still structured the emerging EC polity (national/European; public/private; legal/political), as well as by quoting each other regardless of their different responsibilities, Euro-lawyers of the different breeds (politicians of the law, corporate lawyers, law professors, ECJ judges, the Commission's legal advisers) jointly redefined what it meant and what it required to access and hold various institutional roles within European Communities (commissioners, members of parliament, ECJ Judges, high-ranking officials, but also consultants, etc.), thereby redefining a new 'integration programme' for Europe.

In that respect, it might not be coincidental that it is precisely when the '*Van Gend en Loos–Costa* doctrine' was first discussed in the Parliament (15–16 June 1965) that the requirement for EC elites to possess strong legal credentials became most explicit. Although the Parliament at the time was still weakly institutionalized, the debates generated by the above-mentioned Dehousse report on the issue of supremacy quietly grew into academic exchanges – and accordingly, the Parliament itself turned into an academy of law. The national and political diversity of the thirteen participants in the discussion could not hide the fact that all of them (except one) were, or had been, legal professionals. Written by a renowned academic, the report itself had set the stage for such a 'legal-only' debate. It outlined that 'the science of law and, in particular legal scholarship, play[ed] a decisive role in this framework because it contributes to define and clarify a political situation'.[91] Speaking 'as a lawyer and in the name of the Commission', Hallstein did not go off message either – quite to the contrary. Right from the start, he praised the report for being a 'document of scientific quality'. He also insisted that this 'big political issue' could only 'be answered along legal criteria with the help of a legal methodology and only a solution validated by this method can be the right one'.[92]

Certainly, such a legalistic formulation of the parliamentary debate raised some criticisms. Emmanuel Sassen, a member of the Euratom Commission and himself a doctor of law, expressed some irony about 'the professor's [Hallstein] real law course', and more seriously then remarked that 'neither the Euratom Commission, nor its sister institutions are academies of law'. Similarly, Italian MEP Edoardo Battaglia, himself a former judge and trial lawyer, tried to restore a *political* order by recalling that 'this Assembly is not a scientific academy of public law specialists. We are in a Parliamentary assembly and we are politicians'.[93] However, he also ended up referring to the various law professors and legal doctrines at stake. And, in fact, the metamorphosis of the Parliament into an academy of law seemed to have been conspicuous enough during that particular session that the chairman felt obliged to adjourn it when it occurred to him that there were not enough lawyers present in order to keep a good debate going: '[L]ook around you, it will convince you that, in order to be able to discuss a matter of such importance, there should be more lawyers present'.[94] In other words, while stressing the political stakes of the judicial branch, the theory of European integration was at once promoting a specific representation of the EC polity in which legal competence was deemed essential to anyone wishing to exert leadership within that nascent political system.

[91] Fernand Dehousse, *Rapport fait au nom de la commission juridique sur la primauté du droit communautaire*, Parlement européen, documents de séances, 1965, p. 2.

[92] Walter Hallstein, in *ibid.*, pp. 218 and 220.

[93] *Ibid.*, p. 231. [94] *Ibid.*, p. 243.

Simultaneously, but equally importantly, this integration programme was offering the dispersed and variegated set of Euro-jurists that promoted it (judges of the Court, law professors, lawyers, but also many of the MEPs, commissioners, EC civil servants coming from the legal professions) a common place through which they could think and conceive of themselves as one group – that of 'Euro-lawyers' – endowed with specific functions (social, economic and, *in fine*, political integration). Thereby, reframing the role of the ECJ in Europeanization processes also meant for lawyers reframing their own role within the EC polity. While building a legal theory of Europe, the otherwise segmented and often antagonistic ensemble of Euro-lawyers was therefore constituting itself as a specific EC elite. To quote Lecourt, addressing members of FIDE:

> If Law possesses such an ability to approximate – to the point of integrating in one unique body – separate and sometimes adversary nations, if it has the power to mould and fuse them, to animate them with one unique soul, if it is endowed with a unificatory power, then let's rejoice, Gentlemen, that this power has been in great part delegated to you.[95]

In a very characteristic *effet de théorie*, the emergence of the integration-through-law narrative therefore offered Euro-lawyers a unitary understanding of their variegated, and often conflicting, set of experiences and practices as one unique contribution to the grand project of leading European integration. This does not imply that from then onwards Euro-lawyers would tend to agree on issues and would form one collective profession acting in a rational and unitary way. Rather, it means that, as policy instruments, professional identities and institutional functionalities were now defined in line with and on the basis of that '*Van Gend en Loos–Costa* theory of EC law', the latter served as a blueprint for action, orienting actors' perceptions, anticipations and (competing) strategies *vis-à-vis* the European Communities.

From this perspective, Europe's new integration programme is far from being just an abstract set of principles strategically mobilized by self-interested actors (companies, States, EU institutions, interest groups, associations, etc.), as it is too often conceived of in political science. It is the bearer of specific representations of the European Union, of its specific professional canons and political models. In other words, what is usually considered as the mere surface of the social processes that shape EU government is in fact one of the very terrains on which it is built.

[95] R. Lecourt, 'Le rôle du droit dans l'unification européenne', *Bulletin de l'Association des juristes européens*, 17–18, 1964, pp. 5–23, p. 22.

Part II

Jurisprudence, code, constitution: Europe's building blocks in the making

Let us not, however, delude ourselves on the 'integration programme': EU actors know very well that Europe is not 'driven' by law itself, and that the former exerts its power by virtue of the actors and the contexts in which it is used. They know well that the inter-institutional struggles are not primarily determined by legal stakes. They know well that the daily functioning of the EU polity can be simply deduced from the underlying logic of the European Treaties as 'codified' in the 'integration programme'. All the more so that this programme does not have the consistency nor the clarity that many learned interpretations grant it. And EU actors certainly do not equally 'believe' and support a law-centred vision of Europe: while some actors do heartily embrace the constitutional theory of Europe, others simply formally comply with it, or reluctantly cope with it. These forms of partial acceptance or even resistance change as one is more or less distanced from the heart of the daily politics of Brussels. And yet, no matter how individual actors position themselves *vis-à-vis* this 'integration programme', opposing or praising it, there is no denying its perennial existence at the heart of the definition of what Europe is. Even scholars such as Andrew Moravcsik acknowledge the persistence of what he refers to as the 'European constitutional settlement',[1] namely, the lasting constitutional platform on which all enlargements and deepenings of Europe have so far occurred. It all occurs as if this cognitive and normative arrangement was the unescapable template with which Euro-implicated actors were deciphering and assessing, thinking and acting, anticipating and reforming Europe and its reform. The 'logical' implications of the constitutional doctrine can seem so imperious as for the Court to correct the Treaties themselves, where it appears that

[1] Andrew Moravcsik, 'The European Constitutional Settlement', *World Economy*, 31(1), 2008, pp. 158–83.

they do not fully comply with their own underlying rationale. This has famously been the case of the *Les Verts* decision of the ECJ of 23 April 1986 in which the former unilaterally engaged in a 'judicial revision of the Treaties'[2] granting the European Parliament a right of legal action that was absent from the Treaties, by mere virtue of the fact that it logically derived from their constitutional 'logic'.

How can one explain that such a constraining 'integration programme' has had such enduring effects? The enigma is all the more compelling in view of the fact that in the meantime the EC, and later the EU, have been subjected to an intense and almost uninterrupted activity of Treaty revision. A countless number of bilateral meetings, European Councils, intergovernmental conferences, and European Conventions have taken place. As a result, States, political leaders, and diplomats have had a large number of opportunities to reorient and reboot the very software of the EU polity, thereby dispossessing the integration programme's support groups of their jurisdiction over Europe's normative and cognitive grammar. From the 1966 'Luxembourg compromise' up until the 2007 Lisbon Treaty, Member States' representatives (most of them, at least) have repeatedly tried to resist or curb the full recognition of this 'integration programme' within the black-letter of the European Treaties;[3] yet, none has managed to alter or reorient the general understanding of what the Treaties are about.

Neo-institutionalist theories may seem most adequate to account for such a persistence as they point at social mechanisms of *lock-in* and self-reinforcing feedbacks that prompt a path dependency. And though indeed it may be true that treaty reformers as well as lawyers value references to previously established legal and institutional solutions and tend to frame their own proposals within the boundaries of precedents, it is not enough of an explanation when it comes to account for *how* such persistence was made possible. A constraining institutional arrangement such as the 'integration programme' does not hold by itself, nor has it a life of its own, unless its underlying creeds and credos are perpetuated and revitalized through continuous social and political *mobilizations*. By insisting essentially on the *endogenous*

[2] Jean-Paul Jacqué, 'Note sous Les Verts. Affaire 294/83', *Revue trimestrielle de droit européen*, 1986, p. 503.

[3] See for example the blocks on the various attempts made to include the 'supremacy' principle within the European Treaties, and, in particular, the recent move from the initial inclusion of the supremacy principle in the treaty establishing a European Constitution to become a mere declaration in a protocol to the Lisbon Treaty.

dynamics of EU judicial decision-making, this neo-institutionalist account therefore over-estimates the inherent stability of the 'integration programme'. I argue in this second part of the book that, rather than self-perpetuation, the persistence of the 'DOS and Windows of the European Community'[4] is better explained in terms of *maintenance strategies* engaged by its various support groups. Over the years, they have framed and reframed its form and implications, carving out new cognitive and normative narratives, agendas and instruments in light of the changing contexts and opportunities. Interestingly, these maintenance strategies are not built erratically: they tend to be moulded along the templates that have historically been the most legitimate legal instruments of States ever since the rebirth of legal science in twelfth-century Bologna:[5] the jurisprudence, the code and the constitution. This classic triptych of law's legitimacy in modern polities has become the focal point for a variety of strategies aiming at the institutionalization of the 'integration programme' at the core of the EU polity. The first challenge to the persistence of this constitutional doctrine lies in the generational change and the ever-growing heterogeneity of the composition of the ECJ: Chapter 4, the first chapter in this part, analyzes the means through which the *Van Gend en Loos* decision is consolidated into a limited set of abstract principles at the core of emerging ECJ 'jurisprudence'. Similarly, the emergence of the so-called *acquis communautaire* is not the natural outcome of a spontaneous process of legal aggregation; rather, Chapter 5, the second chapter of this part, shows how it has been produced in the context of the enlargement to the United Kingdom, through a variety of codification instruments (legal databases, judicial compendia, policy indicators, etc.) that aimed at securing EU law as an objective and computable 'body of law' valid *erga omnes*. Last but not least, the European Constitution project that we consider in Chapter 6, the third chapter of this part, has been shaped in the context of an increasing crumbling of Europe's institutional structure in the post-Maastricht period, and put forward by different professional groups and institutions in order to circumvent the

[4] Joseph Weiler, 'The Reformation of European Constitutionalism', *Journal of Common Market Studies*, 37(1), 1997, p. 97.

[5] Ernst Kantorowicz, 'Kinship Under the Impact of Scientific Jurisprudence', in M. Clagett, G. Post and R. Reynolds (eds.), *Twelfth-Century Europe and the Foundation of Modern Society*, Madison, WI, University of Wisconsin Press, 1961, pp. 89–111; and Max Weber, *On Law in Economy and Society*, Cambridge, MA, Harvard University Press, 1954.

increasingly numerous attempts by Member States to secure opt-outs and flexible arrangements in the EU polity. In other words, what we follow is the multifaceted and contested process of objectivization and naturalization of this 'integration programme' at the core of EU standard operating procedures.

4 'Jurisprudence': transnational esprit de corps and the Court's perpetual momentum

There is no possible doubt nowadays about the fact that the ECJ has a 'jurisprudence'. Built along a limited set of founding principles drawn from early decisions, the ECJ jurisprudence has progressively extended and deepened its scope, spilling over to a large variety of domains. From competition policies to the Internal Market, from the environment to non-discrimination or inter-institutional litigation, there are no policy domains that have not been produced or co-produced by it.[1] Although the Member States have repeatedly refused to authenticate in the European Treaties some of its most important principles starting with the 'direct effect' and 'supremacy',[2] its jurisprudence has provided some of the essential bricks for Europe's daily proceedings, from general definitional issues ('Union of law', 'institutional balance') to sector-specific issues (in domains such as free movement or antitrust). Casebooks and textbooks have continuously heralded the success story of this 'jurisprudence' which seems to have remained the last unalterable reference point in the context of an ever-changing European Union.[3] There is more. By all accounts,[4] the steering potential of the early judgments actually seems still to be actively operating. Recent examples have

[1] See for example Rachel Cichowski, *The European Court and Civil Society*, Cambridge, Cambridge University Press, 2007.

[2] The story repeated itself once again when the 'supremacy' principle – which had been expressly included in the treaty establishing a European Constitution – was removed therefrom and relegated to a Protocol to the Lisbon Treaty.

[3] To a point that the European Court of Justice is regarded as a model for the new generation of international courts that has emerged since 2000: see Karen Alter, 'The Global Spread of European-Style International Courts', *West European Politics*, 35(1), 2012, pp. 135–54.

[4] See most recently Bruno de Witte, Elise Muir and Mark Dawson (eds.), *Judicial Activism at the European Court of Justice*, Cheltenham, Edward Elgar Publishing, 2013; and the special issue entitled 'Perpetual Momentum? Reconsidering the Power of the European Court of Justice', *Journal of European Public Policy*, 19(1), 2012.

confirmed that, despite the various waves of enlargement that have affected the Court's organization and composition, the ECJ continues to defend and expand the scope of the fundamental principles of its jurisprudence, pushing its constitutional doctrine further in a number of ground-breaking decisions – from *Kadi* to *Laval* and *Viking*.[5]

And yet, while the ECJ has firmly maintained the essential principles of its jurisprudence over the past five decades, everything has changed. Not only has the European Union dramatically expanded in geographical reach and policy scope in the meantime, but the Court itself has undergone stringent transformations throughout the eight reform treaties that have marked its existence to the six waves of enlargement, including the recent doubling of the Court's membership within a span of just three years (2004–7). How is it then that a Court whose jurisdictions (from one to three tribunals), judges (from seven to sixty-three), nationalities (from six to twenty-eight), and competences (from coal and steel to an almost general competence) have evolved in such a dramatic manner can actually maintain its jurisprudence so constantly over time? Suffice it to consider the increasing turnover: although only two judges were leaving the ECJ every three years during the 1950s, 1960s and 1970s, the average rate of departure rose to two per year in the 1980s and 1990s, and to more than three per year in the past decade. Such instability was made even more obvious by the fact that the group of *référendaires*, until then regarded as the permanent figures of the institution, not only grew in number to more than 200 members,[6] but also lost their stability as their time in office was drastically reduced to five years on average in the late 1990s.[7]

What is it then that makes the Court's jurisprudence so consistent over time when it is grounded on such shaky foundations? The enigma is all the more salient in view of the fact that the Court lacks a supranational judicial profession from which to recruit new members socialized to its core legal principles. Strangely enough, such a research puzzle has essentially remained unaddressed: the neo-rationalists and neo-institutionalists that have dominated the study of the ECJ in the

[5] Among the recent examples of such a continuity, see the ECJ's much debated *Kadi* decision that was considered as 'a direct, if late, offspring of the *Van Gend en Loos* and *Costa* v. *ENEL* jurisprudence': A. Gattini, 'Joined Cases Yassin Abdullah Kadi et al. v. Council and Commission, 3 September 2008', *Common Market Law Review*, 46(1), 2009, p. 224.

[6] Roger Grass, 'Les ressources humaines à la Cour de justice des Communautés européennes', in *Mélanges en l'honneur de Philippe Léger*, Paris, Pedone, 2006, p. 76.

[7] Sally Kenney, 'Beyond Principals and Agents: Seeing Courts as Organizations by Comparing Référendaires at the European Court of Justice and Law Clerks at the US Supreme Court', *Comparative Political Studies*, 33(5), 2000, pp. 593–662.

realm of political science have, so far, taken 'the Court' as their basic unit of analysis without questioning its very existence as one cohesive entity.[8] Although they may disagree about whether the ECJ is an agent of the Member States or a more independent and strategic actor, they assume the existence of *a* Court, analyzed in an anthropomorphic manner, that is, as a unitary and trans-historical collective with a clear-cut idea of its own interests in the EU polity.[9] More often than not, the fifty-year-long continuity of ECJ constitutional jurisprudence has been taken as a postulate and a point of departure. Yet, there are no accounts as to how such a diverse group of twenty-eight judges from different European countries with distinct legal traditions and professional backgrounds would spontaneously and continuously converge on what a 'rational' judicial decision means for the Court. Truly enough, some legal and political science works have pointed at the particular relevance of path-dependent mechanisms in the realm of EU judicial decision-making. It is well known that judges, in both civil law and in common law systems, value references to previously established legal principles, and tend to frame their own judgments within the boundaries of precedents (be they labelled *stare decisis* or *jurisprudence constante*, depending on the specifics of one's national legal culture). Alec Stone has authored interesting publications on the development of precedent-based practices in the case of the ECJ, with *Van Gend en Loos* (1963) standing out as the critical juncture, and the EU litigation arena being the site of a long-term self-reinforcing process.[10] Recently, legal scholars have pointed at the existence of a 'judicial style' specific to the ECJ when it comes to framing legal suits authoritatively:[11] Euro-lawyers need to draw from a limited set of previously established legal sentences that form the commonly accepted bricks of EU law reasoning. However, the fact that EC lawyers do not work in an unpredictable and chaotic manner is not enough of an explanation when it comes to understanding why

[8] For a more detailed discussion of the literature in this regard, see Antoine Vauchez, 'Keeping the Dream Alive: The European Court of Justice and the Transnational Fabric of Integrationnist Jurisprudence', *European Political Science Review*, 4(1), 2012, pp. 51–71.

[9] For an interesting critique of this underlying rationalism, see Andreas Grimmel, *Judicial Interpretation or Judicial Activism? The Legacy of Rationalism in the Studies of the European Court of Justice*, Center for European Studies Working Papers Series, Harvard University, No. 176, 2010.

[10] Alec Stone, *The Judicial Construction of Europe*, Oxford, Oxford University Press, 2004, pp. 30–41.

[11] Loïc Azoulai, 'La fabrication de la jurisprudence communautaire', in P. Mbongo and A. Vauchez (eds.), *Dans la fabrique du droit européen*, Brussels, Bruylant, 2009, pp. 153–70.

and how 'the Court' maintains and repeatedly revives its pan-European agenda in the context of so many internal and external changes. Legal principles do not hold by themselves unless their underlying creeds and credos are perpetuated and revitalized through continuous social and political mobilizations.

To answer the enigma of ECJ 'perpetual momentum',[12] it is first necessary to change our conception of what 'jurisprudence' means and entails. Rather than just an abstract set of free-floating and disembodied legal principles, it is suggested that we consider 'jurisprudence' as a cognitive frame on which basis a constellation of actors have grounded their specific identity. As shown in the previous chapter, *Van Gend en Loos* is not just a famous ECJ judgment opening the way to a broad stream of case law. Its building into the core of the EC polity has helped to coalesce a configuration of legal and non-legal support groups around a new institutional identity for the ECJ defined from then onwards as a cardinal institution of the EU polity. The judicial revolution of the mid-1960s landmark decisions is tightly connected to the formation in Luxembourg of a small, stable and cohesive EU judicial world composed of a variety of legal professionals (judges, *référendaires*, lawyers, law professors, etc.) committed to the defence of a constitutional reading of the EU Treaties. What is today retrospectively referred to as the 'golden age' of the Court ended, however, with the departure of a small group of judges and *référendaires* (described at the time by the Court's president, Robert Lecourt, as a 'judicial battalion') who were closely linked with the adoption and the consolidation of the '*Van Gend en Loos–Costa* doctrine'. Accounting for the perennial development of this doctrine therefore requires an understanding of how this initial constellation of actors was maintained and survived after the disappearance of its initial entrepreneurs. The remainder of the chapter is organized in the following way. First, I analyze the development of commemorations from the 1970s onwards as a collective *strategy* from the most integrated judges of the ECJ, thereby reacting to the progressive dismantling of the internal cohesion and external 'permissive consensus' on which the Court had grounded its initial expansion. The next chapter depicts how *Festschriften*, eulogies and jubilees have been instrumental to perpetuating the Court's 'tradition', covering its core legal principles, its political functions, and its more authoritative representatives.

[12] Dan Kelemen and Susanne Schmidt, 'The European Court of Justice and Legal Integration: Perpetual Momentum', *Journal of European Public Policy*, 19(1), 2012, pp. 1–7.

Perpetuating the founding fathers' spirit

The perpetuation of the principles underlying the '*Van Gend en Loos–Costa* doctrine' soon became a salient stake. From the end of the 1970s, that is, when the early constellation of actors that had coalesced around the doctrine started disaggregating, a series of transformations took place which have gradually chipped away at its internal unity, thereby putting at risk its doctrine. Below, I analyze the commemorative undertaking that was set in motion in this context, and its contribution to the consolidation of the jurisprudential and institutional *acquis*.

A precarious setting

By any standards, the mid-1970s constitutes a turning point for the ECJ. Within the span of three years, four of the judges from the 'revolutionary period' reached the end of their mandate. The departure of both Italian members, judge Riccardo Monaco and advocate general Antonio Trabucchi, was followed by that of both presidents from that period (1958–76), Andreas Donner and Robert Lecourt, who respectively left the Court in 1976 and 1979. By the end of the 1970s, none of the judges and only a handful of the *référendaires* that had taken part in the discussions around the ECJ landmark decisions were still in Luxembourg. Generally speaking, the relative homogeneity and stability that was a feature of the Court for its initial two decades was progressively giving way to a more diverse and changing group. Looked at with hindsight, this opened a phase of continuous changes, both internally and externally. Throughout the five enlargements of the EC and the subsequent steady increase of its caseload, the ECJ experienced a process of internal differentiation which has today transformed the Court into a complex constellation of institutions (the Court of Justice, the Court of First Instance created in 1991 and the Civil Service Tribunal), internal departments, associations (the *Amicale des référendaires et anciens référendaires* created in 1991, the permanent delegation to the ECJ of the Council of European Bar Associations and Law Societies, etc.) and specialized professional groups. The creation of two new tribunals and the successive enlargements, which never challenged the rule of one judge per country, thus took the ECJ from thirteen members (judges and advocate generals) in 1976 to seventy-two today coming from the twenty-eight Member States. This transformation is even more obvious when looking at the number of *référendaires* which has grown from one to two (1979), then three (1985) per judge,[13] to currently make up a group of around 200 members. This category of professionals, which until then had been regarded as the permanent figures of the institution, lost the stability and unity that had characterized it until the end of the 1970s.[14] The drastic reduction of their time in office, down to five years on average in the year 2000, according to the numbers provided by Sally Kenney, has been matched by a pronounced diversification of their profile. In contrast to the first generation, the majority of which had come straight from university, today's *référendaires* come from a wide variety of professions. Indeed, out of the seventy-seven *référendaires* recruited from outside the Court between 1 January 1997 and 19 September 2001, twenty-one came straight from university, seventeen from the bar, thirteen from the judiciary, sixteen from public authorities in the Member States, and ten from other 'institutions'.[15]

This diversification of the ECJ and the now intense mobility of its members have made it more difficult for the Court to exist as a unit. This is further increased by the public exposure that the Court progressively acquired, which has taken it far beyond the semi-public sphere to which it had previously been gravitating. This has put the Court at the centre of a number of controversies of EU politics. Whereas for a long time, the Court's activity was exclusively followed by specialized legal journals (dealing with international or EC law), it is now scrutinized by the whole of the legal doctrine and by professional legal journals. As the object of critical assessment by other strands of legal science, or even assessed by disciplines such as economics[16] or political science,[17] the Court has encountered its first opponents. Here again the mid-1970s probably constitute a turning point. The judicial and academic conference organized by the Court to celebrate twenty-five years of its existence

[13] Sally Kenney, 'Beyond Principals and Agents: Seeing Courts as Organizations by Comparing Référendaires at the European Court of Justice and Law Clerks at the US Supreme Court', *Comparative Political Studies*, 33(5), 2000, pp. 593–662, p. 605.

[14] The change in the status of *référendaires* at the beginning of the 1970s surely constitutes a turning point: the positions were thus 'provided for a duration limited to that of the judge's mandate', with furthermore the position of each *référendaire* being subject to termination with immediate effect.

[15] On this, see Pascal Mbongo and Antoine Vauchez (eds.), *Dans la fabrique du droit européen*, Brussels, Bruylant, 2009.

[16] Anne-Lise Sibony, 'La jurisprudence de la Cour de justice au prisme de la science économique', in Pascal Mbongo and Antoine Vauchez (eds.), *Dans la fabrique du droit européen*, Brussels, Bruylant, 2009.

[17] Lisa Conant, 'Review Article: The Politics of European Legal Integration', *Journal of Common Market Studies*, 45(1), 2007, pp. 45–66.

in 1976 resulted in the Court facing a first barrage of criticism from those who questioned its '*Van Gend en Loos–Costa* doctrine', arguing that the Court had 'severed itself from the real world'.[18] Moreover, the exponential growth of the number of preliminary references brought before the Court by the national courts indicates that a 'dialogue' has thus been engaged with the judicial elites of the different Member States, the contents of which show a number of disagreements interpreted as 'resistance' to the '*Van Gend en Loos–Costa* doctrine'.[19] Finally, the same national authorities which hitherto only paid nominal attention to the ECJ to the point of allowing some of its most spectacular judgments to pass by without much ado,[20] have all – in one form or another – set up specialized services focusing on the case law of the European Communities.[21] Beyond the circle of the legal and judicial professions, the Court has famously become the target of a variety of many political controversies. This is not the place to provide a complete history of the political and governmental campaigns that have been aimed at the Court. However, the bitter attacks by former prime minister Michel Debré in 1979 denouncing the 'legal abnormalities', the 'politicization' and the 'abuse of power' of the Court probably constitute an important step.[22] Hence, the ironic statement delivered later in that same year by the Court's president, Hans Kutscher: '[T]he Court has been astonished to find that it can attain a degree of publicity, hitherto unknown, in a different way, namely as a result of more or less justified attacks on its case law, delivered publicly'.[23] Since then, each government has taken it in turn to challenge the judicial activism of the Court to the extent of

18 C.-J. Hamson, 'Methods of Interpretation: A Critical Assessment of the Results', in Court of Justice of the European Communities, *Judicial and Academic Conference 27–28 September 1976*, Luxembourg, Office des publications officielles des Communautés, 1976.

19 Karen Alter, *Establishing the Supremacy of European Law: The Making of an International Rule of Law in Europe*, Oxford, Oxford University Press, 2001.

20 For an example, see Billy Davis, 'Meek Acceptance? The West German Ministries' Reaction to the Van Gend en Loos and Costa decisions', *Revue d'histoire de l'intégration européenne*, 14(2), 2008, pp. 57–76.

21 Marie-Pierre Granger, 'From the Margins on the European Legal Field: The Governments' Agents and their Influence on the Development of European Union Law', in Antoine Vauchez and Bruno de Witte (eds.), *Lawyering Europe: European Law as a Transnational Social Field*, Oxford, Hart Publishing, 2013.

22 Michel Debré, 'Question au Premier ministre', *Débats parlementaires*, Assemblée nationale, 13 January 1979, pp. 5–6.

23 Hans Kutscher, 'Address Delivered by H. Kutscher, President of the Court, on Judge T. Koopmans' Taking up Office. 29 March 1979' in, *Formal Sittings of the Court of Justice. 1978 and 1979*, Luxembourg, Curia, 1979. p. 33.

threatening, on several occasions, to redefine the Court's powers, in the context of intergovernmental conferences. Even though all these indicators may be of an impressionist nature, they all confirm a widening of the audiences interested in the activity of the Court. As a result of its growing sphere of influence, the Court had become the focal point of a series of sectoral conflicts – in particular a great deal of inter-institutional rivalry – in which its decisions were discussed and scrutinized, thereby putting the Court under public surveillance.

The commemorative undertaking

This new internal and external context in which the Court was operating can also be read in the judges' self-perceived need to codify the judicial *acquis* of the 'revolutionary years' and, relatedly, to centralize the judicial decision-making process of the Court. A variety of studies show that, starting from the early 1980s, and increasingly so after the 2000s, all sorts of 'rationalization' tools have been used in order to define and codify rules for typing, quoting, writing, and, more broadly, arguing within the Court. A whole set of standard operating procedures have been promoted by the Court's most central figures (the president, the registrar, the presidents of chambers, most senior judges, clerks, etc.) in order to face the increase diversity of the Court, in particular in preparation for the periods of enlargement that have raised great fears over the potential weakening of the Court's capacity to maintain both the quality of its decisions and the consistency of its jurisprudence. Such a process of rationalization has gone hand in hand with a progressive centralization of the judge-making power in the hands of few centrally placed judges, from the president to the presidents of the three five-member Chambers and the Grand Chamber.[24] The story of this quest for more coordination and rationalization in the judicial decision-making, from a more interpersonal, decentralized and informal logic to a more bureaucratized, centralized and formal logic through legal databases, judicial compendia and standard operating procedures remains to be written.[25]

Given the difficulties in accessing the internal material of the ECJ, I have chosen to track the Court's maintenance strategies through its

[24] Biliyina Petkova, 'Structural Changes and Decision-Making at the European Court of Justice After the Eastern Enlargement', Paper presented to the European Consortium of Political Research conference in Dublin, 2010 (on file with the author).

[25] See, however, Karen McAuliffe, 'Enlargement at the European Court of Justice: Law, Language and Translation', *European Law Journal*, 14(6), 2008, pp. 806–18.

discursive strategies, that is to say, the set of devices through which the Court narrates itself and aims at securing the continuation of its core legal principles and values. While they may be regarded as essentially formal and ceremonial moments, I suggest that we consider commemorations (tributes, jubilees, *Festschriften*) as one of the rare occasions on which 'the Court', or at least a large part of its members, is publicly brought together. Drawing on the abundant literature on the sociology of rituals,[26] I contend that these commemorative venues are critical for the symbolic maintenance of institutions such as the European courts that are deprived of long-standing historical roots; the eulogizing of the departing judges allows for a codification of the impersonal and ahistorical features of the institution and provide an opportunity to select and authenticate 'founding fathers', institutional leaders and putative heirs faithful to the Court's core principles. For this reason, these celebrations – which could appear as purely idiosyncratic in that they refer to the profile of the addressee, the specifics of a given moment in history, and the singularity of the genre (discourse, written article, short biographical note, etc.) – are integral to the continuation and the transmission of the Court's institutional identity as a whole and its jurisprudence more particularly.

Commemorations are not new to the Court. Ever since the first ECJ judges left the Court in 1958, 'formal sittings' praising the departing judges and welcoming the newcomers have been held, and the related speeches published by the Court's publishing department. Yet, from the mid-1970s onwards, there has been growth in the variety and number of commemorative venues. The gradual reduction in the term of office of the judges and the arrival of new judges following the various enlargements automatically multiply the occurrence of these rites of passage.[27] In addition, the Court also celebrates itself as an institution, by marking its anniversaries, for example the twenty-fifth anniversary in 1976 and the fiftieth anniversary in 2002, not forgetting the thirty-fifth anniversary in 1987 – with as many ceremonies and commemorative editions. Even more striking is the new genre that has gradually established itself,

[26] See for example Marcel Mauss, 'Essai sur la nature et la fonction du sacrifice', *L'année sociologique*, 1, 1897, pp. 35–138; and, on the legal profession, Wendy Espeland and Terry Halliday, *Death Becomes Them: Commemoration, Biography and the Ritual Reconstruction of Professional Identity Among Chicago Lawyers in the Late 19th Century*, Working Paper, Northwestern University, 1994.

[27] The speeches that mark the inauguration and retirement ceremonies as well as tributes in honour of deceased judges are published annually in the Court's report.

namely, that of the judicial *Festschriften* in honour of retiring judges offered by their former colleagues.[28] Some of the professors who were judges at the Court had previously received *Festschriften* in the 1970s (Otto Riese, Riccardo Monaco), but this was usually in recognition of a long *academic* career. The judicial year 1981–2 saw the beginning of what was to become part of the Court's own tradition.[29] Between 1981 and 2008, no less than fifteen judges (i.e. nearly one-quarter of the sixty-one departing judges) were honoured with *Liber Amicorum*, *Studi in onore*, *Mélanges*, *Festschriften* or even *Essays in Honour of* . . . All in all, commemorations are no longer exceptional; from the early 1980s onwards, they constitute an almost uninterrupted internal practice. At first sight, the development of these forms of intervention might seem to be surprising. Indeed, they do not correspond to any of the traditional formats that are valued for their legal or judicial contribution: they are neither procedural acts (such as the Opinion of the advocate general or the *rapport* of the reporting judge), nor are they case-notes. Moreover, they are often published in publishing houses of secondary importance and are thereby destined to remain almost as confidential as the inauguration and retirement speeches. Their growing number from the beginning of the 1980s indicates that there is more to these publications than just a contribution to the legal debate or a formal commemoration of the addressee. I will argue that it is indicative of a strategy to perpetuate the institutional identity of the 'Court of the *Van Gend en Loos–Costa* doctrine'.

What allows us to consider these various forms of commemorations as a part of one collective undertaking lies in the fact that those involved in paying or in receiving these tributes all come from the most integrated

[28] Originally German, *Festschriften* emerged in the second half of the twentieth century as a legal genre of its own in most Western countries, and particularly in the field of international law. The number of *Festschriften* grew rapidly after the 1960s, amounting to 300 volumes in that specific branch of law: see P. Macalister-Smith and J. Schwietzke, 'Festschriften in Public International Law: An Annotated Bibliographical Compilation of Titles (1930–2000/2001)', *Nordic Journal of International Law*, 71(3), 2002, pp. 349–430.

[29] Although the first two recipients of such an honour, Jossé Mertens de Wilmars and Verloren van Themaat, had both taught and actively participated in debates on legal doctrine, neither of them had spent most of their career in academia. The former, Jossé Mertens de Wilmars, had made a name for himself as a lawyer and as a Christian Democrat politician. He had been very active in the European Movement in Belgium before joining the Court for a long period (1967–84) and was president of the Court when his mandate ended. The latter, Verloren van Themaat, had built a reputation as a high-ranking lawyer, first in the German civil service dealing with economic issues, then in the EC civil service where he was the first director of DG Competition, a position he held for nearly twelve years, before working as an academic and then being made a judge at the ECJ.

members of the Court's milieu. First of all, both current and former members of the Court, be they judges or *référendaires*, play a significant role, as they are responsible for over two-thirds of the 406 contributions that are contained in these fifteen volumes. Second, the honours such as the organization, editing and membership of the honorary committee of these *Festschriften* are first and foremost the presidents (or former presidents) of the Court (or of one of its chambers) who are of course elected by their peers and therefore represent an emanation of the Court. Third, the *Festschriften* honour only a selected part of the former judges, i.e. one-quarter of the fifty-two judges who left the Court during the period 1982–2007. Among them are the four presidents of the Court who succeeded one another at the helm between 1980 and 2003, and, in total, a group of judges whose average seniority in Luxembourg (twelve years) is significantly higher than that of their peers. This longevity is illustrated by the Court's former president, Lord Mackenzie Stuart, who 'served with no less than 42 Judges and Advocates General, not to mention three Registrars'.[30] This puts them in a prime position to speak on behalf of the Court. Conversely, through their close connection with the Court, they are also the most exposed to the threats (both genuine and perceived) that affect its perpetuity. Thereby, this commemorative undertaking can be understood as part of a collective effort by a group of centrally placed ECJ judges and Euro-lawyers to maintain the Court's institutional identity in a context where its mission and its *raison d'être* cannot be taken for granted anymore but is at stake in a growing number of political and social conflicts.

The making of jurisprudence: the Court's invented tradition

Interestingly enough, these ritualized celebrations of judges' departure are characterized by a continuous return to the decisions of the Court's 'revolutionary years' (1963–4). While tributes are privileged occasions for the formalization of the ECJ core principles, they are rarely just a simple codification of legal notions taken out of their historical context; most of the time, they are grounded in a particular narrative of the Court's turning points: there are hardly any of these commemorations that do not refer back to the Court's golden age of the early 1960s when

[30] Jack Mackenzie Stuart, 'Address by Lord Mackenzie Stuart, President of the Court, on the Occasion of His Retirement from Office', *Synopsis of the Work of the Court of Justice in 1988 and 1989*, Luxembourg, Curia, 1989, p. 201.

the Court delivered its most renowned decisions: *Van Gend en Loos* and *Costa* v. *ENEL*. For instance, the reference to the sector-specific jurisprudence of the Court in domains such as non-discrimination, competition or State aid ritually involves going back to the period of the seminal cases. Hence the comment by president Iglesias on the occasion of the fiftieth anniversary of the Court: '[I]f there was just one judgment that should be cited on this historic occasion, it would without a shadow of a doubt be the Court's decision of 5 February 1963 in the *Van Gend en Loos* case, which represents the cornerstone of the successive developments of the EC's legal order'.[31] However, this return to the sources is not so much about remembering the past history of the Court but is more about constantly reactivating an 'original prophecy'[32] that provides the Court and its judges with a timeless truth regarding their critical role within the European Union. While all contributors agree that the Court's revolutionary years are now behind it, nevertheless they agree in considering them as a lasting message to which the Court needs constantly to return in order to remain true to itself. Thereby, they are elevated to the status of an 'original prophecy' providing lasting cognitive and normative truths about the nature of Europe's judicial power, its office-holders and its jurisprudence. Hence the comment by former judge Pierre Pescatore: '[A]fter the declarations of principle of the 1960s, which put EC law permanently on the right road, came the period of deep immersion in the practical problems which we, as judges of the second or even third generation, have to master'.[33] By working to bridge the gap between current cases and the constitutional cases of the past, by going over the stages of a jurisprudence that remains in line with its first steps, eulogists continuously design the Court's 'invented tradition',[34] that is, one jurisprudential *acquis*[35] consistent over time and across

[31] Gil Carlos Iglesias, 'Address by Mr Gil Carlos Iglesias, President of the Court of Justice of the European Communities', in *1952–2002: 50th Anniversary of the Court of Justice of the EC. Formal sitting 4 December 2002*, Luxembourg, Curia, 2003, pp. 40–1.

[32] On the fruitfulness of the analogy between religion and the study of professional undertakings, see the seminal piece by Pierre Bourdieu, 'Genèse et structure du champ religieux', *Revue française de sociologie*, 12(2), 1971, pp. 295–334.

[33] Pierre Pescatore, 'Address by Mr Pierre Pescatore Delivered at the Formal Sitting Held on the Occasion of Mr Everling taking Office as Judge', in *Formal Sittings of the Court of Justice 1980–1981*, Luxembourg, Curia, 1980–1981, p. 25.

[34] Eric Hobsbawm and T. Ranger (eds.), *The Invention of Tradition*, Cambridge, Cambridge University Press, 1983.

[35] The index of the judgments cited in certain *Mélanges* allows one to spot the now spontaneous convergence of its contributors – most of them judges or *référendaires* – around such a 'jurisprudential *acquis*'.

policy domains. By exalting the *legal* continuity and the unity of its case law ever since the 1960s, the eulogists help eclipse the many *political* ruptures (enlargements, revisions of the Treaties) and their effects on the course of the ECJ (increase in the number of judges, changes in its competences, etc.). By constantly placing the construction of current judicial strategies as direct descendants of these two judgments, the tributes therefore grant the Court a truly *juridical* foundation that is likely to supersede its political foundations and contributes to distance the Court from the highly controversial and insecure currents of EU politics and join the far more stable and 'apolitical' world of courts and jurisdictions. Such a continuous return to the foundational years of ECJ jurisprudence helps to locate the Court *outside* of the various political and social conflicts that make up the EU polity. Through the building of this 'invented tradition', the many different ECJs (the European Court of Coal and Steel born in 1952 from the Paris Treaty, the Court of Justice of the European Communities born in 1958 from the Rome Treaties, the current Court of Justice of the European Union born in 2009 from the Lisbon Treaty) are indeed superseded by one *unique* 'European Court' featured by an invariant and trans-historical mission started more than sixty years ago 'in service of Europe'.

Yet, there is more to this 'original prophecy' than just the general willingness to ground ECJ case law in a distinctively *legal* tradition. It is integral to the building of a sense of belonging to one unique legal community whose collective task it is to defend and enrich the Court's jurisprudential *acquis*. Under the aegis of praising such common judicial patrimony, *Festschriften* or departure ceremonies symbolically mark the cohesiveness of a group of otherwise diverse perspectives and backgrounds (national and European, public or private, academics and practitioners of EU law). Beyond their many differences, ECJ law clerks, judges, senior members of the national supreme courts, business lawyers and renowned academics are reunited through these ritualized occasions. This bond is intensely praised throughout commemorative discourses. By 'ensuring a link that unites us in the memory and the recognition of our great colleague and unforgettable friend',[36] *Festschriften* and tributes enable the contours of this symbolic EC to be defined and maintained. No doubt, the recurrence of the metaphor of

[36] Gil Iglesias, in Gil Rodrigues Iglesias, Ole Due, Romain Schitgen and Charles Elsen (eds.), *Mélanges en hommage à Fernand Schockweiler*, Baden Baden, Nomos Verlag, 1999, p. 19.

the Court as a 'family' and/or as a 'community' takes here its full meaning in order to reactivate a transversal solidarity beyond the multiplicity of differences, and (potential) conflicts that now afflict the Court as a complex organization now placed under public scrutiny. We are reminded of the 'atmosphere of collegiality, one might even say of brotherhood – since, unfortunately, we [the Court] have only had one sister' and of the congenial rapport between the judges when carrying out their common task'.[37] Reference is thus made to 'our Court of Justice'.[38] We are told about the congenial atmosphere within the cabinet of each of the judges – 'one big happy family'[39] – and their habitual lunchtime parade to the *cantine* of the Court: '[W]e were the first *Cabinet* to *dine en masse*, but the Sevóns and the Ragnemalms followed suit'. Some 'disagreements and highly debated questions'[40] were sometimes on the menu, but these would always take the form of a disinterested legal discussion 'based on the esteem and friendship forged in the joint fulfilment of the task of ensuring the observance by all ... of EC law and thus contributing to the structure of an EC legal order in accordance with the principles of the rule of law'.[41] On the whole, the Court is staged as 'a collegiate body made up not of different nationalities but of individual persons'[42] who 'put aside their national allegiance on accepting appointment to this institution [the Court]'.[43] United despite the diversity of the judicial and extra-judicial functions they carry out in the field of European law (as judges, lawyers, experts, civil servants, professors, etc.), they

37 Ole Due, 'Address by Ole Due, President of the Court, on the Occasion of His Departure', *Report of Proceedings. 1992–1994*, Luxembourg, Curia, 1995, p. 156.

38 Melchior Wathelet, in Ninon Colneric, David Edward, Jean-Pierre Puissochet and Dámaso Ruiz-Jarabo Colomer (eds.), *Une Communauté de droit. Festschrift für Gil Carlos Rodrigues Iglesias*, Berlin, BWV, 2003, p. 443.

39 Mark Hoskins and William Robinson, 'Introduction', in *A True European: Essays for Judge David Edward*, Oxford, Hart Publishing, 2004, p. xv.

40 Fernand Grevisse, in Gil Iglesias, in Gil Rodrigues Iglesias, Ole Due, Romain Schitgen and Charles Elsen (eds.), *Mélanges en hommage à Fernand Schockweiler*, Baden Baden, Nomos Verlag, 1999, p. 151.

41 Jossé Mertens de Wilmars, 'Address by President J. Mertens de Wilmars on the Occasion of the Retirement from Office of Mrs Advocate General Simone Rozès. 13 February 1984', in *Synopsis of the Work of the Court of Justice in Synopsis of the Work of the Court of Justice in 1984 and 1985*, Luxembourg, Curia, 1986, p. 117.

42 Ole Due, 'Address by Ole Due, President of the Court, on the Occasion of the Entry into Office of Judge Paul Kapteyn', in *Synopsis of the Work of the Court of Justice in 1990*, Luxembourg, Curia, 1991, p. 61.

43 Jack Mackenzie Stuart', Address by Lord Mackenzie Stuart, President of the Court, on the Occasion of His Retirement from Office', in *Synopsis of the Work of the Court of Justice in 1988 and 1989*, Luxembourg, Curia, 1989, p. 201.

know and recognize each other as *insiders* of the Court for whom they have worked in the past, present or future. The apparent multiplicity of points of view contributes to overshadowing the reason for the communal presence in the *Festschrift*, namely, their professional experience at the Court and, just as importantly, the subscription to the '*Van Gend en Loos–Costa* doctrine'. Therefore, the *Festschriften* and tributes draw a transnational 'judicial circle', a protected space where symbolic exchanges take place.

Stratifying and profiling the Court

The founding fathers: the Court's spokesmen and putative heirs

Within such a transnational judicial circle drawn throughout the *Festschriften* and tributes, symbolic and material exchanges take place across national, generational and professional lines. What makes them particularly relevant to our purposes is indeed that current, former and – as I argue below – future members of the Court are the central players in these venues. They constitute the editors coordinating the written volume in honour of their former mentor; and the vast majority of the contributors as they are responsible for almost half of the 511 contributions contained in these volumes with 68 (current or former) ECJ *référendaires*, 57 former ECJ judges and 113 current ones. To this number should be added the 21 *future* judges and advocate general s that took part in such venues. Most of the time, a select number of 'founding fathers' whose role in the Court's history is widely recognized are present at the celebration. Their participation (68 out of 511 contributions) is more than just an accolade. Through their presence, they knit an invisible thread that connects all of those, alive or dead, in office or in retirement, who belong to the 'big family' of the Court. Here, the great alumni are not the former university professors, but the survivors of the 'generation of judges of the early 1960s ... which resolutely worked out the basic principles of our case law',[44] and who are thus elevated to the rank of 'founding fathers' of the Court. Among these, Pierre Pescatore is the one most frequently invited to contribute to these collective publications (four out of fourteen). Through his role in the negotiation of the

[44] Hans Kutscher, 'Address Delivered by the President of the Court of Justice, H. Kutscher, at the Formal Sitting of the Court on 29 March 1979 on the Occasion of the Retirement of Judge Andreas M. Donner. 29 March 1979', in *Formal Sittings of the Court of Justice. 1978 and 1979*, Luxembourg, Curia, 1979, p. 17.

Treaties of Rome, his numerous publications and his twenty years spent at the Court, he has become one of the main figures of European law, a genuine trustee of Europe's judicial spirit. His statements show that he embraced this role enthusiastically: '[A]lthough for a long time I remained the youngest of the company [of judges], I am now aware of being in EC terms one of the oldest. Indeed today, I have been connected with the EC for exactly 29 years, of which I have spent 18 years as a judge [at the ECJ]'.[45] Over the years, former judges such as Andreas Donner, Riccardo Monaco and Robert Lecourt have also been repeatedly invited as the institution's 'great old men'. By their presence, they certify the intergenerational continuity of the Court. Most often heading the honorary committee that supervises the *Festschriften*, the current members of the Court are in a position to make sure that the heritage of these 'great alumni' is passed on and that the flame of the '*Van Gend en Loos–Costa* doctrine' is kept alive. As such, they act as the spokesmen of the Court's tradition, as is the case when the then ECJ president, Gil Iglesias, remembered 'our predecessors whose contributions to the Court's rulings remain alive in our daily work'.[46] Indeed, the special value of this continuing historic thread stems from the fact that, by referring back to those who shaped the Court's history, the new generation of judges is able to perpetuate that tradition and thus act as heirs to this heritage. In other words, the various discourses on the Court's institutional identity are also an opportunity to designate those who can usefully invoke this common judicial heritage. By replicating for their own account 'a university tradition that reserves this rare distinction for the elite of its professors',[47] the judges of the Court have to some extent copied this rite of passage where alumni and peers both praise and appropriate this heritage together. Yet, not all current judges or advocates general benefit from such commemorative undertaking: out of the sixty-one leaving the Court between 1981 and 2008, only fifteen (one-quarter) were given such an honour. Those involved in paying these tributes – whether as a speaker during the eulogies (president of the Court or president of

[45] Pierre Pescatore, 'Address by Mr Pierre Pescatore on the Occasion of His Retirement from Office', in *Synopsis of the Work of the Court of Justice in 1984 and 1985*, Luxembourg, Curia, 1986, p. 170.

[46] Gil Carlos Iglesias, 'Address by Mr Gil Carlos Iglesias, President of the Court of Justice of the European Communities', in *1952–2002: 50th Anniversary of the Court of Justice of the EC. Formal sitting 4 December 2002*, Luxembourg, Curia, 2003, p. 44.

[47] Division de la presse et de l'information de la Cour, 'Présentation du Liber amicorum scritti in onore di G. Federico Mancini', Press release No. 17/98, March 1998 (http://curia.europa.eu/fr).

Chambers)[48] or as a member of the *Festschriften* editorial committee – are the most integrated judges: their position within the Court (presidents or former presidents of the Court or of one of its chambers) and their seniority (an average of 12.6 years) are significantly higher than that of their peers. Such longevity, illustrated by the Court's former president, Lord Mackenzie Stuart, who 'served with . . . no less than 42 Judges and Advocates General, not to mention three Registrars',[49] puts them in a prime position to perceive the threats that affect the Court's continuity and to react to them. This rite of remembrance may thus be conceived as a means used by a number of judges to establish the legitimacy of their *temporal* powers (as *de facto* spokesmen of the ECJ) by becoming the interpreters of the *timeless* ideals of the Court as embodied by the Court's 'founding fathers'. The rest of the participants (from the law clerks organizing the *Festschriften* volume to the various authors) in these tributes, those who are neither former nor current judges in Luxembourg are not just merely a public attending this transmission ceremony. Most often, they are fellow countrymen of the addressee, reminding us of the double bonds of each of the Court's judges to transnational and national legal circles of EU law practitioners, a feature more generally characteristic of Euro-lawyers. The participants convened around the addressee thereby form a select group of EU lawyers from the same country sharing a special relationship with the addressee: depending on the latter's original profession, they can be former university colleague (assistant or acquaintance), former law firm partners, or former judicial fellow colleagues, etc. Yet, while they praise the 'Italian', 'German' or 'French' tradition at the Court, these networks of friendships identify a *national* pool of persons who possess the professional and social qualities required from those who aspire to eventually inherit this tradition through an appointment at the ECJ. Among the twenty-two contributors, all of whom were Dutch-speaking (including those of Flemish origin) to the *Festschriften* in honour of Baron Jossé Mertens de Wilmar, there were one former judge, five judges in office and three *référendaires* also in office, and seventeen other participants, including two future judges. Thus, the intergenerational bonds that have been forged through these

[48] The past five presidents – Hans Kutscher, Josse Mertens de Wilmar, John Mackenzie Stuart, Ole Due and Gil Iglesias – who presided over the Court from 1976 to 2003 have been honoured by a *Festschrift* upon their leaving office.

[49] Jack Mackenzie Stuart, 'Address by Lord Mackenzie Stuart, President of the Court, on the Occasion of His Retirement from Office', in *Synopsis of the Work of the Court of Justice in 1988 and 1989*, Luxembourg, Curia, 1989, p. 201.

tributes establish genuine national career paths to the Court. The fellow countrymen and former *référendaires* called upon to celebrate the outgoing judge therefore appear as his natural heirs. Tasked with coordinating the *Festschrift* for their former master, they stand out as future candidates for the office of EC judge as shown by the fact that, from the middle of the 1980s, a growing number of *référendaires* became judges at the Court.[50] Far from being illegitimate, these national breeding grounds, through which European judicial capital is accumulated, are often praised in speeches and in *Festschriften* as a mark of excellence. When addressing the outgoing president Ole Due (a Danish judge), Judge Federico Mancini recalled: 'that wonderful essay on the constitutional consequences of the accession of the Kingdom of Denmark to the European Communities which – a sign of destiny – bears, next to your signature, that of our colleague Claus Gulmann who today (22 years later) succeeds you as judge ... May I add that Mr Gulmann was legal secretary to Max Sørensen, the first Danish judge ... ? Here we have an example of continuity almost virtually unrivalled in the 42 years of the Court's existence'.[51] All in all, *Festschriften* and eulogies sanction both contours of a judicial community and its spokesmen, be they 'founding fathers' authoritatively embodying the Court's 'eternal yesterday', spokesmen tasked with leading the Court's current work, or (putative) 'inheritors', each one of these sub-groups calling the other into existence in a sort of circular affirmation of legitimacy.

Paths of European judicial glory

The continual reference back to the Court's *jurisprudential acquis* also allows us to profile the Court's formal missions and most-suited spokesmen. While the Court's members do not participate in the election of their successors,[52] commemorations offer a rare opportunity to publicly

50 The phenomenon appeared relatively late as it was only in 1988 that a former *référendaire* was for the first time appointed as a judge of the Court. However, it became far more widespread following the creation of the Court of First Instance and of the Civil Service Tribunal. Thus, if one considers the sixty-five judges in office at the Court in 2006, more than one-fifth of them previously exercised the role of *référendaire* at the Court: cf. Roger Grass, 'Les ressources humaines à la Cour de justice des Communautés européennes', in *Mélanges en l'honneur de Philippe Léger*, Paris, Pedone, pp. 69–77.

51 Federico Mancini, 'Address by Federico Mancini, President of Chamber, on the Occasion of the Departure of President Ole Due', in *Synopsis of the Work of the Court of Justice in 1991*, Luxembourg, Curia, 1992, p. 151.

52 The Lisbon Treaty introduced a change in this through the creation of an advisory panel headed by the Court's president, obliging it to 'give an opinion on candidates' suitability to perform the duties of judge or advocate general' (article 255). On the first

set the unofficial parameters of what makes a 'good EC judge'. Indeed, eulogists delineate ideal types of judges particularly capable of embodying the EU's judicial spirit. As they praise the individual, they tend to recall mostly 'individual accomplishments in building a *collective* undertaking',[53] thereby defining specific criteria of professional worth in holding Europe's judicial office. In paying his respects in memory of an advocate general who had died a few days earlier, the president of the Court referred to his Opinions as follows: 'Karl Roemer's monument surrounds us in this building and it lies on our bookshelves'.[54] On each such similar occasion, the person's life is celebrated as if they were the incarnation *par excellence* of the legal person that the Court constitutes as a whole. In this regard, the construction of the biography of the judge – of the character-defining moments, the key stages, etc. – contributes towards the construction of the *office* of judge at the Court.

Most of the time, the spotlight of the commemoration is on the person's role as an accomplished practitioner *and* a renowned academic, as a typical representative of his or her national legal culture *and* as a convinced European. In other words, both the 'internal aspect of his responsibilities' *and* the 'international aspect of his activities'[55] are remembered. Thereby, EU judicial excellence thus consists of the capacity to engage – throughout one's career – in a balancing act between an anchorage in one's national legal culture as the basis of the 'representativeness' of the judge within the EC field together with European (or even international) experience and goodwill. In other words, the Court's judges do not seek to derive legitimacy only from their independence from the groups (EU institutions, Member States) that they are meant to judge; indeed they seek to draw in equal measure upon their attributes as renowned legal scholars and experienced practitioners. This capacity

recruitments made through this procedure, see Tomas Dumbrovsky, Bilyana Petkova and Marijn van der Sluis, 'Judicial Appointments: The Article 255 TFEU Advisory Panel and Selection Procedures Among Member States', *Common Market Law Review*, 51, 2014, pp. 450–82.

[53] Gil Carlos Iglesias, 'Address by Mr Gil Carlos Iglesias, President of the Court of Justice of the European Communities', in *1952–2002: 50th Anniversary of the Court of Justice of the EC. Formal sitting 4 December 2002*, Luxembourg, Curia, 2003, p. 44.

[54] Jack Mackenzie Stuart, 'Address in Commemoration of Karl Roemer, a Former Member of the Court, Delivered by Lord Mackenzie Stuart, President of the Court. 5 February 1985', in *Synopsis of the Work of the Court of Justice in 1984 and 1985*, Luxembourg, Curia, 1986, p. 161.

[55] Gil Iglesias, in Gil Rodrigues Iglesias, Ole Due, Romain Schitgen and Charles Elsen (eds.), *Mélanges en hommage à Fernand Schockweiler*, Baden Baden, Nomos Verlag, 1999, p. 19, p. 17.

to combine a variety of experiences is repeatedly underlined: 'Nor at that time of fruitful academic work did [the former judge] stand aloof from the world of practical law';[56] 'it is scarcely possible to imagine a more valuable addition to the Court in the task entrusted to it of declaring the law than this rare blend of experience in an official capacity, legal learning, insight and belief in the great venture which has now united our States and peoples for a generation'.[57] It is this 'wealth of experience [that] will enable [the appointed judge] to discharge to the full the duties of office',[58] over and above the proof of their independence from those who are the potential subjects of the Court's rulings. It all occurs as if the fact of having successively represented directly each of the EC-implicated actors present would give the judge full legitimacy to rule on the disputes among them. In this context, the key factor is reflected in the comment by the German judge Ulrich Everling with regard to his own career: 'my work always lay on the dividing line between the EU and the Member States. In Brussels, I represented German interests and in Bonn I represented EC interests'.[59] Hence, the 'good EU judge' is neither the one who declares his pan-European beliefs – the reference to European militancy, a rare thing, disappears almost entirely during the 1990s – nor is it the one who demonstrates his independence from the EU political and social games; instead, it is the one who has managed to serve equally all the interests that are present in the EU polity while only ever serving the law. This model of excellence was emphasized by advocate general Van Gerven when he retired from the Court: '[F]or a jurist who has dedicated his life to the study and the practice of law, in particular to EC law, leaving an institution is nothing out of the ordinary, even if that institution is the Court of Justice. To give up one particular type of legal practice is not to renounce the law. For someone whose ideal is to practice law in varied contexts and in different posts, it is normal to close one chapter and move on to the next . . . That is what

[56] Hans Kutscher, 'Address by Mr Hans Kutscher on 29 March 1979 on Judge Thijmen Koopmans' Taking up Office", in *Formal Sittings of the Court of Justice. 1978 and 1979*, Luxembourg, Curia, 1979, p. 26.

[57] Jossé Mertens de Wilmars, 'Address by J. Mertens de Wilmars, President of the Court on the Occasion of the Taking up of Office by Advocate General Peter Verloren van Themaat. 4 June 1981', in *Formal Sittings of the Court of Justice 1980–1981*, Luxembourg, Curia, 1980–1981, p. 86.

[58] *Ibid.*

[59] Ulrich Everling, 'Address by Judge Ulrich Everling on the Occasion of His Retirement from Office', in *Synopsis of the Work of the Court of Justice in 1988 and 1989*, Luxembourg, Curia, 1989, p. 181.

I have been doing for 33 years.'[60] In other words, it is through a subtle mixture of proximity to and distance from the various Euro-implicated groups that 'the ECJ judge' will be able to fully fulfil his role transcending each of them. Thus, the model of excellence, which gathers strength with each tribute, praises the ECJ judge as a *pontiff* of Europe, with the idea that he or she is able to build bridges between all the different interests and groups present in the EU polity.[61]

On the whole, the building of a continuing ECJ constitutional momentum is not a self-reinforcing process: it is the outcome of multi-faceted strategies of maintenance aimed at securing the continuity of the Court's core legal principles. While this chapter only captures part of them, it shows how the maintenance of the Court's specific social and professional ecosystem of spokesmen and support groups is instrumental to the continuous reviving of the ECJ's progressive jurisprudential narrative staging a limited set of constitutional cases.

[60] Walter van Gerven, 'Address by Walter van Gerven on the Occasion of His Retirement from Office', in *Synopsis of the Work of the Court of Justice. 1992–1994*, Luxembourg, Curia, 1995, p. 149.

[61] Bastien François, 'Le président, pontife constitutionnel. Charisme d'institution et construction juridique du politique', in Jacques Lagroye and Bernard Lacroix (eds.), *Le président de la République*, Paris, Presses de Sciences Po, 1992, pp. 303–30.

5 'Code': the formation of the acquis communautaire and the legal objectification in Europe

A central term in 'Euro-speak', and the immutable working basis for a multitude of European negotiations (expert working groups preparing new Member States for accession, parliamentary commissions, committees, DGs, etc.), the *acquis* (previously referred to as the '*acquis communautaire*', but now called the '*acquis* of the Union') is, however, a word which remains difficult to define. As two European scholars put it, it is 'something that everybody has heard about, but nobody knows what it looks like'.[1] And yet, the continual efforts deployed to ensure its 'preservation' or 'respect' in the face of Europe's centrifugal tendencies makes it clear that the apparent simplicity of its legal definition – 'the full body of law in force in the Union' – exhausts neither its meaning nor its scope. Difficult to circumscribe (being at best the object of 'estimates') and oft considered to be opaque and poorly readable,[2] the huge ensemble of around 80,000 pages of treaties, resolutions, directives, regulations, judicial decisions, etc. which make it up is far more than a simple collection of texts. Ritually exalted at each enlargement, integrated into the most banal operations of the Union and officially consecrated ever since the Treaty of Maastricht as something 'to maintain in full ... and build [up] on', it constitutes an object of core value to EU actors. 'A sacred cow among sacred cows', it is considered a 'remarkable measure of the hold

[1] Anna Michalski and Helen Wallace, *The European Community: The Challenge of Enlargement*, London, Royal Institute of International Affairs, 1992, p. 35.

[2] Communication from the Commission to the European Parliament and Council, *Codification of the Acquis Communautaire*, 21 November 2001, COM/2001/0645. According to the estimates of the Commission, 'it should be possible to reduce the acquis to around 30,000 to 35,000 pages if it were codified. Around 70,000 pages of the *acquis* could benefit from this operation (around 10,000 pages having never been modified and therefore not codifiable)' (*ibid.*). The implementation of this codification would be in the hands of the Commission's legal service.

of European integration itself'.[3] This sacredness of the *acquis* never reveals itself more clearly than when it is threatened, such as in the preparatory phases of an enlargement or a Treaty revision as it seems that its 'calling into question' would affect the existence of the European project itself. The term is actually so entangled with the Union itself that linguists in Brussels most often consider it both untranslatable *and* inescapable in all the working languages of the institutions.[4] It all occurs as if this apparently purely formal gauge of the obligations assumed by the Member States within the framework of the EU contained an essential truth about the Union itself.

It would therefore be misleading to consider the *acquis* purely as a surface phenomenon, a product of the natural and logical accumulation of EC texts and acts over time.[5] It is not sufficient to merely refer to the *acquis* as 'the total sum of obligations that have accumulated since the founding of the European Coal and Steel Community', as all sorts of textbooks, multiple-choice questionnaires and European glossaries habitually do today, if one is unable either to recover what this 'sum' is made of (namely, that which it includes/excludes, the operations it necessitates, and the devices and instruments it mobilizes, etc.) or to enumerate the networks of users and alternative modes of calculating 'Europe'. In other words, the transformation of the Union's 'past', from an irregular succession of texts and decisions considered for their political or economic relevance into one normative stock organized as a unique and self-sufficient body of law ordered along a hierarchy of norms is certainly not trivial. If we assume that codification always implies, in addition to the technical process of compilation, an act of authentication and formalization of a 'power' (its foundations, its central institutions),[6] then the

[3] Joseph Weiler, 'The Reformation of European Constitutionalism', *Journal of Common Market Studies*, 37(1), 1997, p. 97, p. 98.

[4] The term is actually used in the English, Dutch and Italian versions of the Treaties. The syntactic evolution is interesting here: initially employed with inverted commas, the expression later lost its qualification '*communautaire*' and came to form an integral part of the English language as an essential component of 'Euro-speak' (the stylesheets of translators, however, recommend to only use it 'internally'). Cf. Francisco Peryo, 'Le qui-dit-quoi de l'acquis communautaire', *Terminologie et traduction*, 1999, p. 59.

[5] However, in this respect, see the work of Knud Jorgensen, 'The Social Construction of the Acquis Communautaire: A Cornerstone of the European Edifice', *European Integration Online Papers (EIoP)*, 3(5), April 1999.

[6] For a comparative analysis of the processes of codification, see the remarks of Dominique Bureau, 'Codification' in Denis Alland and Stéphane Rials (eds.), *Dictionnaire de la culture juridique*, Paris, Presses Universitaires de France, 2003, pp. 225–30.

construction of the *acquis*[7] involves a specific conception of EU power that magnifies the unificatory capacity of the law. The *acquis* in effect paints a stable figure of Europe (a legal community), of its essential structure (a constitutional order), of its protectors (the Court, Commission, legal professionals, etc.) and, *in fine*, the competences (legal) necessary for those who intend to speak in its name.

This chapter therefore tracks the historical trajectory of the notion of *acquis* and explores how it came to epitomize the very foundations on which the EU polity is grounded. Born out of the enlargement negotiations for third countries by a European Commission wary of impinging upon the politically critical phase of negotiating the Acts of Accession, the *acquis* progressively reincorporated itself 'inside' the EU polity as the common working basis for all Euro-implicated (political, administrative, economic) actors. As the notion becomes integral to the definition of an entire series of routine instruments, policy domains and institutional identities, the *acquis* gradually detached itself from its initial creators, thereby ensuring its diffuse institutionalization as an official representation of the European Union of which all Euro-implicated actors would have to take account.

Calculating Europe

By forcing European institutions to make explicit the 'Europe' to which the candidate countries were applying for membership, phases of enlargement have always been moments of self-definition and, thereby, privileged points for observing the conflicts over the (political, economic and legal) nature of the Union. Until the third attempt at enlarging Europe to include the United Kingdom, Denmark, Ireland and Norway, that of the late 1960s, the issue of the *legal* nature of Europe had hardly been part of the debate. When, in December 1961, MEPs attempted to define which elements should be non-negotiable during the negotiations, they framed the stakes in exclusively *political* terms: refusing a strictly *legal* interpretation of the Treaties as implying the *entire* adoption of previously adopted legislations ('it is possible to reserve a difference in treatment for certain questions'),[8] the rapporteur of the European

[7] Barbara Delcourt thus notes that the notion of *acquis* has always been employed in the singular: Barbara Delcourt, 'The Acquis Communautaire: Has the Concept Had Its Day?', *Common Market Law Review*, 38(4), 2001, pp. 829–70.

[8] 'But the accession agreements should in every case define this derogation with precision', Report made in the name of the political commission of the European Parliamentary

Parliament, Willi Birkelbach, had placed the very heart of the Rome Treaty in its *political* ambitions. In the post-*Van Gend en Loos* context, this had changed dramatically, as a whole constellation of actors, from the Commission to the Court and a varied palette of Euro-lawyers, now conceived of Europe as a 'Community of law'. Below, I show how the creation of the *acquis* has been instrumental for this transnational coalition to gain a say in enlargement negotiations from which they had previously been excluded. A *technical* tool forged by the Commission in order to establish its *political* authority during the negotiation of the Accession Treaties of new Member States, the *acquis* progressively acquired a capacity for the 'authentication' of Europe: by ordering (legally) the informal ensemble of tests, resolutions, decisions and declarations that made up EC law, the Commission endowed itself with a power of 'veridiction' of the very nature of the EC project.

A legal artefact

It must be said that many Euro-implicated actors perceived the coming wave of enlargements as a potential risk for the permanence of the 'integration programme' that had been painstakingly defined in the mid-1960s. The enlargement negotiations opened not long after the 1965 'empty chair' crisis by which Gaullist France had put a halt to the development of EC supranational institutions starting with the European Commission. The 'Luxembourg compromise' that French diplomacy had famously managed to impose upon their five fellow EC members (January 1966) undermined the constitutional interpretation of the Rome Treaties that had emerged in the wake of the *Van Gend en Loos* decision. The mere claim that 'a vital interest' was at stake could suffice to block the normal functioning of EC institutions. Thereby, it acknowledged the idea that the heads of States and governments could escape from the legal prescriptions of the Treaties by virtue of a simple diplomatic protocol. Truly enough, FIDE lawyers had tried to counterbalance this political interpretation of the Treaties' scope by nuancing and qualifying the legal value of the 'compromise': Pierre Pescatore, on the verge of being nominated to the ECJ as well as Hermann Mösler, Walter Hallstein's former legal adviser at the *Auswärtiges Amt*, and at the time a judge at the

Assembly on the political and institutional aspects of accession to or association with the EC by M. Willi Birkelbach, Rapporteur (19 December 1961), *Assemblée parlementaire européenne, Documents de séance 1961–1962*, 15 January 1962, Doc. 122.

European Court of Human Rights, both considered the protocol as a mere 'political *modus vivendi*', a *gentlemen's agreement* decided outside of the institutional framework and deprived of any binding value.[9] 'The machinery is intact', said Pierre Pescatore, adding that 'these agreements did not entail any formal change of the Treaty of Rome'.[10]

In this post-crisis context, the starting of the enlargement negotiations generated a widespread concern among pan-European lawyers regarding a further dismantling of the 'integration programme' that had painstakingly constructed from *Van Gend en Loos* onwards. Nothing seemed to guarantee the fact that the new Member States would accept to act in agreement with the constitutional theory of the Treaties that had been defined jointly by the ECJ and the European Commission. Furthermore, the context of treaty negotiations, a terrain *par excellence* of State sovereignty, provided little room in the discussion for non-diplomatic actors.[11] This was especially clear in a context where the main candidate country was the United Kingdom, whose accession to the European Communities had famously been, ever since the constitution of the Europe of Six, an extremely sensitive political and diplomatic issue. Moreover, the candidate countries, beginning with the United Kingdom – marked as it was by parliamentary sovereignty – did not appear culturally and politically well equipped to accept the doctrine of direct effect, much less the supremacy of EC law, leading Judge Pierre Pescatore to opine in 1970 that 'this new combination of direct impact with priority of EC law – which was accepted, though not without difficulties, on the continent – will require a fundamental revision of some deep-rooted habits of political and legal thinking in Great Britain ... I am under the impression that this has not yet been fully realized in the United Kingdom'.[12]

This perceived danger was made all the greater since the essentially diplomatic and intergovernmental character of the accession process left

[9] On this, see Julio Baquero Cruz, 'The Luxemburg Compromise from a Legal Perspective', in Helen Wallace and Pascaline Winand (eds.), *Visions, Votes and Vetoes: The Empty Chair Crisis and the Luxembourg Compromise Forty Years On*, Brussels, Peter Lang, 2006, pp. 251–77.

[10] Pierre Pescatore, 'La perspective du développement institutionnel à la suite de "la crise du Marché commun"', in *La fusion des Communautés européennes au lendemain des accords de Luxembourg*, Liège, Faculté de droit de Liège, 1966, p. 66.

[11] For a chronicle of the multiple political and diplomatic conflicts which surrounded the question of enlargement to include the United Kingdom throughout the 1960s, see in particular Uwe Kitzinger, *Diplomacy and Persuasion: How Britain Joined the Common Market*, London, Thames and Hudson, 1973.

[12] Pierre Pescatore, 'The Common Market', *The Scots Law Times*, 1970, p. 66.

little room for the Commission, not to mention the Court, to express its point of view. It should be said that, during the negotiations of 1961–2, the six Member States had 'simply engaged in presenting, if possible, common points of view',[13] thereby maintaining complete freedom of action and reducing the European Commission to the role of an adviser in the coordination process. It was thus not surprising that, once reopened in 1969 after two failed attempts (in January 1963 and November 1967), negotiations remained first and foremost a matter of national diplomacies. Truly enough, the Commission did try to put itself forward to lead the process in an Opinion of 1 October 1969, arguing from the precedent set by the first Kennedy Round (1964–7) whereby it had received a mandate to negotiate on behalf of the Member States. However, the six Member States refused such a procedure, preferring the more classic method of the Diplomatic Conference.[14] Although it was this time 'the European Communities', and not the six Member States separately, that were negotiating with the four candidate countries, the 'Conference between the European Communities and the States which have requested accession to these Communities', which opened on 30 June 1970, did not grant any role to the European Commission. The strong hold that States' diplomats firmly maintained over the negotiations suggested that nothing good would come out of it, particularly as far as the official recognition of the 'integration programme' was concerned.

To be sure, a political agreement was quickly reached among the six Member States on requiring that the four candidates accept *all* the texts and norms enacted since the creation of the ECSC, thereby refusing the repeated claims by the United Kingdom for an accession *à géométrie variable* in the name of the special links it maintained with the Commonwealth countries (The Hague conference of heads of States and of government, 1–2 December 1969). On that occasion, the six Member States made it clear that the condition for reopening negotiations was the unconditional acceptance of extant EC legislation (point 13).[15]

[13] Jean-Pierre Puissochet, *L'élargissement des Communautés européennes. Présentation et commentaire du Traité et des Actes relatifs a l'adhésion du Royaume-Uni, du Danemark e de l'Irlande*, Paris, Editions techniques et économiques, 1974, p. 22.

[14] For a detailed account of these debates, see Michael Geary, *Enlarging the European Union: The Commission Seeking Influence (1961–1973)*, Basingstoke, Palgrave MacMillan, 2013.

[15] From its first Opinion on the accession negotiations of 29 September 1967, the Commission had put pressure on the six Member States for them to avoid any form of *ad hoc* adaptation or compromise with one or other of the four candidates. The entry of the new Members could only be facilitated by 'the adoption of transition measures', and not

However, the inclusion of the then emerging '*Van Gend en Loos–Costa*' doctrine in the text of the accession treaties was equally quickly rejected in the name of the 'probable political difficulties [such a recognition] would have posed'[16] and because it was deemed impossible to impose more obligations on the new Member States than those imposed upon the six when they had initially signed the Rome Treaties. In other words, the legal doctrine of the Rome Treaties that had been painfully defined in the 1963–5 period was threatening to disaggregate almost completely for the lack of recognition by the 'High Contracting Parties'. This is the context in which the notion of the *acquis communautaire* first appeared in the European Commission's parlance.

Side-lined from the highly political game of diplomatic horse-trading, the Commission turned its legal expertise into one of the essential levers for affirming its political authority.[17] In his account of the negotiations, the director of the Legal Service of the Council recalls the 'essential role [of the Commission] in a dry and complex domain, namely that of examining the totality of secondary EC legislation',[18] as it 'looked over, with the candidate states, all of the existing EC legislation'. As the negotiations continuously called for an objective assessment of the state of EC law to which the four were subscribing, the Commission engaged in a systematic screening, gauging and compiling of Europe's existing normative stock.[19] Interestingly, however, it did not compile this legislation randomly but insisted on recalling its underlying interpretation of EU Treaties. In an Opinion addressed to the Council on 1 October 1969,[20] the European Commission first used the term *acquis*: the notion was in line with the political directives issued by the Member States at the

by 'a modification of existing rules'. This principle would be taken up verbatim by the Council in its declaration of 6 March 1970, *3ème rapport sur les activités des CE*, 1970, p. 523.

[16] In the words of the director of the Council's Legal Service, Jean-Pierre Puissochet, in *ibid*.

[17] This is generally in line with the recent account by Patrick Geary pointing at the expert profile strategically chosen by the Commission in the context of the enlargement to the United Kingdom: Michael Geary, *Enlarging the European Union: The Commission Seeking Influence (1961–1973)*, Basingstoke, Palgrave MacMillan, 2013, in particular Chapters 6 and 7.

[18] In the words of the then director of the Council's Legal Service at the time, Jean-Pierre Puissochet, *L'élargissement des Communautés européennes. Présentation et commentaire du Traité et des Actes relatifs à l'adhésion du Royaume-Uni, du Danemark et de l'Irlande*, Paris, Editions techniques et économiques, 1974, p. 26.

[19] See *Rapport d'activité de la Commission*, 1971, para. 28; and *Rapport 1970*, p. 523.

[20] See European Commission, *Rapport d'activité de la Commission*, 1969, Suppl. No. 9–10, 1969, p. 27. Legal search engines (Eur-Lex, Heinonline, etc.) indicate that the term '*acquis*' only made its appearance in legal scholarship in 1972 or later.

opening of the negotiations which pointed to the overall acceptance of EC law by the new Member States. The Commission, however, added to this political principle a legal twist defining the notion of *acquis* in line with the principles of the 'integration programme'. On the eve of the signature of the Acts of Accession in the Egmont Palace in Brussels, a precise content was eventually provided to the *acquis* in the Commission's Opinion to the Council of 19 January 1972. Remarking the 'silence of the negotiators as to the problems'[21] of the doctrine of direct effect and the supremacy of EC law, despite 'the importance of the question', the Commission sought to avert the risk of contradictory interpretations of the Accession Acts by defining the *acquis* against the yardstick of the 'integration programme'. By accepting, 'without reserve, the Treaties and their political objectives', goes the text, the new Member States at the same time accepted:

> the legal order created by the Treaties establishing the Communities [which] is essentially characterised by the direct applicability of certain of their provisions and of certain acts, the primacy of EC law over national measures which contradict them, and the existence of procedures for ensuring the uniformity of interpretation of EC law ... the binding nature of these rules, the respect of which is indispensable for guaranteeing the effectiveness and unity of EC law.[22]

Defined in such a way, the *acquis* differed significantly from a mere 'sum' or 'compilation' of previously adopted texts (acts, political resolutions, directives, etc.); it meant that the new Member States would also have to accept a *unified* normative *stock* organized along the Treaties' 'underlying logic' as had been specified by the Commission and the Court through the direct effect and supremacy doctrines. The affirmation of the existence of such an *acquis*, common to all three Communities, and founded upon the principles of the 'integration programme', enabled the definition of EC accession treaties (and even more so its future interpretation) as treaties qualitatively different from classic international treaties precisely because they left no freedom of contract to the candidate country, the latter being constrained to accept *en bloc* the European Communities such as it was. As it undermined one core pillar of public international law, that is, the contractual freedom of sovereign states, the *acquis*

[21] Jean-Pierre Puissochet, *L'élargissement des Communautés européennes. Présentation et commentaire du Traité et des Actes relatifs a l'adhésion du Royaume-Uni, du Danemark e de l'Irlande*, Paris, Editions techniques et économiques, 1974, p. 96.

[22] European Commission, 'Avis du 19 janvier 1972', in *Actes relations aux adhésions aux Communautés européennes*, vol. II, Luxembourg, Office des publications officielles des Communautés européennes, 1987.

concretely marked the highly specific nature of the European project, combining the various bits and pieces of Europe into one unique template.

Europe's corpus juris

The formation of the *acquis* as a new legal construct allowing the Commission to assert its authority in enlargement processes goes along with the creation of new instruments (legal databases and statistics) able to calculate the content and contours of the European Union.[23] Too often, scholars concentrate exclusively on legal concepts, as if they were free-floating, and underestimate the *constitutive* role of the concrete instruments that may turn legal theories into standard and daily operating procedures. In this section, I argue that EU law owes an essential part of its existence to the development of techniques that have helped compile the *acquis* and put into one ordered whole the vast chaos of texts and judicial decisions that have accumulated over the decades of integration. If EU law today appears as a specific and self-standing 'body of law', it owes this not to legal ideas and doctrines but also to the instruments, legal *and* non-legal, that have shaped EU law as a consolidated set of decisions and principles. There is a whole story that remains to be told here on how these techniques have contributed to shape and produce EU law, turning it into a limited number of key words and key legal sentences that today form its building blocks. In this section, I highlight particularly on how a computerized tool helped frame the *acquis* as an objective representation of Europe *as it is*, turning the constitutional doctrine into EC law's daily standard operating procedures. As they provided a concrete basis for the informational prerogative of the Commission over EU law, these early computerized instruments constituted a critical basis for its claim for expertise in the context of the politically sensitive preparation of the Acts of Accession.

This requires a little historical detour. Several years earlier, The Legal Service of the Commission started to develop a *database* of EC texts, acts and resolutions named Celex (*Communitatis Europae Lex*). In 1967, returning from a training course in legal information technology at the

[23] On policy instrumentation, see the research strand developed by Pierre Lascoumes and Patrick Le Galès, 'Understanding Public Policy through Its Instruments – From the Nature of Instruments to the Sociology of Public Policy Instrumentation', *Governance*, 20 (1), 2007, pp. 1–27.

University of Michigan,[24] Belgian lawyer Hélène Bernet, although still a very young member of the Legal Service, effectively developed a computing tool on the 'all new IBM 360' thanks to its 'document processing system' software: this new system allowed one 'to analyse thousands of acts to enable them to be recorded mechanically: no data, no system'. 'The Commission's lawyers themselves', she recalled recently, 'had begun to encounter "retrieval" problems, therefore some I. T. assistance in distribution and research of legal information appeared sensible'.[25] The new technology produced its first results in December 1969, presented on the occasion of a European conference on computerized legal tools organized at the initiative of the Commission's Legal Service.[26] These first steps towards the pooling of legal resources and standardization of the mass of EC texts and norms adopted since 1952 were certainly not trivial. In arranging and ordering EC law by type of document (treaties, international agreements, secondary legislation, supplementary acts, preparatory acts, jurisprudence, national measures implementing directives and parliamentary questions), year of adoption, duration and legal value, and so on,[27] the database effectively aggregated as much as it distinguished, bringing into being classes of equivalence between acts and texts originally produced by a wide range of actors in very different circumstances and for very different reasons. Importantly, it brought together what had previously remained scattered, anchoring Treaties and directives to their judicial interpretation by the ECJ. Thereby, it excluded other sources of interpretation (such as national supreme courts), progressively bringing into existence Europe's new legal compact. It ran counter to a more flexible representation of the European Communities' past as a relatively informal ensemble of *political*

[24] In 1972, she would defend a doctoral thesis in German law at the University of Frankfurt am Main on the logic applied in international multilingual law. Cf. *25 années de droit européen en ligne*, Luxembourg, Publications Office, 2006. Generally speaking, the period sees the rapid development of information technologies in the context of the modernization of national bureaucracies and due to the emergence of computerized tools of legal information. See, on this point, Evelyne Serverin, *De la jurisprudence en droit privé. Théorie d'une pratique*, Lyon, Presses universitaires de Lyon, 1985.

[25] Hélène Bernet, email exchange, 14 November 2008.

[26] Hélène Bernet, 'Histoire de Celex de 1963 à 1986. Les racines', in EUR Publications Office, *25 années de droit européen en ligne*, Luxembourg, EUR Publications Office, 2006.

[27] Its net was drawn much wider than that of the *Official Journal* (Series L and C) to progressively include all sorts of documents of indeterminate legal status, including judicial decisions (resolutions, Commission reports, preparatory texts, parliamentary questions, opinions of Advocates General, etc.). *The Celex Database: Celex 2. User Guide*, EUR OP, 1994.

resolutions (such as Treaties, the 'packets' issuing from the 'marathons' of negotiation within the Council, etc.) of widely differing legal scope and value[28] that constituted a diplomatic *acquis*. Conversely, Celex defined Europe as a set of legally binding norms ordered in line with the constitutional principles of the 'integration programme'. In that framework, the diplomatic importance or the economic relevance weighed less than the legal value as defined by the position of the texts in Europe's new hierarchy of norms. Thus, the computing tool Celex became concretely engaged in the transformation of the *maquis* of texts and acts of the EC institutions into a veritable legal corpus. Through this instrument, the approximately 2,000 acts that were in force at the time[29] became a long series of punch-cards (1kg or more), paving the way to the publication from 1972 onwards of the annual *Repository of Acts in Force*. The creation of this 'inter-institutional system of automatic documentation of EC law'[30] – as the Celex database was officially labelled – thus gave a concrete substance to the notion of *acquis*.

Armed with such technology, the Commission could claim to have a mode of access to EU law that no other institution, public or private, could provide. As it was able to take into account the periods of validity of the acts in question, Celex allowed for the calculation of the *current* 'state of the law'. There was no other mode of establishing the totality of 'rights and duties' that came with membership of the European Communities. At the time, there was not even an Index that would allow the retrieval of the consolidated state of EC law on a particular policy matter. The issue was becoming critical in a context were EC law was growing in an exponential manner making it more and more difficult to keep track of the normative stock, even in a sector-specific domain, by traditional means of information (informal contacts, participation in academic conferences, reading of law journals or consulting a collection of the *Official Journal*, etc.). Certainly, there were private publishers providing legal information on the development of the European Communities: besides the semi-official commentaries on the Treaties or case law Repositories, most often published jointly by the high civil servants of the Commission

[28] For an enlightening parallel, see the historical account of the creation of the *Official Journal* in France: Pascal Gougeon, '"Nul n'est censé ignoré la loi". La publication au Journal Officiel. Genèse d'un mode d'universalisation de la "puissance publique"', *Politix*, 32, 1995, p. 76.

[29] Hélène Bernet, 'Histoire de Celex de 1963 à 1986. Les racines', in EUR Publications Office, *25 années de droit européen en ligne*, Luxembourg, EUR Publications Office, 2006, p. 17.

[30] As acknowledged by the Council (of Justice Ministers) in its meeting of 26 November 1974, *Bulletin des Communautés européennes*, 11/1974, p. 1108.

and academics,[31] there was a vast array of practice-oriented compendia which had been published in a variety of policy domains covered by EC legislation.[32] However, although regularly updated, these compilations remained often limited in their scope, infrequently updated and hardly accessible to the individuals and firms. In this context, information and knowledge of EC law was becoming an ever more sensitive issue: the *Official Journal*, which had 7,905 pages in 1960, had grown to more than 45,000 pages ten years later. In the midst of the mass of highly technical and ephemeral regulations on the Common Agricultural Policy, it was really difficult to get a general sense of the evolutions of the law. As a result, various MEPs from the Legal Committee of the European Parliament, beginning with its president, the Christian-Democrat (CDU) attorney Arved Deringer, had become concerned with the many difficulties encountered in retrieving EC law. In a written question to the Commission in 1967, he asked: 'Does the Council or the Commission possess a survey ... of their own law?' However, the question raised little interest among EC institutions, and the Commission barely responded, indicating that such an inventory was unnecessary ('no more than generally informative') since everything of legal value was already published in the *Official Journal*, and tedious as 'it would require much time and energy'.[33]

The enlargement negotiations created a new context, however, whereby the Commission's Legal Service renounced the diffuse knowledge of Europe's normative stock on which it had relied up to then and instead developed Celex in order to obtain an objective, panoptical, view of the 'state of the law'. As the accession of the new Member States involved important industrial and agricultural interests, the different

[31] By way of example, see the *Répertoire de la jurisprudence relative aux traités instituant les Communautés européennes* published from 1962 onwards by two administrators of the European Court of Justice in the collection of the Institute of European Community Law of Cologne.

[32] In France, a lawyer and former attaché at UNESCO, William Garcin, launched a book series in 1958 entitled *Recueil pratique du droit des affaires dans les pays du Marché commun*, known at the time as the 'Collection Jupiter', which did not content itself merely with compiling EC acts but also covered the whole of commercial law by presenting national laws in parallel. Designed by and for legal practitioners, this collection was supposed to 'allow producers to participate without embarrassment in the practical works of the Common Market ... They are more than a simple legislative repository: they strive to place the law in the service of the economy'. Cf. 'Droit des affaires et Marché commun', *Le Monde*, 9 April 1958.

[33] Written Question No. 155/67 by Arved Deringer to the Commission of the European Communities, 20 September 1967; and the response thereto dated 22 November 1967; published in H. A. H. Audretsch, *Supervision in European Community Law*, 2nd edn, Amsterdam, Elsevier, 1986, pp. 460–3.

working groups charged with the preparations were particularly keen on 'providing the new Member States with a list of acts in force, that they would have to accept and introduce in their national legislations'.[34] As the director of the Legal Service of the Council of Ministers indicated at the time, the 1972 enlargement was 'a prodigious occasion for looking over the whole of EC law and to arrive at a sort of radioscopy or spectral analysis of "secondary law" and the *acquis communautaire*'.[35] By the continual updating it enabled and the digital accounting of the temporal validities of the different types of acts, Celex allowed one 'to establish, at any given moment, the state of the law, to publish consolidated, or codified, versions of EC law'.[36] Thereby, it offered a representation of EC law that was far more reliable than that of the Member States which essentially kept track of their own national measures for implementing EC norms, and which was also much more up-to-date than the traditional means of legal compilation (commentaries, *recueil*, etc.).

In the highly sensitive arena of the diplomatic negotiations preparing for the accession of the four candidates, the digital formatting of the *acquis* in a single legal matrix therefore constituted an essential platform for the general expertise that the Commission sought to affirm during the preparatory phase of enlargement. This knowledge instrument conferred on the Commission a specific authority to disclose the state of Europe *as it actually was*. Moreover, it allowed for the new principles of the '*Van Gend en Loos–Costa* doctrine' to be concretely and fully integrated into Europe's normative stock. While the Commission had failed to obtain the official recognition of this doctrine in the Acts of Accession themselves (and repeatedly so up until the fifth wave of enlargement to the countries of Central and Eastern Europe),[37] the latter had

[34] Hélène Bernet, 'Histoire de Celex de 1963 à 1986. Les racines', in EUR Publications Office, *25 années de droit européen en ligne*, Luxembourg, EUR Publications Office, 2006, pp. 10–11.

[35] Jean-Pierre Puissochet, *L'élargissement des Communautés européennes. Présentation et commentaire du Traité et des Actes relatifs à l'adhésion du Royaume-Uni, du Danemark et de l'Irlande*, Paris, Editions techniques et économiques, 1974.

[36] Hélène Bernet, email exchange, 14 November 2008.

[37] However, the Commission would continuously recall the importance of this doctrine, copying and pasting its January 1972 Opinion on each of the following waves of enlargement: European Commission, 'Avis du 27 mai 1979' on Greece, in *Actes relatifs à l'adhésion de la Grèce*, Luxembourg, Office des publications officielles des Communautés européennes, 1981, p. 119, in which, following the Copenhagen declaration of 1973, the notion of common patrimony was added ('the principals of pluralist democracy and the respect for human rights'). See also: European Commission, 'Avis du 31 mai 1985 sur l'entrée de l'Espagne et du Portugal', in *Actes relatifs à l'adhésion de l'Espagne et du Portugal*, Luxembourg, Office des publications officielles des Communautés européennes, 1986,

nevertheless secured its durability, finding a place for itself at the core of Europe's standard operating procedures.

A common platform for Europe's polity

Having passed the test of the first enlargement negotiations, where its representativeness had been both tested and given the official seal of approval, the *acquis* progressively became the working foundation for all EC-implicated actors, be they political, economic or administrative. By a sort of boomerang effect, the notion, initially aimed outwards, would progressively become an essential benchmark for the Communities' *internal* affairs. Below, I follow three different, yet interdependent, scenes that, during the 1970s and the early 1980s, have contributed to turn the *acquis* into Europe's ubiquitous tool: the definition and standardization of the ECJ's 'judicial style', the increasing control by the Commission and the European Parliament over the implementation of EC directives by Member States, and the emerging attempts to frame a political Union that would unite all Communities into one institutional structure.

Shaping jurisprudence

The *acquis* and the related Celex database became the anchor-point for a variety of attempts to standardize the production of EC law at a moment of growth and development where the risk of dispersion and heterogeneity was felt acutely. From the mid-1970s onwards, the *acquis* would become the foundation for various projects aimed at methodically building ECJ jurisprudence. The context is certainly of importance here: as we have pointed out in the previous chapter, by the end of 1980, there were no more judges and few *référendaires* at the Court who had taken part to the 1963–4 'legal revolution'. Between 1976 and 1980, Riccardo Monaco, Alberto Trabucchi, and former presidents Andreas Donner and Robert Lecourt, left Luxembourg and their faithful *référendaires* (Paolo Gori, Sergio Neri, Roger-Michel Chevallier) would do the same shortly afterwards. A new period therefore started at the Court, characterized by an increased turn-over of judges and *référendaires*. As the ECJ progressively lost its initial social cohesiveness and stability, the need for standards

p. 203; European Commission, 'Avis du 19 avril 1994 sur l'entrée de l'Autriche, de la Finlande et de la Norvège', in *Actes relatifs à l'adhésion de la république d'Autriche, de Finlande et du royaume de Suède*, Luxembourg, Office des publications officielles des Communautés européennes, 1995, p. 13.

and templates was felt acutely and a variety of attempts to codify ECJ jurisprudence were engaged by the most active entrepreneurs of the '*Van Gend en Loos–Costa* doctrine'. One could mention the publication in 1974 by Lecourt's highly productive *référendaire*, Roger-Michel Chevallier, of the first edition of the *Grands arrêts de la Cour de justice des Communautés européennes*, following a template, well known to any French lawyer, of the so-called 'GAJA' (*Grands arrêts de la jurisprudence administrative*). But it is first of all Pierre Pescatore, former Rome Treaty negotiator, whom we left earlier gravitating effortlessly between the first European legal milieus, and member of the ECJ (1967–84), who engaged systematically in framing the Court's jurisprudence. First, he theorized the existence of a 'judicial *acquis*' structured around a limited number of landmark decisions of constitutional value, which is superior to Europe's political *acquis*:

> [This is a] jurisprudential *acquis* of a higher rank, since these decisions are directly attached to the Treaties' notions and principles themselves and are aggregated with them. In other words, it is not an ordinary acquis, but an acquis of fundamental character, that is, of constitutional rank ... The political and legislative acquis that is referred to in the Accession Acts are in a lower legal rank than the jurisprudential acquis in so far as this acquis is directly connected with the Treaties themselves. Everything originates from four decisions: *Commission* v. *Luxembourg and Belgium* (1962), *Van Gend en Loos* (1963), *Costa* (1964) and *Consten and Grundig* (1966). This is therefore a solid basis to address the more fundamental disputes of the Community's life.[38]

At roughly the same time, Pierre Pescatore gave practical backing to this theory by writing an internal paper, only recently made public, aimed at his colleagues and their *référendaires* entitled *Vade-mecum – Recueil de formules et de conseils pratiques à l'usage des rédacteurs d'arrêts*.[39] While it would never have any official status within the Court, the paper is known for having had three editions during the years of Pierre Pescatore's presence at the Court. At first sight, the *Vade-mecum* is essentially a guide defining the Court's judicial style. To this end, it suggests a variety of templates and standard operating procedures in order to avoid 'production defects', 'semantic dispersion' and 'verbosity'.[40] However, there

[38] Pierre Pescatore, 'Aspects judiciaires de "l'acquis communautaire"', *Revue trimestrielle de droit européen*, 21, 1981, pp. 620 and 648.

[39] It was only twenty-two years later that the text was published: Pierre Pescatore, *Vade-mecum. Recueil de formules et de conseils pratiques à l'usage des rédacteurs d'arrêts*, Brussels, Bruylant, 2007.

[40] *Ibid.*, pp. 46–8.

is much more to the document than just norms about judicial writing style. As all ECJ decisions and the Opinions had just been integrated into the Celex database (1974), Pierre Pescatore pushed for more consistency and rationality in the making of ECJ jurisprudence. The new digital context (and also that of translation which required the standardization of linguistic equivalencies) served as an essential lever for defining a stable lexicon ('*une bibliothèque de phrases*') and a limited collection of 'style clauses' and 'typical formulations':

> The decisions of the Court are not referable by computer, nor can they achieve their greatest influence as 'precedents' unless they are created in terms which include easily identifiable elements ... [The] consequence for drafting – at the level of textual structure ... is to avoid ambiguous or overlong logical equations. 'Yes, but' and 'no, but' can be useful in politics; in jurisprudence they create confusion. Zigzag, corkscrew, and tiered reasoning, and the accumulation of exceptions and qualifications, constitute a difficulty for computing.[41]

Pescatore's compendium of best practice also suggested a list of all 'relevant articles' of the EEC Treaty to be quoted when it came to building 'general principles' of EC law. Interestingly, it even indicated '*une clé passe-partout*', one drawn from the Dassonville decision (11 July 1974), that purportedly enabled ECJ judges to overcome almost any national legal challenge.[42] Last but not least, Pescatore insisted on the fact that judges had to frame their decisions within the framework of previous decisions, thereby marking a continuous 'chain of decisions': '[W]hen a decision conforms, specifies, or develops a previous jurisprudence, we recommend to always explicitly quote the previous decisions to which it refers in order to avoid any rupture in the *jurisprudential chain*'.

The rare traces available on the internal functioning of the Court do not allow us to follow how this *Vade-mecum* was actually used. Interestingly, however, this is part of an overall process of codification of the Court's jurisprudence around a limited number of highly standardized formulas now routinely used by and before the Court.[43] The creation of new structures such as the *Cellule des lecteurs d'arrêts* specifically devoted to polishing and mainstreaming the decisions, as much as the growing control exerted by the jurist-linguists of ECJ translation directorate have

[41] *Ibid.*, p. 30. [42] *Ibid.*, p. 300.

[43] On this, see Loïc Azoulai, 'La fabrication de la jurisprudence communautaire', in Pascal Mbongo and Antoine Vauchez (eds.), *Dans la fabrique du droit européen*, Brussels, Bruylant, 2009, pp. 178–97.

created interlocking formats (legal databases, writing software, key word indexes, etc.) with which all lawyers, *référendaires* and judges still have to operate nowadays.[44] While these techniques have resulted in the ECJ's much-lamented 'formulaic style' and have ignited a sense of frustration among *référendaires* ('we must draft using the language that has been used by the Court for over 50 years', '[we are] under pressure to cite word-for-word when taking material from source documents ... in particular from past judgments', 'we are so bound to what has been said before that we can hardly even use a new verb or express the same thing in a slightly different way', etc.),[45] they have secured the striking linguistic and legal stability of EU case law along the lines of the '*Van Gend en Loos–Costa* doctrine'.

Monitoring implementation

Initially constructed for the sole benefit of the Commission's Legal Service (the latter had long kept hold of the only Celex terminal), Celex saw its network of users increase significantly in the mid-1970s with the installation, in each of the directorates general, of 'Celex correspondents' running the programme and capable of 'calculating' the state of the law. The asymmetry of information which it generated (until 1981, only the Commission had direct access to the database) provided EC civil servants with an essential instrument to authoritatively intervene in the framework of their daily negotiations with national expert-delegates throughout the amorphous nebula of comitology. As the *acquis* was becoming a tool necessary in a multiplicity of operations of the Commission's daily life and as 'EU civil servants appreciated the service it gave in return',[46] the *acquis* became instrumental to the empowerment of both the Commission and the Parliament *vis-à-vis* Member States. In pretty much the same way it had allowed the Commission to involve itself in the diplomatic discussions on accession candidacies, the *acquis* became one of the essential levers by which the Commission claimed increasing supervisory powers over EC law implementation (transposition of directives, compliance with ECJ decisions, etc.) in each of the Member States, thereby substantiating its role as 'guardian of the Treaties'.

[44] Karen McAuliffe, 'Precedent at the ECJ: The Linguistic Aspect. Law and Language', *Current Legal Issues*, 15, 2013.

[45] *Ibid.* [46] Hélène Bernet, email exchange, November 2008.

This transformation can in part be traced back to the arrival of a new director at the Commission's Legal Service, Claus-Dieter Ehlermann, in parallel with the appointment of a new college of commissioners under the presidency of the Englishman Roy Jenkins. Coming from an academic background (a PhD in law and a former assistant at Heidelberg University between 1954 and 1959), Ehlermann belonged to the second generation of high functionaries, the first that had spent most of its career in EC circles.[47] A member of the Legal Service for more than a decade (1961–73), then a director at the DG for financial control (1973–7), his accession to the head of the Commission's Legal Service brought an end to twenty-five years of French presence in that position.[48] His succession is more important than may appear at first sight when one considers that some of his predecessors, all coming from the *Conseil d'État*,[49] had displayed a certain lack of enthusiasm about the 'constitutionalist' rhetoric and had been wary of some jurisprudential developments at the ECJ. Ehlermann had none of this cautiousness. Weaned on the constitutionalist arguments of German scholarship, and linked to ordo-liberal circles (he was in fact chosen by the competition commissioner Hans von der Groeben as his co-author for the new editions of his *Legal Commentary* on the Rome Treaties),[50] he championed a strengthening of the legal and judicial oversight of the EC law implementation. Under his lead, not only would the Commission develop an autonomous policy for detecting violations (no longer based exclusively on complaints brought by external actors[51]), but also it would begin to systematically prosecute cases of violation which had not been resolved in the conciliatory

[47] On the first generation of EC functionaries to complete their entire career within the 'institutions', see Katja Seidel, *The Process of Politics in Europe: The Rise of European Elites and Supranational Institutions*. London, IB Tauris, 2010.

[48] It is worth recalling that he took up his position as director of the Commission's Legal Service the very same year in which Hans Kutscher, of whom he had been a legal clerk for three years at the German Constitutional Court (1959–61), acceded to the Presidency of the ECJ (1977–80).

[49] On the role of *conseillers d'État* in the history of European integration, see Michel Mangenot, 'The Conseil d'État and Europe: Adapting the French Administrative State', in Helen Drake (ed.), *French Relations with the European Union*, London, Routledge, 2005, pp. 86–104.

[50] Hans von der Groeben, Hans von Boeckh, Jochen Thiesing and Claus-Dieter Ehlermann (eds.), *Kommentar zum EWG-Vertrag*, Baden-Baden, Nomos, 1983.

[51] Thus, the number of cases brought by the Commission to the ECJ increased from 28 in 1980 to 145 in 1984; cf. H. A. H. Audretsch, *Supervision in European Community Law*, 2nd edn, Amsterdam, Elsevier, 1986, p. 290.

phases.[52] While the progression through the different phases (from filing a case of violation up to commencing a legal action before the ECJ) was still ultimately under the control of the college of commissioners which carried out the most important arbitrations, the Legal Service efficiently advocated a quasi-automatic prosecution, bringing the more recalcitrant States more often before the Court.[53] This resulted in concrete legal consequences: while a total of only thirty actions had been filed by the Commission between 1958 and 1977 on this basis, 100 were submitted in the period from 1977 to 1983 alone.[54] Here again, the amplification of the Commission's monitoring powers[55] rested on the development of new databases like Asmodee (Automated System for Monitoring Directives Execution) that allowed for a continuous control over the implementation of directives (now more than 500 in stock) in each of the Member States. Although the gathering of this information was not without difficulties and caused tensions with national bureaucracies, this new technical equipment allowed one for the first time to systematically follow and compare the pace with which the different Member States were conforming to EC law.

The European Parliament also contributed to this increase in the supervisory powers of EU institutions. While it had essentially lost interest in the question of implementation ever since a parliamentary report by Fernand Dehousse on the subject in 1967,[56] the growing number of violations of EC law brought to light by the reinforcement of the policing of the EC law implementation provided the statistical material for reports in which the Commission of Legal Affairs at the

[52] *Ibid.*, p. 289. Cf. Claus-Dieter Ehlermann, *Les procédures en manquement contre les États membres. Articles 169 et 1970 du traité CEE*, Lectures given on 7 and 8 July 1980 at the Institut Universitaire de Luxembourg.

[53] The new control procedure put in place from 1977 onwards gave each DG and each service the obligation – in close collaboration with the Legal Service – to establish procedures and inquiries into the non-application of EU law in the three months following the detection of a violation. On this transformation of the policy in respect of violations, see H. A. H. Audretsch, *Supervision in European Community Law*, 2nd edn, Amsterdam, Elsevier, 1986, pp. 275–315.

[54] *Ibid.*, p. 161.

[55] As defined by the Commission, non-compliance covered the violation of Treaty obligations and of EC legislation, but also the non-application of decisions of the ECJ, and the non-transposition, incorrect transposition or incorrect implementation of EC law; cf. Tania Börzel, 'Participation Through Law Enforcement: The Case of the European Union', *Comparative Political Studies*, 39(1), 2006, pp. 128–52.

[56] Fernand Dehousse, *Rapport sur l'application du droit communautaire par les États membres fait au nom de la commission juridique*, Documents of the European Parliament, 38, 1967.

Parliament became alarmed at States' non-respect of their obligations (1981 and 1982).[57] Supporting the Commission's new course of action, the Parliament called upon it to report annually on the state of national violations of EC law (Resolution of 9 February 1983).[58] Thanks to the Asmodee database that allowed for a continuous evaluation, sector by sector, country by country, and act by act, of the implementation of EC texts,[59] the Parliament became the arena in which, each year, MEPs and commissioners, numbers and data in hand, would point the finger at malfunctions and deficiencies, praising and denouncing the Member States (the latter mainly to Mediterranean countries, perceived as being systematically late or at fault), thereby substantiating the new political role it claimed for itself after 1979.[60]

Envisioning political unity

The *acquis* was not only an instrument of supervision; it soon became the functional equivalent for Europe's institutional unity, thereby becoming an essential component of the EC reformer's glossary. One must remember that, throughout the 1970s, the institutional reform of Europe had come to stand at the top of the political agenda. The many conflicts that developed over the decade (from the United Kingdom's contribution to the EC budget, to reform of the Common Agricultural Policy, the increase of Europe's '*ressources propres*', or the institution of the so-called 'European monetary snake', etc.) had made it clear that the European Communities were facing a moment of serious political and institutional crisis. From the Vedel committee in 1972 on the competences of the

[57] See H. A. H. Audretsch, *Supervision in European Community Law*, 2nd edn, Amsterdam, Elsevier, 1986, pp. 266–71.

[58] Helmut Sieglerschmidt (SPD), *Report on Behalf of the Legal Affairs Committee of the European Parliament on the Responsibility of the European Court of Justice for the Uniform Application of EC Law in the Member States*, European Parliament Working Documents, Doc. 1-414/81, 1 February 1981; and Helmut Sieglerschmidt, *Report on Behalf of the Legal Affairs Committee of the European Parliament on the Responsibility of Member States for the Application of EC Law*, European Parliament Working Documents, Doc. 1–1052/82, 10 January 1982.

[59] European Commission, *Premier rapport annuel au Parlement européen de la commission contrôlant la mise en œuvre du droit communautaire*, 1983, COM(84), 181.

[60] In turn, the publication of compliance data in the Annual Reports enabled the development of a large academic literature which engaged in quantitative studies identifying the gap between the law and its implementation. On this point, see Tania Börzel, *Non-Compliance in the European Union: Pathology or Statistical Artefact*, Working Paper, Robert Schuman Centre for Advanced Studies, European University Institute, 2001/28.

European Parliament to the Dodge committee of 1985 tasked with proposing a complete redefinition of the EC institutional system, more than thirteen expert (or 'wise men') groups were constituted with a view to addressing Europe's institutional dysfunctions. Following the Paris meeting of the heads of states and governments in October 1972, in which the 'transformation … of the relations between Member States into one European Union' was set as the 'major objective' to be accomplished 'before the end of the decade',[61] the idea of unifying the variegated set of Communities, institutions and policies under one unique institutional umbrella – a European Union – became central.

The acquis and the 'political Union' agenda: reports and expert working groups (1972–85)

- 'Comité Vedel', *ad hoc* committee examining the increase of the European Parliament's competences (March 1972)
- 'Rapport Davignon', on European political cooperation (October 1970 and July 1973)
- 'Rapport Marjolin', on the economic and monetary union (March 1975)
- Report of the European Commission on the project of establishing a European Union (June 1975)
- Report of the European Parliament on the project of establishing a European Union (July 1975)
- Report of the European Court of Justice on the project of establishing a European Union (July 1975)
- Report of Leo Tindemans on the project of establishing a European Union (December 1975)
- 'Rapport Spierenburg', on the reform of the European Commission (September 1979)
- 'Rapport Marjolin', from the so-called 'three wise men committee' on EC institutions (October 1979)
- Genscher–Colombo Project of a European Act (November 1981)
- Draft Treaty establishing a European Union, also called the 'Spinelli Constitution' (February 1984)
- Report of the Ad Hoc Committee for Institutional Affairs from the Dodge Committee (March 1985)

In this framework, in which EC reformers devised the building of a European Union, the notion of *acquis* became of proxy for the constitutional understanding of the Treaties. It does not come as a surprise

[61] *Bulletin des Communautés européennes*, 10, 1972.

that the European Commission was first in bringing the notion to the debate over institutional reform, turning the *acquis* into the essential basis on which any project of establishing a European Union would have to be built. In a report of 1975, the Commission suggested two opposite pathways for reform, one that would turn Europe into 'a network of specific agreements to which the Member States, or only some of them, would participate depending on the policy domain involved', and another, referred to as an *authentic* political Union, which would establish 'a unique institutional structure covering all domains of EC competence' and be grounded on the *acquis*. This foundational function granted to the notion would later be acknowledged in all reports and working groups, turning it into a collective good that all policies and reforms needed to protect and consolidate. In this regard, the 1975 report by the European Parliament on the creation of a European Union is very telling, as it indicates that 'the EU should be completed starting from the *acquis communautaire* and through the establishment of a unique organization';[62] similarly, the report commissioned in July 1976 by the heads of States and governments from the former Belgium prime minister Leo Tindemans on the same issue stated that 'an incomplete institutional structure cannot last for long: it needs to be completed, otherwise it falls apart. Today, it is no less than the *acquis communautaire* that is in question'.[63] Three years later, the so-called 'wise men report' of October 1979 established as Europe's 'first priority, its maintenance through the preservation of the *acquis communautaire*'.[64] Unsurprisingly, the proposals that would ultimately be drafted as a result of this decade-long series of reports turned the *acquis* into Europe's building block: the Spinelli draft treaty establishing a European Union of 14 February 1984 actually devoted one of its very first articles (article 7) to the *acquis*, solemnly declaring that 'the Union recognizes all the *acquis communautaire*'. In a similar vein, the 1985 Dodge committee suggested that the Intergovernmental conference that it proposed in order to establish a political Union should be 'grounded on the *acquis communautaire*'.[65] An overall agreement therefore seemed to emerge in this 1975–85 decade to consider this legal and institutional artefact as the best safeguard against the irreversibility and integrity of the European integration process.

[62] *Bulletin des Communautés européennes*, 3, 1985, p. 102.

[63] Leo Tindemans, in Commission institutionnelle du Parlement européen, *Recueil de documents institutionnels de la Communauté, 1950–2*, Luxembourg, European Parliament, 1982, p. 326.

[64] *Bulletin des Communautés européennes*, 3, 1985, p. 102.

[65] *Ibid.*

When the term finally appeared in a legally binding text, that is with the Acts of Accession of Spain and Portugal, almost fifteen years after it was initially coined, its meaning had become embedded in various layers of legal, political and institutional significance.

Representing Europe

This progressive enlargement of the functions as well as of the audiences of the *acquis* triggered a growing demand for publicity and accessibility. This demand was not totally new. As early as 1974, some MEPs, such as Belgian businessman Baron Paul de Keersmaeker, began noting 'how difficult it is for the administrations, legal authorities, and lawyers of the Member States to keep track of all the provisions of EC law',[66] asking that a 'computerized system of legal documentation covering the whole body of EC law (Treaties, acts of the institutions, Agreements with third countries, Judgments of the Court of Justice, etc.)', be accessible to all. In the late 1970s, the situation in this regard was described by an American law librarian as follows: '[T]he enormous mass of papers produced by the European Communities is in part diffused for free and in part not; only one part of the documents are printed while others are mere *duplicata* of dactylographed texts'.[67] National bureaucracies, parliamentary committees and research institutes often engaged in a supervision of the evolution of EC law, but the instruments were discontinuous in time and limited in scope to one country.[68] Hence, this call to the Official publications office of the European Communities (OPOCE): '[R]egarding your legal texts, have you nothing which codifies legislation by subject? For instance, where can we find in one place EC laws and Member States' laws on copyright? Have you anything like a citation system, such as Shephards in the US? We need common sources to refer to ... We literally beseech you, in the light of the pollution of Communities' publications, to do something about this aspect!' This produced an embarrassed answer from the director of the OPOCE: 'I fully recognize the problem, I personally cannot solve it'.[69] Truly enough, from 1981

66 Written Question No. 350/74 by Mr De Keersmaeker to the Commission of the European Communities, 16 September 1974; and the response thereto dated 31 October 1974, in *ibid.*, pp. 476–8.

67 Volker Heydt, 'How to Use the Primary Source Material of the European Communities', *International Journal of Law Libraries*, 5(1), 1977, p. 57.

68 *Ibid.*

69 F. Fitzgerald, 'Publications Policy and Activities of the OPOCE', *International Journal of Law Libraries*, 5(1), 1977, pp. 73–4.

onwards, the Celex database would be opened to users external to the EC institutions, but the database was commercialized by a private company (Honeywell Bull) and the access remained *de facto* limited to 'ministers and para-state organs, parliamentary assemblies, law firms, industrial and commercial groups, research centres and universities'[70] who could afford the payment of the fees. With the 1992 Agenda and the exponential growth of EC law both in scope and in number, this situation soon became untenable. The completion of the *paquet Delors* had led the normative production of the EC to reach new highs, with more than 500 new texts (regulations and directives) per year in the 1986–91 period.[71] The need for a continuous supervision of EC legislation became even more stringent for an increasingly diverse set of interest groups, firms and bureaucracies. Suffice it to mention here the number of subscriptions to the *Official Journal* as a good proxy for the level of interest in EC normative production: after stagnating around 10,000 subscriptions from 1974 (9,500) to 1985 (9,727), the number rose to 12,000 in 1988 and to more than 14,000 in 1991.[72] However, as the *Official Journal* provided no overall Index, accessibility to EC law would logically become a matter of growing concern. In 1990, a British lawyer, John Jeffries, echoed a growing frustration among legal practitioners: '[I]n spite of the continuing volume of published material by and about the EC, academic lawyers, research students, practitioners and legal advisers to governments, companies and other organizations have often found difficulties in ascertaining the current state of internal market programme; this problem has not been resolved by wider access to Celex' which is certainly 'not a database for novices' as its 'language is quite inaccessible'.[73] Publishing houses as well as law firms would not leave this demand unsatisfied. They created new species of European law publications, such as volumes compiling EEC legislations (Blackstone's EEC legislation, first published in 1990), law firms' loose-leafs, newsletters on European law, and even databases (such as Deloitte, Haskins & Sells' database, 'EC 1992') – all sorts of information devices that were intended to 'provide

[70] European Commission, *Seizième rapport général sur l'activité des Communautés européennes*, Luxembourg, Office des publications officielles des Communautés, 1982, p. 358.

[71] On this point, see the data produced by Alec Stone on the annual and cumulative production of acts (directives or regulations) by the Communities since 1958, in Alec Stone, *The Judicial Construction of Europe*, Oxford, Oxford University Press, 2004, p. 59.

[72] Data taken from the Annual Reports of the *Official Journal*.

[73] John Jeffries, 'France and the European Communities', *Law Library Journal*, 83, 1991, p. 241.

information and comment in greater or lesser details on the current state of EC law'.[74]

These challenges to Celex were not trivial as they questioned the capacity of EC institutions to authoritatively 'reveal' the state of European law. They called for better 'coverage' of acts, meaning that it should not be merely inter-institutional and inter-Communities, but also multilingual, thus pushing its administrators to expand the database to new languages and new types of acts.[75] Similarly, as EC legislation was continuously expanding in scope and number, the Commission's monopoly over the Celex database became difficult to accept. This led to an increasing autonomy of the database in relation to its initiators: under pressure from the secretariat general of the Commission, and then from the 'legal IT' group created in the Council in 1974, Celex would progressively be detached from the Legal Service, before finally joining, in 1991, the Office of Official Publications of the Communities.[76] With the growing salience of 'transparency', accessibility grew remarkably, the database becoming accessible via the Internet (1997) and then free to access (2004), and culminating in its fusion with Eur-Lex into a unique portal of legal information on the Union.[77] In turn, these various technical and administrative adjustments sheltered the database from most criticisms (incompleteness, bias towards the interests of the service which had produced it, linguistic bias, etc.), thereby eventually authenticating Eur-Lex as both an objective and an official representation of the 'Union of law' that is Europe.

The capacity of the *acquis* to 'officially' measure, if not to 'represent', Europe, is therefore not the result of a spontaneous process of accumulation of texts, but rather the result of a series of strategies and transactions with a large variety of EC-implicated actors (DGs, comitology

[74] *Ibid.*, p. 665.

[75] cf. Terry Hanson, 'An Introduction to Celex: The Database of European Community Law', *European Access*, 2, June 1989, pp. 29–32.

[76] This explains the disputes which emerged around the administrative ownership of the database. Initially created by the Legal Service and under its sole control, Celex would be under the supervision of the personnel and administration service (in the Information and Documentary Research Centre of the European Communities, CIRCE) which would attempt, without success, a merger with ECDOC, the documentary system of the Commission's Secretariat General. Then, in 1991, the Official Publications Office would finally obtain, 'thanks to the support of the "Legal Informatics" service of the Council' for the integration of Celex, marking a certain distancing from the central space of the Commission.

[77] Michaël Duro, 'Celex Grows Up', in *25 Years of European Law Online*, Luxembourg, Publications' Office of the European Union, 2006, pp. 24–35.

committees, the European Parliament and Court of Justice, etc.). At the same time as they sought to mobilize, fend off or even circumvent for their own advantage the *acquis*, identifying its 'fundamental principles', 'ambiguities' or 'gaps', they acknowledged its 'reality' as a faithful representation of 'Europe'. As it became the common pedestal for EC policies and institutional identities, the *acquis* stood as the essential prism through which actors defined the state of Europe and envisaged its reform.[78] Inserting itself into the most routine operations of the Communities, it was therefore progressively turned into 'the constitutional operating system ... axiomatic, beyond discussion, above the debate, like the rules of democratic discourse, or even the very rules of rationality themselves, which (until challenged by postmodern normative and epistemological precepts) seemed to condition debate but not to be part of it'.[79] An evolving notion in nature (representing the *updated* state of law) *and* an immobile concept by definition (embodying the Union's underlying *logic*), the *acquis* involved much more than the sole acceptance of a corpus of texts; it came with the recognition of the existence of a 'Union of law' and of the transversal magisterium of law and lawyers in that singular transnational polity. Conserving of the *past* through its preservation of some 80,000 pages of the *Official Journal* since the beginning of the ECSC,[80] but equally representing the *present* through the never-ending process of screening and updating of its content (particularly in moments of enlargement),[81] the *acquis* provides a social and cognitive basis for the authority of law and lawyers in European polity.

[78] For an illustration, see the study by Cécile Robert on the negotiations preceding the enlargement to the Central and Eastern European States which shows that the *acquis* was used as a 'filter through which the treatment of issues was organized', meaning that 'the actors had the feeling of assisting in a form of inexorable contraction of the debates', in Cécile Robert, 'L'Europe sociale face à son élargissement. Les déterminants institutionnels du débat communautaire sur la dimension sociale de l'élargissement à l'Est', *Annuaire français des relations internationales*, 4, 2003, pp. 434–5.

[79] Joseph Weiler, 'The Reformation of European Constitutionalism', *Journal of Common Market Studies*, 37(1), 1997, p. 97.

[80] According to the estimates of the Commission in European Commission, 'Codification de l'acquis communautaire', COM(2001)645, 21 November 2001.

[81] Each enlargement is an occasion to re-found the *acquis* through a screening of the entirety of the legislation in force, therefore sparking off a recomposition of its structure. The fifth wave of enlargement (2004) thus led to an *acquis* constructed in thirty-one chapters, while, for the negotiations with Croatia and Turkey, it was decomposed into thirty-five chapters expected to form the basis for negotiation in the different groups of experts.

6 'Constitution': the fragmentation of the Treaties and Europe's constitutional fetishism

> I like constitutions. Reading the most beautiful ones – I use this word deliberately – I feel the same pleasure as Stendhal reading the Civil Code.[1]

It is with this genuine declaration of love that prominent French politician of the law and member of Parliament Robert Badinter opened his proposed European Constitution. Indeed, in the first years of the millennium, all of Europe seemed to be in the throes of a 'constitutional fever'.[2] This frenzy at the turn of the century was exceptional, even compared to the pan-European enthusiasm that animated the 'constituents' of the *ad hoc* European Assembly of 1952. This time, the constitutional rhetoric spread well beyond pan-European circles and the world of law: rare indeed was the political group, think tank, university or 'personality' who did not have a 'turn-key' constitution to propose. Among these apprentice constituents can be mentioned – in addition to more obvious players such as the European Commission and Parliament – former French prime minister Alain Juppé,[3] *The Economist*,[4] the University of Cambridge,[5] the Federal Trust, the Friedrich Naumann Foundation,[6] the

1 Robert Badinter, *Constitution européenne*, Paris, Fayard, 2002, p. 9.
2 Renaud Dehousse, *Une Constitution pour l'Europe*, Paris, Presses de Sciences Po, 2002, p. 11.
3 'Europe: le projet de Constitution Juppé-Toubon', *Le Figaro*, 16 June 2000.
4 'A Constitution for the European Union', *The Economist*, 28 October 2000, pp. 22–8.
5 Alan Dashwood and Angela Ward, 'CELS (Cambridge) Draft Constitutional Treaty of the European Union', *European Law Review*, 22(8), 1997, pp. 395–516.
6 See the projects of the European Constitutional Group chaired by the director of the Foundation, Count Otto Lambsdorff: www.la.fnst-freiheit.org/webcom/show_page.php/_c-1203/_nr-1/i.html (accessed 25 August 2011).

European People's Party,[7] and, a few years later, the Action Committee for European Democracy supported by the Robert Bosch Foundation,[8] among others. Even the British government, Euro-sceptic *par excellence* in many respects, in turn participated in this game of rising constitutional bids, presenting its own European 'Constitution', albeit styled as a 'Constitution for a Union of Sovereign States'.[9] In the space of a few years, between Joshka Fisher's speech at Humboldt University on 1 May 2000 calling for the adoption of a common Constitution, and the European Summit in Berlin on 21–22 June 2007 where the draft treaty was shorn of any reference to the constitutional lexicon,[10] the political, administrative and academic actors in Europe let go all semantic prudence. Whereas a few years earlier the boldest think tanks had wondered 'Does Europe need a Constitution?',[11] it was now a matter only of determining what should or should not figure in the constitutional framework that was henceforth accepted by all. There was no longer any hesitation to invoke a vast body of glorious precedents and parallels, starting with the inevitable reference to the Philadelphia Convention. A veritable constitutional fetishism seized Europe, and invested the reworking of its legal architecture with a set of properties and intrinsic virtues, to begin with the solution to the European deficits – democratic, social, symbolic, etc. For a moment, the European Constitution thus defined the horizon of reform towards which all European hopes and ambitions were turned. After years when the constitutional lexicon had remained essentially the domain of Euro-lawyers and EC institutions, it had finally made its way to the forefront of EU politics as a full-fledged political agenda with the ambitioned to reboot the whole system into one constitutional order.

A few months earlier, however, the constitutional lexicon was still a political taboo. As summed up by Joseph Weiler, 'the C word

[7] Wilfried Martens and Elmar Brok, *A Constitution for a Strong Europe*, Draft Constitution of the European People's Party adopted at the Estoril congress, 12 November 2002 (available at www.eppgroup.eu).

[8] Committee of experts chaired by Giuliano Amato and tasked with proposing a new version of the reform treaty following the referendum votes in France and the Netherlands.

[9] Alan Dashwood, *A Constitution for a Union of Sovereign States*, Report for the UK government, October 2002. Concerning this project, see 'Faint-Hearted and Far from the Heart of Europe', *The Independent*, 16 October 2002.

[10] On this point, see Thomas Christiansen and Christine Reh, *Constitutionalizing the European Union*, Basingstoke, Palgrave Macmillan, 2009, p. 14.

[11] Philip Morris Institute for Public Research, *Does Europe Need a Constitution?*, Brussels, June 1996.

(Constitution) was just as bad as the F word (Federalism)'.[12] As late as October 1999, the French government, through its deputy minister for constitutional affairs, mocked with irony the strategy of the 'constitutional *grand soir*',[13] and just a year later the British prime minister Tony Blair ruled out the possibility of taking this direction, in a speech in Warsaw that garnered attention. Even the Euro-lawyers themselves, despite their long-standing inclination to think of the Rome Treaties as a *de facto* Constitution, used this terminology only sparingly, preferring in most instances the adjective to the noun ('constitutional charter', 'constitutional law', 'constitutional treaty', etc.), a locution that was more ambivalent as to the scope of this term.

How did such a strong 'need' for a Constitution come about? How did the constitutional form, long brandied as a shibboleth, make its way to the top of Europe's reform agenda, to the point that it appeared as the mother of all reforms? The abundant literature on this subject offers all sorts of explanations. Some retrace a chronology of politics that highlights the 'gestures' or 'haggling' of a small number of European leaders and sees them as no more than a one-off public relations exercise deliberately organized for the purposes of self-legitimation by a small group of beleaguered political leaders;[14] others emphasize the short-term legal idealism of a small pan-European elite;[15] still others identify an incremental process that, from one intergovernmental conference to the next, set the groundwork for the constitutional breakthrough.[16] None, however, really took the constitutional project itself and its proponents seriously. If the Constitution thus appeared for a while as a mandatory passage towards the 'relaunching' of Europe, it was because this cause rallied a group of advocates, intellectuals and institutional engineers who were eager to lay realistic plans for a new institutional system.

In this light, the nature of the enigma changes. The question is henceforth one of understanding how the object of the predilection of the

[12] Joseph Weiler and Marlene Wind, 'Introduction', in *European Constitutionalism Beyond the State*, Cambridge, Cambridge University Press, 2003, pp. 1–5, p. 1.

[13] Pierre Moscovici, Deposition before the Committee of the French Senate on the European Union, 17 October 1999.

[14] Andrew Moravcsik, 'What Can We Learn from the Collapse of the European Constitutional Project?', *Politische vertieljaresschrift*, 47(2), 2006, pp. 219–41.

[15] Stefano Bartolini, *Taking Constitutionalism and Legitimacy Seriously*, Eurogov Discussion Paper Working Paper No. 1-2008, Connex Research Network.

[16] Thomas Christiansen and Christine Reh, *Constitutionalizing the European Union*, Basingstoke, Palgrave Macmillan, 2009.

federalists,[17] long held to be thoroughly taboo, came to impose itself as the common denominator of reform. I argue below that this constitutional fetishism stemmed less from a sudden federalist whim of European leaders than from a progressive depoliticization of the constitutional 'red flag' itself. This is what seems to be indicated by an eminent high civil servant of the European Commission in the introduction to the draft European Constitution that he himself wrote in 2003 on behalf of the Commission: there is 'a growing awareness – muddled at first, but dispassionate – that this instrument [the Constitution] can be perceived, not exclusively as the expression of a federal political system, but also as a technical mode of simplifying and ordering the EC *acquis*'.[18] It was undoubtedly necessary that 'the Constitution' would die as an object of essentially political value, to take on the trappings of a legal tool and institutional technique and thus be reborn as a necessary horizon of EU institutional reform.

The constitutionalist push

In the 1990s, a decisive *aggiornamento* transformed the 'ontological status' of the constitutional form: it was the fruit of undertakings that were carried out at the crossroads of the parliamentary, bureaucratic and academic spaces of Europe. To understand this operation, one must remember that, between the early 1990s and the adoption of the Lisbon Treaty, the Communities were continually 'under construction': six intergovernmental conferences and two Conventions on institutional reform mobilized in their wake an ever more dense nebula of specialists – civil servants, academics, diplomats, members of parliament – and proposals – committees, reports, works and colloquia. It was in this sublocus of reform, with its continual institutional brainstorming, that the conviction was forged that the revamping of the legal architecture of the Treaties was the alpha and omega, the end-all and be-all, of the political renovation of Europe.[19]

[17] Cf. Antonin Cohen, 'La Constitution européenne. Ordre politique, utopie juridique et guerre froide', *Critique internationale*, 26, 2005, pp. 119–32.

[18] François Lamoureux, 'Introduction', in François Lamoureux (ed.), *Étude de faisabilité. Contribution de la Commission européenne à un avant-projet de Constitution de l'UE*. Document de travail 4-12-2002, Luxembourg, Publications' Office of the European Union, 2002, p. 12.

[19] Bruno de Witte, 'The Question of Treaty Architecture: From the Spinelli Draft to the Lisbon Treaty', in Alexander Trechsel (ed.), *EU Federalism and Constitutionalism: The Legacy of Altiero Spinelli*, Lanham, MD, Lexington Books, 2011, pp. 87–101.

The academic aggiornamento and the 'constitutionalization of Europe'

We must first consider those who were the core intellectuals of this constitutional reform, who forged a notion of 'European Constitution' that was conceptually autonomous from what the notion means in national constitutional traditions. This reinvention that we can conveniently place under the banner of 'the constitutionalization of Europe' flourished most particularly in the hills of Fiesole between Badia Fiesolana and the Villa Schifanoia, the home of the law department of the European University Institute (EUI) since its creation in 1976. Working to detach the constitutional terminology from its State matrix, this undertaking rendered the notion of 'European Constitution' thinkable and conceivable both in terms of scholarly debate and in terms of the institutional agenda for reform.

It is hard to comprehend this renovation of European constitutionalism without situating it in the context of the profound renewal of European studies whereby the overriding pre-eminence of law studies was for the first time contested. Driven by substantial EC funding (Jean Monnet Chairs, Framework Programmes for technological research and development, etc.) and the revival of interest in Europe in the wake of the Single European Act, the modest semi-political, semi-academic 'boutique'[20] of the early years gave way to a vast transnational ensemble dominated by universities, scholarly societies and English and American publishing houses.[21] This evolution was not neutral from a disciplinary point of view, as it went hand in hand with the ramping up of political science: whereas legal studies had comprised nearly half (45 per cent) of academic publications on the European Communities in the mid-1960s, twenty-five years later this discipline was only one of three poles, representing 34 per cent of published work, alongside 31 per cent in economics and 25 per cent in political science.[22] The centre of gravity of European studies had progressively shifted: while in the 1960s observers saw this work as 'tinted by legalism, and in particular legal positivism',[23] henceforth European

[20] John Keeler, 'Mapping EU Studies: The Evolution from Boutique to Boom Field 1960–2001', *Journal of Common Market Studies*, 43(3), 2005, pp. 551–82.

[21] Ioana Popa, 'La structuration internationale des études européennes. Un espace scientifique dissymétrique', in Didier Georgakakis, Marine de Lassalle (eds.), *The Political Uses of Governance: Studying a White Paper*, Leverkusen, Barbara Budrich Publishers, 2012.

[22] Cf. Jacqueline Lastenouse, 'La Commission européenne et les études universitaires', *Temas de Integracao*, 15–16, 2003, pp. 13–36, p. 22.

[23] Joseph Kaiser, 'L'Europe des Savants. European Integration and Social Sciences', *Journal of Common Market Studies*, 43(3), 2005, pp. 36–46.

studies could hardly escape from the 'poli-sci' jargon then in vogue in this transnational academic sphere.[24] Furthermore, this new generation of Euro-scholars was calling into question the explanatory capacity of EC law scholarship, deemed to be incapable of apprehending the multiple social and political dynamics of Europeanization that made the Single European Act so successful. American political scientist Martin Shapiro was one of the first to sound the charge when in 1980 he denounced the uncritical views of some EC law scholars who propounded, in his eyes, a '[European] constitutional law without politics' and turned the ECJ into 'the disembodied voice of juridical reason and a constitutional teleology'.[25] Political scientists underscored the unrealistic character of EC law narrative, pointing to its inability to take into account the multilevel and cross-cutting nature of EC policy networks. The notion of the 'European governance' which became the new flag of European studies was particularly instrumental in this criticism of the law's inability to provide useful knowledge tools to describe Europe *as it is*.[26]

This is the context in which a new academic paradigm of 'constitutionalism' emerged. The epicentre of this new form of European constitutionalism was the EUI, a university born in 1976 after several decades of efforts to obtain the creation of a European university. This interdisciplinary institution, which described itself as 'definitely "European" through and through', became one of the key places where the mutations of European studies could be observed. This was especially true of the law department that stood out in the early 1980s for its combination of a 'contextual approach to law', a dense web of trans-Atlantic exchanges and an active expertise in the field of Europe's institutional reform. This specific identity was sealed on two occasions. The first of these was the institution's association with the debates over the Spinelli draft treaty in the early 1980s. In 1983, EUI law professor Joseph Weiler, close to US 'pioneer' of EC law Eric Stein, drafted, along with two other jurists, Jean-Paul Jacqué and Meinhard Hilf, the declaration of rights that

[24] On this, see the irritation manifested by German law professor and long-time scholar of the European Communities, Christian Joerges, in the face of the development of Anglo-American political science parlance: Christian Joerges, *Integration Through De-legalization: An Irritated Hacker*, European Governance Papers, no. 7-3, 2007.

[25] Martin Shapiro, 'Comparative Law and Comparative Politics', *Southern California Law Review*, 53, 1980, p. 538.

[26] Didier Georgakakis, 'Studying the Political Uses of a White Paper', in Didier Georgakakis and Marine de Lassalle (eds.), *The Political Uses of Governance: Studying a White Paper*, Leverkusen, Barbara Budrich Publishers, 2012. pp. 9–20.

was supposed to go along with the treaty instituting the European Union that was to be adopted by the Parliament in February 1984. In addition, the EUI also hosted various seminars related to the development of the draft text, attended by Altiero Spinelli, lawyers, top civil servants from the Commission, parliamentary rapporteurs and the president of the institutional committee of the European Parliament.[27] This event was the first of many institutional debates that positioned the EUI law department as a core provider of expertise over the reform of Europe.

In parallel, the law department, under the impetus of Italian-American law professor Mauro Cappelletti, undertook a vast research programme funded by the Ford Foundation, known as the 'Florence Integration Project', that brought together a score of young European and American professors such as Joseph Weiler, Martin Shapiro, David and Louise Trubek, Yves Mény, Renaud Dehousse, Monica Seccombe and others who shared a 'contextual' and non-positivist approach to law. This work was published in eight volumes in 1985 under the title *Integration Through Law: Europe and the American Experience*, and established the existence of a truly trans-Atlantic academic group specialized in the analysis of EC institutions. This network was later expanded and consolidated with the launch in 1991 of the Academy of European Law and, in 1995, of the *European Law Journal*, bearing the emblematic subtitle of 'Review of European law in context'. As announced by a former head of the law department, 'if you are looking for legal scholars passionate about a strict legal positivistic, "black-letter" legal analysis only – you will not find them here. We do not apologize for this'.[28] The journal and the law department thus became the privileged locus of a relationship between the European Union and the United States, whereby political science and 'law in context' would continuously mingle.[29]

In this interdisciplinary and trans-Atlantic hub emerged a paradigm of 'constitutionalism' that profoundly renewed the scholarly debate on the relationships between 'Constitution' and 'European Communities'. At the risk of oversimplifying a rich body of scholarship that is often also quite disparate, one could sum up its main traits in three essential elements. First

[27] On these meetings, see Altiero Spinelli, *Diario europeo (1976–1986)*, vol. 3, Bologna, Il Mulino, 1992, pp. 1096–7.

[28] Wojciekh Sadurski, 'Teaching Law in a European University Institute', *EUI Review*, Autumn 2005, pp. 1–2, p. 2.

[29] For a brief summary, see Alec Stone, 'Integration and Constitutionalism in the European Union', in Antonin Cohen and Antoine Vauchez (eds.), *La Constitution européenne. Élites, mobilisations, votes*, Brussels, Presses de l'Université libre de Bruxelles, 2007, pp. 7–14.

of all, this scholarship claims there exists a *de facto* Constitution, a view supported by the jurisprudence of the Court that qualified the Treaties as, successively, the 'internal Constitution of the European Communities' (Opinion No. 1/76 of 26 April 1977), a 'basic constitutional charter' (Case *Les Verts* v. *Parlement européen* of 23 April 1986) and a 'constitutional charter of a European Community of law' (Opinion No. 1/91 of 14 December 1991). The second feature is more explanatory in nature: in a pathbreaking paper,[30] Anne-Marie Slaughter and Walter Mattli reoriented the functionalist narrative of Europeanization from the realm of economics to that of law, pointing at how economic and social interests had seized ECJ *constitutional* jurisprudence and triggered a process of constitutionalization of Europe. From these lenses, the 'European Constitution' was no longer an object of political value subject to partisan debate and controversy, but an objective legal and sociological 'fact' that was both already accomplished *and* continually being enacted, both descriptive *and* prospective. Many argued that this socio-legal account led to a third point, namely, that Europe (and international organizations in general) were in need of a supranational constitutionalist theory that would detach the constitutional lexicon from its State-centred roots. Proclaiming a post-Westphalian reading of international law, criticizing the archaic nature of the *volkish* conceptions underlying national constitutionalisms,[31] Joseph Weiler, a figurehead of this movement, posited a multilevel and polyarchic constitutional order.[32] Within the walls of the Villa Schifanoia, this new constitutional offer found a space that was relatively protected from the scepticism of national doctrines and supreme courts' jurisprudence. Many colloquia were held there and became the rallying point of all those, whether they be political scientists or legal scholars, who sought to strip the notion of Constitution of its national trappings. Benefiting from the position of the EUI at the crossroads of European studies, it was not long before the paradigm of 'constitutionalism' found its way into the manuals and handbooks of 'theories of European integration'.[33]

[30] Anne-Marie Burley and Walter Mattli, 'Europe Before the Court: A Political Theory of Legal Integration', *International Organization*, 47(1), 1993, pp. 41–76.

[31] See the important critique by Joseph Weiler of the ruling on the Maastricht Treaty by the German Constitutional Court: Joseph Weiler, *The State Über Alles. Demos, Telos and the German Maastricht Decision*, Working Paper, New York University, 1995.

[32] Joseph Weiler and Marlene Wind, 'Introduction', in *European Constitutionalism Beyond the State*, Cambridge, Cambridge University Press, 2003.

[33] See Anthony Arnull, 'The Americanization of EU Law Scholarship', in *Continuity and Change in EU Law: Essays in Honour of Sir Francis Jacobs*, Oxford, Oxford University Press, 2008.

This scholarly undertaking went hand in hand with the central position that the law department (and the related research institute founded in 1994, the Robert Schulman Centre) progressively acquired in the field of Europe's institutional reform. EUI law professors like Joseph Weiler, Giuliano Amato, Claus-Dieter Ehlermann, Jean-Victor Louis, Yves Mény (and many others) all took part, together or separately and more or less actively depending on the case, in the writing of one or more of the following constitutional projects: the Spinelli Constitution (1984), the Declaration of Human Rights and Liberties (1989), the Herman Constitution (1994), the Robert Schuman Centre for Advanced Studies reports on reform of the Treaties for the Parliament (1996 and 1999) and for the Commission (2000), of the Convention on the Future of Europe (2002–3) and the draft Lisbon Treaty, etc. While they did not all agree, of course, on the necessity of an authentic 'European Constitution' (for instance, Joseph Weiler considered the Constitution as both superfluous and counterproductive), they all shared the conviction that it was necessary to '*reinforce* the constitutional character of the Treaties' with a palette of solutions ranging from the simple constitutional codification of the existing Treaty articles ('à droit constant') to an overall political rebooting of the Union via a constitutional treaty.

The rationalizing pressure of EU jurisconsults

This new scholarship that cast off the national and State-centred origins of constitutionalism combined with the formation of a supranational constitutional technique, at the heart of the EU institutions. Through the multiple intergovernmental conferences and conventions that marked almost without interruption the period from 1992 to 2007, the legal confection of the Treaties came to be a relatively specialized activity conducted by a small number of jurisconsults drawn from the EU institutions and mindful of the overall rationality of the EC Treaties.

EC jurisconsults traditionally had their homeport at the Commission. It was here, as we have seen above, under the aegis of Michel Gaudet, that a corps of jurists was formed specialized in the legal and judicial defence of the European Communities. This began to change at the end of the 1980s with the development of equally important Legal Services at the Parliament and foremost at the Council. An essential part of this development related to the growing judicialization of the inter-institutional conflicts within the Communities that were spurred in the wake of the attribution to the European Parliament of a right of recourse before the Court (*Les Verts*, April 1986) and the increasing conflicts over the 'legal basis' in the three pillars of the post-Maastricht Europe.[34] Advising both the Council of Ministers and the European Council, the Legal Service of the Council also benefited from the rising influence of the Council's general secretariat in the EC decision-making process from the late 1980s onwards. The growing importance of the rotating presidencies and the new missions assigned to both the European Council and the Council of Ministers in managing the so-called second and third pillars – the Common Foreign and Security Policy (CFSP) and Justice and Home Affairs (JHA) – conferred a pivotal role on the secretariat, notably for the preparation of the European meetings of the two Councils, a process in which the secretariat gradually replaced diplomatic missions and the Committee of Permanent Representatives (Coreper).[35] This progression was consecrated in the role taken on by the secretariat in drafting the Treaties: whereas the secretariat of the Single European Act had been assured jointly by the services of the Commission and of the Council, with the Maastricht Treaty the Council was henceforth alone in handling the intergovernmental conferences, and its Legal Service thereby became the Legal Service of the intergovernmental conferences.[36]

A small group of members of these Legal Services (Commission, Parliament and Council) emerged in the course of the 1990s in the framework of the uninterrupted series of negotiations over Europe's future, and this group came to be the indispensable engineers of the treaty drafting process. As they 'knew each other perfectly and were accustomed to working together, regardless of their institutional origins',[37] these

[34] On this point, see Jean-Paul Jacqué, 'Quelques réflexions sur le contentieux interinstitutionnel', in *Festschrift für Roland Bieber*, Baden-Baden, Nomos, 2007, pp. 338–55; and Guillaume Sacriste, 'Un Parlement européen de droit. Comment un service juridique est devenu "nécessaire" au Parlement européen?', Communication presented at the study day organized by the Polilexes group, *Capitales et capitaux juridiques en Europe* (15 September 2006, CRPS-CURAPP).

[35] See Michel Mangenot, 'The Invention and Transformation of a Governmental Body: The Council Secretariat', in Jay Rowell and Michel Mangenot (eds.), *A Political Sociology of the European Union: Reassessing Constructivism*, Manchester, Manchester University Press, 2010, pp. 46–67.

[36] In the abundant literature on the growing power of the Council Secretariat, see Derek Beach, 'The Unseen Hand in Treaty Reform Negotiations: The Role and Influence of the Council Secretariat', *Journal of European Public Policy*, 11(3), 2004, pp. 408–39.

[37] Jean-Paul Jacqué, 'The Role of the Legal Services in the Elaboration of European Legislation', in Antoine Vauchez and Bruno de Witte (eds.), *Lawyering Europe: European Law as a Transnational Social Field*, Oxford, Hart Publishing, 2013, pp. 43–54.

specialists of European institutional engineering formed a tight circle of *repeat players*. The set comprised jurisconsults such as Roland Bieber, Alan Dashwood,[38] Claus-Dieter Ehlermann, Jean-Paul Jacqué, François Lamoureux, Michel Petite, Jean-Claude Piris, Roland Reich and John Temple Lang,[39] the latter two of whom had in common their past service as director or director general in the Legal Services of one of the major EC institutions. From upstream to downstream, from preliminary working groups for intergovernmental conferences to drafting committees tasked with finalizing the wording of the Treaties, they were nearly continuously at work on the reform of EC institutions. In the course of the 1990s, they led the work of countless expert groups: the working group tasked with simplifying the Treaties in the framework of the intergovernmental conference (1996), the task force under the secretariat of the Convention for the Charter of Fundamental Rights (2000), the secretariat of the Praesidium of the Convention (2002) or the drafting committee presided over by the Council's jurisconsults charged with formulating the terms of the final agreement that would pave the way for the Treaty of Lisbon (2007), to name just a few examples. The opening remarks of the *Festschrift* recently offered to Jean-Claude Piris, the head of the European Council's Legal Service for more than twenty-two years, and emblematically entitled 'A Man for All Treaties', give a glimpse of these multifarious activities:

> This volume pays a tribute to Jean-Claude Piris, who held for more than 22 years, from April 1988 to November 2010, when he retired, the high functions in the Legal Service of the European Council. He became, on the 1st January 1990, Jurisconsult to the European Council and to the Council of the European Union, and director general of the Council's Legal Service. Jean-Claude Piris has been one of the craftsmen of European integration. He has lived at the core of EU institutions of whom he knows all details. He has brought his legal advice by taking part in more than 1,000 meetings of the Coreper, serving for 46 European semesters, and taking part in hundreds of meetings of the European Council. He has also been the Jurisconsult of the last 5 Intergovernmental conferences that met in order to reform the European Treaties. Each time that the European Union faced a serious difficulty, Jean-Claude Piris has contributed to craft a solution both legally correct and politically acceptable (for example, the solution for Denmark in 1992, the 1994 Ioannina compromise, the solution for Ireland in 2002, the Lisbon Treaty in 2007, the 2009 solution for Ireland, the decision on the

[38] Alan Dashwood, 'The Elements of a Constitutional Settlement for the European Union', *Cambridge Yearbook of European Legal Studies*, 4, 2001, pp. 1–13.

[39] John Temple Lang, *Is There a Rational European Constitution Now?*, Oxford, Oxford University Press, 1998.

European External Action Service and the mechanism for the debt crisis in 2010). He also presided over the workings of the expert groups that were set up during the 2003–2004 and 2007 [intergovernmental conferences].[40]

In the context of the many intergovernmental conferences and Conventions of the 1990s and 2000s, these jurisconsults worked almost uninterruptedly on reform of the EU institutional system, thereby acquiring a central position in the fabric of the Treaties as both intellectuals of the institutional reform process and craftsmen able to translate these ideas into technical arrangements. While they usually acted in the shadow of governments and diplomats, these treaty engineers started to play a new role 'acting at the border between the "*pouvoir constitué*" and "*pouvoir constituant*"',[41] thereby reviving what had been the prominent role of the Commission's Legal Service in the 1950s and 1960s under the leadership of Michel Gaudet. While 'the DNA of the Legal Service did include a pro-active role',[42] to put it in the words of one of the directors of the Council's Legal Service, these jurisconsults assumed an increasingly visible role, such as when, in December 1992, Piris intervened at a meeting of the European Council, the first time a jurisconsult of the Council was permitted so to do; similarly, Piris would take over the chairmanship of the expert working groups of intergovernmental conferences, a position previously held by representatives of the country holding the rotating presidency, which even took their name from him: 'Groupe Piris' and 'Groupe Piris II'.[43] It must be said that, in addition to this institutional expertise, they also usually pursued activities in think tanks or universities, speaking sometimes in their own name, sometimes under a pseudonym, or in the name of their institution. They would also take on the role of assisting as experts at the European Conventions of 2000 and 2004, specialists consulted by the constitutional affairs committee of the European Parliament, professors called upon to discuss the state of European institutions in conferences, or as top civil servants coordinating the work of committees of experts. These jurisconsults, who were in practice constantly at the bedside of Europe and its

[40] Jean-Claude Piris (ed.), *A Man for All Treaties. Liber Amicorum en l'honneur de Jean-Claude Piris*, Brussels, Bruylant, 2012.

[41] Herman von Rompuy, 'Préface', in Jean-Claude Piris (ed.), *A Man for All Treaties. Liber Amicorum en l'honneur de Jean-Claude Piris*, Brussels, Bruylant, 2012, p. XVIII.

[42] Giorgio Maganza, 'Un seul homme pour cinq traités', in Jean-Claude Piris (ed.), *A Man for All Treaties. Liber Amicorum en l'honneur de Jean-Claude Piris*, Brussels, Bruylant, 2012, pp. 405 and 409.

[43] *Ibid.*, p. 413.

institutions, thus occupied a crucial position in framing how reform of the Treaties could be conceived of. Table 3 sets out in detail the projects and careers of this group of 'legal architects of the Union'.

It should be said that, in the course of the 1990s, the architecture of the Treaties became increasingly baroque: from opt-outs and reinforced cooperations or pillars, Europe was turning into a crazy-quilt patchwork, thereby undermining the legal and political unity of the Union promised by the 'integration programme'.[44] In the context of the five intergovernmental conferences and the two Conventions of the 1990s and 2000s, the jurisconsults found themselves pushed to the forefront of Europe's institutional fabric, having to reshape a mixed bag of texts (Treaties, annexes, protocols, declarations), simplify them by flushing out the repetitions, redundancies and contradictions in thousands of pages, and knit them altogether via cross-referencing and tables of substitution article by article.[45] Of course, there was no question of imposing abstract models: in the words of the jurisconsults, the art of institutional reform required a keen sense of political *à propos* and clarity so as to 'be understood by ambassadors and ministers as well as by one's students!', and intellectual flexibility that led to 'accepting that, sometimes, while a perfect legal solution existed, it would have to be abandoned to give way to another solution that would allow a viable political decision, all the while complying with the law'.[46] Collectively, they defined pragmatic ways to harmonize, if not unify, the pillars, Communities and Treaties aiming at rationalizing Europe's legal architecture,[47] including concision of expression, simplification by deleting outdated provisions of the Treaties, clarification of the hierarchy of standards, reducing the variety of types of legal acts and instruments (either 'law' or 'regulation'), granting a sole and unique legal personality to Europe, establishing clear rules for the division of competencies (with States, with the European Convention on Human Rights), formalizing treaty amendment procedures, etc. In this framework, the constitutional form – because it allowed the highest degree of formal unity by assembling all these texts under a single umbrella – appeared as the 'regulating

[44] See the assessment by Deidre Curtin, 'The Constitutional Structure of the Union: A Europe of Bits and Pieces', *Common Market Law Review*, 30(1), 1993, pp. 17–69.

[45] Thérèse Blanchet, '1997–2007. D'une simplification des traités à l'autre', in *Mélanges en l'honneur de Jean-Paul Jacqué*, Paris, Dalloz, 2010, pp. 113–25.

[46] Jean-Claude Piris, 'En hommage à Jean-Paul Jacqué', in *Mélanges en l'honneur de Jean-Paul Jacqué*, Paris, Dalloz, 2010, p. XXVI.

[47] Jean-Paul Jacqué, 'La simplification et la consolidation des traités', *Revue trimestrielle de droit européen*, 33(4), 1997, pp. 902–13.

Table 3 *The legal architects of the Union*

	Reform projects	Highest administrative position	Other positions
Roland Bieber (Germany)	'Spinelli Constitution' draft (Parliament, 1984); 'Simplification of the Union Treaties' (Parliament, 1984)	Legal consultant to the European Parliament for twenty years	Professor, University of Lausanne; Cabinets of Presidents Spénale and Dankert (European Parliament)
Alan Dashwood (UK)	Draft Constitutional treaty (University of Cambridge, 1997); Draft Constitution (UK Government, 2002); Deposition at the Convention on legal personality	Référendaire, CJEC; Director, Legal Service, Council (1987–95)	Professor, University of Cambridge; Editor, *Common Market Law Review* and *European Law Review*; law firm
Claus-Dieter Ehlermann (Germany)	Strategies to reinforce the constitutional character of the Treaties (European Parliament, 1996); Study on the reorganization of the Treaties (European Commission, 2000)	Director-General, Legal Service (1977–87); Director-General, DG Competition (1990–5)	Delors Cabinet; Professor, European University Institute; law firm
Jean-Paul Jacqué (France)	'Spinelli Constitution' draft (Parliament, 1984); Treaty simplification group, IGC (Council, 1996); Charter of Fundamental Rights (Convention, 2000); Drafting group, Lisbon Treaty (Council, 2007)	Director of Legal Service, Council (1990–2008)	Professor, University of Strasbourg; Editor, *Revue trimestrielle de droit européen*
François Lamoureux (France)	'Penelope Constitution' draft (Commission, 2002)	Director, Legal Service, Commission; Director, DG Relex	Delors and Cresson Cabinets; Notre Europe (think tank)
Michel Petite (France)	Intergovernmental task force, Amsterdam Treaty (Council, 1996)	Director-General, Legal Service, Commission (2001–7)	Scriener and Prodi Cabinets; law firm
Jean-Claude Piris (France)	Drafting group, Amsterdam Treaty (Council, 1996); Drafting group, constitutional treaty (Council, 2003); Drafting group, Lisbon Treaty (Council, 2007)	Director-General, Legal Service, Council (1988–2010)	
Charles Reich	Constitutional projects (Comafco, Parliament)	Director, Secretariat Cominst, then Comafco, Parliament	
John Temple Lang (Ireland)	Worked on Spinelli draft	Référendaire, CJEU; Legal Service; Director, DG Competition	Professor, University College Dublin; Federal Trust (law firm); law firm

horizon' that was unattainable but still the compass point guiding the strategies. As the standard bearers, in various forms, of this concern for rationalization, they were in many ways the modern manifestation of 'those prince functionaries, authors of systematic codifications ... naturally interested in systematicity for its own sake' described by Max Weber.[48] The main feature of this new constitutional repertoire lay in the belief in the political virtues of legal rationalization both in terms of efficiency in the decision-making process and in terms of accessibility of the Treaties by ordinary citizens. Only in this way can we understand the special satisfaction felt by these jurisconsults when they contemplated 'the architectural elegance of a project both ordered and well structured',[49] or the satisfaction to be had in having conducted an '*aggiornamento* of the Treaties that, starting with a body of material, an *acquis* (Treaties, Charter) of roughly 225 pages (not including the Protocols) led to reducing this body of material by half, to about 124 pages',[50] or when it resulted in 'deleting 533 provisions'.[51]

This rationalizing pressure certainly found its clearest expression in the project for a constitutional treaty henceforth defined as first and foremost a technique of codification putting an end to the dysfunction resulting from the stratification of Treaties, pillars and policies. The major shift came in the middle of the 1990s during the preparation of the intergovernmental conference that would lead to the Amsterdam Treaty. Contributing in 1995 under a pseudonym (albeit a not very discreet one, since he chose the name 'Justius Lipsius', the name of the building where the Council secretariat met), the director of the Council's Legal Service, Jean-Claude Piris, evoked for the first time the utility of a 'Treaty-Constitution' – a 'single short text that would provide for the fusion of the EU and the three European Communities in a single entity, and would be as brief and as legible as possible'.[52] A couple of months later, his main collaborator for institutional matters, EU law professor and Legal Service director, Jean-Paul Jacqué, mentioned what he called

[48] Max Weber, *Sociologie du droit*, Paris, Presses universitaires de France, 1986, p. 197.

[49] Alfonso Matera, in European Commission, *Étude de faisabilité. Contribution de la Commission européenne à un avant-projet de Constitution de l'UE*, Document de travail 4-12-2002, Luxembourg, Publications' Office of the European Union, 2002, p. 50.

[50] François Lamoureux, in *ibid.*, p. 21.

[51] Roland Bieber (ed.), *Simplification des traités de l'Union*, European Parliament, 2 October 1994.

[52] Justius Lipsius, 'La conférence intergouvernementale de 1996', *Revue trimestrielle de droit européen*, 2, 1995, pp. 175–206.

'la Constitution communautaire'.[53] As professionals of institutional coherence, they did not hesitate to show what such a Constitution would entail. At the close of the negotiations for the Amsterdam Treaty, the *groupe des amis de la présidence* coordinated by Jean-Paul Jacqué and the legal adviser to the Dutch government at Coreper, Jaap de Zwaan, drew up a fictitious treaty (that would be made public in application of a declaration annexed to the new Treaty). Truly a legal 'bad conscience', this model constitution showed, like a photographic negative, what a single text would look like that merged *à droit constant* the provisions of all the existing Treaties, while putting the 'constitutional aspects' of the Union at the top of the document. These first drafts were echoed by other members of the Legal Services' 'family', starting with the legal adviser to the European Parliament, Roland Bieber, who had already been associated with the Spinelli draft treaty in 1984 and who in 1996 presented his *Rapport sur la simplification des traités*, or former director of the Commission's Legal Service, Claus-Dieter Ehlermann, who had in the meantime joined the EUI who in the same year had published *Strategies and Options for Reinforcing the Constitutional Character of the Treaties* with a group of law professors at the EUI. In so doing, they – one after the other – joined in a dynamic circle that gave credence to the notion that there was such a thing as a technical need for a European constitution. Thereby, the constitutional solution no longer took the form of a federal political scheme, but was rather a mere technical solution to the institutional dysfunction of the EU.

The European Parliament's constitutional strategy[54]

Since the Spinelli draft treaty of 1984 the European Parliament had also staked a claim to be an essential locus for the formalization of a constitutional agenda for Europe, to the extent that it deemed this to be a fundamental element of its political identity.[55] This activity has essentially taken place within the Committee on institutional affairs (Cominst), an avatar of the *Commission permanente pour les problèmes institutionnels chargée d'élaborer une modification des traités existants* that Altiero Spinelli had created in July 1981 to prime the pump of parliamentary

53 Jean-Paul Jacqué, 'La Constitution communautaire', *Revue universelle des droits de l'homme*, 1995, pp. 397–423.

54 Olivier Costa, 'La contribution de la composante "Parlement européen" aux négociations de la Convention', *Politique européenne*, 13(2), 2004, pp. 21–41.

55 European Parliament Press Service, 'L'ambition constitutionnelle du Parlement européen', 12 January 2005, www.ena.lu (accessed 13 July 2011).

talks on his draft Treaty-Constitution. Over the years, this committee has had a special position among the European Parliament's committees. Unlike the sectoral committees caught up in the co-decision procedure through the European Parliament's increasing legislative role, the Cominst has remained essentially outside the legislative process, asserting itself first and foremost through its constitutional expertise, launching successive trial balloons for treaty revision.[56] A 'political' commission *par excellence* where the most federally inclined could give free rein to their aims, this committee became the rallying point of the most assiduous MEPs, such as Klaus Hänsch elected in 1979 and member of the Commission from 1982 to 2009, Karel de Gucht who had participated in the Spinelli draft (1982–94), Fernand Herman (1985–99) or Jean-Louis Bourlanges (1989–2007). Indeed, the presidents of the European Parliamentary Assembly had often been recruited from its ranks over the years, for example Klaus Hänsch and José Maria Gil-Robles.

All the signs show, however, that in the decade from 1994 to 2004 (fourth and fifth legislatures) the Cominst entered a new phase of constitutional activism. This was certainly related to the failure of the 1994 Herman Constitution through which the European Parliament had sought to renew the 'constituent' ambition of the Spinelli draft. Sponsored by a long-term Belgian Socialist MEP (first elected in 1979) and PhD in law, Fernand Herman, this European Constitution drafted by Cominst was a direct descendant of the Spinelli draft from which it took over the aim of making the European Parliament into nothing less than the constituent assembly of the European Union. However, when it was finally introduced in plenary session, in February 1994, that is, at the very end of the third legislature, it garnered only modest support in the form of a mere resolution.[57] Confronted with this rebuff, the Cominst group of the fourth and fifth legislatures sharply reoriented the committee's strategy, renouncing the idea of embodying alone the 'constituent power' in favour of a strategy of influencing the intergovernmental

[56] Laurent Godmer and Guillaume Marrel, 'The Creation of Institutional Expertise at the European Parliament: Legal and Political Resources of the Members of the Constitutional Affairs Committee', in Antoine Vauchez and Bruno de Witte (eds.), *Lawyering Europe: European Law as a Transnational Social Field*, Oxford, Hart Publishing, 2013, pp. 153–76; and Antonin Cohen and Julien Weisbein, 'Laboratoires du constitutionnalisme européen. Expertises académiques et mobilisations politiques dans la promotion d'une Constitution européenne', *Droit et société*, 60, 2005, pp. 353–71.

[57] Jean-Victor Louis, *Les institutions dans le projet de Constitution de l'Union européenne (Rapport Herman, 1994)*, in Jean-Victor Louis and Denis Waelbroeck (eds.), *L'Union européenne et l'avenir de ses institutions*, Brussels, Presses de l'Université libre de Bruxelles, 1996.

conferences on Treaty reform. The constitutional ambition remained omnipresent, as shown by the renaming of the Cominst to the Committee for *Constitutional* Affairs (Comafco) at the beginning of the fifth legislature (1999) in the run-up to the preparations for the intergovernmental conference that was opening in Nice.[58] However, the Parliament's constitutional strategy now aimed at influence: the tone was given as early as November 1999 in a European Parliament Resolution 'on the preparation of the reform of the Treaties and the next [intergovernmental conference]'. Drafted by German social-democratic MEP and former lawyer trained at the College of Bruges, Jo Leinen, the resolution asked for the 'launching of a constitutional process that encompasses simplification and ratification of the Treaties with a view to the transparency and intelligibility of the Treaties for citizens'.[59] Through the fits and starts of the constitutional process, the Cominst/Comafco maintained throughout the fifth and sixth legislature (1999–2009) a steady vigilance overseeing the preparation and unfolding of the intergovernmental conferences and Conventions, and denouncing any attempt to weaken the constitutional project for the EU.

This new constitutional strategy was accompanied by a claim to intellectual authority in constitutional matters, and the Cominst/Comafco asserted itself – in reports, resolutions and hearings – as a hybrid space, acting both as 'expert group' and pan-European activist. This muddling of lines was not surprising for a Parliament that had appropriated new powers in the legislative field (the 'cooperation' and 'co-decision' procedures), advancing as an argument its expertise in the fields of EU governance.[60] But it also stemmed from the personal traits of the most active members of the committee. Over the course of the legislatures, Cominst had gained in legal credentials what they had lost in political weight within the Parliament. A new group had formed in the committee, that beyond its political affiliations was marked by a very high level of qualification (in 2004, 27 per cent of its members held doctoral degrees), by the decisive weight of its legal expertise (more than two-thirds of members held law degrees) and continued close ties with federalist

[58] Giorgio Napolitano, 'Entretien', *Revue du Marché commun et de l'Union européenne*, October–November 2001, p. 586.

[59] Dimitrakopoulos-Leinen Report on Treaty Reform and the Next IGC, European Parliament, A5-0058/199, 18 November 1999.

[60] Willy Beauvallet, *Profession: Eurodéputé. Les élus français au Parlement européen et l'institutionnalisation d'une nouvelle figure politique et élective (1979–2004)*, University of Strasbourg, 2007.

groups.[61] Among the most active members were: vice-president of the European Movement Jo Leinen, rapporteur under the fourth mandate of many resolutions on the constitutionalization of the Treaties and Comafco president under the fifth mandate (2004–9); law professor Inigo Mendez de Vigo, who was to head the parliamentary delegations to both of the European Conventions (the Charter of Fundamental Rights and the Constitutional Treaty); and the three members who would later represent the European Parliament at the 2007 intergovernmental conference in Lisbon, Elmar Brok, Enrique Baron Crespo and Andrew Duff, all of them active members of pan-European movements and playing on both sides of the law-and-politics fence.[62] This blurring of the lines favoured a special proximity between the Cominst/Comafco MEPs, their legal advisers (or former legal advisers) and the experts they mobilized. The committee could rely on its secretary general, the jurist Charles Reich, who had already taken a part (although modest) in the Spinelli draft and who was a staunch supporter of the 'constitutionalization' cause. The committee also called upon numerous experts that were heard as 'qualified personalities' and commissioned to write reports on the reworking of the Treaties. Among these personalities the law professors of the EUI had a special place, judging by the fact that Joseph Weiler, Jean-Victor Louis, Claus-Dieter Ehlermann and the Robert Schuman Centre for Advanced Studies directed at the time by Yves Mény were solicited in this context. At once mindful of the political stakes involved in affirming the Parliament in treaty revision processes, and responsive to offers of constitutional expertise from academic spheres, the Cominst/Comafco became a singular venue, both a powerhouse for European constitutionalists and an activist group deploying its constituent strategy via roadmaps, memos and other resolutions. The double constitutional repertoire combined a politicization of the stakes, the only level that could interest their MEP colleagues, and an increasing technicization of the terms of debate, that was in phase with the new scholarship in European constitutionalism. This double-faced constitutional project is admirably captured by the constitutional law professor and French

[61] Guillaume Marrel and Laurent Godmer, 'The Creation of Institutional Expertise at the European Parliament: Legal and Political Resources of the Members of the Constitutional Affairs Committee', in Antoine Vauchez and Bruno de Witte (eds.), *Lawyering Europe: European Law as a Transnational Social Field*, Oxford, Hart Publishing, 2013, pp. 153–76.

[62] See Antonin Cohen and Julien Weisbein, 'Laboratoires du constitutionnalisme européen. Expertises académiques et mobilisations politiques dans la promotion d'une Constitution européenne', *Droit et société*, 60, 2005, pp. 353–71, p. 362.

socialist MEP, Olivier Duhamel, in his 2000 report on the 'constitutionalization of the Treaties' adopted by Comafco: '[T]he existence of a European Constitution', underscored the rapporteur, 'would have the double advantage of giving European citizens a reference text and of accomplishing the indispensable simplification of the standards governing European institutions'.[63]

A shared assumption? The 'need' for a European Constitution

Should we conclude that these streams of Constitution entrepreneurs actually dictated their ambitions to the heads of government and the diplomats through what would eventually become the Constitutional Treaty? The situation was assuredly more complex than that. The various types of reformers, whether EU law professors, EU institutions' jurisconsults, or Comafco MEPs, set their actions in their own specific timeframes, repertoires of discourse and logic; and it is therefore difficult to revive them as constituting just one homogeneous agent. For instance, we cannot ignore the reserve and cautiousness of jurisconsults *vis-à-vis* their political constituents and their legitimate embodying of 'the will of the peoples and the States'.[64] Furthermore, the relationships between these three groups were changeable, and not always cooperative, depending on the circumstances and situations. Rather than looking for some sort of conspiracy by constitutional entrepreneurs, it is suggested that we consider their capacity to collectively shape a new space of possibilities for EU reform, one that national political leaders and diplomats would then have to take into account in the intergovernmental conferences themselves.

A common constitutional ethos

The capacity of the constitutional project to become, for a period of time at least, Europe's commonsensical idea of treaty reform, can be traced back: it relates to the intense cross-sectoral interactions that played out over a decade of colloquia, parliamentary committees and other EU institutions' working groups. Important in this has been the striking mobility of certain protagonists in the debate, whom we find circulating between the different poles and assuming different (political, scholarly,

[63] Constitutional Affairs Committee, *Rapport sur la constitutionnalisation des traités*, Rapporteur Olivier Duhamel, Doc PE A5-289/2000, 12 October 2000, p. 8.

[64] Michel Petite, 'Le métier de Directeur général du Service juridique de la Commission européenne', *Revue des affaires européennes*, 3, 2007–8, p. 517.

technical) roles all along Europe's constitutional saga. How does one distinguish between former prime minister Giuliano Amato who went back to being a law professor at the EUI, and law professor Inigo Mendez de Vigo acting as the European Parliament's representative at the Convention for the Future of Europe? Who is more academic, the 'politician' Oliver Duhamel (albeit a professor of constitutional law and MEP) insisting upon the logical consequences of the fragmentation of the Treaties, or the 'jurist' Claus-Dieter Ehlermann, former spokesman for Jacques Delors and director general of the competition DG who as long ago as the distant 1970s had defended a constitutional interpretation of the European Treaties? Whom should one follow here in this perpetual game of role-playing: 'the friend Giuliano (who) told me that as a professor of constitutional law he would commit suicide if the unanimity rule (for treaty revisions) was maintained (in the constitutional treaty)', or the 'political Amato (who) would survive'?[65] As it is impossible to identify one single group, one must instead refer to a 'pro-reform nebula',[66] a space that was poorly unified, with fuzzy outlines, but which was united by a common vocabulary and traversed by a single 'constitutional ethos'[67] that turned all EU existential problems into a matter of constitutional reform.

The Constitution entrepreneurs agreed above all on the diagnosis: in their view, Europe's enduring crisis lay in the traditional intergovernmental method of reforming Treaties, and its related set of actors, first and foremost national politicians and diplomats, deemed incapable of accomplishing an authentic European Union. The fruit of laborious haggling that perverted the spirit of the European project, the Treaties were the favourite target of the constitutional reformers. Academic work, legal assessments and political verdicts would all denounce the irrational nature of the inter-State dynamics and the resulting 'constitutional chaos'. 'Each of us admits', stated the director of the Council's Legal Service in 1995, 'that the outcome of the Maastricht conference, i.e. the Treaty of the European Union, is not adequately formulated: the form and presentation of the Treaty lack the clarity necessary for it to

[65] Remarks by Jean-Luc Dehaene, reported by Olivier Duhamel, *Pour l'Europe. La Constitution européenne expliquée et commentée*, Paris, Seuil, 2005, p. 124.

[66] Christian Topalov (ed.), *Laboratoires du nouveau siècle. La nébuleuse réformatrice et ses réseaux en France 1880–1914*, Paris, Éditions de l'EHESS, 1994, pp. 12–58, p. 13.

[67] Paul Magnette, *Au nom des peuples. Le malentendu constitutionnel européen*, Paris, Cerf, 2006, p. 80.

be understood, and hence accepted, by public opinion'.[68] And less than a decade later, the 330-hour marathon of the Nice conference provided a *reductio ad absurdum* that the diplomatic method had reached its limits. It suffices to note the comments of the Comafco MEP Andrew Duff, an ardent advocate of 'parliamentarizing' the treaty revision process who denounced governments' 'cynical manoeuvres', and issued a final verdict: '[I]f proof were needed that intergovernmentalism does not work well in the common European interest, we need look no further than Nice'.[69] It is no surprise to find in these transnational circles the most fervent advocates of the 'conventional method', a method that had been initially tested with the 1999 Convention on the Charter of Fundamental Rights, which for the first time opened the treaty-revision process to MEPs and representatives of 'civil society'.

A second commonality of the Constitution entrepreneurs was the remarkable stability of the arsenal of institutional solutions proposed, throughout the many reports, draft treaties and resolutions produced over the period. It all occurred as if there were a sort of reform catalogue that was adjusted as circumstances changed, suggesting novel combinations and arrangements on each occasion, but which remained essentially the same. It is no easy task to determine the origin of this reform arsenal from which the Constitution entrepreneurs so regularly drew their ideas. From the 1975 report of the European Commission on the European Union project to the 1984 Spinelli draft of the European Union Treaty, from the 1994 Herman Constitution of the European Parliament to the 1999 Dehaene report for the Commission, a consistent reform portfolio progressively consolidated. Among the solutions envisaged, the adoption of a Framework Treaty or a Treaty-Constitution went hand in hand with the recognition of the legal personality of the Union, the inclusion of fundamental rights in the Treaties, the recognition of the supremacy principle, or the adoption of simplified terminology for EC norms ('laws', 'regulations'), etc. All reformers actually did identify in each new treaty elements borrowed from that catalogue. As the head of the Commission's Legal Service stated:

> [M]any of the ideas [contained in the draft treaty that came out of the Convention on the Future of Europe] were already in the air, and sometimes well known to

[68] Justius Lipsius, 'La conférence intergouvernementale de 1996', *Revue trimestrielle de droit européen*, 2, 1995, pp. 175–206.

[69] See Andrew Duff, 'From Amsterdam Leftovers to Nice Hangover', March 2001, www.ena.lu.

specialists. Examples: dividing the Treaty into a 'constitutional' Part 'I', and a Part 'II' that would be less so, is an idea that harks back to 1995, before Amsterdam. The Commission had even at the time commissioned the European University Institute to work up a model intended to prove the feasibility of this presentation and to evaluate the resulting simplification.[70]

The most experienced constitutional reformers actually nourished a sort of practical wisdom, recalling that 'reforms mature slowly in the Union and many of the points claimed to be new have already been broached, marginally or in the framework of earlier intergovernmental conferences'.[71]

Last but not least, Constitution entrepreneurs shared a form of constitutional fetishism that endowed the legal reorganization of the Treaties' internal structure with an array of intrinsic properties and virtues: more efficiency as the EC norms would become more accessible for professionals, more 'acceptance by public opinion',[72] and eventually more explicit political legitimacy for a European polity that had been grounded so far essentially on a mere simple 'permissive consensus'.[73] Relatedly, Constitution entrepreneurs felt somehow legitimized in their undertaking by what they perceived as a 'need for a Constitution': as indicated by the head of the Council's Legal Service, 'after forty years the people of our countries now feel the need for some clarification'.[74] The most zealous proponents would even identify such 'need' in the 'European opinion', sponsoring Eurobarometers' polls on the proposed 'future Constitution';[75] others, like the president of the Committee on Constitutional Affairs at the European Parliament, went so far as to calculate the 'costs' and 'risks' that would result from the non-adoption of the Constitution,[76] along the lines of the 1988 Cecchini report that a few years earlier

70 Michel Petite, 'La Convention européenne sur l'avenir de l'Europe', in Christine Kaddous and Andreas Auer (eds.), *Les principes fondamentaux de la Constitution européenne*, Geneva, Helbing and Lichtenhahn, 2006, pp. 39–46.

71 Jean-Paul Jacqué, 'Les dispositions générales et spéciales du Traité établissant une Constitution pour l'Europe', *Revue trimestrielle de droit européen*, 2, 2005, pp. 549–56, p. 550.

72 Justius Lipsius, 'La conférence intergouvernementale de 1996', *Revue trimestrielle de droit européen*, 2, 1995, pp. 175–206, p. 204.

73 Claus-Dieter Ehlermann and Armin von Bogdandy, 'Un traité unique pour le marché unique', *Revue du Marché commun*, 405, February 1997, p. 82.

74 Justius Lipsius, 'La conférence intergouvernementale de 1996', *Revue trimestrielle de droit européen*, 2, 1995, pp. 175–206, p. 177.

75 'La future Constitution européenne (Vague 1)', *Flash Eurobaromètre*, January 2004.

76 On the 'gains' side of the ledger, the adoption of a constitutional charter would avoid the delays of European leaders in responding to the Lebanese crisis, enable the leaders to

had evaluated the 'costs of non-Europe' in the run-up to the completion of the Internal Market. On the whole, in this nebula of EU reforms the constitutional horizon was an accepted fact and inevitably the starting point of all reform arguments and plans.

There is no better sign of the dynamic and endogenous force of this nebula than the capacity of the constitutional agenda to perpetually rise from its ashes as it has been doing for nearly twenty years or so, despite various streams of academic criticism, referendum failures and legal invalidations before national supreme courts. There are many factors explaining this enduring presence in Europe's reform debates: the Constitution entrepreneurs of the Comafco employed the full arsenal of 'reports', 'declarations of intent' and other 'roadmaps' to continuously boost the constitutional impetus. Academics have also had a specific contribution to the many revivals of the constitutional project, periodically attempting to spark the European constitutional debate through colloquia through workshops and congresses on themes such as: 'Does the European Constitution Exist?', 'What Constitutionalization of the Treaties?', 'What Is a Constitution?', etc. Last but not least, one should not underestimate the specific contribution of institutional techniques used to keep the constitutional agenda alive. Suffice it to mention here the *forward linkage* articles included in European Treaties pre-empted the agenda of the next following intergovernmental conference by listing a set of reform items to be accomplished in the future.[77] For instance, the Amsterdam Treaty (1996) left pending a series of questions listed in the 'Amsterdam Left-Overs', and the Nice Treaty (2000) inscribed the 'reorganization of the Treaties' into the agenda of the following intergovernmental conference already scheduled for 2004, etc. All in all, this created a self-maintaining salience of the constitutional agenda at the core of Europe's political debate.

Constitutionalizing Europe

The reorientation of the European reform agenda in constitutional terms actually happened in a relatively short time span: from the European

better anticipate terrorist attacks in the United Kingdom and Germany at the time, and to react more effectively to illegal immigration and to the energy crisis, etc. Cf. Jo Leinen, *The Cost of No-Constitution*, Constitutional Affairs Commission, European Parliament, 19 September 2006.

[77] See Yves Buchet de Neuilly, 'Des bâtisseurs de traités. Continuités et discontinuités du processus conférentiel', in Antonin Cohen and Antoine Vauchez (eds.), *La Constitution européenne. Élites, mobilisations, votes*, Brussels, Presses de l'Université libre de Bruxelles, 2007.

Council declaration in Laeken (December 2001) to the 'constitutional skeleton' proposed by Valery Giscard d'Estaing, president of the brand-new Convention on the Future of Europe (October 2002). In less than a year, the space of possible reforms for the 'future of Europe' shrank rapidly. Yet nothing had presaged this reorientation. In late 1999, the Council jurisconsult Jean-Claude Piris, well versed in EC politics, stated that the question of the EU Constitution 'is not going to come up in the short term . . . It is not really a subject of discussion between the governments and the Member States'.[78] Accordingly, the conclusions of the group of 'wise men' presided over by Jean-Luc Dehaene, suggesting in October 1999 that a constituent strategy be engaged, were received with scepticism by the European chancelleries, that were above all worried about completing the difficult negotiations on the Nice Treaty that were to anticipate the future waves of enlargement to Eastern and Central Europe. Two years later, the Laeken declaration marked a first step, when the Belgian presidency, which was very active on the constitutional front,[79] let the term 'Constitution' appear in a statement by heads of State. However, the reference remained very vague: among some sixty other questions raised, the Laeken declaration questioned, in rather speculative terms, 'whether this simplification and reworking [of the Treaties] should not lead at term to the adoption of a constitutional text; what essential elements should be found in such a Constitution?' The mandate given to the Convention on the Future of Europe in the wake of this declaration seems singularly imprecise: the European Constitution was initially evoked only as a distant eventuality, while the Convention itself was not conceived as 'constituent' but simply preparatory to the 2004 intergovernmental conference. It must be said that, in the context of the period 2000–1, there were more concerns about Europe's social and democratic deficits: the large demonstrations that had taken place at the summits in Nice in December 2000 and then in Göteborg in June 2001 marked the rising impact of anti-globalization criticism of the European Union. Moreover, the Convention opened in a context of uncertainty as to its own usefulness. One of the most enthusiastic participants, the MEP Olivier Duhamel, pointed out the many unknowns: if

[78] Jean-Claude Piris, 'L'Union européenne a-t-elle une constitution? Lui en faut-il une?', *Revue trimestrielle de droit européen*, 35(4), 1999, p. 630.

[79] Xavier Landrin, 'Sortie de crise et construction du changement. Les usages du projet conventionnel sous la présidence belge du Conseil', in Antonin Cohen and Antoine Vauchez (eds.), *La Constitution européenne. Élites, mobilisations, votes*, Brussels, Presses de l'Université libre de Bruxelles, 2007, pp. 33–52.

the Convention were to choose to adopt a single text, 'many options are available: "final document", draft of a "new treaty", "fundamental treaty", "constitutional treaty", "constitutional charter", "constitution", etc.'.[80] And yet, the Convention very quickly turned towards the path of constitutional reform. Although it cannot really be called 'accidental',[81] in light of the mobilization of the many Constitution entrepreneurs listed above, the constitutional *volte face* within the Convention occurred with surprising ease and rapidity: as early as October 2002, that is, eight months after the Convention began its work, there was no longer any doubt that the final product would have to be a Constitution.[82]

This is difficult to understand without referring to the fact that, by its very structure, the Convention for the Future of Europe constituted an unprecedented opening of the arena of treaty negotiations to the Constitution entrepreneurs, whether they be jurisconsults, MEPs or academics. Members of the EU institutions' Legal Services were on the front lines of the treaty-making process: while the secretariat of the Council of Ministers did not this time assume the secretariat of the Convention, the secretariat of the Praesidium of the Convention nonetheless included many jurists from the three institutions who thus mingled with the diplomats.[83] They were all old hands in the theatre of the European institutional debate,[84] and most shared a common fund of diagnostics and solutions in terms of 'simplification', 'transparency', 'governance' or 'integration'. Hence, and even though they came from institutions that frequently had divergent interests, they were progressively able to replicate within this *ad hoc* secretariat the consensual work methods and habits so characteristic of the 'institutional triangle',[85] a non-negligible feat considering that they were charged with writing nearly all the texts

80 Olivier Duhamel, 'Une Constitution pour l'Europe. 4 février 2002', in Olivier Duhamel, *Pour l'Europe. La Constitution européenne expliquée et commentée*, Paris, Seuil, 2005, p. 23.

81 Peter Norman, *The Accidental Constitution: The Story of the European Convention*, Brussels, Eurocomment, 2003.

82 Michael O'Neill, *The Struggle for the European Constitution: A Past and Future History*, London, Routledge, 2009.

83 See Florence Deloche-Gaudez, 'Le secrétariat de la Convention européenne. Un acteur influent', *Politique européenne*, 13, 2004, pp. 43–67.

84 The chief officer of the Secretariat, John Kerr, was the permanent representative of the United Kingdom to the EU (1990–5) and his deputy, Annalise Giannalla, worked for the Council of Ministers for over thirty-one years.

85 Yves Buchet de Neuilly, 'Des bâtisseurs de traités. Continuités et discontinuités du processus conférentiel', in Antonin Cohen and Antoine Vauchez (eds.), *La Constitution européenne. Élites, mobilisations, votes*, Brussels, Presses de l'Université libre de Bruxelles, 2007.

that served as the basis for discussion in the plenary sessions. In addition to these 'counsellors to the Prince', there were the members of the European Parliament who were on this occasion admitted to the negotiating table without reservation. While these were only 16 out of the 105 members of the Convention, some of them were senior members (Elmar Brok, Andrew Duff, Klaus Hänsch, Inigo Mendez de Vigo) and key rapporteurs (Olivier Duhamel) of the Comafco.[86] From the outset they deployed their constitutional activism, launching all sorts of test balloons and other doomed texts,[87] such as that circulated by British free-market federalist Andrew Duff,[88] or the Constitution proposed in November 2002 by the German Conservative Elmar Brok. Together they ploughed the constitutional field in which the Convention was gradually inscribed. Not without provoking 'the great surprise of many observers [as they saw] many of the positions of the European Parliament prevail as the mainstream thinking of the Convention, beginning with the legal personality of the Union, the inclusion of the Charter of Fundamental Rights, the rejection of the renationalization of competencies, and a broad EC scope for the third pillar'.[89] And finally, EU studies' scholars, and in particular law professors, found an unprecedented echo in the Convention. In addition to the fact that they were frequently tapped as experts for the different working groups, there were innumerable research programmes, conferences and dossiers devoted to the novelty of the Convention process. The public nature of the sessions, breaking with the secrecy of diplomatic talks, put the Convention under the scrutiny of EU experts in institutional matters who were in fact the main, if not the only audience of a constitutional saga that sparked little interest outside EU circles.

The convergence of these different streams of Constitution entrepreneurs in the forum of the Convention had an immediate effect: it led to a sort of closure of the discussion around the 'language of public law',[90] the rhetoric of Treaties' simplification and, *in fine*, the constitutional agenda, with the risk of disappointing a large proportion of the reform ambitions that the Convention had sparked. The clear predominance of

[86] Olivier Costa, 'La contribution de la composante "Parlement européen" aux négociations de la Convention', *Politique européenne*, 13(2), 2004, pp. 21–41.

[87] Andrew Duff, *The Struggle for Constitution*, London, The Federal Trust, 2009, p. 14.

[88] 'A Model Constitution for a Federal Union of Europe', Conv 234/02.

[89] Peter Norman, *The Accidental Constitution: The Story of the European Convention*, Brussels, Eurocomment, 2003.

[90] Paul Magnette, *Au nom des peuples. Le malentendu constitutionnel européen*, Paris, Cerf, 2006.

law graduates and legal professionals in this forum was certainly no stranger to this prevalence of a legal framing of Europe's issues for the future.[91] But it also reflected the fact that the Constitution entrepreneurs were the only ones to offer the Praesidium and its president a way towards a trans-partisan and transnational agreement. It was they who offered the first compromises at the Convention, through their hard work in the working groups devoted to 'simplification', the 'Charter', the 'legal personality of the Union' and to 'subsidiarity'. As these settings were beyond the reach of political and diplomatic balances (they were constituted on a purely voluntary basis), and often affected by absenteeism,[92] they were often marked by an over-representation of the constitutional reformers who had long appropriated these themes as their preferred battlegrounds. Thereby, Constitution entrepreneurs secured a considerable room to manoeuvre and promote the constitutional agenda.[93] This was particularly true for the 'legal personality' working group presided over by the former Socialist prime minister of Italy and EUI law professor, Giuliano Amato. Supported by the recommendations of various academic reports, in particular from the Robert Schuman Centre for Advanced Studies,[94] the working group from the start adopted a singularly technical outlook, even as it imposed itself as the locus of formation of an extremely ambitious consensus, in that its final report saw the constitutional revamping of Europe as a 'logical' consequence of endowing the Union with legal personality: '[A]lthough it would be conceivable to merge the legal personalities without merging said Treaties, on this point the group has concluded that the merger of these two Treaties would be a logical consequence of the fusion, and would help simplify the Treaties'. The conclusion was praised by the Constitution entrepreneurs: EUI law professors saw here the mark 'of the first EUI

[91] Antonin Cohen, 'Legal Professionals or Political Entrepreneurs? Constitution Making as a Process of Social Construction and Political Mobilization', *International Political Sociology*, 4(2), 2010, pp. 107–23.

[92] The 'Legal Personality' group had only twenty-nine members, as opposed to forty members in the 'Liberty and Security' group: cf. Michal Frzyzanowski and Florian Oberhuber, *(Un)Doing Europe: Discourses and Practices of Negotiating the EU Constitution*, Brussels, Peter Lang, 2007.

[93] See the working group on the Charter (presided over by Antonio Vittorino), the subsidiarity group (presided over by Inigo Mendez de Vigo) and the groups on 'simplification' and on the 'legal personality of the Union', both presided over by Giuliano Amato.

[94] Cf. Communication of the Convention Commission dated 22 May 2002, 'Un projet pour l'UE', COM(2002)247 (p. 18); and Giuliano Amato, *Rapport du président du groupe de travail III 'Personnalité juridique'*, Brussels, Conv 305/02, 1 October 2002.

work on simplification [that] had been carried out by Giuliano Amato';[95] former head of the Commission's Legal Service, Michel Petite, welcomed 'the expert experience of these [four] groups that gave me the strong impression of [having] the rare possibility of explaining certain orientations to a Convention that had no political or dogmatic *a priori* assumptions, and ultimately of being able to convince them'.[96] Introduced during the plenary session of 2–3 October, the ambitious Amato Group report[97] – the first from a working group – placed the Convention in the constitutional furrow, much to the displeasure of the Eurosceptics who seemed to belatedly take the measure of this *coup de force*. British Conservative David Heathcoat-Amory expressed his position a few days later: 'Is a working party on simplification the right place to make big changes to the institutional balance?'[98] These first forms of agreement were all the more important given that at the same time the other working groups dealing with more substantial issues (economic governance, defence, exterior action, social Europe) were divided by irreconcilable differences in the economic and social domains that rapidly jeopardized the chances of renewal on this front.[99] As Olivier Duhamel noted in the course of October 2002: '[I]t seems more and more clear that the content of policies will not be much discussed'.[100] A few weeks later, Valery Giscard d'Estaing referred explicitly to this first compromise when he presented a 'preliminary draft of a constitutional treaty' (28 October 2002), thereby confirming the constituent path taken by the Convention. Olivier Duhamel commented with the constitutional zeal that was his at the time: '[O]ne year after Laeken, the members of the Convention in their vast majority had appropriated their mission, and there was no longer any question of alternatives or options'.[101] The rare Eurosceptics who had carved out a place in the parliamentary delegations, those whom

[95] Jacques Ziller, *La place du droit matériel dans le projet de Constitution. Pourquoi une troisième partie?*, Working Paper, Robert Schuman Centre for Advanced Studies, European University Institute, 2004, p. 11.

[96] Michel Petite, 'La Convention européenne sur l'avenir de l'Europe', in Christine Kaddous and Andreas Auer (eds.), *Les principes fondamentaux de la Constitution européenne*, Geneva, Helbing and Lichtenhahn, 2006, pp. 44–5.

[97] In the working group, only William Abitbol, a French 'sovereignist', rejected the report.

[98] Quoted in Paul Magnette, *Au nom des peuples. Le malentendu constitutionnel européen*, Paris, Cerf, 2006, p. 87.

[99] Michal Frzyzanowski and Florian Oberhuber, *(Un)Doing Europe: Discourses and Practices of Negotiating the EU Constitution*, Brussels, Peter Lang, 2007, p. 78.

[100] Olivier Duhamel, *Pour l'Europe. La Constitution européenne expliquée et commentée*, Paris, Seuil, 2005, p. 69.

[101] *Ibid.*, p. 45.

Giuliano Amato called 'the three solitary horsemen of anti-Europeanism, the Dane Bonde, the Frenchman Abitbol, and the British Heathcoat-Amory',[102] were now completely marginalized. The rest was just a matter of detail, it seemed, starting with the drafting of the third part of the Constitution – a codification of the existing Treaties *à droit constant* – that was entrusted to a group of jurists from the three Legal Services (Commission, Council, Parliament), who were given the task of going through the Treaties with a fine-toothed comb. Indeed, prudence was no longer necessary a few months later when, in February 2003, the first articles of the treaty proposed by the Praesidium referred almost naturally to the 'Constitution'. Nothing is more revealing of this imperceptible convergence than the joint letter addressed to Valery Giscard d'Estaing in July 2003 by Giuliano Amato, Elmar Brok and Andrew Duff, who, in the name of their respective parties (Socialists, Conservatives and Liberals), concluded their participation in the Convention, speaking with one voice of this 'Constitution' that they had just passed by consensus.[103]

The constitutional form was indeed the main result of the Convention moment. While the draft treaty did touch upon specific policies and competences of the Union, the overall institutional balance was not profoundly affected by the changes introduced in the European Treaties. The innovation of the Convention draft treaty lay first and foremost in the ambition to engrave in stone the multifarious ensemble of the Treaties, institutions and policies that had accumulated over the decades. In this light, the controversies of the French referendum campaign in the spring of 2005 debating whether the constitutional treaty was neo-liberal or social-democrat in nature, missed the point of the main novation: it was under the aegis of the law (and, *in fine*, of judges) that the different segments and periods of the European Union were woven together. Denounced by the proponents of national constitutional 'authenticity' who saw it as a perverted form of 'Constitution', the treaty established the law and its legitimate interpreters as the privileged enunciators of Europe, and at the same time the geometric locus where the articulation of powers and groups (and their eventual conflicts) would be voiced and regulated. A conceptual map of Europe, like any constitution, the Treaty establishing a Constitution for the European

[102] Giuliano Amato, in 'Le regard de deux professeurs de l'IUE sur la Convention', *EUI Review*, Winter 2003, p. 8.

[103] Giuliano Amato, Elmar Brok and Andrew Duff, 'Letter to Valery Giscard d'Estaing', 24 July 2003, available on the website of the Convention for the Future of Europe (www.european-convention.eu).

Union was thereby sealing the integrating function of the law. Its failure on the occasion of the French and Dutch referenda, followed by a Lisbon Treaty which was explicitly deprived of any constitutional rhetoric, seemingly condemn – once again – the constitutional project, and marked the still incomplete institutionalization of the 'integration programme' that had initially emerged under the guise of the '*Van Gend en Loos–Costa* doctrine'.

However, while the constitutional rhetoric was once again becoming a political taboo, *officially* banned from treaty reform vocabulary by a declaration of the European Council of 22 June 2007,[104] it remained, however, still very vivid through a number of essential categories (the *acquis*, the 'Union of law', the Fiscal Compact's 'golden rule', etc.), instruments (the Court's case law, the Eur-Lex database, etc.), and specialized groups which have linked their destiny to the promotion of the constitutional understanding of Europe.[105] Even though it was officially banned from public discourse over Europe's future, the constitutional paradigm continued to pursue its path in semi-public arenas. Transnational academic settings still valued the 'constitutionalization of Europe'. EU jurisconsults, called upon as they have been to formalize new institutional mechanisms to deal with the euro crisis, started their rationalizing undertaking all over again. And, there again, in the political field, the question of the legal foundations of the EU appeared through the discussion over the reform of the European Treaties. While a couple of months earlier, it seemed that 'the Treaties would not be modified for at least another generation',[106] the constitutional rhetoric surged once more; just as it seemed that the euro crisis was calling for more budgetary coordination, again the constitutional toolbox would appear as the most authoritative governance tool to restore Europe's credibility before the markets; the new rules were elevated to the status of a 'golden rule' of constitutional value placed under the control of the

[104] The Conclusions of the European Council solemnly stated: 'The constitutional concept, which consisted in repealing all existing Treaties and replacing them by a single text called "Constitution", is abandoned ... The TEU and the Treaty on the Functioning of the Union will not have a constitutional character. The terminology used throughout the Treaties will reflect this change: the term "Constitution" will not be used': European Council, 'Conclusions of the Presidency', Brussels, 21 and 22 June 2007 (available at http://europa.eu/rapid/press-release_DOC-07-2_en.htm).

[105] See also Thomas Christiansen and Christine Reh, *Constitutionalizing the European Union*, Basingstoke, Palgrave Macmillan, 2009.

[106] Herman van Rompuy, 'Préface', in *A Man for All Treaties. Liber Amicorum en l'honneur de Jean-Claude Piris*, Brussels, Bruylant, 2012, p. XVII.

ECJ. And it does not come as a surprise that the head of German diplomacy, Guido Westerwehle, eventually brought the constitutional solution back into the political debate over Europe's future. '*La Constitution est morte, vive la Constitution!*', one could conclude, thereby pointing at how deeply entrenched in the political thinking of Europe the constitutional paradigm is.

Conclusion: constitutio non moritur!

'Jurisprudence', 'Code', and 'Constitution' are thus the habitual denizens of the EU polity. Essential operators of the historic evolution of the Treaties into an institutional *system* with its own logic, these legal constructs are today the basic building blocks of a specifically European political lexicon, as much as the true markers of the relative autonomy acquired by Europe. They are Europe's 'boundary objects',[1] sufficiently malleable and adaptable to circulate between Euro-implicated groups, institutions, and policies, and at the same time sufficiently robust and coherent to preserve a relatively stable set of meanings across this transnational social space. They are henceforth essential practical handbooks for decoding a European ensemble that is ritually presented as complex and *sui generis*, offering cross-sectoral grids for identification and classification that make it possible to conceive the *unity* of the EU polity as a whole, above and beyond the fragmentation of policies and levels of government. Objects of value common to many groups and actors, they are inscribed in a single 'arch of legitimacy' that associates the integrity of Europe to the long-term stability of this legal infrastructure, a veritable conservatory of the fundamental principles of the European project itself ('Union of law', *méthode communautaire*, 'constitutional charter'). Enmeshed in an ever denser network of significations that associate them to the very nature of the Union, these objects are deemed indispensable for its 'equilibrium' and its 'revival'; if one of the pillars of the Jurisprudence–Code–Constitution triptych wobbles it seems all of Europe that is in danger. In other words, they form in many ways an

[1] Susan Leigh and James Griesemer, 'Institutional Ecology, "Translations" and Boundary Objects: Amateurs and Professionals in Berkeley's Museum of Vertebrate Zoology (1907–1939)', *Social Studies of Science*, 19, 1989, pp. 387–420.

essential part of the EU's specific cognitive and normative infrastructure. Because they are among the few objects of value that Europe can claim as its own, they are the 'blocks of granite' on which most, if not all, *relances* of its administrative, political, economic integration are grounded. Thereby, they are not so much a hindrance blocking change, or a force of institutional inertia, but rather the very stage upon which change is determined. Take the recent Fiscal Compact born, in a time of deep economic crisis, of the Franco-German desire to forge instruments to control the deficits of Member States, and that, *in fine*, has resulted in a constitutional 'golden rule' placed under the double control of the Commission and the ECJ, once more deemed to be the only institutions capable of embodying, by the medium of the law, Europe's general interest.[2] All in all, the constitutional function that has historically been granted to law is Europe's 'moving constant': a fixed point that has seemed to resist all attempts to renegotiate and reorient Europe's integration path over the past five decades, as much as a transmission belt for all projects that have the ambition to strengthen Europe's unity.

[2] On this, see Antoine Vauchez, *Démocratiser l'Europe*, Paris, Seuil, 2014.

Bibliography

Printed sources

Amato (Giuliano), *Rapport du président du groupe de travail III 'Personnalité juridique'*, Brussels, Conv 305/02, 1 October 2002

'Le regard de deux professeurs de l'IUE sur la Convention', *EUI Review*, Winter 2003, p. 8

Amato (Giuliano), Brok (Elmar) and Duff (Andrew), 'Lettre à Valery Giscard d'Estaing', 24 July 2003, available on the website of the Convention for the Future of Europe (www.european-convention.eu)

Angelo (Homer), 'Developments in the European Common Market', *International and Comparative Law Bulletin*, 7(2), 1963, pp. 10–13

Angelo (Homer) and Waelbroeck (Michel) (eds.), *Brevets et marques au regard du droit de la concurrence en Europe et aux États-Unis. Colloque organisé les 15 et 16 novembre 1966*, Brussels, Presses universitaires de Bruxelles, 1968

Arithmos, 'Propos européens', *Cahiers du droit européen*, 1(1), 1965, pp. 95–6

Badinter (Robert), *Constitution européenne*, Paris, Fayard, 2002

Balladore Pallieri (Giorgio), 'Problèmes juridiques de la CECA', in Centro italiano di studi giuridici, *Actes officiels du congrès international sur la CECA, Milan-Stresa, 31 mai–9 juin 1957*, 7 vols., Milan, Giuffrè, 1959

Bieber (Roland) (ed.), *Simplification des traités de l'Union*, Luxembourg, European Parliament, 2 October 1994

Bieber (Roland), Jacqué (Jean-Paul) and Weiler (Joseph), *L'Europe de demain, une union sans cesse plus étroite: analyse critique du projet de traité instituant l'Union européenne*, Luxembourg, Office des publications officielles des Communautés européennes, 1985

Birkelbach (Willi), *Rapport fait au nom de la commission politique sur les aspects politiques et institutionnels de l'adhésion ou de l'association à la Communauté*, 122, European Parliament, 15 January 1962

Blanchet (Thérèse), '1997–2007. D'une simplification des traités à l'autre', in *Mélanges en l'honneur de Jean-Paul Jacqué*, Paris, Dalloz, 2010, pp. 113–25

Bowie (Robert) and Friedrich (Carl) (eds.), *Studi sul federalismo*, Milan, Comunità, 1959

Catalano (Nicola), *Manuel de droit des Communautés européennes*, Paris, Dalloz-Sirey, 1962

'L'inserimento diretto delle disposizioni contenute nel Trattato istitutivo della Comunità economica europea negli ordinamenti giuridici degli Stati membri', *Foro padano*, 5, 1963, pp. 33–42

'Le Traité d'Union européenne. Légitimité juridique et institutionnelle', Crocodile. Lettre aux membres du Parlement européen, 11, June 1983

Catalano (Nicola) and Monaco (Riccardo), 'Rapport italien', in FIDE, *Deuxième colloque international de droit européen. La Haye, 1963*, The Hague, W. E. J. Tjeenk Willink, 1966, pp. 115–35

Chevallier (Roger-Michel), 'Commentaire d'arrêt', *Gazette du palais*, 19–22 January 1963, pp. 1–2

College of Bruges, 'Droit communautaire et droit national. Semaine de Bruges', *Cahiers de Bruges*, 14, 1965

Colliard (Claude-Albert), 'L'irréductible diplomatique', in *Études de droits des Communautés européennes. Mélanges offerts à Pierre-Henri Teitgen*, Paris, Pedone, 1984

Colneric (Ninon), Edward (David), Puissochet (Jean-Pierre) and Ruiz-Jarabo Colomer (Dámaso) (eds.), *Une Communauté de droit. Festschrift für Gil Carlos Rodrigues Iglesias*, Berlin, BWV, 2003, p. 443

Comité de réflexion sur le préambule de la Constitution – 'Comité Veil', *Rapport au président de la République*, Paris, La documentation française, 2008

Conseil de l'ordre du barreau de Bruxelles, 'Installation des juristes étrangers à Bruxelles', *Ordre des avocats. Barreau de Bruxelles*, March 1968, pp. 47–8

Curtin (Deidre), 'The Constitutional Structure of the Union: A Europe of Bits and Pieces', *Common Market Law Review*, 30(1), 1993, pp. 17–69

Da Cruz Vilaça (José), 'Address by Mr Advocate General José da Cruz Vilaça on the Occasion of His Departure', *Synopsis of the Work of the Court of Justice in 1988 and 1989*, Luxembourg, Curia, 1990

Dashwood (Alan), 'The Elements of a Constitutional Settlement for the European Union', *Cambridge Yearbook of European Legal Studies*, 4(1), 2001, pp. 1–13

Dashwood (Alan) and Ward (Angela), 'CELS (Cambridge) Draft Constitutional Treaty of the European Union', *European Law Review*, 22(8), 1997, pp. 395–516

Dehousse (Fernand), *La ratification des traités. Essai sur les rapports des traités et du droit interne*, Paris, Sirey, 1935

Rapport établi au nom de la Commission des affaires politiques et des questions institutionnelles sur l'élection de l'Assemblée parlementaire européenne au suffrage universel direct, Assemblée parlementaire européenne, documents de séance, 30 April 1960, Doc. 22

Rapport fait au nom de la commission juridique sur la primauté du droit communauté, Parlement européen, documents de séance, 1965, p. 14

L'avenir institutionnel des Communautés européennes, Nancy, Centre européen universitaire, 1967

Deringer (Arved), 'Les règles concernant la concurrence dans le cadre du Marché commun entrent en vigueur', *Revue du Marché commun*, 5(2), 1962, pp. 70–82

Dimitrakopoulos (Giorgos) and Leinen (Jo), *Rapport sur la réforme des traités et la prochaine Conférence intergouvernementale*, Parlement européen, A5-0058/199, 18 November 1999

Donner (Andreas), *Audience solennelle du 8 mars 1962 à l'occasion du départ de M. le juge Nicola Catalano et de la prise de fonctions de M. le juge Alberto Trabucchi*, Luxembourg, Curia, 1962, 18 p

'National Law and the Case-Law of the European Court of Justice', *Common Market Law Review*, 1(1), 1963, pp. 8–14

'Les rapports entre la compétence de la Cour de justice des Communautés européennes et les tribunaux internes', *Recueil des cours de l'Académie de droit international de La Haye*, 115(2), 1965, pp. 1–61

The Role of the Lawyer in the European Communities, Chicago, IL, Northwestern University Press, 1968

'Funeral Oration in Honour of Mr Jacques Rueff Given by Judge A. M. Donner on 11 May 1978', in *Formal Sittings of the Court of Justice. 1978 and 1979*, Luxembourg, Curia, 1979

Due (Ole), 'Address by Ole Due, President of the Court, on the Occasion of the Entry into Office of Judge Paul Kapteyn', *Synopsis of the Work of the Court of Justice in 1990*, Luxembourg, Curia, 1991

'Address by Ole Due, President of the Court, on the Occasion of His Departure', in *Report of Proceedings. 1992–1994*, Luxembourg, Curia, 1995

Duff (Andrew), 'From Amsterdam Leftovers to Nice Hangover', March 2001, published on www.ena.lu

The Struggle for Constitution, London, The Federal Trust, 2009

Duhamel (Olivier), *Rapport sur la constitutionnalisation des traités. Rapport pour la Commission des affaires constitutionnelles*, Doc. PE A5-289/2000, Luxembourg, European Parliament, 12 October 2000

'Une Constitution pour l'Europe. Le texte intégral de la Constitution expliqué et commenté', *Pour l'Europe*, Paris, Seuil, 2003

Duro (Michaël), 'Celex Grows Up', in *25 Years of European Law Online*, Luxembourg, Publications' Office of the European Union, 2006, pp. 24–35

Ehlermann (Claus-Dieter) and von Bogdandy (Armin), 'Un traité unique pour le marché unique', *Revue du Marché commun*, 405, 1997, pp. 81–5

Everling (Ulrich), 'Address by Judge Ulrich Everling on the Occasion of His Retirement from Office', in *Synopsis of the Work of the Court of Justice in 1988 and 1989*, Luxembourg, Curia, 1990

Everling (Ulrich) and Wohlfart (Ernst), *Die Europäische-Wirschaftsgemeinschaft: Kommentar zum Vertrag*, Berlin, Vahlen, 1960

Fédération internationale pour le droit européen, 'Résolution finale de la FIDE', *Bulletin de l'Association des juristes européens*, 15–16, 1st trimester 1964, pp. 78–9

Deuxième colloque international de droit européen. La Haye, 1963, Zwolle, NV Uitgeversmij, 1966

Fitzgerald (F.), 'Publications Policy and Activities of the OPOCE', *International Journal of Law Libraries*, 1977, pp. 64–75

François (J. P. A.), 'La juridiction européenne dans la communauté internationale', in *Mélanges offerts à Henri Rolin. Problèmes de droit des gens*, Paris, Pedone, 1964, pp. 95–103

Galmot (Yves), 'Address by Judge Yves Galmot on the Occasion of His Retirement from Office', in *Synopsis of the Work of the Court of Justice in 1989*, Luxembourg, Curia, 1990

Gattini (Andrea), 'Joined Cases Yassin Abdullah Kadi et al. v. Council and Commission. 3 September 2008', *Common Market Law Review*, 46(1), 2009, pp. 213–39

Gaudet (Michel), 'Le Marché commun devant les juges', *Annales de droit et sciences politiques*, 2, 1961, pp. 133–49

'Incidences des Communautés européennes sur le droit interne des États membres', *Annales de la Faculté de droit de Liège*, 1, 1963, pp. 5–26

'Exposé de Michel Gaudet devant la Commission juridique du Parlement européen en sa réunion du 18 février 1965', *Revue trimestrielle de droit européen*, 2(2), 1965

'The Challenge of the Changing Institutions', *Common Market Law Review*, 3(3), 1965–6, pp. 143–57

'Entretien avec Gérard Bossuat', *INT 603 of 14th April 1988, Voices of Europe Collection*, accessible on the website of Historical Archives of the European Union

Gori (Paolo), 'Una pietra miliare nell'affermazione del diritto europeo', *Foro italiano*, 1963, p. 10

'La preminenza del diritto delle Comunità europee sul diritto interno degli Stati membri', *Giurisprudenza italiana*, 1964, pp. 1071–86

Grass (Roger), 'Les ressources humaines à la Cour de justice des Communautés européennes', in *Mélanges en l'honneur de Philippe Léger*, Paris, Pedone, 2006, pp. 69–77

Grewe (Wilhelm), 'The Lawyer as Diplomat', *Society of International Law Proceedings*, 54, 1960, pp. 232–6

Gurman (Hannah), *The Dissent Papers: The Voices of Diplomats in Cold War and Beyond*, New York, Columbia University Press, 2012

Hallstein (Walter), 'Economic Integration: An Example of the Association of States', *International Law Association Conference Report. August 1960*, 1960, pp. 13–32

United Europe: Challenge and Opportunity, Cambridge, MA, Harvard University Press, 1962

'The European Economic Community', *Political Science Quarterly*, 78(2), 1963, pp. 161–78

'La Communauté européenne, nouvel ordre juridique', *Les documents de la Communauté européenne*, Luxembourg, Publications officielles des Communautés européennes, 27, November 1964, pp. 1–12

'L'unité de l'action européenne (discours du 15 octobre 1964 aux VIIe états généraux des communes d'Europe)', Lausanne, Centre de recherches européennes, 1965

'Zu den Gründlanden und Verfassungsprinzipien der Europäischen Gemeinschaften', in *Zur Integration Europas, Festschrift für Carl Friedrich Ophüls*, Karlsruhe, CF Müller, 1965, p. 5

Hamson (C. J.), 'Methods of Interpretation: A Critical Assessment of the Results', in Court of Justice of the European Communities, *Judicial and Academic Conference 27–28 September 1976*, Luxembourg, Office des publications officielles des Communautés européennes, 1976

Hansen-Ingram (Diane), 'Tales from the Tartan Chambers', in *A True European: Essays for Judge David Edward*, Oxford, Hart Publishing, 2004, pp. 2–7

Heydt (Volker), 'How to Use the Primary Source Material of the European Communities', *International Journal of Law Libraries*, 5(1), 1977, p. 57

Hoskins (Mark) and Robinson (William) (eds.), *A True European: Essays for Judge David Edward*, Oxford, Hart Publishing, 2004

Iglesias (Gil Carlos), Due (Ole), Schitgen (Romain) and Elsen (Charles) (eds.), *Mélanges en hommage à Fernand Schockweiler*, Baden-Baden, Nomos, 1999

'Address by M. Gil Carlos Iglesias, President of the Court of Justice of the European Communities', in *1952–2002: 50th Anniversary of the Court of Justice of the EC. Formal Sitting 4 December 2002*, Luxembourg, Curia, 2003

Institut d'études juridiques européennes, *Le Parlement européen. Pouvoirs, élections, rôle futur*, Liège, Université de Liège, 1976

Institut für das Recht der europäischen Gemeinschaften, *Zehn Jahre Rechtsprechung des Gerichtshofs der Europäischen Gemeinschaften. Congrès de Cologne des 24–26 avril 1963*, Cologne, Carl Heymanns Verlag, 1965

Jacqué (Jean-Paul), 'La Constitution communautaire', *Revue universelle des droits de l'homme*, 1995, pp. 397–423

'La simplification et la consolidation des traités', *Revue trimestrielle de droit européen*, 33(4), 1997, pp. 902–13

'Les dispositions générales et spéciales du Traité établissant une Constitution pour l'Europe', *Revue trimestrielle de droit européen*, 41(2), 2005, pp. 549–56

Jeantet (Fernand-Charles), 'Commentaire de l'arrêt Van Gend & Loos', *La semaine juridique*, 1963, p. 13177

Jeffries (John), 'France and the European Communities', *Law Library Journal*, 83, 1991, pp. 237–51

Kutscher (Hans), 'Address by President Hans Kutscher Delivered at the Formal Sitting Held on 30 October 1980 on the Occasion of Mr Everling Taking Office as Judge', in *Formal Sittings of the Court of Justice 1980–1981*, Luxembourg, Curia, 1982

'Address Delivered by the President of the Court of Justice, H. Kutscher, at the Formal Sitting of the Court on 29 March 1979 on the Occasion of the Retirement of Judge Andreas M. Donner', in *Formal Sittings of the Court of Justice. 1978 and 1979*, Luxembourg, Curia, 1979

'Address Delivered by H. Kutscher, President of the Court, on Judge T. Koopmans' Taking up Office. 29 March 1979', in *Formal Sittings of the Court of Justice. 1978 and 1979*, Luxembourg, Curia, 1979

Lagrange (Maurice), 'Conclusions sous Fédération charbonnière de Belgique c. Haute autorité de la CECA. Affaire No. 8/55', in Cour de justice des Communautés européennes, *Recueil de la jurisprudence de la Cour*, Luxembourg, Curia, 1955, p. 263

'Conclusions sous Gouvernement de la République française contre Haute autorité de la CECA. Affaire No. 1-54', in *Recueil de la jurisprudence de la Cour*, Luxembourg, Curia, 1955, pp. 53–5

'L'ordre juridique de la CECA vu à travers la jurisprudence de sa Cour de justice', *Revue de droit public*, 84, 1958, pp. 841–65

'Le rôle de la Cour de justice des Communautés européennes tel qu'il se dégage de sa jurisprudence', *Revue du Marché commun*, 4(32), 1961, pp. 39–53

'Conclusions sous Confédérations nationales des producteurs contre Conseil des CEE, Affaire 16-62, 14 décembre 1962', in European Court of Justice, *Reports of Cases before the Court*, Luxembourg, Curia, 1962, p. 486

'L'organisation, le fonctionnement et le rôle de la Cour de justice des Communautés européennes', *Bulletin de l'Association des juristes européens*, 13–14, 1963, pp. 5–35

'Conclusions sous Costa c. ENEL. 25 juin 1964', in Cour de justice des Communautés européennes, *Recueil de la jurisprudence de la Cour*, Luxembourg, Curia, 1964, pp. 1169–93

'La CJCE du Plan Schuman à l'Union européenne', in *Mélanges Fernand Dehousse*, Paris, Nathan et Labor, 1979, pp. 127–37

Lamoureux (François) (ed.), *Étude de faisabilité. Contribution de la Commission européenne à un avant-projet de Constitution de l'UE*, Document de travail 4-12-2002, Luxembourg, Publications' Office of the European Union, 2002

Lecourt (Robert), 'L'Europe dans le prétoire', *Le Monde*, 23 February 1963, p. 1

'L'unification du droit européen est aussi un moyen de construire l'Europe', *France-Forum*, March–April 1963, pp. 27–31

'Le rôle du droit dans l'unification européenne', *Bulletin de l'Association des juristes européens*, 17–18, 1964, pp. 5–23

'La dynamique judiciaire dans l'édification de l'Europe', *France-Forum*, April–May 1965, pp. 20–2

'Allocution prononcée à l'audience solennelle du 23 octobre 1968 à l'occasion du Xe anniversaire de la CJCE', *Revue trimestrielle de droit européen*, 4(4), 1968, pp. 746–62

'Speech Delivered by Mr Robert Lecourt on 7 October 1976 on the Occasion of His Departure', in *Formal Hearings of the Court of Justice*, Luxembourg, Curia, 1976

'Qu'eut été le droit des Communautés sans les arrêts de 1963 et 1964?', in *L'Europe et le droit, Mélanges Boulouis*, Paris, Dalloz, 1991, pp. 349–61

Leinen (Jo), *The Cost of No-Constitution, Commission des affaires constitutionnelles*, Luxembourg, European Parliament, 19 September 2006

Lipsius (Justius), 'La conférence intergouvernementale de 1996', *Revue trimestrielle de droit européen*, 31(2), 1995, pp. 175–206

Louis (Jean-Victor), 'Compte-rendu', *Cahiers du droit européen*, 1(1), 1965, pp. 74–82

L'ordre juridique communautaire, Commission des Communautés européennes, Luxembourg, Publications' Office of the European Union, 1993

Mackenzie Stuart (Jack), 'Address in Commemoration of Karl Roemer, a Former Member of the Court, Delivered by Lord Mackenzie Stuart, President of the Court. 5 February 1985', in *Synopsis of the Work of the Court of Justice in 1984 and 1985*, Luxembourg, Curia, 1986

'Éloge funèbre de Maurice Lagrange prononcé par le président Lord Mackenzie Stuart', in European Court of Justice, *Aperçu des travaux de la Cour en 1986 et 1987 et audiences solennelles*, Luxembourg, Curia, 1988

'Address by Lord Mackenzie Stuart, President of the Court, on the Occasion of His Retirement from Office', in *Synopsis of the Work of the Court of Justice in 1988 and 1989*, Luxembourg, Curia, 1989

Mancini (Federico), 'Address by Federico Mancini, President of Chamber, on the Occasion of the Departure of President Ole Due', in *Synopsis of the Work of the Court of Justice in 1991*, Luxembourg, Curia, 1992

Martens (Wilfried) and Brok (Elmar), *Une Constitution pour une Europe forte. Projet de Constitution du PPE adopté au Congrès d'Estoril*, 12 November 2002 (accessible on the website of the EPP)

Mégret (Jacques), 'La spécificité du droit communautaire', *Revue internationale de droit comparé*, 19(3), 1967, pp. 565–77

Mégret (Jacques), Louis (Jean-Victor), Vignes (Daniel) and Waelbroeck (Michel), *Le droit de la Communauté économique européenne. Commentaire du traité et des textes pris pour son application*, vol. 1, Brussels, Presses universitaires de Bruxelles, 1970

Mertens de Wilmars (Jossé), 'Address by J. Mertens de Wilmars, President of the Court on the Occasion of the Taking up of Office by Advocate General Peter Verloren van Themaat. 4 June 1981', in *Formal Sittings of the Court of Justice 1980–1981*, Luxembourg, Curia, 1982

'Address by President J. Mertens de Wilmars on the Occasion of the Retirement from Office of Mrs Advocate General Simone Rozès. 13 February 1984', in *Synopsis of the Work of the Court of Justice in 1984 and 1985*, Luxembourg, Curia, 1985

'Souvenirs externes sur les débuts de la Cour', *XXXV anni (1952–1987)*, Luxembourg, Curia, 1987

Mestre (Achille), 'Commentaire sous Arrighi, Conseil d'État. 3 novembre 1936', *Recueil Sirey*, 3, 1937, p. 33

Miller (Arthur Selwyn), 'Foreword', in *Doing Business in the Common Market*, George Washington University and Commerce Clearing House Inc., 1963, pp. iii–x

Monaco (Riccardo), 'Nicola Catalano (1910–1984)', *Rivista di diritto europeo*, 23(1), 1984, pp. 104–5

Memorie di una vita, memorie per l'Europa, Rome, Ledip, 1996

Mösler (Hermann), 'Der Vertrag über dei Europäische Gemeinschaft für Kohle und Stahl', *Zeitschrift für Ausländisches Recht und Volkerrecht*, 14, 1951, pp. 3–22

Munch (Fritz), 'Prolégomènes à une théorie constitutionnelle des Communautés européennes', *Rivista di diritto europeo*, 1(1), 1961, pp. 127–37

Napolitano (Giorgio), 'M. Giorgio Napolitano répond aux questions de la Revue sur Le large débat', *Revue du Marché commun et de l'Union européenne*, 452, 2001, pp. 586–8

Olivier (Gérard), 'Entretien avec Gérard Bossuat et Myriam Rancon', *INT 714 of 4 December 2003*, accessible on the website of Historical Archives of the European Union

Ophüls (Carl Friedrich), 'Juristische Grundgedanken des Schumanplans', *Neue Juristische Wochenschrift*, 15 April 1951, pp. 288–92

Padis (Pierre), 'Introduction à un colloque de juristes européens', *Problèmes juridiques et pratiques du Marché commun*, Lyon, Imprimerie des petites affiches lyonnaises, 1962

Pescatore (Pierre), 'Les aspects fonctionnels de la Communauté économique européenne, notamment les sources du droit', in Commission vie et droit des affaires, *Les aspects juridiques du Marché commun*, Liège, collection scientifique de la Faculté de droit de Liège, 1958, pp. 51–84

'La Cour en tant que juridiction fédérale et constitutionnelle', in Institut für das Recht der Europäischen Gemeinschaften, *Zehn Jahre Rechtsprechung des Gerichtshofs der Europäischen Gemeinschaften*, Cologne, Carl Heymanns Verlag, 1965, pp. 520–58

'The Common Market', *The Scots Law Times*, 1970, pp. 65–8

Le droit de l'intégration. Émergence d'un phénomène nouveau dans les relations internationales selon l'expérience des Communautés européennes, Leiden, Sijthof, 1974

'L'Exécutif communautaire. Justification du quadripartisme institué par les traités de Paris et de Rome', *Cahiers du droit européen*, 14(4), 1978, pp. 387–406

'Les objectifs de la Communauté européenne comme principes d'interprétation dans la jurisprudence de la Cour de justice', in *Miscellanea Ganshof van der Meersch*, Brussels, Bruylant, 1979, pp. 325–63

'Address by Mr Pierre Pescatore Delivered at the Formal Sitting Held on the Occasion of Mr Everling Taking Office as Judge', in *Formal Sittings of the Court of Justice 1980–1981*, Luxembourg, Curia, 1980–1

'Les travaux du "groupe juridique" dans la négociation des Traités de Rome', *Studia diplomatica*, 24(1–4), 1981, pp. 159–78

'Address by Mr Pierre Pescatore on the Occasion of His Retirement from Office', in *Synopsis of the Work of the Court of Justice in 1984 and 1985*, Luxembourg, Curia, 1986

'Une révolution juridique. Le rôle de la Cour de justice européenne', *Commentaire*, 59, 1992, pp. 569–74

'Le traité CECA. Origine et modèle de l'unification européenne', in *CECA (1952–2002)*, Luxembourg, Publications' Office of the European Union, 2002, pp. 181–8

'Robert Lecourt (1908–2004)', *Revue trimestrielle de droit européen*, 41(3), 2005, pp. 989–96

Vade-mecum. Recueil de formules et de conseils pratiques à l'usage des rédacteurs d'arrêts, Brussels, Bruylant, 2007

Études de droit communautaire européen (1962–2007), Brussels, Bruylant, 2008

Petite (Michel), 'La Convention européenne sur l'avenir de l'Europe', in Christine Kaddous and Andreas Auer (eds.), *Les principes fondamentaux de la Constitution européenne*, Geneva, Helbing and Lichtenhahn, 2006, pp. 39–46

'Le métier de directeur général du service juridique de la Commission européenne', *Revue des affaires européennes*, 3, 2007–8, pp. 517–21

Phelan (William), 'Supremacy, Direct Effect and Dairy Products in the Early History of European Law', EUI Working Paper, 2014/11

Philip Morris Institute for Public Research, *Does Europe Need a Constitution?*, Brussels, June 1996

Piris (Jean-Claude), 'L'Union européenne a-t-elle une Constitution? Lui en faut-il une?', *Revue trimestrielle de droit européen*, 35(4), 1999, pp. 599–636

'En hommage à Jean-Paul Jacqué', in *Mélanges en l'honneur de Jean-Paul Jacqué*, Paris, Dalloz, 2010

(ed.), *A Man for All Treaties. Liber Amicorum en l'honneur de Jean-Claude Piris*, Brussels, Bruylant, 2012

Puissochet (Jean-Pierre), *L'élargissement des Communautés européennes: Présentation et commentaire du traité et des Actes relatifs à l'adhésion du Royaume-Uni, du Danemark et de l'Irlande*, Paris, Éditions techniques et économiques, 1974

Quardi (Rolando), Monaco (Riccardo) and Trabucchi (Antonio) (eds.), *Trattato istitutivo della Comunità economica europea*, Milan, Giuffrè, 1965

(eds.), *Trattato CECA. Commentario*, Milan, Giuffrè, 1970

Reuter (Paul), *La Communauté économique du charbon et de l'acier*, Paris, LGDJ, 1957

'Techniciens et politiques dans l'organisation internationale', in *Politique et technique*, Paris, Presses Universitaires de France, 1958, pp. 181–96

'Communautés européennes et techniques d'unification', in *Les problèmes juridiques et économiques du Marché commun*, Lille, Librairies techniques, 1960, pp. 15–25

Rey (Jean), 'Les juristes et le Marché commun', *Journal des tribunaux*, 81, 1961, pp. 1–2

Roemer (Karl), 'Conclusions sous NV Algemeine Transport Van Gend en Loos contre Administration fiscale néerlandaise. 12 décembre 1962. Affaire No. 26-62', in Cour de justice des Communautés européennes, *Recueil de la jurisprudence de la Cour*, Luxembourg, Curia, 9, 1963, pp. 29–58

Rolin (Henri), 'La Cour du charbon et de l'acier', *Journal des tribunaux*, 71, 1951, pp. 345–6

Rueff (Jacques), 'Une mutation dans les structures politiques. Le marché institutionnel des Communautés européennes', *Le monde économique et financier*, 9–10 February 1958, p. 5

Sadurski (Wojcieh), 'Teaching Law in a European University Institute', *EUI Review*, Fall 2005, pp. 1–2

Servan-Schreiber (Jean-Jacques), *Le défi américain*, Paris, Denoël, 1967

Sieglerschmidt (Helmut), *Report on Drawn on Behalf of the Legal Affairs Committee of the European Parliament on the Responsibility of the European Court of Justice for the Uniform Application of EC Law in the Member States*, European Parliament, Docs. 1-414/81, 1981 and 1-1052/82, 10 January 1982

Simon (Denys), 'Retour du mythe du gouvernement des juges?', *JurisClasseur-Europe*, February 2006, p. 1

Snyder (Francis), 'Book Review', *Modern Law Review*, 53(5), 1990, pp. 706–7

Sorensen (Max), 'Obligations conventionnelles et droit interne', in *Les droits de l'homme en droit interne et droit international*, Brussels, Presses universitaires de Bruxelles, 1968, pp. 46–8

Spinelli (Altiero), 'La beffa del Mercato comune. 24 sett. 1957', *L'Europa non cade dal cielo*, Bologna, Il Mulino, 1960, pp. 282–7

Diario europeo (1976–1986), vol. 3, Il Mulino, 1992

Stein (Eric), 'The European Parliamentary Assembly: Techniques of Emerging "Political Control"', *International Organization*, 13(2), 1959, pp. 233–54

'The New Institutions', in Eric Stein and T. L. Nicolson (eds.), *American Enterprise in the European Common Market*, Ann Arbor, MI, University of Michigan Press, 1960

'European Communities', *American Journal of Comparative Law*, 22(3), 1974, pp. 573–5

'The Making of a Transnational Constitution', *American Journal of International Law*, 75(1), 1981, pp. 1–27

Steindorff (Ernst), 'Schuman-Plan und Europäischer Bundesstaat', *Politisches Archiv*, 20 May 1951, pp. 3955–86

'Der Beitrag Walter Hallstein zur europäische integration', in *Probleme des Europäische Recht. Festschrift für Walter Hallstein zu seinem 65 Geburstag*, Frankfurt am Main, Klostermann, 1966

'The Grundig–Consten Case, a Landmark Decision of the European Court of Justice on Common Market Antitrust Law', *American Journal of Comparative Law*, 15(4), 1966, pp. 811–22

Stendardi (Gian Galeazzo), *I rapporti fra gli ordinamenti giuridici italiano e delle Comunità europee*, Milan, Giuffrè, 1958

Teitgen (Pierre-Henri), *Rapport fait au nom de la Commission des affaires politiques et des relations extérieures de la Communauté sur les pouvoirs de contrôle de l'Assemblée commune et leur exercice*, Assemblée commune de la CECA, 5 November 1954

'Préface', in Fernand Dehousse, *L'Europe et le monde. Recueils d'études, de rapports et de discours 1945–1960*, Paris, LGDJ, 1960

Temple Lang (John), *Is There a Rational European Constitution Now?*, Oxford, Oxford University Press, 1998, 38 p

Ter Kuile (L. F. D.), 'Rapport néerlandais', in FIDE, *Deuxième colloque international de droit européen. La Haye, 1963*, Zwolle, NV Uitgeversmij, 1966, pp. 49–113

Thorp (René-William), *Vues sur la justice*, Paris, René Julliard, 1962

Timberg (Sigmund), 'Antitrust in the Common Market: Innovation and Surprise', *Law and Contemporary Problems*, 37(2), 1972, pp. 329–40

Touffait (Adolphe), 'Maurice Rolland, européen', *Bulletin de l'Association des juristes européens*, 38, 1978, pp. 15–18

Trabucchi (Antonio), 'Un nouveau droit. Conférence faite le 6 avril 1963, Université de Ferrare', *Rivista di diritto civile*, 9(3), 1963, pp. 259–72

'Note à MM. les juges. Affaire 26/62 Tariefcommissie', in Giuseppe Perini, 'Alberto Trabucchi giurista europeo. Alle radici del diritto in Europa: una testimonianza inedito', *Quaderni della rivista di diritto civile*, 2008, pp. 174–6

Van der Goes van Naters (Marinus), 'Les fondements du droit parlementaire européen', *Nederlands tijdschrift voor international recht*, 10, 1956, pp. 324–41

Van Gerven (Walter), 'Address by Walter van Gerven on the Occasion of His Retirement from Office', in *Synopsis of the Work of the Court of Justice. 1992–1994*, Luxembourg, Curia, 1995

von der Groeben (Hans) and von Boeckh (Hans) (eds.), *Kommentar zum EWG-Vertrag*, Baden-Baden, Nomos, 1958

von der Groeben (Hans), von Boeckh (Hans), Thiesing (Jochen) and Ehlermann (Claus-Dieter) (eds.), *Kommentar zum EWG-Vertrag*, Baden-Baden, Nomos, 1983

Waelbroeck (Michel), *Peut-on parler d'un droit constitutionnel européen?*, Brussels, Travaux et conférences de l'Université de Bruxelles, 1964

Weiler (Joseph), *The State Über Alles. Demos, Telos and the German Maastricht Decision*, Working Paper, New York, New York University, 1995

Weiler (Joseph) and Wind (Marlene), 'Introduction', in *European Constitutionalism Beyond the State*, Cambridge, Cambridge University Press, 2003, pp. 1–5

Wissenschaftliche Gesellschaft für Europarecht, *Aktuelle fragen des europäische gemeinschaftsrechts: Bensheim. 10–14 Juli 1964*, Stuttgart, Enke Verlag, 1965

Wyatt (D.), 'Publications for Solicitors' Firms', *Yearbook of European Law*, 10(1), 1990

Ziller (Jacques), *La place du droit matériel dans le projet de Constitution. Pourquoi une troisième partie?*, Working Paper, European University Institute, Robert Schuman Centre for Advanced Studies, European University Institute, 2004

General bibliography

Abbott (Andrew), *Systems of Profession: Essay on the Division of Expert Labor*, Chicago, IL, University of Chicago Press, 1988

'Linked Ecologies: States and Universities as Environments for Professions', *Sociological Theory*, 23(3), 2005, pp. 245–74

Aldrin (Philippe), 'L'invention de l'opinion publique européenne. Genèse intellectuelle et politique de l'Eurobaromètre', *Politix*, 1, 2010, pp. 79–101

Alter (Karen), *Establishing the Supremacy of European Law: The Making of an International Rule of Law in Europe*, Oxford, Oxford University Press, 2001

The European Court's Political Power: Essays on the Influence of the European Court of Justice on European Politics, Oxford, Oxford University Press, 2009

'The Global Spread of European-Style International Courts', *West European Politics*, 35(1), 2012, pp. 135–54

Alter (Karen) and Meunier-Aitshalia (Sophie), 'The New Constitutional Politics of Europe: European Integration and the Pathbreaking Cassis de Dijon Decision', *Comparative Political Studies*, 26(4), 1994, pp. 535–61

Arnull (Anthony), 'The Americanization of EU Law Scholarship', in *Continuity and Change in EU Law: Essays in Honor of Sir Francis Jacobs*, Oxford, Oxford University Press, 2008, pp. 405–31

Audéoud (Olivier), 'L'acquis communautaire, du "mythe" à la pratique', *Revue d'études comparatives Est–Ouest*, 33(3), 2002, pp. 67–77

Audretsch (H. A. H.), *Supervision in European Community Law*, 2nd edn, Amsterdam, Elsevier, 1986

Azoulai (Loïc), 'La fabrication de la jurisprudence communautaire', in Pascal Mbongo and Vauchez Antoine (eds.), *Dans la fabrique du droit européen. Acteurs, scènes et publics de la Cour de justice des Communautés européennes*, Brussels, Bruylant, 2009, pp. 178–97

'La révolution introduite par Pierre Pescatore dans l'étude du droit communautaire européen', *Revue de la faculté de droit de l'Université de Liège*, 4, 2010

Baquero (Cruz Julio), 'The Luxemburg Compromise from a Legal Perspective', in Jean-Marie Palayret, Helen Wallace and Pascaline Winand (eds.), *Visions, Votes and Vetoes: The Empty Chair Crisis and the Luxembourg Compromise Forty Years On*, Brussels, Peter Lang, 2006, pp. 251–77

Bailleux (Julie), 'How Europe Came to Law', *Revue française de science politique*, 60(2), 2010, pp. 295–318

Penser l'Europe par le droit. L'invention du droit communautaire en France, Paris, Dalloz, 2014

Baisnée (Olivier) and Smith (Andy), 'Pour une sociologie de l'apolitique': acteurs, interactions et représentations au cœur du gouvernement de l'Union européenne', in Antonin Cohen, Bernard Lacroix and Philippe Riutort (eds.), *Les formes de l'activité politique. Éléments d'analyse sociologique XVIIIE–XXE siècle*, Paris, Presses Universitaires de France, 2006, pp. 39–64

Bancaud (Alain), 'La haute magistrature. Une constance mobile', *Actes de la recherche en sciences sociales*, 76–7, 1989, pp. 30–48

La haute magistrature judiciaire entre politique et sacerdoce, Paris, LGDJ, coll. 'Droit et société', 1993

Barbou Desplaces (Ségolène), 'La *summa divisio* en droit communautaire', in Xavier Bioy (ed.), *l'identité en droit public*, Paris, LGDJ, 2010

Barnard (Catherina) and Sharpston (Elenor), 'The Changing Face of Article 177 References', *Common Market Law Review*, 34, 1997, pp. 1113–71

Bartolini (Stefano), *Taking Constitutionalism and Legitimacy Seriously*, Eurogov Discussion Paper, 1, 2008

Bauman (Jon R.), *Pioneering a Global Vision, Baker & Mc Kenzie*, Chicago, IL, Harcourt Professional Education Group, 1999

Beach (Derek), 'The Unseen Hand in Treaty Reform Negotiations: The Role and Influence of the Council Secretariat', *Journal of European Public Policy*, 11(3), 2004, pp. 408–39

Beaud (Olivier) and Wachsmann (Patrick) (eds.), *La science juridique française et la science juridique allemande de 1870 à 1918*, Strasbourg, Presses universitaires de Strasbourg, 1997

Beauvallet (Willy), *Profession: Eurodéputé. Les élus français au Parlement européen et l'institutionnalisation d'une nouvelle figure politique et élective (1979–2004)*, Strasbourg, University of Strasbourg, PhD political science, 2007

Becker (Howard), *Les mondes de l'art*, Paris, Flammarion, 1985

Bélot (Cécile), Magnette (Paul) and Saurugger (Sabine) (eds.), *La science politique de l'Union européenne*, Paris, Economica, 2008

Berger (Peter), *The Sacred Canopy. Elements of a Sociological Theory of Religion*, Garden City, NY, Doubleday, 1967

Bitsch (Marie-Thérèse), *La construction européenne. Enjeux politiques et choix institutionnels*, Brussels, Peter Lang, 2007

Boerger (Anne), 'La Cour de justice dans les négociations du Traité de Paris instituant la CECA', *Journal of European Integration History*, 14(2), 2008, pp. 7–33

Boerger-De Smedt (Anne), 'Negotiating the Foundations of European Law (1950–1957): The Legal History of the Treaties of Paris and Rome', *Contemporary European History*, 21(3), 2012, pp. 339–56

Boltanski (Luc), 'L'espace multipositionnel. Multiplicité des positions institutionnelles et habitus de classe', *Revue française de sociologie*, 14(1), 1973, pp. 3–26

Bonini (Francesco), 'Studi, materiali e prospettive per una storia delle amministrazioni comunitarie', in *Storia amministrazione costituzione, annale dell'Istituto per la scienza dell'amministrazione pubblica*, 8, 2000, pp. 57–67

Börzel (Tania), 'Guarding the Treaty: Compliance Strategies of the European Commission', in Tania Börzel and Rachel Cichowski (eds.), *The State of the European Union VI: Law, Politics and Society*, Oxford, Oxford University Press, 2003, pp. 197–209

'Participation Through Law Enforcement: The Case of the European Union', *Comparative Political Studies*, 39, 2006, pp. 128–52

Bourdieu (Pierre), 'Genèse et structure du champ religieux', *Revue française de sociologie*, 12(3), 1971, pp. 295–334

'La force du droit. Élément pour une sociologie du champ juridique', *Actes de la recherche en sciences sociales*, 64, 1986, pp. 3–19

La noblesse d'État. Grandes écoles et esprit de corps, Paris, Minuit, 1989

Sur l'État. Cours au Collège de France (1989–1992), Paris, Seuil, 2012

Bruno (Isabelle), *À vos marques, prêts... cherchez ! La stratégie européenne de Lisbonne, vers un marché de la recherche*, Bellecombe-en-Bauges, Éditions du Croquant, 2008

Buchet de Neuilly (Yves), *L'Europe de la politique étrangère*, Paris, Economica, 2005

'Des bâtisseurs de traités. Continuités et discontinuités du processus conférentiel', in Antonin Cohen and Antoine Vauchez (eds.), *La Constitution européenne. Élites, mobilisations, votes*, Brussels, Presses de l'Université libre de Bruxelles, 2007

Buch-Hansen (Hubert) and Wigger (Angela), 'Revisiting 50 Years of Market-Making: The Neoliberal Transformation of EC Competition Policy', *Review of International Political Economy*, 17(1), 2010, pp. 20–44

Buffet-Tchakaloff (Marie-France), *La France devant la Cour de justice des Communautés européennes*, Paris, Economica, 1985

Burt (Ronald), 'Le capital social, les trous structuraux, l'entrepreneur', *Revue française de sociologie*, 36(4), 1995, pp. 599–628

Carbonnier (Jean), *Essais sur les lois*, Paris, Répertoire du notariat Defrénois, 1995

Carlier (Philippe), 'Fernand Dehousse et le projet d'Union politique', in Gilbert Trausch (ed.), *The European Integration from the Schuman Plan to the Treaties of Rome*, Baden-Baden, Nomos, 1993, pp. 365–77

Cayla (Olivier), 'Le coup d'État de droit?', *Le Débat*, 100, 1998, pp. 108–33

Charle (Christophe), 'Pour une histoire sociale des professions juridiques à l'époque contemporaine. Note pour une recherche', *Actes de la recherche en sciences sociales*, 76–7, 1989, pp. 117–19

Chélini (Michel-Pierre), 'Le plan de stabilisation Pinay–Rueff 1958', *Revue d'histoire moderne et contemporaine*, 48(4), 2001, pp. 102–23

Christiansen (Thomas) and Reh (Christine), *Constitutionalizing the European Union*, Basingstoke, Palgrave Macmillan, 2009

Cichowski (Rachel), *The European Court and Civil Society*, Oxford, Oxford University Press, 2007

Cini (Michele), 'La Commission européenne comme lieu d'émergence de cultures administratives. L'exemple de la DG IV et de la DG XI', *Revue française de science politique*, 46(3), 1996, pp. 457–73

Clement-Wilz (Laure), *La fonction de l'avocat général près la Cour de justice des Communautés européennes*, Brussels, Bruylant, 2011

Cohen (Antonin), 'Constitutionalism without Constitution: Transnational Elites between Political Mobilization and Legal Expertise (1940s–1960s)', *Law and Social Inquiry*, 23(1), 2007, pp. 109–35

'Le "père de l'Europe". La construction sociale d'un récit des origines', *Actes de la recherche en sciences sociales*, 166–7, 2007, pp. 14–29

'Ten Majestic Figures in Long Amaranth Robes: The Formation of the Court of Justice of the European Communities', *Revue française de science politique*, 60(2), 2010, pp. 227–46

'Legal Professionals or Political Entrepreneurs? Constitution Making as a Process of Social Construction and Political Mobilization', *International Political Sociology*, 4(2), 2010, pp. 107–23

De Vichy à la Communauté européenne, Paris, PUF, 2012

'L'autonomisation du "Parlement européen". Interdépendance et différenciation des assemblées parlementaires supranationales (années 1950-années 1970)', *Cultures et conflits*, 85–6, Spring 2012, pp. 13–33

'Juge et expert. L'Affaire Rueff ou la production des frontières institutionnelles', *Critique internationale*, No. 59, 2013

Cohen (Antonin) and Dezalay (Yves) and Marchetti (Dominique), 'Ésprits d'État, entrepreneurs d'Europe', *Actes de la recherche en sciences sociales*, 166–7, 2007, pp. 5–13

Cohen (Antonin) and Vauchez (Antoine), 'Anatomie du "moment constitutionnel"', in Antonin Cohen et Antoine Vauchez (eds.), *La Constitution européenne. Élites, mobilisations, votes*, Brussels, Presses de l'Université libre de Bruxelles, pp. 15–32

Cohen (Antonin) and Weisbein (Julien), 'Laboratoires du constitutionnalisme européen. Expertises académiques et mobilisations politiques dans la promotion d'une Constitution européenne', *Droit et société*, 60, 2005, pp. 353–71

Commun (Patricia) (ed.), *L'ordolibéralisme allemand. Aux origines de l'économie sociale de marché*, Paris, Ciera, 2003

Conant (Lisa), 'Review Article: The Politics of European Legal Integration', *Journal of Common Market Studies*, 45(1), 2007, pp. 45–66

Condorelli-Braun (Nicole), *Commissaires et juges dans les Communautés européennes*, Paris, LGDJ, 1972

Costa (Olivier), *Le Parlement européen, assemblée délibérante*, Brussels, Éditions de l'Université de Bruxelles, 2001

'La contribution de la composante "Parlement européen" aux négociations de la Convention', *Politique européenne*, 13, 2004, pp. 21–41

Courty (Guillaume) and Michel (Hélène), 'Interest Groups and Lobbyists in the European Political Space: The Permanent Eurocrats', in Didier Georgakakis (ed.), *The Field of Eurocracy: Mapping EU Actors and Professionals*, Basingstoke, Palgrave, 2013, pp. 166–87

Darendorf (Ralf), 'The Education of an Elite: Law Faculties and the German Upper Class', in *Transactions of the Fifth World Congress of Sociology*, Louvain, 1964, pp. 259–74

Davies (Bill), 'Meek Acceptance? The West German Ministries' Reaction to the Van Gend en Loos and Costa decisions', *Revue d'histoire de l'intégration européenne*, 14(2), 2008, pp. 57–76

Resisting the European Court of Justice: West Germany's Confrontation with European Law (1949–1979), Cambridge, Cambridge University Press, 2012

Dehousse (Renaud), *La Cour des justices des Communautés européennes*, Paris, Montchrestien, 1997

'L'Europe par le droit', *Critique internationale*, 2(2), 1999, pp. 133–50

Une Constitution pour l'Europe, Paris, Presses de Sciences Po, 2002

'La méthode communautaire a-t-elle encore un avenir?', in *Mélanges Jean-Victor Louis*, Brussels, Presses de l'Université libre de Bruxelles, 2003, pp. 95–107

Delcourt (Barbara), 'The Acquis Communautaire: Has the Concept Had Its Day?', *Common Market Law Review*, 38(4), 2001, pp. 829–70

Deloche-Gaudez (Florence), 'Le secrétariat de la Convention européenne. Un acteur influent', *Politique européenne*, 13, 2004, pp. 43–67

Denord (François) and Schwartz (Antoine), *L'Europe sociale n'aura pas lieu*, Paris, Raisons d'agir, 2009

'L'économie (très) politique des Traités de Rome', *Politix*, 1, 2010, pp. 35–56

de Witte (Bruno), 'Retour à "Costa". La primauté du droit communautaire à la lumière du droit international', *Revue trimestrielle de droit européen*, 20(3), 1984, pp. 425–54

'The Question of Treaty Architecture: From the Spinelli Draft to the Lisbon Treaty', in Alexander Trechsel (ed.), *EU Federalism and Constitutionalism: The Legacy of Altiero Spinelli*, Lanham, MD, Lexington books, 2011, pp. 87–101

Dezalay (Yves), *Marchands de droit. La restructuration de l'ordre juridique international par les multinationales du droit*, Paris, Fayard, 1992

'Les courtiers de l'international. Héritiers cosmopolites, mercenaires de l'impéralisme et missionnaires de l'universel', *Actes de la recherche en sciences sociales*, 151–2, 2004, pp. 5–35

'Vendre du droit en (ré)inventant de l'État. Stratégies constitutionnelles et promotion de l'expertise juridique dans le champ du pouvoir d'État', in Antonin Cohen and Antoine Vauchez (eds.), *La Constitution européenne. Élites, mobilisations, votes*, Brussels, Presses Université de Bruxelles, 2007

Dezalay (Yves) and Garth (Bryant), 'Re-structuring States by Exporting Law: American Law Firms and the Genesis of a European Legal Market', in Petersen Hanne *et al.* (eds.), *Paradoxes of European Legal Integration*, Aldershot, Ashgate, 2008, pp. 76–88

Dezalay (Yves) and Madsen (Mikael), 'La construction européenne au carrefour du national et de l'international', in Antonin Cohen, Bernard Lacroix and Philippe Riutort (eds.), *Les formes de l'activité politique. Éléments d'analyse sociologique XVIIIE–XXE siècle*, Paris, PUF, 2006, pp. 277–96

Dezalay (Yves) and Sugarman (David) (eds.), *Professional Competition and Professional Power: Lawyers, Accountants and the Social Construction of Markets*, London, Routledge, 1995

Dulong (Delphine), 'Mourir en politique. Le discours politique des éloges funèbres', *Revue française de science politique*, 44(4), 1994, pp. 629–46

Sociologie des institutions politiques, Paris, La découverte, coll. Repères, 2012

Dumoulin (Michel) *et al.* (eds.), *La Commission européenne 1958–1972*, Luxembourg, Office des publications officielles des Communautés européennes, 2007

Farneti (Paolo), *Sistema politico e societa civile: Saggi di teoria e ricerca politica*, Turin, Giappichelli, 1971

Fligstein (Neil) and Mara-Drita (Ioana), 'How to Make a Market: Reflections on the Attempt to Create a Single Market in the European Union', *American Journal of Sociology*, 102(1), 1996, pp. 1–33

Fligstein (Neil) and McNichol (Jason), 'The Institutional Terrain of the European Union', in Wayne Sandholtz and Alec Stone (eds.), *European Integration and Supranational Governance*, Oxford, Oxford University Press, 1998, pp. 59–91

Fligstein (Neil) and Stone (Alec), 'Constructing Polities and Markets: An Institutionalist Account of European Integration', *American Journal of Sociology*, 107(5), 2002, pp. 1206–43

Foret (François), *Légitimer l'Europe. Pouvoir et symbolique à l'ère de la gouvernance*, Paris, Presses de Sciences Po, 2008

François (Bastien), 'Le président, pontife constitutionnel. Charisme d'institution et construction juridique du politique', in Jacques Lagroye and Bernard Lacroix (eds.), *Le président de la République*, Paris, Presses de Sciences Po, 1992, pp. 303–30

Naissance d'une Constitution. La Cinquième République 1958–1962, Paris, Presses de Sciences Po, 1996

'Le Conseil constitutionnel et la Ve République. Réflexions sur l'émergence et les effets du contrôle de constitutionnalité en France', *Revue française de science politique*, 47(3–4), 1997, pp. 377–404

Frzyzanowski (Michal) and Oberhuber (Florian), *(Un)Doing Europe: Discourses and Practices of Negotiating the EU Constitution*, Brussels, Peter Lang, 2007

Gaïti (Brigitte), *De Gaulle, prophète de la Ve République*, Paris, Presses de Sciences Po, 1998

'Entre les faits et les choses. La double face de la sociologie politique des institutions', in Antonin Cohen, Bernard Lacroix and Philippe Riutort (eds.), *Les formes de l'activité politique. Éléments d'analyse sociologique XVIIIE–XXE siècle*, Paris, PUF, 2006, pp. 39–64

Galanter (Mark), 'Why the Have's Come Out Ahead: Speculations on the Limits of Legal Change', *Law and Society Review*, 9(1), 1974, pp. 95–160

Gaxie (Daniel) and Godmer (Laurent), 'Cultural Capital and Political Selection: Educational Backgrounds of Parliamentarians', in Heinrich Best and Maurizio Cotta (eds.), *Democratic Representation in Europe: Diversity, Change and Convergence*, Oxford, Oxford University Press, 2007, pp. 106–35

Geary (Michael), *Enlarging the European Union: The Commission Seeking Influence (1961–1973)*, Basingstoke, Palgrave Macmillan, 2013

Gemelli (Giuliana), 'American Foundations and European Scientific Integration: Actors and Networks (1920s–1970s)', in Michel Dumoulin (ed.), *Réseaux économiques et construction européenne*, Brussels, Peter Lang, 2004

Georgakakis (Didier), 'A New Map for New Research Horizons', in Didier Georgakakis (ed.), *The Field of Eurocracy: Mapping EU Actors and Professionals*, Basingstoke, Palgrave, 2013, pp. 226–47

'French Historical and Political Sociology of the European Union', *French Politics*, 7, 2009, pp. 437–51

'Studying the Political Uses of a White Paper', in Didier Georgakakis and Marine de Lassalle (eds.), *The Political Uses of Governance: Studying a White Paper*, Leverkusen, Barbara Budrich Publishers, 2012

Georgakakis (Didier) and de Lassalle (Marine), 'Where have all the lawyers gone? Structure and transformations of the top European Commission officials' legal training', in Antoine Vauchez and Bruno de Witte (eds.), *Lawyering Europe: European Law as a Transnational Social Field*, Oxford, Hart Publishing, 2013, pp. 137–52

Gerber (David), 'Constitutionalizing the Economy: German Neo-liberalism, Competition Law and the "New" Europe', *American Journal of Comparative Law*, 42(1), 1994, pp. 25–84

Law and Competition in 20th Century Europe: Protecting Prometheus, Oxford, Oxford University Press, 2003

Godmer (Laurent) and Marrel (Guillaume), *La construction de l'expertise institutionnelle au Parlement européen Capital juridique et ressources politiques des députés de la Commission des Affaires constitutionnelles*, Centre Robert-Schuman, Working Paper, 2009

Gottlieb (Léo), *Cleary, Gottlieb, Steen & Hamilton: The First Thirty Years*, New York, Cleary Gottlieb, 1993

Gougeon (Pascal), '"Nul n'est censé ignorer la loi". La publication au Journal officiel. Genèse d'un mode d'universalisation de la "puissance publique"', *Politix*, 8(32), 1995, pp. 66–88

Granovetter (Mark), 'The Strength of Weak Ties: A Network Theory Revisited', in Peter Marsden and Nan Lin (eds.), *Social Structure and Network Analysis*, Beverly Hills, CA, Sage Publications, 1982, pp. 105–30

Granger (Marie-Pierre), 'Les stratégies contentieuses des États devant la Cour', in Pascal Mbongo and Antoine Vauchez (eds.), *Dans la fabrique du droit communautaire*, Brussels, Bruylant, 2009, pp. 64–124

Greaves (Rosa), 'The First Advocate General: Maurice Lagrange', in Noreen Burrows and Rosa Greaves (eds.), *The Advocate General and EC Law*, Oxford, Oxford University Press, 2007, pp. 59–88

Green Cowles (Maria), 'The EU Committee of AmCham: The Powerful Voice of American Firms in Brussels', *Journal of European Public Policy*, 3(3), 1996, pp. 339–58

Grilli (Antonio), *Le origini del diritto dell'Unione europea*, Bologna, Il Mulino, 2010

Gueguen (Laurent), *L'invention du droit des affaires. La construction doctrinale d'un savoir spécialisé alliant la rationalité gestionnaire au langage juridique*, Paris, Université Paris I, thèse de science politique, 2005

Guiraudon (Virginie) and Favell (Adrian), 'The Sociology of the European Union: An Agenda', *European Union Politics*, 10(4), 2009, pp. 550–76

Günther (Frieder), *Denken vom Staat her. Die bundesdeutsche Staatsrechtslehre zwischen dezision und integration (1949–1970)*, Munich, Oldenbourg, 2004

Halpérin (Jean-Louis), *Avocats et notaires en Europe. Les professions judiciaires et juridiques dans l'histoire contemporaine*, Paris, LGDJ, 1996

Heilbron (Johan), 'Qu'est-ce qu'une "tradition nationale" en sciences sociales?', *Revue d'histoire des sciences humaines*, 18, 2008, pp. 3–13

Hennette-Vauchez (Stéphanie), 'L'Europe au service (du droit) des droits de l'homme', *Politix*, 1, 2010, pp. 57–78

La Convention européenne des droits de l'homme vue d'ailleurs, Paris, mission Droit et Justice, 2010

'Divided in Diversity: National Legal Scholarship(s) and the European Convention on Human Rights', in Antoine Vauchez and Bruno de Witte (eds.), *Lawyering Europe: European Law as a Transnational Social Field*, Oxford, Hart Publishing, 2013, pp. 117–36

Horwitz (Morton), 'The History of the Public/Private Distinction', *University of Pennsylvania Law Review*, 130(6), 1982, pp. 1423–8

Jabko (Nicolas), *Playing the Market: A Political Strategy for Uniting Europe (1985–2005)*, Ithaca, NY, Cornell University Press, 2006

Jacqué (Jean-Paul), 'L'arrêt Les Verts', in Loïc Azoulai and Miguel Maduro (eds.), *The Past and Future of EU Law: The Classics of EU Law Revisited on the 50th Anniversary of the Rome Treaty*, Oxford, Hart Publishing, 2009

'The Role of the Legal Services in the Elaboration of European Legislation', in Antoine Vauchez and Bruno de Witte (eds.), *Lawyering Europe: European Law as a Transnational Social Field*, Oxford, Hart Publishing, 2012, pp. 43–53

Joana (Jean) and Smith (Andy), *Les commissaires européens. Technocrates, diplomates ou politiques*, Paris, Presses de Sciences Po, 2002

Joerges (Christian), 'La Constitution économique européenne en processus et en procès', *Revue internationale de droit économique*, 20(3), 2006, pp. 245–84

'Integration through De-legalisation: An Irritated Heckler', European Governance Papers, No. 07-3 (www.connex-network.org)

Jorgensen (Knud), 'The Social Construction of the Acquis Communautaire: A Cornerstone of the European Edifice', European Integration Online Papers (EIoP), 3(5), 1999

Kaiser (Joseph), 'L'Europe des Savants. European Integration and Social Sciences', *Journal of Common Market Studies*, 43(3), 2005, pp. 551–82

Kaiser (Wolfram), *Christian Democracy and the Origins of European Union*, Cambridge, Cambridge University Press, 2007

'History Meets Politics: Overcoming Interdisciplinary Volapük in Research on the European Union', *Journal of European Public Policy*, 15(2), 2008, pp. 300–13

Kaiser (Wolfram), Leucht (Brigitte) and Rasmussen (Morten) (eds.), *The History of the European Union: Origins of a Trans- and Supranational Polity 1950–1972*, London, Routledge, 2008, pp. 129–47

Karpik (Lucien), *Les avocats entre l'État, le public et le marché: xiiie-xxe siècle*, Paris, Gallimard, 1995

Keeler (John), 'Mapping EU Studies: The Evolution from Boutique to Boom Field 1960–2001', *Journal of Common Market Studies*, 43(3), 2005, pp. 551–82

Kelemen (Daniel), *Eurolegalism: The Transformation of Law and Regulation in the European Union*, Cambridge, MA, Harvard University Press, 2011

Kelemen (Dan) and Schmidt (Susanne), 'The European Court of Justice and Legal Integration: Perpetual Momentum', *Journal of European Public Policy*, 19(1), 2012, pp. 1–7

Kenney (Sally), 'The Members of the European Court of Justice', *Columbia Journal of European Law*, 5(1), 1998, pp. 101–33

'Beyond Principals and Agents: Seeing Courts as Organizations by Comparing Référendaires at the European Court of Justice and Law Clerks at the US Supreme Court', *Comparative Political Studies*, 33(5), 2000, pp. 593–625

Kitzinger (Uwe), *Diplomacy and Persuasion: How Britain Joined the Common Market*, London, Thames and Hudson, 1973

Koskenniemi (Martti), *La politique du droit international*, Paris, Pedone, 2007

Krynen (Jacques), *L'emprise contemporaine des juges. L'État de justice XIII–XXème siècle*, Paris, Gallimard, 2012

Lacroix (Bernard) and Lagroye (Jacques) (eds.), *Le président de la République. Usages et genèses d'une institution*, Paris, Presses de Sciences Po, 1992

Lagroye (Jacques), 'L'institution en pratiques', *Revue suisse de science politique*, 8(3–4), 2002, pp. 114–28

Lahusen (Christian), 'Commercial Consultancies in the European Union: The Shape and Structure of Professional Interest Intermediation', *Journal of European Public Policy*, 9(5), 2002, pp. 695–714

Landrin (Xavier), 'Sortie de crise et construction du changement. Les usages du projet conventionnel sous la présidence belge du Conseil', in Antonin Cohen and Antoine Vauchez (eds.), *La Constitution européenne. Élites, mobilisations, votes*, Brussels, Presses de l'Université libre de Bruxelles, 2007

Lascoumes (Pierre) and Le Galès (Patrick), 'De l'innovation instrumentale à la recomposition de l'État', in Pierre Lascoumes Pierre and Patrick Le Galès (eds.), *Gouverner par les instruments*, Paris, Presses de Sciences Po, 2004, pp. 11–44

Lastenouse (Jacqueline), 'La Commission européenne et les études universitaires', *Temas de Integracao*, 15–16, 2003, pp. 13–36

Latour (Bruno), *La fabrique du droit. Ethnographie du Conseil d'État*, Paris, La découverte, 2002

Le Boulay (Morgane), 'Investir l'arène européenne de la recherche. Le groupe de liaison des professeurs d'histoire contemporaine auprès de la Commission des Communautés européennes et la promotion de l'histoire de l'intégration européenne', *Politix*, 1, 2010, pp. 103–24

Le Beguec (Gilles), *La république des avocats*, Paris, Armand Colin, 2003

Lehingue (Patrick), 'Mais qui a gagné? Les mécanismes de production des verdicts électoraux', in Jacques Lagroye *et al.* (eds.), *Mobilisations électorales*, Paris, PUF, 2006, pp. 323–60

Leigh (Susan) and Griesemer (James), 'Institutional Ecology, "Translations" and Boundary Objects: Amateurs and Professionals in Berkeley's Museum of Vertebrate Zoology (1907–1939)', *Social Studies of Science*, 19, 1989, pp. 387–420

Leucht (Brigitte), 'Tracing European Mentalities: Free Competition and Cartels in Transatlantic Europe 1950–51', in Marie-Thérèse Bitsch (ed.), *Cultures politiques, opinions publiques et intégration européenne*, Brussels, Bruylant, pp. 337–53

Leucht (Brigitte) and Seidel (Katia), 'Du Traité de Paris au règlement 17/1962: ruptures et continuités de la politique européenne de concurrence, 1950–1962', *Histoire, économie et sociétés*, 27(1), 2008, pp. 35–47

Lindsay (Kenneth) (ed.), *European Assemblies: The Experimental Period 1949–1959*, London, Stevens and Sons, 1960

Lindseth (Peter), 'The Law–Regulation Distinction and European Integration. Reflections on the German Jurisprudence from the 1960s to the Present', *Jus Politicum*, 2(4), 2009, www.juspoliticum.com/The-Law-Regulation-Distinction-and.html

Power and Legitimacy. Reconciling Europe and the Nation-State, Oxford, Oxford University Press, 2010

Löffler (B.), *Soziale Marktwirtschaft und administrative praxis: das Bundeswirtschaftsministerium unter Ludwig Erhard*, Stuttgart, Steiner, 2002

Loth (Wilfried), Wallace (William) and Wessels (Wolfgang) (eds.), *Walter Hallstein: The Forgotten European?*, Basingstoke, Palgrave Macmillan, 1998

(ed.), *Crises and Compromises: The European Project 1963–1969*, Baden-Baden, Nomos, 2001

Louis (Jean-Victor), 'Les institutions dans le projet de Constitution de l'Union européenne (Rapport Herman, 1994)', in Jean-Victor Louis and Denis Waelbroeck (eds.), *L'Union européenne et l'avenir de ses institutions*, Brussels, Presses de l'Université libre de Bruxelles, 1996

Ludlow (Piers), 'De-Commissioning the Empty Chair Crisis: The EC Institutions and the Crisis of 1965–66', in Jean-Marie Palayret, Helen Wallace and Pascaline Winand (eds.), *Visions, Votes and Vetoes: The Empty Chair Crisis and the Luxembourg Compromise Forty Years On*, Brussels, Peter Lang, 2006, pp. 79–96

'A Supranational Icarus: The Early Commission and the Search for an Independent Role', in Antonio Varsori (ed.), *Inside the European Community: Actors and Policies in the European Integration 1957–1972*, Baden-Baden, Nomos, 2006, pp. 37–54

'Value, Flexibility and Openness: The Treaty of Rome's Success in Historical Perspective', in Julio Baquero Cruz and Carlos Closa Montera (eds.), *European Integration in Historical Perspective from Rome to Berlin (1957–2007)*, Brussels, Peter Lang, 2009, pp. 17–39

MacIntosh (Wayne) and Kate (Cynthia), *Judicial Entrepreneurship: The Role of Judges in the Marketplace of Ideas*, Westport, CT, Greenwood Press, 1997

MacMullen (Andrew), 'European Commissioners: National Routes to a European Elite', in Neil Nugent (ed.), *At the Heart of the Union: Studies of the European Commission*, Basingstoke, Palgrave Macmillan, 2000, pp. 28–50

Maddalon (Philippe), *La notion de marché dans la jurisprudence de la Cour de justice des Communautés européennes*, Paris, LGDJ, 2007

Madsen (Mikael), 'La Cour qui venait du froid: les droits de l'homme dans la genèse de l'Europe d'après-guerre', *Critique internationale*, 25, 2005, pp. 133–47

La genèse de l'Europe des droits de l'homme. Enjeux juridiques et stratégies d'État (France, Grande-Bretagne et pays scandinaves, 1945–1970), Strasbourg, Presses de l'Université de Strasbourg, 2010

Magnette (Paul), *Au nom des peuples. Le malentendu constitutionnel européen*, Paris, Cerf, 2006

Malandrino (Corrado), *'Tut etwas Tapferes': compi un atto di coraggio: l'Europa federale di Walter Hallstein, 1948–1982*, Bologna, Il Mulino, 2005

Malatesta (Maria), *Professionisti e gentiluomini: storia delle professioni nell'Europa contemporana*, Turin, Einaudi, 2006

Mangenot (Michel), 'Le Conseil d'État et l'Europe. Conditions et effets d'un ralliement', in Philippe Raimbault (ed.), *La puissance publique à l'heure européenne*, Paris, Dalloz, 2006, pp. 173–90

'The Invention and Transformation of a Governmental Body: The Council Secretariat', in Michel Mangenot and Jay Rowell (eds.), *A Political Sociology of the European Union: Reassessing Constructivism*, Manchester, Manchester University Press, 2010, pp. 46–67

'La présidence du Conseil. Sociologie d'une institution de l'Union européenne', *Politique européenne*, 35, 2011, pp. 7–28

Mangenot (Michel) and Schirmann (Sylvain) (eds.), *Les institutions européennes font leur histoire. Regards croisés, soixante ans après le Traité de Paris*, Brussels, Peter Lang, 2012

Marchand (Christèle) and Vauchez (Antoine), 'Lawyers as Europe's Middlemen? A Sociology of Litigants Pleading to the European Court of Justice (1954–1978)', in Mangenot Michel and Rowell Jay (eds.), *A Political Sociology of the European Union: Reassessing Constructivism*, Manchester, Manchester University Press, 2010

Mbongo (Pascal) and Vauchez (Antoine) (eds.), *Dans la fabrique du droit européen. Acteurs, scènes et publics de la Cour de justice des Communautés européennes*, Brussels, Bruylant, 2009

Michalski (Anna) and Wallace (Helen), *The European Community: The Challenge of Enlargement*, London, Royal Institute of International Affairs, 1992

Michel (Hélène), 'Le droit comme registre d'européanisation d'un groupe d'intérêt. La défense des propriétaires et la Charte des droits fondamentaux', *Politique européenne*, 6, 2002, pp. 9–42

Moravcsik (Andrew), 'What Can We Learn from the Collapse of the European Constitutional Project?', *Politische vertieljaresschrift*, 47(2), 2006, pp. 19–241

'The European Constitutional Settlement', *World Economy*, 31(1), 2008, pp. 158–83

Mudge (Stéphanie) and Vauchez (Antoine), 'Building Europe on a Weak Field: Law, Economics and the Scholarly Constitution of Europe', *American Journal of Sociology*, 118(2), 2012, pp. 449–92

Nay (Olivier) and Smith (Andy), 'Les intermédiaires en politique. Médiation et jeux d'institutions', in Olivier Nay and Andy Smith (eds.), *Le gouvernement du compromis. Courtiers et généralistes dans l'action publique*, Paris, Economica, 2002, pp. 1–20

Norman (Peter), *The Accidental Constitution: The Story of the European Convention*, Brussels, Eurocomment, 2003

Osiel (Mark), 'Lawyers as Monopolists, Aristocrats, and Entrepreneurs', *Harvard Law Review*, 103(8), 1990, pp. 2009–66

O'Neill (Michael), *The Struggle for the European Constitution: A Past and Future History*, Abingdon, Routledge, 2009

Page (Edward C.) and Wright (Vincent) (eds.), *Bureaucratic Elites in Western European States: A Comparative Analysis of Top Officials*, Oxford, Oxford University Press, 1999

Parsons (Talcott), 'A Sociologist Looks at the Legal Profession', in *Essays in Sociological Theory*, 3rd edn, New York, The Free Press, 1964, pp. 370–85

Patel (Kiran) and Schweitzer (Heike) (eds.), *Historical Foundations of EU Competition Law*, Oxford, Oxford University Press, 2013

Peryo (Francisco), 'Le qui-dit-quoi de l'acquis communautaire', *Terminologie et Traduction*, 2, 1999, pp. 52–75

Pierson (Paul) and Skocpol (Theda), 'Historical Institutionalism in Contemporary Political Science', in Ira Katznelson and Helen Miller (eds.), *Political Science: The State of the Discipline*, New York, Norton, 2002, pp. 693–721

Polanyi (Karl), *La grande transformation*, Paris, Gallimard, 1998

Poidevin (Raymond) and Spierenburg (Dirk), *Histoire de la Haute autorité de la CECA*, Brussels, Bruylant, 1993

Popa (Ioana), 'La structuration internationale des études européennes. Un espace scientifique dissymétrique', in Didier Georgakakis and Marine de Lassalle (eds.), *The Political Uses of Governance: Studying a White Paper*, Leverkusen, Barbara Budrich Publishers, 2012, pp. 117–48

Preda (Daniele), 'Hallstein e l'amministrazione pubblica europea', *Storia amministrazione costituzione, annale dell'Istituto per la scienza dell'amministrazione pubblica*, 8, 2000, pp. 79–104

'The Movements for European Unity (1958–1972)', in Antonio Varsori (ed.), *Inside the European Community: Actors and Policies in the European Integration 1957–1972*, Baden-Baden, Nomos, 2006, pp. 177–93

Rasmussen (Hjalte), *On Law and Policy in the European Court of Justice*, Dordrecht, Nijhoff, 1987

'Past and Future European Judicial Problems after Enlargement and the Post-2005 Ideological Revolt', *Journal of Common Market Studies*, 44(1), 2007, pp. 1661–87

Rasmussen (Morten), 'The Origins of a Legal Revolution: The Early History of the European Court of Justice', *Journal of European Integration History*, 14(2), 2008, pp. 77–98

'Establishing a Constitutional Practice of European Law: The History of the Legal Service of the European Executive (1952–1965)', *Contemporary European History*, 21(3), 2012, pp. 375–97

Robert (Cécile), 'L'expertise comme mode d'administration communautaire', *Politique européenne*, 11, 2003, pp. 57–78

'L'Europe sociale face à son élargissement. Les déterminants institutionnels du débat communautaire sur la dimension sociale de l'élargissement à l'Est', *Annuaire français des relations internationales*, 4, 2003, pp. 426–37

Robert (Cécile) and Vauchez (Antoine), 'L'Académie européenne. Savoirs, experts et savants dans le gouvernement de l'Europe', *Politix*, 1, 2010, pp. 9–34

Sacriste (Guillaume), 'Un Parlement européen de droit. Comment un service juridique est devenu "nécessaire" au Parlement européen?', communication à la journée d'étude du groupe Polilexes 'Capitales et capitaux juridiques en Europe', 15 September 2006, CRPS-CURAP

La république des constitutionnalistes (1870–1914), Paris, Presses de Sciences Po, 2011

'L'Europe est-elle un État comme les autres? Retour de la distinction public/privé au sein de la commission juridique du Parlement européen des années 1960', *Cultures et conflits*, 85–6, 2012, pp. 33–60

Sacriste (Guillaume) and Vauchez (Antoine), 'Les "bons offices" du droit international. Analyse de la Constitution d'une autorité non politique dans le concert diplomatique des années 1920', *Critique internationale*, 25, 2005, pp. 101–17

Saurugger (Sabine), 'Sociology and European Studies', *Journal of European Public Policy*, 16(6), 2009, pp. 937–50

Scheingold (Stuart), *Law and Politics in Western European Integration*, Berkeley, CA, University of California Berkeley, PhD, 1963

Schepel (Harm) and Wesseling (Rein), 'The Legal Community: Judges, Lawyers, Officials and Clerks in the Writing of Europe', *European Law Journal*, 3(2), 1997, pp. 165–88

Schmitter (Philippe), 'Imagining the Future of the Euro-Polity with the Help of New Concepts', in Gary Marks, Fritz Scharpf and Philippe Schmitter, *Governance in the European Union*, London, Sage, 1996, pp. 121–50

Schönwald (Matthias), 'Walter Hallstein and the "Empty Chair" Crisis 1965/1966', in Wilfried Loth (ed.), *Crises and Compromises: The European Project 1963–1969*, Baden-Baden, Nomos, 2001, pp. 157–71

Seidel (Katia), 'DG IV and the Origins of a Supranational Competition Policy: Establishing an Economic Constitution for Europe', in Wolfram Kaiser, Brigitte Leucht and Morten Rasmussen (eds.), *The History of the European Union: Origins of a Trans- and Supranational Polity 1950–1972*, London, Routledge, 2008, pp. 129–47

The Process of Politics in Europe: The Rise of European Elites and Supranational Institutions, Basingstoke, Palgrave Macmillan, 2010

Serverin (Evelyne), *De la jurisprudence en droit privé. Théorie d'une pratique*, Lyon, Presses universitaires de Lyon, 1985

Shapiro (Martin), 'Comparative Law and Comparative Politics', *Southern California Law Review*, 53, 1980, pp. 536–42

Slinn (Judy), *A History of Freshfields*, London, Freshfields, 1984

Linklaters & Paines: The First One Hundred and Fifty Years, Harlow, Longman, 1987

Clifford Chance: Its Origins and Development, Cambridge, Granta Editions, 1993
Smith (Andy), *Le gouvernement de l'Union européenne. Une sociologie politique*, Paris, LGDJ, 2004
Snyder (Francis), 'The Effectiveness of European Community Law: Institutions, Processes, Tools and Techniques', *Modern Law Review*, 56(1), 1993, pp. 19–54
Stone (Alec), *The Judicial Construction of Europe*, Oxford, Oxford University Press, 2004
'The Juridical Coup d'État and the Problem of Authority', *German Law Review*, 8(10), 2007, pp. 915–28
'Integration and Constitutionalism in the European Union', in Antonin Cohen and Antoine Vauchez (eds.), *Anatomie d'un 'moment constituant' européen. Élites, mobilisations, votes*, Brussels, Presses de l'Université libre de Bruxelles, 2007
'The European Court of Justice and the Judicialization of EU Governance', *European Governance: Living Review* (http://blog.europeangovernance.livingreviews.org)
Stone (Alec), Sandholtz (Wayne) and Fligstein (Neil) (eds.), *The Institutionalisation of Europe*, Oxford, Oxford University Press, 2001
Topalov (Christian), *Laboratoires du nouveau siècle. La nébuleuse réformatrice et ses réseaux en France 1880–1914*, Paris, Éditions de l'EHESS, 1994, pp. 12–58
Uitz (Renata), *Constitutions, Courts and History*, Budapest, Central European University Press, 2005
Vauchez (Antoine), *Démocratiser l'Europe*, Paris, Seuil, 2014
L'institution judiciaire remotivée. Le processus d'institutionnalisation d'une 'nouvelle justice' en Italie (1960–2000), Paris, LGDJ, coll. 'Droit et société', 2004
'Une élite d'intermédiaires. Genèse d'un capital juridique européen (1950–1970)', *Actes de la recherche en sciences sociales*, 166–7, 2007, pp. 54–65
'Review Article: Democratic Empowerment through Euro-Law?', *European Political Science*, 7, 2008, pp. 444–52
'The Force of a Weak Field: Law and Lawyers in the Government of the European Union (for a Renewed Research Agenda)', *International Political Sociology*, 2(2), 2008, pp. 128–44
'Pouvoir judiciaire', in Antonin Cohen, Bernard Lacroix and Philippe Riutort (eds.), *Nouveau manuel de science politique*, Paris, La découverte, 2009, pp. 242–55
'Interstitial Power? A Weak Field Approach to Transnational Settings', *International Political Sociology*, 5(3), 2011, pp. 340–5
Veenwijk (Virginia), *Coudert Brothers. A Legacy in Law: The History of America's First International Law Firm*, New York, Truman Talley books, 1994
Wagner (Anne-Catherine), 'Les stratégies transnationales en France', Stockholm, Skeptronhäften Working Papers, 13, 1997
Les classes sociales dans la mondialisation, Paris, La découverte, 2008
Waquet (Françoise), 'Les "mélanges". Honneur et gratitude dans l'Université contemporaine', *Revue d'histoire moderne et contemporaine*, 53(3), 2006, pp. 100–21

Warlouzet (Laurent), *The Rise of European Competition Policy, 1950–1991: A Cross-Disciplinary Survey of a Contested Policy Sphere*, European University Institute/RSCAS, 2010, 39 p

Le choix de la CEE par la France. L'Europe économique en débat de Mendès France à de Gaulle (1955–1969), Paris, Comité pour l'histoire économique et financière, 2011

Weber (Max), *On Law in Economy and Society*, Cambridge, MA, Harvard University Press, 1954

Weiler (Joseph), 'Une révolution tranquille. La CJCE et ses interlocuteurs', *Politix*, 32, 1995, pp. 119–38

'The Reformation of European Constitutionalism', *Journal of Common Market Studies*, 37(1), 1997, pp. 97–120

'Rewriting Van Gend en Loos: Towards a Normative Theory of ECJ Hermeneutics', in Ola Wiklund (ed.), *Judicial Discretion in European Perspective*, The Hague, Kluwer Law International, 2003, pp. 151–63

Weisbein (Julien), 'Les mouvements fédéralistes ou les entrepreneurs déçus d'une Europe politique (années 1950–1990)', in Baisnée Olivier and Pasquier Romain (eds.), *L'Europe telle qu'elle se fait. Européanisation et sociétés politiques nationales*, Paris, CNRS Éditions, 2007, pp. 35–54

Weisbrode (Ken), *Four Generations of Extraordinary Diplomats Who Forged America's Vital Alliance with Europe*, Cambridge, Da Capo Press, 2009

White (Jonathan), 'Theory Guiding Practice: The Neofunctionalists and the Hallstein EEC Commission', *Journal of European Integration History*, 9(1), 2003, pp. 111–31

Wilkins (Mira), *The Maturing of Multinational Enterprise: American Business Abroad from 1914 to 1970*, Cambridge, MA, Harvard University Press, 1974

Wright Mills (Charles), *The Power Elite*, Oxford, Oxford University Press, 2000 (originally published 1956)

Index

www.ingramcontent.com/pod-product-compliance
Lightning Source LLC
LaVergne TN
LVHW011523200926
848484LV00001B/128

* 9 7 8 1 1 0 7 0 4 2 3 6 0 *